Charms, Charmers and Char

Charms, Charmers and Charming

International Research on Verbal Magic

Edited by

Jonathan Roper

First published 2009 by
PALGRAVE MACMILLAN
Houndmills, Basingstoke, Hampshire RG21 6XS and
175 Fifth Avenue, New York, N.Y. 10010
Companies and representatives throughout the world

PALGRAVE MACMILLAN is the global academic imprint of the Palgrave
Macmillan division of St. Martin's Press, LLC and of Palgrave Macmillan Ltd.
Macmillan® is a registered trademark in the United States, United Kingdom
and other countries. Palgrave is a registered trademark in the European
Union and other countries.

ISBN-13: 978–0–230–55184–8   hardback
ISBN-10: 0–230–55184–X   hardback

This book is printed on paper suitable for recycling and made from fully
managed and sustained forest sources. Logging, pulping and manufacturing
processes are expected to conform to the environmental regulations of the
country of origin.

A catalogue record for this book is available from the British Library.

Library of Congress Cataloging-in-Publication Data

Charms, charmers and charming / edited by Jonathan Roper.
      p. cm.
   Includes bibliographical references and index.
   ISBN 0–230–55184–X (alk. paper)
   1. Charms. 2. Incantations. I. Roper, Jonathan, 1969–
GR600.C47 2008
133.4′4—dc22
                                                              2008016159

A catalog record for this book is available from the Library of Congress.

10   9   8   7   6   5   4   3   2   1
18   17   16   15   14   13   12   11   10   09

Transferred to Digital Printing in 2013

Contents

Palgrave Historical Studies in Witchcraft and Magic

Series Foreword

The history of European witchcraft and magic continues to fascinate and challenge students and scholars. There is certainly no shortage of books on the subject. Several general surveys of the witch trials and numerous regional and micro studies have been published for an English-speaking readership. While the quality of publications on witchcraft has been high, some regions and topics have received less attention over the years. The aim of this series is to help illuminate these lesser known or little studied aspects of the history of witchcraft and magic. It will also encourage the development of a broader corpus of work in other related areas of magic and the supernatural, such as angels, devils, spirits, ghosts, folk healing and divination. To help further our understanding and interest in this wider history of beliefs and practices, the series will include research that looks beyond the usual focus on Western Europe and that also explores their relevance and influence from the medieval to the modern period.

Notes on Contributors

Paul Cowdell holds an MA from the National Centre for English Cultural Tradition at the University of Sheffield. He is a recent winner of the Folklore Society's *'President's Prize'* for an essay on dating an agricultural protest song. He has recently conducted fieldwork in his native Kent for the Smithsonian Institution Festival on the Roots of Virginia Culture.

Natalia Glukhova is Head of the Finno-Ugric Languages Department of the Mari State University in the Republic of Mari El in the Russian Federation. Her main fields of research are comparative phraseology of the Germanic Languages, methods of teaching English to bilingual students, Mari folklore style, gender studies, and ethnolinguistics. She has published over one hundred works in these fields in international, all-Russian and regional collections and journals.

Vladimir Glukhov's fields of research include radio electronics, the thermography of the human body; mathematical simulation; engineer psychology, ethnic psychology; and methods in linguistics. He has published more than 60 articles in the above mentioned fields of research, published in international, all-Russian and regional collections and journals.

Lee Haring is Professor Emeritus of English at Brooklyn College of the City University of New York. He has conducted folklore research in Madagascar, Mauritius, and the other islands of the Indian Ocean, and is the author of *Verbal Arts in Madagascar, Indian Ocean Folktales, Indian Folktales from Mauritius*, many articles, and the forthcoming *Stars and Keys: Folktales and Creolization in the Indian Ocean*. He is also the translator of *Ibonia, Epic of Madagascar*.

Ritwa Herjulfsdotter is a doctoral candidate of Ethnology at the University of Gothenburg and the Nordic Museum postgraduate school. She has an interest in medical anthropology, popular religion, ethnobotany, curing symbols and magical thought. She is currently working on a thesis on magic medicine, with a focus on magic charms used for snake bite during late nineteenth and early twentieth century Sweden.

David Hunt has recently retired from his post as Visiting Professor at London South Bank University. He is interested in the folk literature of the Caucasus, and has translated a number of books on the folklore of the Caucasus, as well as being the author of various published papers on special aspects of Caucasian folklore.

Henni Ilomäki was formerly Chief Librarian of the Finnish Literature Society. She is now a freelance researcher of ritual folklore, with articles published on topics such as charms, ritual poetry and worldview in Finnish, English and Estonian.

Vladimir Klyaus works at the Institute of World Literature in Moscow. He has published much on charms, including a *Guide to Plots and Plot Situations in Charm Texts of Eastern and Southern Slavs* (1997) and *Slavic Charm Plots in Comparative Perspective* (2000) (both in Russian). He is also a maker of ethnographic films.

Monika Kropej is a Senior Research Fellow of the Institute of Slovene Ethnology at the Scientific Research Centre of the Slovenian Academy of Sciences and Arts in Ljubljana. She has published widely on folkloric topics including folk tales, contemporary legends and charms.

Lea Olsan has published articles on charms in medieval manuscripts, amulets and the role of prayers and charms in medieval medicine. She is Professor Emerita of English at the University of Louisiana at Monroe and serves on the Committee on Charms, Charmers and Charming for the International Society for Folk Narrative Research.

Low Kok On is a Senior Lecturer attached to the School of Arts of the Universiti Malaysia Sabah. The main focus of his research is the folk-literature of the Kadazandusun people in Sabah. His latest publications include a book entitled *Reading Myths and Legends of Kadazandusun* (2005) and an article entitled 'Kadazandusun Folklore' in *The Greenwood Encyclopedia of World Folklore and Folk Life* (2006). He is currently conducting fieldwork on the legends of a Malay saint known as Tunku Syarif Kedah among the Kedayan and Brunei Malay in Labuan Island.

Éva Pócs is Professor Emeritus at the University of Pécs, Hungary. She is the author of numerous publications on popular religion, magic and witchcraft, including *Fairies and Witches at the Boundary of South-Eastern* *and Central Europe* (1989) and *Between the Living and the Dead: a Perspective on Witches and Seers in the Early Modern Age* (1998).

Jonathan Roper is Teaching Fellow in English Language at the University of Leeds. He is interested in traditional linguistic genres, and is the author of *English Verbal Charms* (2005) and editor of *Charms and Charming in Europe* (2004).

Jacqueline Simpson is an active member of the Folklore Society, having served as Editor of *Folklore* for fourteen years and as President for three. She has written on British and Scandinavian folklore, with a particular interest in local legends. Her two most recent books are *A Dictionary of English Folklore* in collaboration with Steve Roud (2000), and *The Lore of the Land* in collaboration with Jennifer Chandler (2005).

T.M. Smallwood was a lecturer in English at the University of Ulster, following temporary appointments at the universities of Manchester and London. His research interests are chiefly in medieval literature and language, and he has a particular interest in the sharing of charm-motifs by different language-communities.

Laura Stark is Professor of Ethnology at the Department of History and Ethnology, University of Jyväskylä, Finland. Her research interests include magic and sorcery, gender studies, nineteenth-century Finnish folk belief, popular Christianity, and the effects of modernization on folk culture.

Andrei Toporkov is researcher at the Institute of the World Literature, Moscow, and a corresponding member of Russian Academy of Sciences. His research interests include Russian and Slavic folklore, Slavic and general Ethnology, and the History of Russian Literature. His chief publications are *The Origins of Etiquette: Ethnological Essays* (in collaboration with A.K. Baiburin) (1990, French translation 2004), *The Theory of Myth in the Russian Philology of the 19th Century* (1997); *Charms in the Russian Manuscript Tradition from the Fifteenth to the Nineteenth Centuries: History, Symbolism, Poetics* (2005).

Mary Tsiklauri is an associate of the Shota Rustaveli Institute of Georgian Literature, Tbilisi, Georgia. Her main research interests include Georgian and Caucasian Folklore and Mythology. She has also conducted comparative research on Georgian–Spanish–Basque and Georgian–British folktales.

Daiva Vaitkevičienė is Senior Researcher at the Institute of Lithuanian Literature and Folklore. A folklorist and mythologist, she has compiled an electronic database of Lithuanian verbal charms and published a book and several articles on Baltic mythology.

Maria Vivod is Associate Researcher at the Centre National de Recherches Scientifiques based in Strasbourg, France. Her fields of research and interest include identity, ethnic and social conflicts, the anthropology of Eastern European and ethno-medicine. She is also interested in Visual Anthropology, and is the director of several ethnographical documentaries.

Ulrika Wolf-Knuts is Professor of Folkloristics and Vice Rector at Åbo Akademi University in Finland. Her main fields of research are the study of folklore and folk religion, and she has specialised on Swedish Finn tradition, and on the situation of cultural minorities, identity and ethnicity, especially among the Swedes of Finland. Her most recent book was *Ett bättre liv. Finlandssvenskar i Sydafrika* (A Better Life. Finnish Swedes in South Africa – on Emigration, Memories, Home Sickness, and Nostalgia, 2000).

Introduction: Unity and Diversity in Charms Studies

Jonathan Roper

While visiting London not so many years ago I was told of an eighteenth century healing manuscript that had recently been purchased at auction. The book was what might be called a 'household book': alongside the medical recipes that dominated its contents (intended 'to cure a brakn beley', 'for the hooping cough', and 'for the inward piles'), its pages had also been used for other purposes. These other purposes included the working out of financial accounts (there was information about the price of 'Sheepseds' and the purchase of '20 burdes at 20 pence'), and doodling (rough jottings filled some pages). But on one particular pair of pages toward the end of the medical recipes, there were some healing-related texts of another sort. Were these by any chance charms I asked, aware that they sometimes figured in the passages of just such house-hold books. Oh no, came the answer, just scraps from the Bible. Meeting the same person a fortnight later, I was struck by their enthusiasm: 'I took another look, and the little stories aren't in the Bible after all!' It was apparent that these texts were not to be dismissed as simple (and misspelt) Biblical paraphrases. They were rather apocryphal healing narratives, known to scholars by such terms as **Flum Jordan**, **Super petram**, and **Crux Christi**, the majority of which were to be found all over Europe, including in Latin versions recorded up to eight and more centuries before.

I begin with this story as it is symbolic of the paradoxical neglect of charms by students of culture, be they historians, anthropologists, folk-lorists, or others. Such 'minor', 'obscure' items have repeatedly been overlooked in favour of (seemingly) more interesting or more significant phenomena. But verbal charms are a cultural near-universal (perhaps even a universal), a way of coping with ill health, with misfortune, and with anxiety about success in fields from agriculture to love. This is a fair claim to their significance. Similarly, while the texts of verbal charms receive remarkably little attention, they nonetheless form some of the earliest, most colourful, and most popular (in both senses) of writings that exist in many languages. Happily, the ending of the story

I began with also expresses the excitement that charms can hold for the researcher when they are recognised for what they are.

Despite the antiquity of charms as a phenomena (and of some charm-types), it is only in the last decades of the nineteenth century that the academic study of charms can be said to get underway. We might choose to see it inaugurated in 1869 with Leonid Maikov's publication on Russian charms.[1] Before this time, while representatives of the educated classes had expressed some interest in charms – during agitation against superstition and False Religion, and during the witch craze – the interest that they showed was not what one might call disinterested, nor was it thorough-going. And while it is certainly the case that late nineteenth-century researchers were not especially disinterested either (their own particular aims and agendas included building Romantic Nationalist monuments of folk poetry, 're'-constructing former models of thought, and scavenging for literary source material), they were relatively thorough-going in their work. In many countries, they managed to record a large number of texts of verbal charms, and sometimes also details of the charming too, which they then shared with a larger scholarly community by placing them in public archives or by publishing them in books and journals. Such collecting activities have sometimes been lightly dismissed as 'butterfly collecting', but it is clear that in areas (England, for example) where this did not take place, a huge swathe of cultural history went largely undocumented.

On top of this, many pseudo-scholarly pitfalls – such as the excessive paganising or nationalising of the material – were successfully avoided, and steadily an international network of researchers and charms research was developed in the first decades of the twentieth century, the Golden Age of charms studies. In this period solid collections of verbal charms were issued by such great names as Bang, Forsblom, Pradel, and Prasendanz,[2] amongst others. Other key works from this time include Franz's collection of medieval church benedictions,[3] many of which (so German, Hungarian, Finnish and other scholars argue) provide the basis for various key charm-types, and Ebermann's early international work concentrating on the development of charms to heal wounds and staunch bleeding in a variety of European languages.[4]

The outstanding figure amidst all this activity is that of Ferdinand Ohrt. He was not one of those who after publishing an exemplary national collection then moved on to other unrelated research topics. Rather, in his case, the national collection (the two-volume *Danmarks Trylleformlers*[5]) was succeeded by a series of works all concentrating upon charms. Refreshingly, the majority of these were international and historical in scope, notably *Da signed Christ, Die ältesten Segen uber Christi Taufe und Christi Tod in religionsgeschichtlichem Lichte* and his masterly series of entries written in German for the *Handwörterbuch des deutschen Aberglaubens*, including his essay-length entry on 'Segen'.[6] Although he never used the word, he was clearly straining towards the concept of *charm-type* in much of his later work, as seen by his grouping of material in the *Handwörterbuch*, and equally by the use of such typological terminology as 'Normalform'.

The half-century following the Second World War exhibited a distinct falling-off in activity in European charms studies. Despite some landmark publications, such as Spamer's historical–philological edition of the *Romanusbüchlein* (with its painstaking documentary research, much of which was shaped by the hand of Johanna Nickel),[7] van Haver's excellent edition of the Netherlandic charms[8] (perhaps the best of the volumes dedicated to a single national or linguistic tradition), and a series of wide-ranging articles by Alfons Barb,[9] the pace of research had clearly flagged. As the pre-war set of researchers died out, their academic successors turned to different topics. In the west, the turn in academic fashion in ethnology and folklore studies to urban, non-textual and emerging traditions led to a corresponding turn away from 'old-fashioned' genres such as charms. In the eastern part of Europe, a similar turning away from charm studies during the era of 'historical materialism' and atheistic communism was somewhat more a matter of ideology rather than of fashion (in as much as the two are distinguishable).

However in the last decade or so, charms studies have undergone somewhat of a revival – a silver age perhaps. There have, for instance, been a series of international charms studies conferences recently, in London in 2003 and 2005, and in Pécs, Hungary in 2007 (indeed, some of the chapters in this book were initially presented at those latter two conferences). A recent development with significant potential is the formation of a special committee on Charms, Charmers and Charming within the International Society for Folk Narrative Research. This, it must be hoped, will encourage and enable international co-operation in the field of charms studies. In Eastern Europe in particular, recent years have seen a torrent of publications on charms and charming. It is no coincidence that this is also the very part of the continent with the most active present-day traditions of charming. A sign of this scholarly vitality is the presence in this volume of chapters dealing with Russian, Georgian, Estonian, Hungarian, Slovene, Lithuanian and Mari charms. At the present time, Russophone scholars seem to be the most active – the lists of the Moscow publishers Indrik positively bulge with publications on charms. German-speaking scholars are also active once again, just as they were at the start of charms studies. While compiling this short work with its nineteen chapters has felt like fitting a quart into a pint-pot, which has necessarily involved some absences and exclusions, the absence I most regret here is that of any Germanophone voices, such as those of significant scholars like Leander Petzoldt, Monika Schultz, Verena Holzmann, etc.

Charms studies today

One advantage this silver age of charms studies has over its predecessor is now that much of the spadework has been done in establishing corpora, a larger variety of topics can addressed. Typical research topics now include the historical relationships between scattered texts, the relationship between text and context, and between the words of the charm and the procedure of charming. Investigations are made into how charms are memorised and into what the traditional rules about their transmission from one person to another might be, and the presence of variation in charm-texts is focussed on (and attempts are made to discern what the invariant elements might be). Pen-portraits of charmers are produced, the internal logic and the poetics of charms debated, the psychology of the users of charms and patients of charmers analysed. And outside of charms studies, the use of charms and charming as historical evidence for other fields of knowledge has begun to grow.

And yet despite this diversity of theme in charm studies, the current work demonstrates that there is a surprising degree of unity. For example, the existence of closely analogous texts in a variety of languages (i.e. the internationality of charm-types) is highlighted here by the work of Toporkov, Vaitkevičienė, Roper and Kropej, amongst others. The poetics of charms are widely covered here, as is (to concentrate on a narrower topic) the theme of impossibility conditions, which Glukhov and Glukhova, Tsiklauri and Hunt, and Pócs all tackle. The psychology behind charming is addressed here by Wolf-Knuts, Herjulfsdotter, Ilomäki and Low Kok On, amongst others. And epistemological problems lurk in the background (or are dissected in the foreground) in various of the pieces found in this book – questions of how accurately and how fully we can be said to know about (secret) knowledge, how we can construct and yet stay at one remove from what (in the absence of additional evidence) we know must be only educated guesses. One topic unaddressed in the present collection that may prove of some use is the possibility of making a divide (and of making connections) between the charmer his- or herself and the *incantatory I*, i.e. between the speaker of the charm and the speaker in the charm. Such a division would mirror that made in studies of poetry between the bundle of accidents and incoherence that sits down to breakfast and the lyrical I of the poem.

The structure of the book is bipartite, consisting of sections on 'Topics in Charms Studies' and 'National Traditions'. But even this division is somewhat artificial, as the topics and issues found in the first section of this book often overlap (and indeed spill over into the book's second section too). And although scholars in the second half of the book concentrate more keenly upon national traditions, many of them explicitly try to position their material in a comparative, international context. While research on national traditions, establishing corpora and their characteristics, is a goal sufficient in itself for some researchers, for others it is a key stepping stone in the development of charms studies more broadly.

The book proper begins with a discussion by Laura Stark, one of the world's leading anthropological folklorists, of 'the dark side' of traditional Finnish rural life. The great folklore archives established by national–romantic fiat in the nineteenth and early twentieth centuries were designed to preserve something of the fast-vanishing culture of traditional rural life, and by extension of national character. But, in some cases at least, they can also offer the historical anthropologist clues as to the darker elements of such a way of life – social pressures, tensions, and attempts at harming others magically. In addition to the first-hand historical testimonies she quotes on the role of the *tietäjä* in village life, she also presents us with some fascinating charm texts in Kalevala metre aimed at 'hardening' the body both against potential harm from magic and from bullets on a battlefield. And Stark is also one of the growing band who attempt to use the evidence that charm texts, records of the practice of charming, and the beliefs of and about charmers can provide in support or contradiction of larger historical theses, in this case about the nature of the self in early modern society.

Paul Cowdell examines charms used to be rid of rats, a form of charm with, as he shows, a remarkable long history, and also with, he argues, a consistent set of structural elements over time. His chapter combines rat-lore with natural history in a fruitful way, reminding us of the real world background to charming. Indeed, one question always lurking in the background of charms studies is the one formulated most eloquently by Brian Murdoch: 'But did they work?'[10] Understandably, academic researchers often do not choose to address this question, but Cowdell touches upon an answer in his chapter, by speculating that the written charms he discusses may in fact work, that the intrusive pieces of paper pushed into their environment may trigger their 'neophobia'.

Ritwa Herjulfsdotter presents us with a short but focussed chapter which concentrates on one theme – uncovering the gender of those involved in charming snake-bites in Suedophone areas. She draws important distinctions between who recorded the charms, knew the charms, and who learnt them, distinctions which are often glossed over in less painstaking work. In addressing the question of the transmission of charms, she shows both that contra-sexual transmission of charms was the desired norm (as is the other Germanic countries of Germany and England[11]), but that the ethnographic record is full of contradictory evidence as to what actually took place. Investigations such as Herjulfsdotter's which involve the interrogation of archival materials in order to wring fresh insights from them must be a key activity for charms scholars, especially those investigating those areas (such as in this case Sweden and Swedish-speaking Finland) where traditional charming is moribund. In subsequent research in much the same vein, Herjulfsdotter has identified that men were more likely than women to use those snake charms that feature Jesus rather than Mary as the chief protagonist.

Ulrika Wolf-Knuts is another who focuses here primarily on the charming rather than the charm, or more exactly upon the preconditions for charming: 'My point of departure is that charms are rituals performed in a crisis, be it illness, bad weather, an attack by vermin or predatory animals, fire or a bad churning experience.' She plausibly suggests that charms can be well understood as a psychological coping mechanism. Although her chapter is not long, it is full of insight, often expressed in passing, and contains ideas worthy of following up at greater length: 'unsuccessful charms are seldom found in the collections, simply because there is no mention of the real effect of charming'. It may be that her most fruitful formulation is the following, which equates the possible effects of great literature and of charms: 'Charms mentioning mythical beings and supernatural actors can function as fictive texts and provide the distressed with the same mechanism for understanding his or her life situation [as novels can]. This understanding is brought about with the help of a culture-specific text containing roles and wordings that suit the actual state.'

Vladimir Klyaus, who has produced an index of the 'plots and plot situations' of Eastern and Southern Slavic charms, discusses the principles behind his work here, presenting examples from Russian, Belorussian and Bulgarian tradition. Arguing that 'opposition is one of the typical characteristics of charm poetry', he outlines a structuralist model based on oppositions reminiscent at times of the work of both Lévi-Strauss and Propp. But Klyaus does not concentrate upon the textual aspect of tradition alone, he also addresses how this is paralleled or filled out by the actions of the charmer. He argues that charms, often included by earlier Russian scholars under the rubric of the 'short genres', are, when considered together with their 'extra-textual' context, more complex that this potentially dismissive description might imply. Indeed Klyaus reminds us that the shorter the charm, the more significant the charming.

T.M. Smallwood is one of the contributors who highlights the Christian background for (what we know of) European verbal charms. Based on the sheer number of charms that survive and on their manuscript context, he makes the claim that charms were 'openly disseminated and perfectly respectable' in the fourteenth, fifteenth and early sixteenth centuries (the period for which the greatest number of English charms survive, the majority, alas, still unpublished). Smallwood's key opposition is found in his title, that of 'conformity and originality', and while accepting that the majority of charms from this period are likely to conform to well-established norms, he chooses to focus on the minority which display originality 'within the bound of conventional doctrine'.

At one point, Smallwood compares the originality of the Middle English charms he examines with that of certain Middle English devotional lyrics – another form for which a large number of examples survive in manuscript form.

Jacqueline Simpson, the *doyenne* of English folkloristics, presents us with a discussion of a charm (or is it a charm?) that occurs in one of the key works of English literature, *King Lear*. It is instructive that the words in question were not recognised as being a charm (or at least charm-like) during the eighteenth and nineteenth centuries, and that it was only a scholar with a sound background in folklore studies (and indeed a student of the great ballad scholar F.J. Child), namely G.L. Kittredge who identified the jingle beginning 'Swithold footed thrice the old' for what it seems to be. Simpson sets the charm-type (which I have called *St George*) against the background of encounter charms (*Begegnungssegen*) involving an encounter with evil more generally. And she uses genuine examples from the Anglophone ethnographic record, both early modern and nineteenth century to show both their similarity to Shakespeare's formulation, and also the comic and grotesque changes he made, changes which would, argues Simpson, have produced 'a brief but loud guffaw from the groundlings'.

Natalia Glukhova and Vladimir Glukhov discuss the folk literature of a European people very little known in the wider world. The Mari, who live in European Russia, have, as many peoples do, an interesting variety of poetic expressions of inevitability and impossibility in verbal folklore in general, and in the language of charms in particular. For instance, the words of the charm may express the idea that the speaker of the charm may be attacked when the bewitcher is able to bewitch the sun, i.e. is able to do the impossible: never. Or, to give an example of an expression of inevitability, the words of the charm may express the idea that the love between two people will grow just as the sun goes round the earth, i.e. the longed-for will occur, just as something natural and inevitable occurs. Such rhetoric is the common currency of charms worldwide. What sets this chapter strikingly apart in its discussion of such universal tropes is its attempt to frame that discussion in the terms of probability theory.

Inasmuch as we would like to see the establishment of an international typology of charms, perhaps the best hope for the creation of such a catalogue might be with the husband and wife research team of Andrei Toporkov and Tatjana Agapkina. In his chapter in the present volume, Toporkov gives a magisterial summary of literature on the topics of both charms studies in Russia and the study of love magic in Europe as a whole, before going on to present an array of examples of this feature in a series of European traditions – adding important eastern European examples such as Czech, Romanian, and Serbian, to the known Italian, Dutch, German and Spanish examples. Whether there is a historical connection between the Russian and the ancient Greek examples, or whether the parallel is something that might be expected to occur given the widespread parallels in the descriptions of the symptoms of love in this area is unsure. Toporkov himself suggests that there was a historical link (Byzantium), although in the absence of fresh manuscript evidence being uncovered in the future, we are in a situation we often find in charms studies: that of uncertainty.

Monika Kropej presents the Slovenian charming tradition to us on the basis of both archival sources and her own fieldwork. But once again, this presentation of a national tradition is happily set in a broader comparative framework, for as Kropej herself notes, 'parallels to Slovene charms can be found in the South Slavic oral tradition, and in the cultures of Central Europe, especially in the Friuli, Romanic, Austrian, and Swiss Alpine heritages'. Her ability to contextualize the charms she recorded during her own fieldwork in the village of Windish Bleiberg/Slovenji Plajberg with the earlier ethnographic record is admirable. She also presents us briefly with data on a key aspect of charms studies that is too often neglected (or is inaccessible), namely data about the charmer. In addition to the brief portrait of the charmer, Marija Wieser, herself, there are also descriptions of the charming too, with mention of Marija's use of a kerchief and oil, her gestures such as making the sign of the cross, and the taboo against thanking her. Many of these features of charming are to be found in other cultures too. And following an interesting presentation of a variety of Slovene healing and weather charms, she concludes, as we would expect of the editor of *Studia Mythologica Slavica*, by attempting to draw out cosmological elements in the charm texts.

Henni Ilomäki discusses snake charms as found in Finnish tradition in her contribution to this volume. After some discussion of the image of the snake in pre-Christian and Christian societies, she presents us with some fascinating Finnish texts drawn from nineteenth-century folklore collections, and in one case, from a seventeenth century court transcript. These are charms with a very different feel to them than the majority of recent European charms. But presentation of such material, fascinating as it is in itself, is not Ilomaki's only goal, she also uses the charms as part of an account of the worldview of nineteenth century Finnish peasants. In particular, she is interested in what the charms reveal about the syncretism between ethnic beliefs and Christian worldview in the minds of charmers. While one need not agree with all the details of the case she sets out, it is at all events an interesting example of another possible use of charms, as evidence in descriptions of *mentalité*.

The author of the next chapter, Jonathan Roper, has been much concerned with the fact that many charms are far from being unique sets of words, but rather have analogues across time and over space, and can indeed be said to show features of typicality, or the membership of a particular charm-type. In his monograph *English Verbal Charms*, he has presented a tentative typology of the English material, with reference to continental analogues. In his chapter in this book, he turns to a rather different set of material, but with the same research goal in mind. On the basis of archival research on the little-known Estonian material, he supplies an outline of Estonian narrative charm-types. As might be expected analogues to such charms can be found widely in that corner of Europe, and on occasion even further afield. Most interesting of all perhaps is the predominant German influence in this corpus of material his analysis reveals. As for the typicality or atypicality of the English and Estonian narrative charm corpora as a whole, this will only emerge, as he suggests, when more data on such national corpora of charms is made available in international languages.

Daiva Vaitkevičienė ploughs a similar furrow in her chapter. She presents information on charm-types shared in both Latvian and Lithuanian traditions. Although these neighbouring countries possess closely related languages, the history of the documentation of charms in the two countries differs. Despite this she is able to present us with examples of internationally known types such as **Flum Jordan** and **Three Roses**, as well as more local texts, as represented for example, by a variety of dialogue charms. The biggest surprise arrives in her conclusion, where she states that, on the basis of the evidence she has, there are more similarities between Lithuanian charms and Russian and Belorussian charms than with Latvian charms. If we knew more about such distributions and could establish the 'isoglosses' (to borrow a term from the study of dialects) of different charm-types in Europe, we would be able to write an important chapter in the history of vernacular culture.

Lea Olsan's chapter presents us with an important study of a related set of late medieval manuscripts containing charms. Although England is somewhat out of step with many continental countries in never possessing a printed chapbook of healing charms, such as the *Romanusbüchlein*, the 'Leechcraft' remedy books that Olsan discusses may well prove to be a close analogy of such works, although somewhat *avant la lettre*. Olsan demonstrates by her painstaking library work (the results of which are set out in tabular form) that these manuscripts had a rather firm core of recurrent charms (albeit subject to internal variation), along with certain other items. A core of shared material (with some variations) together with other matter is just what we find in the later and printed *Romanusbüchlein* tradition too. Olsan, rather than glossing over the substantial variation found in one particular manuscript, examines these differences with the hope that they 'offer insights into the development of the charm set over time'. In the conclusion to her chapter, Olsan addresses the question of why some diseases and conditions were thought to be the fit subject for charming, while others were deemed suitable for herbal remedies. The answer she suggests lies in culture rather than in physiology.

Maria Vivod presents the results of her own fieldwork with the magical healer Biljana in modern-day Serbia. Biljana, a former school secretary, uses methods and texts close to (yet slightly altered from) traditional healing practice and traditional healing texts. Vivod also usefully describes the lead-casting procedure that this charmer uses to diagnose what afflicts those who come to her as patients. Vivod's work provides us with another remind that any system of folk healing (including charming) also depends upon the existence of a system of folk illness: the folk diagnosis of particular illness, and the belief that they are (or might) be amenable to folk treatment. At the conclusion of her chapter, Vivod turns briefly to address the social, economic and cultural factors that have lead to a resurgence of charming, which had fifty years previously been described as being in terminal decline. It is worth noting that Vivod has also documented Biljana's healing on film. The documentation of charming on film, and also the elicitation of information from both charmers and their patients may well prove (where it is possible to undertake) a key new means of expanding our understanding of charms, charmers and charming.

Charms studies have been a rather euro-centric field to date, as this Introduction no doubt has indicated in passing. Indeed the title of this volume's predecessor was explicitly European: *Charms and Charming in Europe*. The presence of two extra-European chapters in this volume may be a hopeful sign of the geographical development of this field of study. Firstly, we have a chapter by Lee Haring, the well-known specialist on the oral traditions of the Indian Ocean, who addresses oral tradition in Madagascar in his chapter. And secondly we have work on a south-east Asian tradition by Low Kok On.

While the main focus of names studies, or onomastics, is names used in the real world, there is a fascinating subfield of names studies, known as 'literary onomastics', which studies the use of names in works of folklore and literature. Some of the extra piquancy that literary onomastics possesses derives from the fact that there is partial but imperfect overlap between literary names and names found in the real world. By analogy, Haring's chapter can be seen a pioneer study in the field of literary charms studies, or to be more precise oral-literary onomastics (since he is concerned with Malagasy oral literature).

The Anglo-Georgian team of David Hunt and Mary Tsiklauri present us with precious information about a fascinating charming tradition (one of several survey chapters in the present work) that to date has been inaccessible for non-Kartvelologists. Their discussion encompasses the etymology of terms for charms, the inner logic of different forms of charms, and the details of actions and objects that form part of the charming procedures. The thirteen charms collected by Mikho Mosulishvili which they present in parallel Georgian and English translation at the conclusion of their chapter form a particular interesting set from the eastern edge of Christendom.

Low Kok On continues on from the *tours d'horizon* presented in the past by W.W. Skeat and K.M. Endicott,[12] by documenting recent and contemporary Malay magic. So contemporary, indeed, is his survey, that it even encompasses some recent internet sources for charms for success in business, but there are also age-old aspects of this tradition, as the Sanskrit etymology for 'mantera', the Malay word for charm, suggests. As well as a generous number of example charms, he also discusses the charmer (in this case the *bomoh* or *pawang* and the *tuk bidan*) and the procedures of charming as well. He also usefully highlights the frequently syncretic nature of these charms, with their Hindu–Buddhist, Islamic, and indigenous Malay characteristics. The question of the continuation of such charming in an era when the majority of the population turn first to modern biomedicine is another aspect of the survey presented here.

The nineteen chapters of this book certainly cover a diverse set of fields, as this overview has attempted to indicate. Encouragingly, there are several attempts in the pages that follow to combine discussion of charm texts with the procedures that accompany them (or perhaps we should say which they accompany?). This two-barrelled focus on the charms and on the charming is much to be welcomed, and gives rise to all sorts of insights and fresh research questions. Which predominates: the words or the actions? Can the words or actions have any effect in isolation? How successfully is the unity of words and actions transmitted from one generation to another? Happily however, one question which is not addressed in the present collection is that of which of the two might have historical precedence whether in particular cases or in general – in other words, which came first the magical procedure or the magical words, the charming or the charm? That question would, I fear, prove as unanswerable as that of the chicken and the egg.

I would like to conclude this introduction by expressing my thanks to the staff of the National Centre for English Cultural Tradition at the University of Sheffield, of the School of English at the University of Leeds, of the Folklore Society, and of the Warburg Institute, and by acknowledging the help and support of my colleagues in charms studies.

Jonathan Roper,
Leeds, November 2007

Notes

1. Maikov, Leonid, 'Velikorusskije zaklinanija' *Zapiski Imp. Russkogo geograficheskogo obshchestva po otdeleniju ethnografij*, II (1869): 417–580. There have been various reprints of this in book form, e.g. in 1992, 1997, etc.

2. Bang, Anton, *Norske Hexeformularer og Magiske opskrifter* (Kristiania: Skrifter udgivne af Videnskabsselskabet i Christiania 2. Historisk-filosofisk Klasse, 1901); Forsblom, Valter, *Finlands Svenska Folkdiktning VII.5 (Folktro och trolldom, Magisk Folkmedicin)*, (Helsingfors: SLS, 1927); Pradel, Fritz, *Greichische und süditalienische Gebete, Beschwörungen und Rezepte des Mittelalters* (Giessen: A. Töpelmann, 1907); Preisendanz, Karl, *Papyri graecae magicae: die griechischen zauberpapyri* (Leipzig [etc.]: B.G. Teubner, 1928-31).
3. Franz, Adolph, *Die kirchlichen Benedictionen im Mittelalter*, 2 vols (Freiburg im Breisgau: Herder, 1909).
4. Ebermann, Oskar, *Blut- und Wundsegen in ihrer Entwicklung dargestellt* (Berlin: Mayer und Müller, 1903).
5. Ohrt, Ferdinand, *Danmarks Trylleformler 1–2* (Copenhagen, Kristiania: F[olklore] F[ellows] publications, northern series 3, 1917, 1921).
6. Ohrt, Ferdinand, *Trylleord. Fremmede og danske*, Danmarks folkeminder 25 (Copenhagen: Det Schønbergske Forlag, 1922); *De Danske Besværgelser mod Vrid og Blod* (Copenhagen: Bianco Luno, 1922); 'The spark in the water: an early Christian legend – a Finnish magic song' *Folklore Fellows' Communications* 65 (Helsinki: Academia Scientiarum Fennica, 1926); *Da Signed Krist: Tolkning af det religiøse Indhold i Danmarks Signelser og Besværgelser* (Copenhagen: Gyldendal, 1927); *Gamle Danske Folkebønner* (Copenhagen: V. Pio, 1928); *Herba, gratiâ plena: die Legenden der alteren Segensspruche uber den gottlichen Ursprung der Heil- und Zauberkrauter* (Folklore Fellows' Communications 82) (Helsinki: Academia Scientiarum Fennica, 1929); 'Fluchtafel und Wettersegen', *Folklore Fellows' Communications* 86 (Helsinki: Academia scientiarum fennica, 1929); 'Trylleformler' in Lid, Nils, ed., *Nordisk Kultur*, vol. 19, 77–94 (Stockholm, Oslo and Copenhagen: Boniers, 1935), 'Über Alter und Ursprung der Begegnungssegen', *Hessische Blätter für Volkskunde* 35 (1936): 49–58; *Die ältesten Segen über Christi Taufe und Christi Tod in religionsgeschichtlichem Lichte* (Det Kgl. Danske Videnskabernes Selskab. Historisk-filologiske Meddelser, 25.1) (Copenhagen: Levin og Munksgaard, 1938); Hoffmann-Krayer, Eduard, and Bächtold-Stäubli, Hanns, eds, *Handwörterbuch des deutschen Aberglaubens* (Berlin: de Gruyter, 1927–42), s.v. 'Segen', and numerous other entries in that work. It should be noted that this is not a full list of this productive scholar's publications in the sphere of charms – there are also numerous articles and reviews which I have not mentioned here.
7. Spamer, Adolf, *Romanusbüchlein: historisch–philologischer Kommentar zu einem deutschen Zauberbuch* (Berlin: Akademie-Verlag, 1958).
8. Haver, J. van, *Nederlandse incantatieliteratuur. Een gecommentarieerd compendium van Nederlandse bezweringsformules* (Gent: Koninklijke Vlaamse Academie voor Taal- en Letterkunde. Publications reeks 6. no. 94, 1964).
9. E.g. Barb, A.A. 'St Zacharias the Prophet and Martyr: a Study in Charms and Incantations', *Journal of the Warburg and Courtauld Institutes* 11 (1948), pp. 35–67; 'Animula Vagula Blandula.... Notes on Jingles, Nursery-Rhymes and Charms with an Excursus of Noththe's Sisters', *Folklore* 61:1 (1950): 15–30; 'Antaura. The Mermaid and the Devil's Grandmother: A Lecture', *Journal of the Warburg and Courtauld Institutes* 29 (1966), 1–23.
10. Murdoch, B. O., 'But did they work?: interpreting the Old High German *Merseburg Charms* in their medieval context', *Neuphilologische Mitteilungen*, vol. 89, no. 3 (1988), 358–69.

11. See Roper, Jonathan, *English Verbal Charms* (Helsinki: Academia Scientiarum Fennica, 2005) (Folklore Fellows' Communications 288).
12. Skeat, W.W., *Malay Magic: Being an Introduction to the Folklore and Popular Religion of the Malay Peninsula* (London: Macmillan, 1900); Endicott, K.M. *An Analysis of Malay Magic* (Kuala Lumpur and Oxford: Oxford University Press, 1970).

Part I

Topics and Issues in Charms Studies

1

The Charmer's Body and Behaviour as a Window Onto Early Modern Selfhood[1]

Laura Stark

Some years ago, in researching images of the human body in traditional Finnish magic, I came across the following text recorded in northern Finland from a male sorcerer born in 1835. This text gave me my first glimpse into the dark side of life in traditional[2] rural Finland, one rarely portrayed in folkloristic and ethnological research:

> If someone commits a terrible wrong against me, then I seize an iron rod and run into the forest, to the sort of place which is half peat bog and half dry land, to the boundary between them. Then I make a hole in the ground with the iron rod and put a live frog in the hole, cover it with peat and step on it three times with my left foot and say:

Te maassaa asuvaiset ja	You who live in the ground,
maanhaltiat,	and earth spirits,
Tarttukaa tuota perkeleen roistoa	Seize that devil's villain and
kivuttamaan,	make him suffer,
Niinkun tuo sammakko kituu tuolla!	Just as that frog suffers!

> One should have terrible *luonto* [=inner supernatural force], anger, and clenched teeth when one does this. Then illness and pain come to the other person. So that they do not see another day of health. At times they are racked with aches in their head, arms and legs, at times with sharp pains in their chest (*pistos*). Even a person who can set the dead and underground beings in motion cannot cure him. Only the person who has bewitched him using the earth can cure him.
>
> (SKVR XII₂:6024. Kittilä. 1920.
> J. Paulaharju 8578 – Johan Aapraham Koskama or
> Takalo, alias 'Jans Päkki', 82 years old)

3

This account is just one of thousands of descriptions of magical harm[3] dating from the nineteenth and early twentieth centuries. Although usually associated with the period of the witchcraft trials (sixteenth–eighteenth centuries), magic continued to live a robust life some two hundred years later, as recent research on Britain, Scandinavia, and Continental Europe has emphasized (e.g. Davies 1999; de Blécourt 1999; Gijswijt-Hofstra 1999). Nearly all rural nineteenth-century Finnish villages appear to have contained witches, healers and quarrelsome neighbors who believed they were able to cause each other magical harm. In some parts of rural Finland people continued to use magic rites to bring harm to their enemies as late as the 1950s (see Stark 2006: 47–9).

Descriptions of magic and sorcery housed in the Finnish Literature Society Folklore Archives in Helsinki provide rare glimpses into the kinds of social pressures and tensions people experienced in their everyday lives. They also serve as windows onto the nature of early modern personhood. The envy and vindictiveness, fears of magical harm bordering on paranoia, and lack of ability to identity with others' suffering which are all evident from these descriptions would appear to most twenty-first-century Europeans as irrational and even pathological. This is because these are no longer the means of achieving the rational long-term aims held by most modern individuals. Yet any scrutiny of what has constituted reasonable behavior in other historical periods must take into account cultural-specific notions of self and agency. How individuals define themselves and what they are seen to be entitled to, as well as whatever culturally constitutes the 'good life' will determine what sort of behavior is viewed as rational versus irrational.

Behaviors and beliefs linked to magic did not disappear from daily life simply because people were educated in new scientific belief systems or materialist modes of thought. It was not simply a mentality or world view that changed, but the very conditions and circumstances which made magic a reasonable strategy in nineteenth-century social life. When these conditions changed, so did modes of thought and experience.

From contemporary reports of persons living in the nineteenth-century countryside, it appears that rural life was characterized above all by poverty, endless toil, and high personal risk. Nineteenth-century rural Finns lived in communities where hunger and disease were common, and there were few formal social institutions to guarantee safety and well-being. Health care was usually unavailable and poor relief too ineffective to prevent mass starvation in times of famine. Rural inhabitants had very little material protection from the harsh natural environment: if they were landowners, they possessed only the farm and its fields carved from the forest through human labour, as well as the minimal technologies of knife, axe, scythe, and horse-drawn plough which extended the body's capabilities. The landless population possessed even less. Severe poverty meant that in many cases there was a sense of competition, rather than cooperation, among neighbours. Policemen were few, criminal detectives unknown, and the courts could not always compel persons to appear before them. As a result, vandalism, theft, assault, fraud and slander often went unpunished and left victims feeling helpless in the face of their neighbors' malice.

It is no surprise, then, that descriptions of magic recorded in rural Finland paint a vivid picture of persons who perceived themselves to be vulnerable and unprotected. In modern society, the individual is protected by laws, practices and institutions which safeguard personal boundaries. These include laws against fraud, defamation, slander, assault, battery, intimidation, violation of privacy, and more recently in some Western societies, laws against sexual harassment, stalking, and the physical punishment of children. Early modern individuals, by contrast, had to protect *themselves* from threats, and magic provided one means of doing this. Those who spread the word that they were magically powerful could sleep more soundly at night believing that because of their dangerous reputations, they were safer from thieves, vandals and other evil-doers.

The lack of institutional protections experienced by rural inhabitants also seems to have led to a perception of the outside world as containing countless dangers waiting attack the human body. The body was not depicted as separate from its surroundings, but as extremely porous, its boundaries weak and fuzzy. Ordinary persons were expected to go to great lengths to protect themselves from magical harm, hostility, and the curses of others. If they suspected that acts of magical harm had already been carried out against them, they hastened to perform counter-sorcery. Even children learned from a young age the importance of guarding themselves against the envy of others by participating in the counter-measures carried out by their parents (Stark 2006: 211–13).

Tietäjä: specialist in magical protection

The person whose behavior best expresses this ideal of self-protection was the *tietäjä* (literally, 'one who knows').[4] The *tietäjä* was a specialist in magic – including sorcery, healing and divination, and was assumed to have secret knowledge others did not possess. Although the majority of *tietäjäs* appear to have been men, some were also women, particularly in the northern areas of Finland.

Minor witches and household healers were abundant in early modern Finland, but it was the *tietäjäs* who possessed the most elaborate knowledge regarding the structure of the supernatural and magical worlds. The *tietäjä* was seen to have the ability to divine the source of illness through dreams, to staunch the flow of blood from a wound, to force thieves to return stolen goods, to battle illness-agents and to send dangerous animals back to the witches who had originally summoned them to attack humans or livestock. *Tietäjäs* were thus the highest level of professionals versed in knowledge of folk illness and supranormal entities. It was they who preserved, in their enormous repertoires of rites and Kalevala-metre charms,[5] knowledge which was partly the legacy of a shamanistic past. The *tietäjä* institution had inherited many features of Eurasian shamanism including altered states of consciousness and the use of helper-spirits and animal spirits. *Tietäjäs* also possessed knowledge of the illness-agent's true origin and essence, of the topography of the other world, and of which supranormal beings to call upon for assistance (see Siikala 2002: 86–90, 178–234). Unlike shamans, however, *tietäjäs* did not need to journey to the worlds of the spirits or the dead in order to communicate with them. *Tietäjäs* instead recited lengthy incantations to invoke, threaten or placate supernatural entities such as the dead, nature spirits, illness-demons, and various deities both Christian and pre-Christian.

The *tietäjä*'s authority derived from his ability to convince others of his superior knowledge. He did this through his feats of memory in reciting lengthy incantations, his ritual performance technique, his use of secrecy and possession of mysterious objects such as human skulls, parts of animals and even so-called 'black Bibles', which were thought to contain black pages with white print, or to be written with unfamiliar characters.[6] The authority of *tietäjäs* in magic rituals was thus based in part on a sense of mystery: *tietäjäs* emphasized their possession of secret knowledge and used actions and objects which were often baffling and opaque to participants.

In nineteenth-century Finnish rural communities, the use of magic functioned to create a sense of security and protect personal boundaries. Constant vigilance and self-protection against magical and supernatural harm were a way of life for many rural inhabitants, but *tietäjäs* took this behavior to new extremes. When *tietäjäs* drove illness-agents from the bodies of suffering individuals and performed counter-sorcery against other magic-workers, they were often in a state of agitated excitation or frenzied anger. When they wished to paint a picture of themselves as quick to defend any encroachment upon their personal boundaries, *tietäjäs* became enraged and displayed this rage for all to see. Anger was a *cultural performance* acted out in order to emphasize the performer's readiness to take action against any perceived threats.

In his work *Mythologia Fennica* (1786), Christfrid Ganander depicted the state of the ecstatic sorcerer as follows: 'Nobody dares to disturb these masters who know everything, for they become enraged, gnash their teeth, their hair stands on end, in their frenzy they leap into the air, mumble some words, stamp their feet and behave totally as if in a fit of rage, for which reason they are called "men of frenzy" (*intomies*)' (in Siikala 2002: 243). A more detailed description can be found from the early nineteenth-century writings of folklore collector and compiler of the *Kalevala*, Elias Lönnrot: 'the *tietäjä* 1) becomes enraged, 2) his speech becomes loud and frenzied, 3) he foams at the mouth, 4) gnashes his teeth, 5) his hair stands on end, 6) his eyes widen, 7) he knits his brows, 8) he spits often, 9) his body contorts, 10) he stamps his feet, 11) jumps up and down on the floor, and 12) makes many other gestures' (ibid. 2002: 244). Similar descriptions were still being recorded from northern and eastern Finland as late as the 1930s. In 1921, a man from rural Eastern Finland wrote down the following written recollection of an event which took place in his childhood. In it, he depicts the ecstatic frenzy of a sorcerer who bathed his family in order to release them from the magical harm perpetrated by an unknown witch:[7]

... And so the sauna was heated and the entire group of us, from the father of the family to the smallest child, went to the sauna with the sorcerer. There the demon-frightener first bathed us, slapping each of one of us separately with the sauna whisk made of birch leaves, and at the same time reciting an incantation so that he foamed at the mouth. Then he put each of us three times through a hoop fashioned from the blades of three scythes, first by lowering the hoop over each of us from head to foot two times, and then one time from bottom to top. While doing this trick, the sorcerer was in an extremely agitated state the entire time, but that was still nothing compared to what happened next. Now, you see, the sorcerer encircled each of our heads with a hunting knife, two times clockwise and one time counterclockwise, and then in a fit of frenzied rage, hurled the knife into the sauna whisk lying on the floor, and then, holding the knife, flung the whisk out of the sauna window and against the cooking hut so that the wall of the cooking hut reverberated. Apparently in this way he flung out our tormentor, supposedly pierced to the core by the knife, thus sending the dog[8] to its own home to bite and gnaw the person who had 'broken' us ...

A *tietäjä*'s power or magical force was seen to come from his wrath, and fear of that wrath ensured that few deliberately dared to offend him. One story tells of a farmhand who, despite warnings from onlookers, vandalized a bird-trap set by an elderly *tietäjä*. The narrator, himself the famous *tietäjä* Pekka Tuovinen, recounts: 'at this the old man became furious. And later, when the farmhand went insane for the rest of his life and the old man was asked to grant mercy, he said, "I became too angry, he cannot be saved".'[9] In another account, a man who verbally offended the *tietäjä* known as 'Doctor Hirvonen' (=Juho Hirvonen, 1866–1930) died of a haemorrhage the same night: 'Doctor Hirvonen said of himself that the person at whom he became angry would die right away.'[10]

Steeling the self against magical harm: bodily 'hardness'

In addition to cultivating reputations for being quick to react aggressively in the face of danger, *tietäjäs* created imagined zones of magical invulnerability around the self. They did this by invoking supernatural protection when reciting incantations. In the incantation below, a *tietäjä* from Archangel Karelia asks water spirits for protective armour against malicious magic-workers living in his vicinity:

... Anna mulle rauta takki,	... Give to me an iron coat,
Rauta takki, rauta lakki,	Iron coat, iron cap,
Rauta hattu hartijoille,	Iron mantle for my shoulders,
Rauta kihttahat käteen,	Iron mittens for my hands,
Rauta saappahat jalkoin,	Iron boots for my feet,
Joilla astun hiien maita,	With which I shall enter the Hiisi's[11] lands,
Maita lemmon leyhyttelen,	Move about in Evil's realm,
Ettei pysty noijan nuolet	So that the sorcerer's arrows will not penetrate,
Eikä velhon veitsirauvat,	Nor the wizard's knives,
Ei asehet ampumiehen	Nor the shooter's weapons,
Eikä tietäjän teräkset.	Nor the *tietäjä's* blades.

(SKVR I₄:2. Kiimasjärvi. 1888. Meriläinen 52 – Risto Nikitin)

It was believed that one of the most important qualities that enabled *tietäjäs* to triumph in struggles against harmful forces and agents was a 'hard' or 'strong' *luonto*. The term *luonto* referred to an inborn supernatural force used to heal, harm, or make magic rites more effective. It was thought that a *tietäjä* possessed a hard luonto if he had been born with teeth. Since *teeth* are the hardest part of the human body, the *tietäjä*'s possession of teeth from birth was a sign of the innate 'hardness' of his being. Numerous accounts also describe how elderly *tietäjäs* needed to have a full set of teeth in order to perform magic. When they lost their teeth, it was believed that they had also lost their supernatural powers:[12]

> Whoever has a full set of teeth can work magic, and otherwise he should be "in all ways strong and powerful in his being", so that the only thing that can cut him is a bullet.
> (Kuusamo. 1938. Maija Juvas 486 – A certain old man, 70 years old)

Tietäjäs were also thought to have the ability to physically 'harden' their bodies in order to withstand the blows of whips and sticks. For instance, it was told of Vagrant-Eeva, a witch from Satakunta, that she could 'make herself so that she felt nothing, even if she were struck with an axe …'.[13] Behind beliefs in the *tietäjä*'s ability to harden his or her body against whips lay a deeper cultural fascination with persons whose bodies were reported to be hard or invulnerable to the heat of fire, freezing temperatures and even the sharpness of metal objects applied to their skin.[14] There appears to have been no shortage of such persons in the late nineteenth- and even early twentieth-century countryside, and particularly from Southwestern Finland come reports of locals who walked barefoot on the sharp edges of scythes, or allowed others to strike them with hard objects. It was not uncommon for such persons to have performed feats demonstrating their bodily hardness in front of onlookers who might pay a small fee to watch the spectacle.

The means by which *tietäjäs* and others 'hardened' their bodies varied, but one common method was to keep in one's mouth a bullet which had killed a person or animal, or to wear a shirt in which a corpse had been buried (which required digging up the corpse).[15] As one informant from Western Finland described,

> Soldier Alatt had been in the 1808–1809 war … Alatt had said that in the war he had brushed handfuls of bullets off his chest when they didn't penetrate his skin. He had sacrificed himself to the cemetery. Before he went off to war he had dug up a consecrated corpse from the cemetery. He took off its shirt and wore it when going off to battle. Then the bullets didn't penetrate him …
> (Länsi-Teisko. 1938. K.H. Färm KT 44:18)

Another man, born in 1842 in Eastern Finland, reported having heard from his grandfather, who was a famous *tietäjä*, how to make oneself hard before leaving for war. According to the grandfather,

> When leaving for war, one takes a shirt from a buried corpse and exchanges it for one's own, a corpse which has died honorably and has been buried, and is older than the person exchanging shirts. Then, when one comes to the battlefield, one says:

Veijon ukko, kultahelma,	Old man, friend, golden-hem,
Vettä vänkillä vetäse,	Draw water with all your might,
Ettei ruutit rupsahaisi,	So that gunpowder will not blast,
Pahat jauhot paukahaisi,	The evil powder will not boom,
Ettei lyijy miestä löisi,	So that lead will not strike this man,
Tinapalli paiskovaisi! ...	The ball of tin will not hit! ...

> Then the bullets will not penetrate, even if one is shot at all day long, they will go through other clothes, but not the shirt. If one wears a second shirt over the first, then the bullets will collect inside it [above the belt]. They should be put aside for safekeeping; they are needed when making salve for animals suffering from bloating or witches' shot: when you scrape bits of them into water, then nothing more is needed than to give [the animal] that water.
>
> (SKVR XII$_2$:7926. Suomussalmi. 1888 – Jeremias Seppänen, 46 years old. Heard from his grandfather ... The narrator had seen these bullets still in his father's keeping ...)

Reputations for magical harm

In an age before law enforcement, a reputation for revenge and danger-ous sorcery discouraged others from attempting to cheat, harm or steal from the *tietäjä* or his property:

> In former times lumber was transported to the city of Pori. When they reached their lodgings, the men transporting the lumber took their belongings inside so they would be safe from thieves. But the *tietäjä* Tilli [=Nikolai Lamminsivu, 1863–1948] left his mittens on top of the load. Nobody dared to touch Tilli's belongings ...
>
> (Teisko. 1961. Frans Kärki TK 52:65 – Mikko Korpula, farmer, b. 1891. Heard as a child from his father Erland Korpula)

Many *tietäjäs* strove to draw a boundary of untouchability around themselves by cultivating reputations as persons not to be trifled with. Informants from various regions of Finland remarked on local *tietäjäs* as follows: 'Tilli is a mighty sorcerer, with whom it does not pay to fool around';[16] '... with Hiltunen there was no sense in being cheeky';[17] 'it wasn't a good idea to make Oskar angry.'[18] Some magic-workers were even said to have boasted with pride – and without remorse – how their sorcery had brought injury, illness or death to their victims:

The girl from Pannula farm went blind because she called me a thief. A piece of straw happened to go into her eye and when she went from the fields into the farmhouse, she had already lost her sight. She injured her other eye on a bundle of leaf-fodder and it went blind too. That's what happened, when she accused me.
> (Perho. 1930. Samuli Paulaharju b)14575 – Maija Sivula,
> old woman cottager, *tietäjä*, 83 years old)

... My father had already been married for twenty years or so, I myself was seventeen, the third child of ten. I went with my father to the remote log-floating site near Haapavaara farm where he worked, and I was there for a week and lived at Haapavaara farm. Tiina [Lyhykäinen] was the mistress in charge of the farm, for she had married a man from somewhere on the Russian side of the border. As a life companion he didn't turn out to be much to write home about. Then Tiina told me the story of her youth and how she had taken revenge on my aunt, since my aunt had not let my father marry her. My aunt had twelve children, of which only three girls were left. Many of the children had drowned and all the boys had died, and my aunt's husband had drowned. Tiina said that it was because of her that this had happened to my aunt's family and said that she had carried out sorcery so that it would happen in precisely that way. After she said this, she added: "Mark my words, your aunt herself will die by drowning." Two years went by and then my aunt, while out fishing on Midsummer's Eve, fell into the water and drowned. Only then did I realize what dreadful things could be concealed in that simple, ordinary person's story.
> (Pielisjärvi. 1961. Hilda Pesonen TK 75:
> 15 – Tiina Lyhykäinen, born circa 1875)

Impoverished and itinerant members of the community, both men and women, were also able to arouse fear and respect in others by presenting themselves as quick to take offence, telling stories of their frightening feats of sorcery, and carrying around 'magic' bundles and pouches. A man from Eastern Finland who wrote to the Finnish Literature Society in the 1920s described the typical contents of such magic pouches as: 'small bones, three snake heads obtained in spring before St. George's Day, a snake's assembly stone,[19] snakes' skin, teeth and claws of a bear, bear grease, the herb asafoetida, arsenic, incense, and Ukko's soil.'[20] He also said of such persons: 'A magic worker (*welho*) who travelled about with a magic pouch was terribly dangerous and terrible to look upon as well. It wasn't good for anyone to make him angry, rather, he was someone to be flattered and fawned over.'[21] Another narrator from South Savo recalled an elderly beggar who visited his childhood home at the end of the 1870s: 'she had been married to four men and then remained a widow and roamed about, begging and telling the most frightening tales of her magical abilities, so that farm mistresses, in their fear, put all kinds of things in her begging-sack ...'.[22] A third account from Ostrobothnia tells a similar story:

> I remember how dreadfully afraid we were of the sorceress named Pykly. I was a small girl on my home farm of Emoniemi. It was a completely different time than now, there were no railroads, nor anything else that was modern. The old beliefs were still alive. Every once in a while our home farm was visited by a tiny, old, extremely dark-complexioned woman with a bundle in her hand. She was the dreaded sorceress Pykly, with her magic objects in her bundle. "Pykly is coming", it was said, "now children, behave." Cold shivers ran up and down my body. I would have wanted to run away, but there was nothing to do but remain in the farmhouse and be good, so that Pykly wouldn't work her magic. The adults tried to curry favour when dealing with Pykly. She was fed and given drink and gifts. Pykly was a malicious old woman, from whose brown face blazed a pair of keen black eyes. And she was capricious and quick to anger. Everyone heaved a sigh of relief when she left the farm. Many people used Pykly's "services" during their lifetime. Pykly was in fact a capable sorceress, so it was said.
>
> (Valtimo<Pyhäjärvi. 1955. Siiri Oulasmaa 3116 – Lempi Suurkoski)

Making the self inviolable

In nineteenth-century rural Finland, individuals had to take steps to ensure that other persons did not violate the boundaries of their body and self. Supernatural attacks on enemies, the cultural performance of anger, self-hardening and supernatural self-protection against attacks were practices which promoted a sense of agency, autonomy and inviolability. From the perspective of our modern society, it may be difficult to understand why individuals strove to display their vindictiveness and pride in causing others' suffering. Yet if nothing outside the self guarantees individual rights, then the individual must contain *within himself* the means to secure these rights, and the result is a very different sort of self.

From the early modern perspective, disorder and threat were almost never located within the individual. The illnesses cured by *tietäjäs* in nineteenth-century Finland were seen to come primarily from some external alien essence intruding into the body, whether a curse, a witch's arrow, or supernatural 'contagion' from the forest, water, or cemetery.[23] By contrast, social and cultural historians have emphasized that as European societies were transformed by modernization and industrialization, the focus of people's anxieties shifted to an internal world of self-awareness. Individuals underwent an 'introspective turn' toward a mental and emotional landscape that had never been experienced before in the same way. This 'interior space' of the psyche was now viewed as the dark realm which threatened social and individual well-being. In the pre-modern era, evil spirits were thought to reside in external reality. With the rise of Freudian psychoanalysis, however, the dark corners of the subconscious came to be seen as the source of mysterious disturbances in self and society. Disorder in the modern self is conceived as a problem in the internal organization of the personality and behavior, and Western individuals in the modern era have come to fear the inner workings of their minds: their emotions, desires and impulses. This is because they are expected to internalize an unprecedented amount of physical and mental control (e.g. Elias 1978; Foucault 1977; Spierenburg 1991). Modern persons must submit themselves to the regimens of educational institutions which, it is hoped, will instill in them modern social conventions to such a degree that the suppression of desires and impulses becomes automatic and unconscious.

We should not, however, assume that just because early modern persons did not exhibit *our* familiar forms of self-control in their behaviors, that they failed to internalize any self-controls at all. Their self-discipline, internalized at a young age, was just as rigorous as ours, but its attention was focused in the *opposite* direction: in the older rural culture, individuals did not direct their attention inward to their psyche but rather concentrated on the outer boundaries of the self and body. Individuals were forced to maintain constant vigilance over the perimeter of their person in the face of external threats (magical harm, supernatural forces, other people's anger and envy). They did this by performing magic rites to protect their person, farm and livestock, and by cultivating reputations for magical violence and revenge in order to discourage their enemies from attempting harm in the first place.

The modern Finn is careful not to let uncontrolled behavior *escape* from the body, whereas his or her great-grandparents would have been more concerned about not letting uncontrolled forces from the *outside in*. An individual living in Eastern Finland in the nineteenth century, for instance, might find our modern body practices horrifyingly lax and unrestrained. We care little where we dispose of the cuttings of our hair and nails, we stand on thresholds, we turn our backs to the fire in the hearth, and pregnant women and small children walk freely in public without fear of the evil eye. We are unconcerned with the order in which we put on our clothes or with which foot we enter a room, not to mention countless other behaviors whose violation was seen to open oneself to the threat of supernatural harm. In the modern period, the personal protections given to us by a wide range of societal institutions have reduced the experience of violence, risk and unpredictability so prevalent in earlier times, allowing us to turn our attention away from the outside world in order to focus on another kind of vigilance: the monitoring of our internal orderliness, and the repression of our impulsive behavior.

Notes

1. The research upon which this study is based was funded by the Academy of Finland and the Helsinki Collegium for Advanced Studies.
2. Finland underwent the processes of modernization relatively late, and during the entire period of industrialization and nation-building (1860–1950), older beliefs and practices continued to survive in rural areas where a significant portion of the population resided. The nineteenth-century rise in Finnish national consciousness, first among the cultural elite and later among the ordinary populace, resulted in popular campaigns to record for posterity the oral–traditional heritage of Finnish speakers. This undertaking was highly successful and resulted in some three million recorded folklore texts, including thousands of descriptions of magic rites.
3. These descriptions were first recorded by educated collectors starting in the 1830s, and from the 1880s onward also by tradition enthusiasts coming from the ranks of the rural population. The latter 'writing folk' collectors sent their written recollections and those of their neighbours and kin directly to the Finnish Literature Society Folklore Archives in Helsinki, where they are still housed today. My analysis in this paper is based on over

1,750 archived memorates and folk narratives recorded from informants throughout Finland, most of who were born between 1850 and 1890.

4. The term *tietäjä* is therefore roughly equivalent to the term 'cunning folk' used in early modern England, since according to Owen Davies (2003: viii) the term 'cunning' derives from the Anglo-Saxon *cunnan*, meaning 'to know.' Like the English cunning-man or -woman, the *tietäjä* was assumed to have secret knowledge others did not possess (cf. ibid.).

5. Over 52,000 variants of Kalevala-metre magic incantations were recorded in the nineteenth and early twentieth centuries from the agrarian populations of Finland and neighbouring Karelia. Thirty thousand incantations were published in the 34-volume series *Suomen Kansan Vanhat Runot* (*Ancient Poems of the Finnish People*). For more on Kalevala meter, see Siikala 2002: 32–34; Stark 2006: 464, note 27.

6. See Stark 2006: 248–49, 297, 473 note 176.

7. For this description in full, see Stark 2006: 181–3.

8. When a *tietäjä* performed counter-sorcery to punish the perpetrator of magical harm, it was believed that the magical harm itself (referred to as a 'dog') would find its own way back to its sender or 'master,' even if this sender had not been identified by the *tietäjä*. The 'dog' was thought to attack its master or mistress even more furiously than it had attacked its original victim, causing sudden pain, illness, or even death, according to the *tietäjä*'s instructions.

9. Valtimo. 1939. Jorma Partanen 1124 – Pekka Tuovinen, 45 years old.

10. Liperi. 1935–36. Tommi Korhola KRK 157:143 – Aapeli Ihalainen, 43 years old.

11. *Hiisi* was another name for the forest spirit, but sometimes had the connotation of 'evil spirit,' or 'devil.'

12. See also Stark 2006: 306–14.

13. Tyrvää. 1935–36. Kauko Upo KRK 46:10 – Emma Bljy, 79 years old.

14. See Stark 2006: 310–14.

15. Some *tietäjäs* in the 19th century also worked as gravediggers, and thus had easy access to corpses.

16. Parkano. 1958. Impi Kyrönviita MT 5: 664.

17. Kuopio. 1946. Otto Räsänen 724 – Antti Räsänen, cobbler.

18. Hankasalmi. 1961. Hankasalmi Folk School. Tuula Tarvainen TK 13:27 – Alma Tarvainen, farm mistress, b. 1887.

19. Another man from Eastern Finland explained the idea of a snake's assembly stone as follows: 'When I was a child the old people told how snakes would gather to hold their general assembly in a fixed place where there was a round, egg-shaped stone. The person who found and took possession of such a snakes' assembly stone would have a powerful tool for magic.' (Nilsiä. 1961. Aatto V. Korhonen TK 37:51 – Collector's father Adolf Korhonen, died 1935).

20. Ukko was the 'highest god' in the pre-Christian Finnish pantheon and was associated with thunder (*ukkonen*). According to the narrator, 'Ukko's soil is the sort of earth taken with an important person's knife from under one's left heel when thunder rumbles for the first time in spring.' (Kitee. 1921. Pekka Vauhkonen VK 107:1, p. 25).

21. Kitee. 1921. Pekka Vauhkonen VK 107:1, p. 26.

22. Sääminki. 1939. J. Vaahtoluoto 419.

23. Stark-Arola 2002: 77–110; Stark 2006: 158–60, 317, 355–56.

References

Davies, Owen. 1999. *A People Bewitched: Witchcraft and Magic in Nineteenth-Century Somerset*. Bruton.

——. 2003. *Cunning Folk: Popular Magic in English History*. London & New York: Hambledon.

De Blécourt, Willem. 1999. 'The witch, her victim, the unwitcher and the researcher: the continued existence of traditional witchcraft,' in Willem De Blecourt, Ronald Hutton & Jean La Fontaine (eds), The *Athlone History of Witchcraft and Magic in Europe: Volume 6, The Twentieth Century*. London: The Athlone Press, pp. 141–219.

Elias, Norbert. 1978. *The Civilizing Process. Volume 1, The History of Manners*. New York: Pantheon Books.

Foucault, Michel. 1977. *Discipline and Punish: The Birth of the Prison*. Sheridan, Alan (trans.). London: Penguin Books.

Gijswijt-Hofstra, Marijke. 1999. 'Witchcraft after the witch trials,' in Gijswijt-Hofstra, Marijke, Brian P. Levack & Roy Porter (eds), *Witchcraft and Magic in Europe: The Eighteenth and Nineteenth Centuries*. Athlone Press, pp. 98–101.

Siikala, Anna-Leena. 2002. *Mythic Images and Shamanism. A Perspective on Kalevala Poetry*. Helsinki: Suomalainen Tiedeakatemia (Academia Scientiarum Fennica).

SKVR = Suomen Kansan Vanhat Runot (Ancient Poems of the Finnish People). 1908–48 (34 volumes). Helsinki: Finnish Literature Society.

Spierenburg, Pieter. 1991. *The Broken Spell: A Cultural and Anthropological History of Preindustrial Europe*. New Brunswick: Rutgers University Press.

Stark, Laura. 2006. *The Magical Self: Body, Society and the Supernatural in Early Modern Rural Finland*. Folklore Fellows Communications 290. Helsinki: Academia Scientiarum Fennica.

Stark-Arola, Laura. 2002. *Peasants, Pilgrims and Sacred Promises: Ritual and the Supernatural in Orthodox Karelian Folk Religion*. Studia Fennica Folkloristica 11. Helsinki: Finnish Literature Society.

2

'If Not, Shall Employ "Rough on Rats" ': Identifying the Common Elements of Rat Charms

Paul Cowdell

In the standard literature we find various references to several charms against rats. Most of these charms are direct invocations of saints, predominantly Saint Gertrude of Nivelles and Saint Nicasius. St. Gertrude is associated with rodents through her devotion to souls in purgatory; rats are often seen as representatives of human souls, so she is often represented with rodents on her garments. Traditions surrounding Saint Nicasius are rather more obscure, but he is 'celebrated ... as an enemy of rats'.[1] In the course of my research I also became aware of a group of charms directed at the rats themselves, and with a rather more secular tone. These will form the main subject of this chapter.

The starting place for most popular beliefs and narratives about rats is their supposed intelligence, allied to their known destructive capacity. In fact, rats are not particularly smarter than other rodents. They are, however, 'neophobic', a term coined by the biologist S. Anthony Barnett. Like other mammals, rats enjoy exploring new terrains, i.e. they can be neophilic. However, they are wary of new objects in familiar terrains, i.e. they are neophobic in familiar surroundings. Barnett offers evidence that neophobia is restricted to those rat species living commensally with humans (which includes both British species). In other words, the neophobia is itself an evolutionary response to the perils of living as a pest on human populations.[2]

This could well explain why rats, despite having such apparently suitable qualities, do not seem to turn up as Trickster figures: those species which live apart from humans (like Trickster figures such as coyotes) have not actually evolved the neophobia which makes domestic rats seem intelligent. To quote Barnett: 'We can now ... see ... clearly why rats have been called diabolically clever, and why today we say that they are nothing of the sort.' Or, as one American psychologist put it: 'Most of the books ... have been all about animal intelligence, never about animal stupidity.'[3]

This has pest-control implications: if you want to poison rats, you cannot just put down poison where you know they go, as that will alarm them. You need to put down food until they get used to it, *then* poison it. Then poison it again, before they can restore the population through reproduction. That useful pointer might seem like an aside, but it has implications for the ways in which charms are delivered.

As with other charms, charms against rats are often 'presented' in written form. Many examples refer to written charms being displayed in some way. In the tenth century, Cornelius Bassus described sticking a charm to a stone in the field afflicted by the rats. In a nineteenth century Baltimore example, a letter addressed to rats was first read out aloud, and then laid on the floor of the infested meat house.

That latter example, cited by William Wells Newell in his pioneering 1892 article on the subject, gives the clearest indication that we *are* dealing with charming.[4] The letter was written by a third party who had specific knowledge of what was required. It was then passed to the householder, who had to deliver it in person under quite specific conditions, namely when no one else was present. Similarly, amongst Dutch examples of charms to be pinned to barn doors, several specify the *time* at which this will be efficacious, particularly around the feasts of Saints Gertrude and Nicasius.

Equally, many written charms are directed to be greased and pushed into rat-holes. Newell gives examples from New England and from the Ardennes, the latter charm directly invoking St. Gertrude again. In 1955, the journal *Folklore* recorded an Irish example of Erse charms being pushed into rat-holes to drive them out.[5]

Given the neophobia already identified, it is quite possible that such an intrusion into their environment could itself cause changes in the rats' behaviour. The examples are divided between pinning up notices and pushing them into holes, with both prose and verse examples being used in both ways. From the point of view of the charm, the key purpose is making it 'public' to the rats. Chambers underlines this when he writes that in Scotland 'a writ of ejectment ... is issued upon them, by being stuck up *legibly* upon the walls' [emphasis added].[6] Bassus also stresses that the writing must face outwards, that is, it must be legible to the rats. This is about intruding into the rats' lives, with predictable results.

One problem with the natural history of the rat as regards the folklore is that in the earliest records rats and mice are conflated. The Latin word *mus* included rats, martens, sable and ermine. One late Latin formulation speaks of 'mures et glires': literally, these are mice and dormice, but the distinction seems to be between good and bad rodents. (Dormice, of course, are edible).[7] Similarly, the Greek term μυσ also includes rats, hamsters and other rodents. Gerald of Wales, writing in the twelfth century, refers to 'the larger species of mice, commonly called rats'.[8] This is the earliest certain literary reference to rats in the British Isles. It had long been assumed that Black Rats arrived here in the thirteenth century on ships returning from the Crusades, but archaeological evidence from York has now definitely established their presence in the fourth century. This suggests that the terminological confusion had existed throughout the intervening period.

This may pose problems in analysing earlier records of superstitions and beliefs, but I do not believe it undermines the assessment we make of them, not least because this conflation continues well into modern times. (I was surprised, for example, to find that many of my London informants were unsure of the difference between rats and mice.) Also, the methods used against both rats and mice are remarkably similar. A 1962 report of mice being requested to leave a house is almost identical to the rat charms we will be looking at. A 1748 dreambook discussing dreams of being attacked by rats, says: 'Mice are pretty much of the same nature, but not in so high a degree.'[9] That is just about their relationship in folklore, too.

So when I refer to rats in earlier writings, this term may well include other rodents. The important thing is that rats have had about 10,000 years of co-habitation with humans (if we accept Barnett's hypothesis that commensal living probably began with the first settled agriculture). The idea that they are smart animals (even if they are conflated with mice) has had a long time to sink in.

Rats have long been supposed to have uncanny knowledge of forthcoming disaster. In the fourth century BC, Theophrastus satirised the Superstitious Man more concerned with the omen of rodents gnawing a hole in his meal-bag than with repairing the hole itself. Theophrastus was describing the effect of natural rodent food-gathering, but superstition attaches to general gnawing right through to the modern period. Pliny in AD77 credited rodents with foreseeing the Marsian war by gnawing shields, and foreseeing the death of the general Carbo at Clusium by gnawing the straps on his shoes. This was taken up by some Christian writers, albeit sceptically. St. Augustine of Hippo described the same superstition in 396. Chaucer mentioned 'Hem that bileeven on divynailes ... by gnawynge of rattes' in the *Parson's Tale* (c.1395).

This belief was also recorded in the seventeenth (e.g. 'It is a great signe of ill lucke, if Rats gnaw a mans cloathes' – Melton, *Astrologaster*, 1620), and the seventeenth centuries (e.g. 'Rats gnawing the hangings of a room, is reckoned the forerunner of a death in the family' – Grose, *Provincial Glossary*, 1787). It even survived into the twentieth century: in 1909 rats nibbling furniture was recorded as an omen of death from Worcestershire.[10]

Note here that it is the *behaviour* that is ominous. General gnawing is a recognised phenomenon of rat behaviour. Rats have a flap of skin that closes behind their teeth when they're gnawing, thus preventing them choking on whatever they chew up. (This is why gnawing on concrete pillars, for example, does not kill them: I would suggest, though, that it might be another good reason for thinking rats are uncanny in some way.) When Gerald of Wales wrote of the cursing of rats by St. Yvorus in Fernigenan, Leinster, he assumed that the rats had aroused the saint's displeasure in the first place by gnawing his books. The Ardennes example refers to rats having eaten the heart of St. Gertrude.

It has been suggested that the foresight of disaster stems from the association of the rodents with the souls of men mentioned earlier. Several European legends have rats either as agents of divine retribution or as souls of the murdered avenging their deaths. One German story tells of a famine in 970 when Bishop Hatto of Mayence confined starving people to a barn and torched it to reduce the demand for food. He was then pursued and destroyed by an army of rats. A Scandinavian legend tells how rats attacked and ate Earl Asbjorn after he had murdered St. Knut at Odense. Charlotte Latham recorded a nineteenth-century Sussex example of a man haunted by evil spirits in the form of rats: every night, his neighbours heard him pleading with them to leave him alone.[11]

It is therefore understandable how sudden movements of rats and mice come to be unlucky. Their foresight of impending disaster makes their exodus from a building or a ship ominous. 'Rats leaving a sinking ship' is, of course, proverbial, but the exodus of rats from a house also presaged disaster, as did their *influx*. In one seventeenth century Irish example, rats over-running a house, in an area where they had formerly been rare, was taken as a portent of the 1641 rebellion. In Mexico, an influx of rats was taken as an indicator of immorality. The tradition is about the general movement, though: in nineteenth century Aberdeen the arrival of rats was seen as a harbinger of money.[12] In many of the narratives, too, rats embody the threat of itinerant populations for a settled community. Although beyond the scope of this paper, that does have some bearing on some of the charms we will see.

It is in this movement of rats that the difference between rural and urban beliefs is clearest. My informants unanimously saw rats as endemic: within a city they are merely an affirmation of urban life. On a 2005 BBC World Service radio programme, speakers from US cities boasted of their rat populations ('We've just as many rats as in New York', said one), while one New Yorker called her home city 'ratropolis'. So, rats move within cities, but they do not move *from* them, which may be why the surviving charm forms are predominantly rural. I think this background is important for several reasons. Here are animals seen as intelligent, uncanny and destructive, with strange quirks of behaviour, and prone to rushing from place to place. If there is available space to remove them, then, this provides some reason why they are prime subjects for charming.

The charms and conjurations fall into two main overlapping groups. The earliest attested clearly is the *written* charm. Cornelius Bassus' Greek agricultural treatise, the *Geoponika*, which almost certainly uses much earlier material, describes an exhortation which incorporates many elements recurring elsewhere:

> I conjure you, O mice who inhabit here, not to injure me yourselves, nor to allow any other mouse to do so; and I give you this field (mention which one it is). But if I find you residing here in the future, with the aid of the mother of the gods, I will cut you up into seven pieces.

Bassus then describes how the exhortation should be presented, although he says he does not believe a word of it. 'Having written this, paste up the paper at a spot where the mice are, against a natural stone, taking care to keep the letters on the outside. I have written this, in order not to leave out anything; but ... I counsel every one not to pay any attention to such rubbish.'[13] The charm described by Bassus has a number of significant elements. There is an appeal to the rodents not to continue their present destruction; this is followed by the offer of a specified alternative accommodation; lastly, there is the threat of violence if the rodents do not accept the kind offer. I would also draw attention to the tone of the letter: it is rather formal, but certainly firm and polite. All of these elements can be seen elsewhere, and this becomes almost a standard model for charming rats from one site to another.

Newell recorded a nineteenth century American example that stands comparison with the description found nearly nine centuries earlier in the *Geoponika*:

> Maine, October 31, 1888
> MESSRS RATS AND CO., – Having taken quite a deep interest in your welfare in regard to your winter quarters I thought I would drop you a few lines which might be of some considerable benefit to you in the future seeing that you have pitched your winter quarters at the summer residence of * * * * No. 1 Seaview Street. I wish to inform you that you will be very much disturbed during cold winter months as I am expecting to be at work through all parts of the house, shall take down ceilings, take up floors, and clean out every substance that would serve to make you comfortable, likewise there will be nothing left for you to feed on, as I shall remove every eatable substance; so you had better take up your abode elsewhere. I will here refer you to the farm of * * * * No. 6 Incubator Street, where you will find a splendid cellar well filled with vegetations of (all) kinds besides a shed leading to a barn, with a good supply of grain, where you can live snug and happy. Shall do you no harm if you heed to my advice; but if not, shall employ 'Rough on Rats'.
> Yours, * * * *[14]

Again, this is polite: it is presented as a *request* to leave that will be in the rats' best interest because of the building work. (Note also the assurance not to harm the rats if they accede. Rolland, who cites several French examples, points out that purpose of such charms is not to exterminate the animals, but 'to cause them to quit the place of their depredations'). Precisely the same element is in use in the 1962 mouse example mentioned earlier, where the mice are told it would not be safe for them to come down because there is a big cat.[15] In the American example there is no explicit appeal to cease the current destruction, as there is in the Greek. I would argue, though, that it is implicit in the overly polite account of their accommodation, not to mention in the account of the creature comforts which will be taken away from the rats (describing their habitat and their food sources), as well as in the description of their replacements in the alternative location.

These are prose examples, but verse examples are used in the same way. Chambers recorded a Scottish example ('Ratton and mouse,/Lea' the puir woman's house,/Gang awa' owre by to 'e mill,/And there ane and a' ye'll get your fill').[16] There are suggestions that they were widely used in Ireland in the sixteenth and seventeenth centuries, as rhyming Irish rats to death seems to have been almost proverbial, the notion turning up in the works of Shakespeare and Jonson. This may, though, not be evidence of ethnographic practice or belief so much as satire against a community.

The threat of violence if the rats do not accede is also consistent with other examples. It is an unspoken threat, but its presence is implied (they should leave before he convinces himself to exterminate them). I therefore think it should be included as a component part of the charm. There is also the important element of the rats being offered a new residence. In the Baltimore example cited by Newell, the rats are given very elaborate directions ('straight to the lane ... past the stone house, and keep on up the hill, right past the church ... until they came to the large white house on the right, and turn in there'), while the Ardennes charm mentioned earlier conjured them in the name of St. Gertrude into the plain of Rocroi. This offer also features in the other main form of charming rats, that is, by noise. In some of the French examples cited by Newell, although the rats are offered an alternative residence, they are 'conjured' there by beating a kitchen pan with a harrow tooth while reciting the appropriate charm. This is similar to Jacqueline Simpson's Worthing example of a man who beat on lamp-posts with his walking stick to drive rats away.[17]

In the earliest verse examples (for example the fourteenth century 'Rats Away' quoted by Sisam), no alternative location is given: the charm is used predominantly to protect a property ('I betweche this place from ratones and from alle other schame. God save this place fro alle other wykked wytes').[18] This is also the case with many of the Dutch examples given by van Haver in his 1964 collection.[19] Many of these charms are appeals to Saints (usually Gertrude and Nicasius) to ward off rats, rather than appeals to the rats themselves to move.

It may be that this tendency of offering alternative accommodation develops as a response to the animals' observed behaviour, it being possible to encourage rats from one place to another within certain limitations. (Charlotte Latham's example of rats as evil spirits, for example, is also predicated on their movement *en masse*). It is not recorded how a nineteenth century Cheshire rat-charmer at Peover led rats from farm to farm, but he said explicitly that he could not make them cross a road.[20]

In this connection, perhaps the most interesting part of Chambers' rhyme is the mention of the mill. Several of the charms refer to crossing water. In one French example, if water is to be crossed a board must be laid down as a bridge for the rats. Newell associates this with the difficulty of evil spirits in crossing water. Certainly a connection is made with rats as representatives of evil spirits: Powell, improbably connecting rats with lemmings, says that Bishop Hatto's rats made straight for the river.[21] Unfortunately, as any Londoner will tell you, rats can swim, which suggests there is more research to be done on this aspect of the subject.

I mentioned briefly conjuration of rats by noise; this is best known as some sort of musical activity. A 1950's rat-charmer in West Cornwall whistled, causing the rats either to come to him, or at least to stop running away: he could then pick them up and dispose of them.[22] That this is still arcane knowledge, however, is clear from the Grimms' *Rattenfänger*, who 'knows a particular tone, which he sounds nine times on his pipe', or the Altmark story *Rats in Neustadt-Eberswalde* where the ratcatcher places 'something in the mill and something else in a secret place'.[23] The Pied Piper of Hameln may be the best-known version of this story, but there are a number of interesting variations. The rats are not always conjured by music, but generally a fife or a flute is used, as in the Austrian *Rat Catcher from Magdalenagrund*.[24] According to Robert Means Lawrence, Thuringian houses were cleared of rats by blowing a tiny whistle made of a rat's thigh bone through each room of a house on Good Friday morning.[25] Some variants of the story do not even feature rats, but are solely about child abduction. Significantly, though, some of these, like the Westphalian *Hurdy-Gurdy Player Abducts Children*, also have a musical motif.[26]

Many of the musical motif stories also involve the conjuring of rats into or across water: the Grimms' *rattenfänger* can make them go 'wherever he wants . . . into a pond or pool'; the rats of Neustadt-Eberswalde swam into the Finow River; a foreign sorcerer drives all the rats to the southern tip of the Isle of Ummanz, whence they fled into the water. Abraham Elder's 1839 *Tales and Legends of the Isle of Wight*, which transplants the Hameln story to Franchville, has the piper lead the rats into the Solent. The tale of *How Ma Hsiang Rid Hangchow of Rats* epitomises this trend. It is often included amongst the Pied Piper literature, although it is not quite analogous to that. It does, though, have traces of the charms, and clearly indicates the relationship between the musical element and the verbal components. It is a literary adaptation, and it is unclear to what extent it actually reflects its source. For our purposes that does not make a great deal of difference: as an embodiment of the charm elements in common usage it is fascinating:

Ma Chih having happened to remark that the city was infested with rats, Hsiang wrote out a charm, and got someone to stick it up on the south wall. Then he drummed on a bowl with a pair of chopsticks, and gave a long whistle. At once an army of rats appeared, scuttled up under the charm, and stopped there cowering. Hsiang commanded one of the rats, larger than the rest, to approach the dais on which he sat, and addressed it thus, 'You diminutive creatures of the furry tribe, heaven supplies you with food in the shape of grain. Why must you burrow your way through walls and gnaw holes in our dwelling houses, making yourselves day and night a nuisance to His Excellency? Being tender hearted, I cannot bring myself to exterminate you utterly, but your leader must in return conduct his hordes away from this town.' The large rat then retired, and all the others came forward to make a sort of prostration, as though in contrition for their guilt. This done, they re-formed their ranks and passed out of the city gates in an unending stream. From that time onward the city has been entirely free from rats.[27]

Ma Hsiang, who has knowledge of the charm, writes it out for a third party to pin up. Then he drums and whistles, causing the rats to appear. He addresses the rats politely (through their leader), describing the benefits that they enjoy. However, he says, they are a nuisance: because he does not want to kill them, he asks them nicely to leave town, which they do. This epitomises most of the elements we have identified, including the musical component. No explicit alternative accommodation is mentioned, but the charm refers to their current good life and the problem that they have become. There is also a quite clear threat of what will become of the rats if they *do not* go.

Although research into rat charms is still at an early stage, there is, I believe, extensive evidence of consistent elements within rat charms. It is not only possible to be specific about these components, but also to identify them as structural elements of a definite group of rat charms.

Notes

1. Sisam, Kenneth, ed. by, *Fourteenth Century Verse and Prose*, 2nd corrected edn, (Oxford: Oxford University Press, 1955), p. 258.
2. S. Anthony Barnett, *The Story of Rats: Their Impact On Us, And Our Impact On Them*, Crows Nest: Allen & Unwin, 2001, pp. 56–62.
3. Barnett, pp. 62–3.
4. Newell, William Wells, 'Conjuring Rats', *Journal of American Folklore*, 5:16 (1892), 23–32.
5. MacGregor, Alasdair Alpin, 'The Pied Piper', *Folklore* 66:4 (1955), 432.

6. Chambers, Robert, *Popular Rhymes of Scotland*, p. 339, quoted by Newell, 25–6.
7. Hoffmann-Krayer, Eduard, and Bächtold-Stäubli, Hanns, eds, *Handwörterbuch des deutschen Aberglaubens* (Berlin: de Gruyter, 1927–42), *s.v.* 'Maussegen'.
8. Giraldus Cambrensis, *Topography of Ireland*, ch. 32.
9. *Every Lady's Fortune Teller*, p. 85, quoted in *A Dictionary of Superstitions*, ed. by Opie, Iona, and Moira Tatem (Oxford: Oxford University Press, 1989), p. 323.
10. Opie and Tatem, pp. 322–3.
11. Radford, E. and M. A., *A Dictionary of Superstitions*, ed. and rev. by Christina Hole (London: Hutchinson, 1961), pp. 279–80; *A Dictionary of English Folklore*, ed. by Simpson, Jacqueline, and Steve Roud (Oxford: Oxford University Press, 2000), p. 290.
12. Opie and Tatem, p. 323.
13. Quoted in Newell, 29–30.
14. Newell, 23.
15. Opie and Tatem, p. 324.
16. Cited by Newell, 26.
17. Newell, 26–7; Simpson and Roud, p. 290.
18. Sisam (1955), p. 258.
19. van Haver, Jozef, *Nederlandse Incantatieliteratuur: Een Gecommentarieerd Compendium van Nederlandse Bezweringsformules* (Ghent: Secretariaat van de Koninklijke Vlaamse Academie Voor Taal- en Letterkunde, 1964).
20. Margaret Baker, *Folklore and Customs of Rural England*, (Newton Abbot: David and Charles, 1974), pp. 54–7.
21. Powell, J. U., 'Rodent-Gods in Ancient and Modern Times', *Folklore*, 40:4 (1929), 392.
22. Thomas, Charles, 'Present-Day Charmers in Cornwall', *Folklore*, 64:1 (1953), 304.
23. Temme, J. D. H., *Die Volkssagen der Altmark, mit einem Anhange von Sagen aus den übrigen Marken und aus dem Magdeburgischen* (Berlin: Nicolaischen, 1839), No. 31, p. 114.
24. Umlauft, Friedrich, *Sagen und Geschichten aus Alt-Wien*, (Stuttgart: Loewes Verlag Ferdinand Carl, 1944), pp. 97–100.
25. Lawrence, Robert Means, *The Magic of the Horse-Shoe with Other Folk-Lore Notes* (Boston: Houghton, Mifflin, 1898), ch. 4 'Charms Against Animals'.
26. Kuhn, A., and W. Schwartz, *Norddeutsche Sagen, Marchen und Gebrauche aus Meklenburg, Pommern, der Mark, Sachsen, Thuringen, Braunschweig, Hannover, Oldenburg und Westfalen, aus dem Munde des Volkes Gesammelt* (Leipzig: F. A. Brockhaus, 1848), pp. 89–90.
27. Giles, Lionel, *A Gallery of Chinese Immortals: Selected Biographies, Translated from Chinese Sources*, (London: John Murray, 1948), pp. 117–19. For this reference, as for many of the Pied Piper analogues, I am indebted to D. W. Ashliman's online resource *The Pied Piper*, <http://www.pitt.edu/~dash/hameln.html> [accessed 18 August 2005].

3
Miracles and Impossibilities in Magic Folk Poetry

Éva Pócs

The aim of this chapter is to discuss a few 'impossibility' motifs know from incantations, with a particular emphasis on their connections with miracle motifs. Some of these connections were observed during my field work in Gyimes county, Transylvania, between 2002 and 2004,[1] while collecting belief legends, legends and incantations. Motifs relevant in this context accrete around the subjects of vegetable and animal fertility (*birth, the sprouting of plants, the breeding of animals*) and infertility (*stones, rocks, rocky, infertile soil, infertile animals, people of stone*). In the context of these subjects I surveyed the material that was available to me regarding incantations in Europe. In the incantations these subject areas are supplemented by an added layer of mythical and cosmological motifs, such as the creation of the world, the birth of Christ, the resurrection, the structure of the universe and its 'infinitude'. All of this is in turn subordinated to the oppositions of *God – Satan, creation – annihilation, created world – chaos* and, ultimately, of *life* and *death*. These motifs occur most frequently in those incantations and demon-averting verbal charms[2] which are commonly referred to in research as 'impossibility formulas'.[3]

Impossibility formulas are a verbal means of magic which express (as is common in incantations) the wish to attain a particular concrete aim (that illness should end, the disease demon should depart or the grain should grow, etc.). These are arranged into some sort of parallel grammatical structure which follows the metaphoric vision of incantations. Similes as well as metaphors, which are syntactically more hidden, are evidently means of analogic magic (may X happen just like Y) and provide the most common structure for incantations worldwide. Impossibility formulas provide very widespread and varied subgroups of this type of magic (at least in European cultures). The lead sentence of the similes refers to some 'impossibility' in an affirmative or negative form, i.e. stating it as 'truth' or 'a lie'. This may be a natural image, process or empirical fact (rocks grow no wool, water will not run backwards). It can also be a reference to a rite which is supposed to be carried out while reciting the text, e.g. this grain of barley (which the charmer throws into the well) will/will not sprout. Finally, and most relevantly to our present subject matter, the simile can refer to a mythical or legendary event or a miracle (such as cannot take place in the present context, e.g. Christ can/cannot be born once more). After the lead sentence the wish is introduced in a clause starting with as/when/if. This wish can be formulated in several different ways in terms of its truth value or logical structure, as compared to the content of the lead sentence. It can be an affirmative, optative or negative statement, depending on the truth value of the lead sentence (the process of recovery, for example, can be connected in a logically straight or a reverse fashion to the impossible condition depending on the concrete content). The text may specifically include an impossible condition (e.g. the onset or return of some trouble may be tied to a condition) or give an 'impossible' task to a belief creature. As we shall see, the possibilities are extremely varied.

Structures of the *if – then, when – then, just as* type can serve as frames for the emergence of spontaneous texts. The 'impossibilities' of the lead sentence, as we mentioned above, are permanent elements of the texts, either as natural images fixed in a poetic form or as fragments from biblical texts or motifs of legendary recoveries. According to twentieth century practice, these are then applied to the familiar structure, or adjusted to the momentary situation of recovery, as textual motifs known from oral tradition (incantations and other genres). In the process of cultural transmission, these motifs find their way into other types of incantations, as well as into different genres.

Some more highly organised texts containing mythic or legendary motifs were also circulated in writing by priests and monks who relied on a spell-book for their healing services. This was true both in the areas of Western and Eastern Christianity, but the monastic spell-book practice of the Eastern Church seems to have been richer in this respect. Individual textual motifs were not tied in irrevocably with a grammatical or logical structure. Any content could appear and in the most varied constructions. It is characteristic to have a great number of transformations between an identical content and different structures and also to alter the logical structure arbitrarily while the content remains the same.[4] This is one reason I give little consideration to formal characteristics and structural frames (as opposed to content) in the present chapter.

The motifs examined below are among the permanent elements of content. Indeed, they are extremely general motifs known all over Europe in several epochs and in a number of genres. It is impossible to examine organic geographical and historical connections, except for in a few cases, as textual material is scanty with regard to each type or variant. I shall only present a few examples of the type of thematic connection mentioned above between impossibilities and miracles from a vast and multi-layered wealth of motifs which has been woven between the folklore and literature of Europe for several thousand years (!), and also has appeared in a number of mixed genres. I shall only very occasionally make allusions to textual connections with other genres (when there is an identity of motifs relevant to our present subject).

Natural impossibilities

Relevant motifs in European charms involve *vegetable and animal fertility* and *infertility*, ideas of *life* and *death*, mainly by invoking *stones* and *plants which will not sprout or bear no fruit*, as well as *insensitive stone persons*. Stone as a material offers itself evidently for condensing this rich symbolism: it is hard, it is difficult to crush, split or crumble; it is infertile, no water springs from it, no plants sprout from it.

According to data from Gyimesközéplok, the following charm is performed (even today) to cure a baby's headache:

Jézus Krisztus megindult egy úton
s találkozott az igézettel.
S azt kérdezte, hová mész te igézet?
Megyek ennek a gyermeknek a fejfájását meghasogatni
S térj vissza te igézet, s nem térek
S Krisztus Jézus letaszította egy sziklán,
és megmondta, hogy akkor fájjon a feje,
mikor ez a kőszikla meg fog hasadni.

Jesus Christ set out along a road
And met the Evil Eye.
And he asked, where are you going, you Evil Eye?
I am going to split this baby's headache.
Come back, you Evil Eye. No, I won't.
And Jesus Christ pushed it off a rock
And said may the headache come
When this rock cracks.

After reciting the above text, the healer said the Lord's Prayer and Hail Mary and then spat and blew on the patient's head three times.[5] We shall later return to the introductory part of this charm (in which Christ sends the demon to a barren, rocky land). The command contained in the second half mentions the cracking of the rock (as an impossibility), setting up a reverse logical parallel with the wish that the malady should pass. (This is the most common logical/grammatical structure for the impossibility formulas).

Perhaps the best known Hungarian impossibility formula is referred to as Szelestei's incantation. It was noted down in the early sixteenth century and contains a whole collection of natural impossibilities. The command mentions a stone-impossibility in close contact with vegetable infertility

> *Contra Thargy Equorum*:
> Erdewn yar wala lebeke tharghy.
> Beka wala ekeye.
> kygo wala oſ tora.
> Zanth wala keweth.
> weth wala kewecheth.
> parancholok en theneked
> hogy my keppen a kew nem ghyekerezhethyk eſ nem lewelezhethyk,
> azon keppen the Ith a lowon ne ghyekerezheſſel eſ erekedheſſel.[6]

To heal a horse's abscess

> *A floating abscess once walked in the forest*
> *Its plough was a frog,*
> *Its whip was a snake*
> *It was ploughing rock*
> *And it was sowing pebbles.*
> *I command thee,*
> *Just as pebbles will not grow roots or sprout leaves,*
> *So you should not grow roots or spread on the horse.*

In a seventeenth century version of this text[7] there is an important extra motif: the words of Jesus Christ with which he commands an illness demon that it should 'have no seeds'. This marks the appearance of the opposition of deity against demon so characteristic of the group of impossibility formulas discussed below. A divine command gives extra weight to the fact that the miracle mentioned is impossible for the human or demon in question.

The *dry branch which will not turn green* is a poetic metaphor for yearn-
ing, which appears as a lyrical image in folk songs and ballads.[8] However,
the motif of a *plant sprouting from a dry branch* as an impossibility also
occurs in incantations as is proven in a paper by Károly Marót. Marót
found a similar impossibility formula in *The Odyssey*, in the text of an
oath. He quotes a parallel from the text of a Hittite contract to show that
the motif is widespread and has a long history.[9]

Vegetable and animal infertility are mentioned alongside each other
in a type of impossibility incantation that has been known ever since
antiquity. The idea of *stone does not grow wool* occurs in a sequence with
the infertile mule, and all of this is stood in parallel with the wish that
illness should not return. The text is quoted by Richard Heim from the
fourth century spell-book of Marcellus of Bordeaux:

Nec mula parit,	*A mule does not bear young,*
Nec lapis lanam fert,	*A stone does not give wool,*
Nec huic morbo caput crescat	*Nor may this head grow ill,*
Aut si creverit, tabescat.	*Only if it has been cut off,*
	may it waste away.

Heim also quotes two variants from late antiquity (this must have been
a widely known and commonly used incantation in the early centuries
of Christianity).[10] And we see the motif of the infertile mule once more
from the spell-book of an early mediaeval Jewish rabbinical healer, where
the infertile mule is used as a precedent for a boil's (desired) lack of
increase.[11]

Mansikka presents several Russian incantations. The author claims
not only that these are related to the Latin incantations which start
Nec mula ..., but also that they originate from these texts (through the
usual path of Eastern European transmission, by monastic spell-books
and through the hands of monk healers). Whatever their origin, these
incantations certainly include images of vegetable and animal infertility
embedded in one and the same simile with infertile stone – similarly to
the images of Marcellus's text. For example, Mansikka presents a Russian
blood-staunching charm that states that the blood will not leave the
patient, any more than water leaves the *Latyr* stone, or anymore than
milk come from hens, or eggs come from cocks, etc.[12]

Man as a biological creature often appears as an insensitive stone-man
with no sensory organs. The figure of the stone woman who cannot
breast-feed is also known from Hungarian folklore. The manuscript spell-
book of the Radvánszky family from 1614 retains a text used to stop

bleeding in a horse, which you have to recite three times over the animal.

> Az Zinaj hegjnek tetejen egj kü aztal,
> az ku aztal meghet egj kü Azonj ember,
> az ku azonjembernek ku karjan egj ku giermek,
> az kü Azonj ember [nek karjan] az ku giermeknek ki uetette az eo kü mellieth,
> ualamind abul az ku meljbul se nem czeordul se nem czepen,
> sinten ugj se ne czeorduljeon se ne czepenien az en kek louamnak az uere.[13]

> *On top of mount Sinai there is a stone table*
> *Behind the stone table a stone woman*
> *On the stone woman's stone arm a stone child*
> *The stone woman has taken out her stone breast for the stone child*
> *And just as no drop comes out of that stone breast*
> *So should the blood of my black horse stop dripping or running.*

This text, rich in Byzantine connections, has relations to the Russian stone cow and stone woman derives from Mansikka's 1909 study, which only includes extracts of the content and abstracts from the text ('A stone maiden on a stone hill'). The texts usually close with a remark to the effect that the staunched blood will only begin to flow again when milk flows from the stone cow.[14]

Another variant cited by Mansikka resembles the Hungarian text in featuring a stone woman sitting on a stone, with a stone child in her lap. The macabre character of the stone is confirmed by its black colour.[15] Given the scanty available textual relics, the exact routes along which charms spread through spell-books are impossible to determine. Nonetheless, a fourth century Latin incantation seems to offer a relatively direct textual parallel (again from the spell-book of Marcellus of Bordeaux):

Stulta femina super fontem sedebat	*A stupid woman sat over a spring,*
et stultum infantem in sinu tenebat,	*holding a stupid child in her lap*
siccant montes, siccant valles, siccant venae,	*mountains dry up, valleys dry up, veins dry up,*
vel quae de sanguine sunt plenae.[16]	*or those things which are full of blood.*

The figure of the *Stulta femina* who renders everything dry and lifeless is used in this text (a blood-staunching charm) as an impossibility by simple logical opposition. The stupid woman and her child are not of stone, but they are insensible: they have 'a dry brain' and by analogy they render everything dry around themselves. Besides drying the waters and the hills, they dry up the wound of whoever is bleeding and, thus, heal the patient. (The motif must have been widespread in early-mediaeval Europe: Heim published another tenth century text which was also used to stop bleeding, and was written on the margin of the original spell-book.)[17] A very similar text, the *Strassburger Tumbo-Spruch*, comes from an eleventh century German spell-book. Written in Old High German, its first words are 'Tumbo saz in berke ...' The translation of the word *Tumbo*, and thus the interpretation of the whole text, are still subject to debate. Haug and Volmann offer a translation and interpretation which talks about *Dummling* – a stupid woman and her stupid child. *Dummling* is supposed to be a 'dead spirit' incapable of mental activity, yet in the context of the present verse it offers healing.

Dummling saß auf dem Berge mit Dummlingskind im Arme,
Dumm hieß der Berg, Dumm hieß das Kind:
Der heilige Dummling heile diese Wunde.[18]

The Dummling *sat on a mountain with a* Dummling *child in its arms,*
The mountain is called Dumm, *the child is called* Dumm,
Holy Dummling, *heal this wound.*

The deep structure, i.e. the real meaning stays unchanged even if, following Monika Schulz,[19] we think not of the *Dummling* as being not a stupid but a deaf woman: in any case we are talking of a person with reduced mental capacity, a dried-up mind. In the light of the above parallels with creation miracles I am inclined to question other interpretations[20] and argue that in this case the insensible child, sitting on the mother's lap, is somehow identified with the infant Jesus, capable of performing a miracle even in his *Dummling* form, bringing himself to life. (Unless, of course, we are talking about a text which has lost its meaning through textual corruption.) If I am right, this text leads on to those below which state the impossibilities as miracles.

In this context we must also mention the figure of the *dry man* mentioned in Russian incantations alongside dry trees, as a positive use of impossibilities to stop bleeding or pain.[21] Russian incantations also talk of *birds with no head or wings* and of *dry trees with no branches or roots* in a structure of one single thought parallel.[22] According to Mansikka some Russian charms used against bleeding also mention a tree which is upside down and has no roots or leaves.[23]

Impossibility formulas using *dead man/carcass* motifs are a distant parallel to stone-man incantations (with no Hungarian examples). These place the living or dead character of the dead body in a straight or reverse logical connection with the wish that the illness should pass or with some negative wish (evil eye, curse). The earliest relevant relics are ancient Greek curse formulas.[24] Contrary to the simple similes known from Central and Western Europe, the Serbian, Bulgarian and Belorussian formulas published by Mansikka integrate the characteristics of a dead body (its inability to speak, move, use hands or legs, to revive, to feel pain or to bleed) into genuine impossibility formulas. In a Bulgarian love magic text, one simile runs *when the dead man begins to speak, only then will N.N. deny me what I desire.*[25]

The motif of a *demonic being which descends from heaven without a mouth or limbs and yet shows signs of life* appears later in Eastern European text types with Byzantine connections. This motif is difficult to interpret and is also considered by Heim and Mansikka to belong in the sphere of dumb and insensible stone persons.[26] The earliest variant is known once again from Marcellus of Bordeaux's fourth century century spell-book:

stolpus a caelo cecidit,	*a* stolpus *fell from the sky,*
hunc morbum pastores invenerunt,	*shepherds found this illness,*
sine manibus collegerunt,	*without hands they collected it,*
sine igni coxerunt,	*without fire they cooked it,*
sine dentibus comederunt.[27]	*without teeth they ate it.*

This motif appears in a similar context in an eighth century Coptic healing charm which contains a legend featuring Isis. The demon tells Isis that he had seen her son Horus going up a hill where a bird descended on a tree, and made a nest; Horus cut it up without a knife, cooked it without a fire and ate it without salt.[28]

Mansikka, and later some other scholars, also included the riddle of 'birds flying without wings' in the sphere of incantations about insensible, infertile stone beings.[29] In this text the bird which changes its place without wings or legs is identified with the snowflakes, while the creature that eats it without a mouth is the sun. Researchers used to think of this riddle as an example of ancient Germanic heritage,[30] until a rich array of variants emerged from all parts of Europe. A summary of these

was published by Antti Aarne.[31] Even before this time, on account of
the similar motifs of the above incantations published by Richard Heim,
the question emerged whether these incantations might be seen as the
pre-formations of later riddles and at the same time as a more archaic
formulation of these impossibilities, or whether we need to imagine a
different chronology. (The first time these appear as riddles is in a Latin
text from a German-speaking area, 'Volavit volucer sine plumis ...') This
problematic is present in the research of the question even today. Forty
years ago Gerhard Eis was still out to prove that incantations are archaic
and primary;[32] this is what has been repeated several times since then.[33]
A German variant published in 1505 and quoted by Eis runs like this,

Es flog ein vogel federloss	*There flew a bird featherless*
Vff ein baum blatloss,	*From a tree leafless,*
Kam die fraw mundtloss,	*There came a woman mouthless*
Frass den vogel federloss.[34]	*And ate the bird featherless.*

Archer Taylor published two articles to add to Aarne's already rich store
of parallels from Eastern and Western Europe.[35] This rich image, however, shows the structure of a riddle which flourished in the European
tradition (most commonly in Central Europe). He draws attention to
the fact that the *bird flying without wings* is a very common motif describing cosmological phenomena and that much could unfold from it in
the oral tradition in a number of contexts. Particular genres were also
likely to meet. This kind of mingling may have taken place between
charms and riddles on account of the metaphoric angle and structure
that they share.[36] More important than the question of primacy is for
us the observation that while in riddles the appearance of the motif is
accidental, in certain types of incantations it seems a regular necessity.
This is particularly true of those types which contain impossibilities of
a cosmogonic scale in relation to the miracles of creation. It is from this
point of view and in this sense that these texts are primary (even if not
earlier) compared to riddles.

The stone world of the satan

In certain incantation motifs the themes of stone/desert/death are elevated into the cosmic sphere and arranged around the thoughts of
divine and satanic power. These motifs appear most frequently in narrative charms which feature some saint or deity on the one hand and
demons on the other. Their appearance is particularly common in those

charms where a 'saint meets evil.'[37] Above we quoted one example from Gyimes county, Transylvania. In these texts, the barren stone desert appears as the dwelling place of demons in a bipartite world which can be described by the oppositions *human – non-human/demonic, divine/Christian – satanic/non-Christian*. These charms are widespread all over Europe, but particularly under the rule of Eastern Christianity, and certain of their motifs also appear in medieval clerical benedictions as demon-avoiding formulas (indeed, they partly arise from such benedictions). The legendary recoveries integrated into the simile depict the duel between the saint and the demon. The duel is fought for the recovery of the patient and serves as an example for that recovery. The demon-averting formulas recited by the healer of the legend describe the absence of the conditions of life, the impossibility of proper living, the uncreated world of chaos as the dwelling place of demons/non-Christian beings.[38]

It is into this barren stone world[39] that demon-expelling charms wish to exile the demons of illness, which are treated as non-divine, non-created, reductive stone beings. This dead world is usually characterised in the texts by the absence of ploughing and sowing, of bread or the sacraments, but it is also common to talk of a desert, rocky land with no domestic animals or cultivated plants. It is inhabited by wild animals and demons. According to Russian charms, under a stone in the middle of the sea we find a snake, or Satan itself in the image of a snake.[40] According to Weinreich's Latin benediction text, for example, the demon is exiled to

| ... profundum desertum, | *a deserted depth,* |
| ut nominibus nihil noceant | *so that may harm nothing by means of names* |

or to a place,

| Ubi nec aratur nec seminatur | *which is not ploughed nor sown* |
| Nec ullus nomen dei invocat.[41] | *nor does anyone invoke the name of God.* |

The motif of sending the demon to rocky, desert places, into rocks or marshes occurs sporadically all over Europe, but the richest material comes from Eastern and South-Eastern Europe, the Orthodox world and its sphere of influence.[42] Brunner also cites several examples of Finnish charms where demons are sent to the hills or the desert of the endless ocean or to a stone lying in the middle of a meadow inhabited by curious 'impossible' animals, creatures with no head, no blood vessels (in other Finnish charms there are demons with no limbs or sensory organs).[43] Our Hungarian examples come mainly from the Eastern groups of the Hungarian population. The following is an extract from a text from Moldova used to avert storms:

. . .

	. . .
menj a kősziklákra,	*go to a rock*
hol kenyérvel nem élnek,	*where no bread is eaten*
és az ótáriszenséget nem használják.[44]	*where no holy sacrament is used.*

A manuscript from Moldova says

. . .

Menny el kősziklába,	*Go to the rock*
Ott száncs, vess mind a	*and plough and sow seeds*
Te vetésed ott ki nem nő,	*Just as your seeds will never grow*
Úgy ne nőjön ki (Jánosnak) a nyakába,	*So should your disease and poison*
Te eved, és a te mérged[45]	*Not grow on (John's) neck.*

The command given to the demon may be to roll the rock, or, what is known as a natural impossibility, to crumble it, crack it or break it. An eighteenth century spell-book contains the following text:

. . .	. . .
Ti gonosz felhők, gonosz homályok a mi határainkba ne jöjjetek,	*You evil clouds, evil darknesses, do not come to our lands*
. . .	. . .
hanem menjetek hegyekre, köveket repegessetek[46]	*but go to the hills to crack rocks*
. . .	. . .

Formulas for sending away demons are known in charms – naturally enough, such formulas were also used directly. The easternmost groups of the Hungarian population have a living belief in the devil and sustain varied forms of these formulas up to the present day. In one form of the demon-averting charms, the stone motif figures as an 'infertility' symbol by showing the sexual act, but *not* as a life-giving action. These have been collected from the whole of the Hungarian-speaking area.

Kő a fülibe	*Stone into thy ears,*
s patkószeg a seggibe,	*Shoe-nail in thy arse,*
s távojz a kősziklák tetejire![47]	*And go thee to the top of the rocks!*

Giving impossible tasks to the demon also occurs in legends of sending away the helping spirits. In this case, we also find in the background another stratum of meaning, whereby the task is going to kill the demon and be left there for ever. Mrs Cs. K. from Gyimesközéplok intertwined the verbal charm of 'sending into stone' with the act of sending away the helping devil *paratika*: 'Unless you fill it with money by the morning, clear out of here and go into a rock.' People here also relate the legend of the tiny helping spirit in red boots. In this story, a grinding stone is made the impossible condition of liberation.[48] At the same time, this legend is the origin myth of an area of the village, known for being strewn with crumbly rocks. The legend explains the emergence of the rocky soil which is forever gliding down on the slopes of the hills. Once again the devil created a barren, stony world.

According to a widely known belief legend, a Hungarian verbal charm is used to send away the helping spirit of the *lidérc* (will-o'-the-wisp) chicken which is overdoing its tasks and has thereby become a burden. It is told, for example, to bring some sand in a rope.[49] This is an impossible task for the *lidérc* and fulfilling it will kill it.

Natural impossibility – divine miracle

The use of poetic images and legendary scenes (legendary *miracles*) as examples in similes is a feature common throughout Europe. These may be formulated as negative images or impossibilities, but also as straight logical parallels of the desired aim. The miracles performed by the deities and saints of Christian mythology are impossible for earthly man. It is common in incantations to use as examples of impossibility the miracles of Christian mythology and hagiography known from other genres or from the Bible itself. The connection is particularly close between miracles and impossibilities, when the task impossible for the demon appears as a divine miracle. (Unlike the demon, the saint is able to perform things which are impossible according to the laws of nature and human experience). Because of this it is particularly relevant to examine the connections between miracles and impossibilities in charms as a genre.

There is a group of charms where the semantic fields of impossibility and miracle accrete over each other within one and the same text. In these charms, miracles and impossibilities usually appear in the opposition of *demonic impossibility – divine miracle*: it is impossible for the demon or ill-intentioned person to carry out the divine miracle. Texts focussing on the birth of Christ usually express this through the opposition of *infertility vs. birth.*

Föld szülte Annát,	*The Earth bore Anne,*
Anna szülte Máriát,	*Anne bore Mary,*
Mária szülte világ Megváltóját.	*Mary bore the Saviour of the Earth,*
Aki ettül nagyobbat szül,	*Anyone who bears someone greater*
Az árthasson nékünk.[50]	*Should alone harm us.*

Both the German and the Hungarian example speak of the unrepeatable, unsurpassable miracle of Mary's immaculate birth. This overcomes any demonic impossibility.

Du sollst nicht schmerzen,	*You will not ache,*
du sollst nicht geschwären,	*you will not swear,*
bis daß die liebe Mutter Gottes	*until the blessed Mother of God*
ihren andern Sohn tut gebären[51]	*bears another son.*

The following text is used against demons threatening the mother in childbed:

Az árthasson, az véthessen,
aki a boldogságos szűznél szebb fiat szült.[52]

May harm be done and ill be done
by anyone who bore a son more beautiful than the Blessed Virgin's.

A variety of logical structures, as well as of grammatical and stylistic solutions, have generated impossibility formulas with the most varied structures in the subject area of the miracle of the birth of Christ. 'The birth of Christ is the most marvellous, this miracle cannot be surpassed' and 'Jesus is the greatest, none can be greater/more powerful than him' are contents which serve as very general bases of European impossibility formulas. Formulations of the 'evidence' or 'testimony' type are also frequent, and take a unique and characteristic structure. Let us look at an example of these incantations. This is a textual type used repeatedly in an eighteenth century Hungarian manuscript spell-book for healing 'horses that had kicked a tendon'. (This text is an exception in that it does not talk of defeating a demon, only of an 'ordinary' illness.)

> Boldogságos asszonyom Szüz maria
> nem csudálkozom azon, hogy szüzen szüléd a te áldott Szt fiadat ...
> De csudálkozom azon, hogy a pej lo ... az ő hátulsó
> lábával az ő első lábának Inát meg ütötte ...[53]

> *My Blessed Lady, Virgin Mary*
> *I do not marvel that you gave birth as a virgin to your blessed holy son ...*
> *But I do marvel that this bay horse ... has kicked the tendon*
> *Of its front leg with its hind leg ...*

Further variants testimonies include, for example, structures such as 'this is a great thing, but that is an even greater miracle', or 'I do not wonder, I even believe that ...'[54] The logical structure may be of many different kinds even within the variants of the same textual form. Positive and negative facts (miracles and impossibilities) can serve equally well as 'proofs'.

It seems that these texts, transmitted in spell-books held by aristocrats, show a close connection with certain types of legendary miracles. One of these is St. Nicholas's bird miracle (the roast bird is revived and flies away) which is analysed by Kretzenbacher. To the saint, the miracle as a *Zeugnis*, proves the truth and the declaration about the power of the saint or deity is related closely to this. This appears in a number of different contexts in the legend which has been widespread all over the Christian West since the eleventh century.[55]

It would be futile to try to decide the question of primacy between the legend and the incantation; this logical structure and the adequate textual structure may well have been transported from the legendary tradition into our written wealth of incantations along with the motifs of the legend which transform the impossibilities of legends into miracles (or it may have happened the opposite way round). It is also characteristic, at least among those miracles which are related to the clerical benedictions of Latin Christianity, that the miracle of Christ's birth (or other events of his life) simply appear as a parallel to a desired event (the passing of the illness) in the text. The frame formula emphasises the true and real nature of the event, stressing that the miracle did take place, as opposed to the impossibility which did not. (Sometimes the above testimonies appear in this context, too.)

One German example is the following,

Ich beschwör dich Mensch, daß du still stehest,
wie das Wasser im Jordan gestanden ist,
da man Jesum Christum taufet im Namen Gottes.[56]

Man, I adjure you to stay still,
Like the water of the Jordan stood
When Jesus Christ was baptized in the Name of God.

Here the reference is to the miracle which took place at the river Jordan, when the water stood solid as a wall at the time of the baptism of Christ. An old German incantation from Bohemia draws a parallel between the impossibility related to infertile stone and the miracle of birth and salvation. The birth and death of Christ is said to have overcome natural impossibilities:

. . .
Wachse nicht . . .
Wie die Steine nicht wachsen,
Seit der Geburt Christi.
. . .
Ich beschwöre dich, Kropf, damit du nicht wachsest,
Wie die Felsen nach dem Tode Christi nicht wachsen.[57]

. . .
Do not grow,
Like the stones have not grown
Since the birth of Christ.
. . .
Goitre, I adjure you not to grow,
As the rocks have not grown since Christ's death.

Cosmic impossibilities – cosmic miracles

In texts based on the opposition of the divine world and the demonic world, impossibilities are the attributes of demons, while miracles oppose them as attributes of the deity. These texts usually move in cosmic dimensions, in the sphere of ideas around creation and recreation. Miracle motifs may appear in them on a number of different semantic levels in varying grammatical and logical structures. The divine miracle questions and subverts the 'devil's miracles', rendering them impossible; it can be the attribute of the healing deity which figures in the example in the centre of the incantation, it can be a simple example in a simile about healing, and so on. In to an Arabic-Coptic text they request God to tie up the enemy who holds back the sun and the moon (cf. stopping the sun and the moon, Joshua 10:12).[58] The same miracle occurs in the simile of a latter-day German incantation used for stopping bleeding:

Blut, stehe still,	*Blood, stand still,*
Wie die Sonne zu Gibeon	*As the sun did over Gibeon*
Und der Mond im Thale Ajalon.[59]	*And the moon did over*
	the valley of Ajalon.

In texts which protect the house and its inhabitants from demons, the duality of the divine and the demonic world is projected onto the microcosm. We know the motifs of this protective system from Hungarian charms and particularly from archaic prayers (as well as from Southeast European amulet texts): the deity descends over the house, or the entrance of the demon is made impossible by consecrated things.[60] The content of the formula 'the deity is present, the demon cannot enter/do harm' may be expressed through other structures, too, but expressing it in impossibility formulas is also characteristic. There exists a special Hungarian structural type which must have been a deep-rooted turn of phrase, as it is known in a great number of variants from latter-day incantations to archaic prayers still known today.

...	...
Mert mellettem van egy Isten,	*For over me is a God*
Előttem van Boldogasszony,	*in front of me is a Blessed Lady,*
Fejem fölött három Mária,	*over my head Three Maries,*
Körülöttem ezer angyal,	*around me a thousand angels*
...	...
Az árthasson s véthessen,	*no one can hurt me*
Éjcakának idején,	*during the night*
Nekem más senkise,	*unless they take*
Aki elvesz mellőlem egy Istent,	*a God from over my head*
Előllem Boldogasszonyt,	*a Blessed Virgin from in front,*
Fejem fölül három Máriát,	*three Maries from over my head,*
Körülöttem ezer angyalt,	*a thousand angels from around me*
A kezemből szent keresztet ...[61]	*and the holy cross from my hand ...*

There are demon-avoiding formulas known all over Europe based on the opposition of *divine creation of the world – demonic chaos/un-creation*. The idea these texts are based on is that the miracles of the created world are greater than the demon can understand or measure by human standards. In the texts, and the rites which frequently accompany them, the demon (*lidérc*, Mora, Mahr, Alp, or another pressing demon or witch) is given an impossible task. In most cases they have to count the stars, the leaves of the trees, the pine needles, the sand in the sea, before they are allowed to do harm. Further tasks include flying across the world, going to the bottom of the sea, drink or spoon out the water of the sea, eat all the sand from the sea or beach, or take the sun or moon off the sky.[62]

All of this can appear in any of the customary structures of impossible conditions. For example, in a protective charm from Belorussia, we find reference to it being as impossible to influence the protected person by magic as it is impossible to eat all the bread in the world, or count all the stars in the sky, or drink all the water in the sea, etc.[63]

In Central Europe this *mora*-incantation (or Alp-Segen to use Spamer's term), which has been known in books of magic ever since the beginning of modernity, becomes contaminated by the thief-binding incantation which Spamer calls *Diebsbann*, also widespread in latter-day Central Europe. This even includes the impossibility of stealing the baby Jesus: St. Peter binds and renders immobile the thieves approaching Jesus:[64]

Remperas, du Meister aller Diebe, bind dich
Mit Teufels Händen,
Mit eisernen Banden,
Daß du mußt stehen wie ein Stock,
Starr stehen wie ein Bock,
Daß du mußt zählen alles Laub an den Bäumen,
Alle Tropfen im Meere,
Alle Sterne am Himmel,
Alle Sandkörnlein der Erde . . .[65]

Remperas, you master of all thieves, I bind you
With devil's hands,
With iron bands,
So that you must stay stock-still,
Stand stiff as a goat,
You must count all the leaves on the trees,

> *All the drips in the seas,*
> *All the stars in heaven,*
> *All the grains of sand on the earth . . .*

The *mora* spell seems to have no close Hungarian variants, and the task of counting stars does not appear in any prayer.[66] Impossible tasks given to related demons (*lidérc*, fairy) are associated in Hungary with genuine anti-demon rites, e.g. with sprinkling millet or poppy-seed around the house. The texts refer to counting *these* seeds as an impossible condition.[67] (The above mentioned formulas for avoiding the *lidérc* contained in legends are used in different contexts.) As we have seen, these texts, which move in cosmic dimensions, set the demons the task of reaching endless divine dimensions: to fly across the whole world, bring the stars down or count the objects of the infinite universe, spoon the sea out or penetrate to the bottom of it. In other words, they need to apply human standards to the endless divine world – all of which is impossible for the demon. In some ancient demon-avoiding incantations, as a miracle counter-pointing these impossibilities, we also encounter the image of the infinite universe which functions without any technical aid from humans. This Egyptian text written in Aramaic in late antiquity is used against the demon of fever:

> . . .
> Be exorcised from the body of Marian the daughter of Esther,
> . . . in the name of He who . . . suspended the sky
> without chains, and set up the earth without
> pillars, and the sea and the wilderness . . .[68]

The motif of spooning out the sea also appears in the German legend of the baby Jesus (at other times an angel child) which seems to have been widespread in the early modern period. St. Augustine sees a little boy next to the sea who is trying to spoon out the water. When he marvels at this, the child pronounces that just as he is incapable of spooning out the sea, so is the saint incapable of comprehending the essence of the Holy Trinity (according to a song from 1657). Next, the boy appears, who turns out to have been an angel (in other variants the infant Jesus).[69] Kretzenbacher also mentions this legend as part of the St. Nicholas legend of Tolentino[70] and publishes a graphic depiction whereby this miracle is shown together with the revival of the roast chicken. Here, too, the description of the event takes place as part of a testimony as mentioned above. As we have seen, this testimony, as a narrative relating a miracle which vanquishes an impossibility, can be related to impossibility incantations in many ways. (Here spooning out the sea, which is impossible even for the angel or baby Jesus, is surpassed by the divine miracle of the Holy Trinity, which is 'incomprehensible' even for the saint.)

* * *

In presenting these examples in this chapter my aim was no more than to outline depictions of impossibilities and miracles in charms. I hope that describing these few cases has not been without its lessons. Despite their wide variability, perhaps I managed at least to give a notion of the complex role that the genre of charms plays in preservation and integration. Charms are a genre of magical texts where textual fidelity and adaptation to a concrete magical task are important traits. They retain a number of basic, general mythic contents or basic ideas and use them, as we might say, in their 'original' meaning almost up till the present day. Besides this, as a practical and 'functional' genre, they use anything that they might need in the service of this concrete aim. It is no accident that they have such a rich and varied web of connections with myth and legend. It would be particularly interesting to identify the threads which lead to motifs with a related meaning or logical content. Motifs of this kind can be miraculous recoveries, which we only mentioned in passing here. These can be used as examples of similes expressing homoeopathic magic, as well as the testimonies that confirm one or other of the articles of faith which, similarly to anti-demon charms, present miracles as the force to vanquish impossibility. And somewhat further afield lies the appearance of impossibilities and miracles in sayings, riddles and humorous tales or tales of lying (or in fact in any genre where these logical structures only appear as poetic metaphors instead of aiming to relate or confirm some truth content).

As far as the connection is concerned between demon-averting impossibilities and creation myths, I think we are talking of an almost inevitable rather than an accidental connection. The encounter between cosmic impossibilities and also dualistic creation myths took place in certain textual types. Miracles are challenged by the Christian devil characterised by impossibilities, but also by a popular world of demons. Demons of illness, of the child-bed and pressing night demons are all mingled with the devil in the world view of the incantations on account of their shared (Babylonian, Hebrew, Iranian) origin as well as by their later close interrelations. This is particularly true in the world of Orthodox Christianity. As figures of belief legends, they have retained some archaic Christian and non-Christian features even in the modern period. These included some apocryphal devil-traits as well which originate in the myths of dualistic creation. Naturally, these processes had to entail a great amount of change. The *devil* who creates rocks instead of a fertile plain is still a divine creature – he had sunk into the bottomless sea and still creates some sort of a world, if not a very attractive one. The *lidérc* who dies in consequence of the failure to bring up sand from the bottom of the sea is a being of lower order bound by human standards. It is not a mythical creature but a belief figure, equal in rank with the *mora* demon who is unable to count the stars. Demon-averting formulas, however, can be very similar and show close textual connections, thanks to the fact that these formulas are passed down without textual change. This is true whether they are of a legendary nature (to do with the humorous figure of the helping devil-servant) or of a realistic type (as, e.g. the present day anti-devil practices of the people of Gyimes county, Transylvania) or fictitious incantations put into the mouths of the healing saints of incantations. Naturally, living demon-averting formulas and incantations show the closest ties with these legendary verbal charms. As far as threads to other genres are concerned, the most exciting one leads from cosmic tasks given to helping spirits to dualistic creation myths. In this respect I have to mention the suspicions of Lajos Vargyas and Ilona Nagy, according to which this motif of Hungarian *lidérc* legends comes from non-Christian (or possibly *Bogomil*) dualistic creation myths. However, as we have seen, similar cosmic tasks are also contained in *mora*-incantations which are wide-spread in Central and South-Eastern Europe. At any rate we are definitely talking about a very old 'basic notion' and the question is interesting for more than its Hungarian aspects.

Notes

1. In three Roman Catholic villages in Rumania, among the easternmost group of the Hungarian population.
2. By 'verbal charms' I mean incantations used as in a fictitious situation for spell-use in a narrative.
3. The so-called impossibility formulas of incantations have received considerable attention in European and Hungarian research. For a summary see Pócs 1988, 648–50. Attention was first drawn to Hungarian 'impossibility formulas' by Bernát Munkácsy, partly based on Krohn 1901, and partly on Votyak (Udmurt) incantations he had collected himself (Munkácsy 1905). In a much later study, Thomas Sebeok offered a semiotic analysis of a Mari ('Cheremis')

charm. This text seems to represent an entire type among Cheremis magic texts (Sebeok 1956, 284–7; 1975). See also Glukhova's chapter in this volume.
 4. For a presentation of all relevant Hungarian textual types known at that time see Pócs 1985–1986, groups Nos IV and V, as well as several types within group XV. The fundamental role that impossibility formulas played in research was recognised a long time ago. According to Krohn, impossibility formulas of what he called the 'if ... then ...' structure, and the 'just as ... so ...' structure are the two most important groups of Finnish incantations (Krohn 1901). The question of the 'emergence' of incantations and, within that, of impossibility formulas is a recurring question even in latest research. Most recently, a large study was devoted by Versnel to the way in which improvised texts are 'created,' using the special stylistic and grammatical devices of incantations: Versnel 2002, 128–9. He envisages the emergence of impossibility formulas as a more or less spontaneous process. However, he sees them as improvised means of magic, just as in the case of similes. 'If you cannot immediately think of a positive analogon, you create a negative one.' As an example he quotes the impossibility related to mules which will be referred to below.)
 5. Mrs B. J., aged 52, Gyimesközéplok, 2004.
 6. From a manuscript noted down in a book marked with the name Szelestei Tamás and the date 1516. First published in: Mészöly, 1917, 274.
 7. Jankovics 1990. 'Frog' is the name of a disease, just like 'lizard in the throat' (diphtheria).
 8. Katona 1978; Vargyas 1976, II. 90–1.
 9. Marót 1958, 515.
 10. The source of all three texts is: Heim 1893, 493. One includes also the remark 'nec palumba dentes habet' ('the dove has no teeth'), according to another 'nec lumbricus oculos habet' ('earthworms have no eyes'); both the 'no eyes' and the 'no mouth' motif of the riddle on 'birds with no wings' are contained herein.
 11. Veltri 1997, 234. Veltri believes most of the (Hebrew) texts of the spell-books to be of Babylonian origin within Jewish culture.
 12. Mansikka 1909, 280–1; the present example comes from p. 281. Similar texts are also found on p. 89. Similar sequences also occur in Lithuanian incantations, e.g. against snake-bite: Mansikka 1929, 74; for similar images of the stone which bled/did not bleed; the son which yielded milk/did not yield milk see ibid. 69.
 13. Máriássy, György: 'Egy néhány rendbeli lóorvosságok' [Some cures for horses], a manuscript spell-book, published (with a simplified orthography) by Radvánszky 1879, III. 81.
 14. See Mansikka 1909, 216.
 15. Mansikka 1909, 218.
 16. Marcellus, X. 35: quoted by Heim 1893, 498.
 17. Heim 1893, 488.
 18. The Old High German original is also included. 11th century manuscript, once kept in the City Library of Strasbourg and subsequently destroyed by fire.
 19. Schulz 2003, 6–88.
 20. In their commentary on the text, Haug and Vollmann cite previous attempts at interpretation, e.g. Jakob Grimm's certainly outdated notions on the 'ghost of the mountains', Haug und Vollmann 1991, pp. 1166–8. Ohrt, another

author to quote this text, also relates it to the motif of 'heavenly fire falling into the Dead Sea' from a Syrian apocriphal legend (about the baptism of Christ in the river Jordan). (Ohrt 1927).

21. Mansikka 1909, 234.
22. See Mansikka 1909, 71–2. For more instances see ibid.
23. Mansikka 1909, 236–7. (Turning a tree upside down or planting it that way is definitely a death symbol in historical legends in Gyimes. If a tree like that still happens to sprout, this means the re-birth or return of the hero.)
24. Faraone 1991, 5. Faraone also offers further examples, as well as simple curse formulas with no simile (all moving in a similar sphere of thought; these texts used to be place in the grave, beside the body).
25. Mansikka 1909.
26. Mansikka 1909, 70. Heim (1893, 494) also includes here an incantation which is very common among Germans, and speaks about animals lacking certain internal organs: 'Die Bienen ohne Lunge, die Störche ohne Zunge, der Taube ohne Gall', hilft für die 77 Fieber all.'
27. Marcellus XXVIII. 16. For a similar instance see: Marcellus XXI. 3; in a spell-book by a fourth century animal healer Pelagonius, VII. 39: 'stulta femina … sine igni coxerunt, sine dentibus comederunt' – all three from Heim 1893, 494.
28. Kropp O. P. 1931, 10. (German translation of the Coptic text cited in Volume I.)
29. Mansikka 1909, 72.
30. See the recent German summaries quoted below. Zsigmond Szendrey (1921) cites the Hungarian and Serbian texts that had been published up to that date and derives them all from the German. (Nevertheless, the possibility of an archaic Hungarian heritage crops up repeatedly in Hungarian research even after this date.)
31. Aarne 1920. Aarne is also trying to establish origin or primacy (according to him it spread from Central Europe toward the peripheries.)
32. According to Eis (1964) the text is likely to have drifted into the German healing repertoire from a 14th century Arabian veterinary medical book.
33. E.g. Tomasek 1994 points out on the basis of summaries by various researchers the primacy of the Latin text, the orally transmitted forms and of incantations as opposed to riddles and the forms spreading in German literary and written forms.
34. Eis 1964, 76.
35. Also with Hungarian data on the basis of Szendrey (1921), (Taylor 1958). He is trying to establish oikotypes (e.g. Italian, Polish/Czech, bipartite and tripartite).
36. Taylor 1958, 288–9.
37. Of the many textual types featuring '*encountering evil*', this is the type which has the highest number of Hungarian variants (the name given to this type of text by Ferdinand Ohrt and accepted all over Europe is *Begegnungssegen:* Ohrt 1936). For a description see: Pócs 1988, 682–5; for textual variants known up till 1985 see Pócs 1985–86, II. 442–503. The healing saint meets the illness or demon and asks it where it is going; the illness tells him whom it is about to harm and in what way. The saint sends it off to a place where no humans live and it can do no harm.

38. For a description of this inhuman, 'raw' world through a few examples of Hungarian incantations see: Pócs 1992.
39. Cf. a modern literary allusion: Borowski's 'stone world' of Auschwitz. (Tadeusz Borowski: *Kővilág. Válogatott versek és elbeszélések* [Stone world. Selected poems and short stories. (Hungarian translation from Polish)]. Budapest, Múlt és Jövő Kiadó, 1999. For a brief account of the archaic past of 'sending places' see Pócs 1986, 686–7.
40. Mansikka 1909, 34–6.
41. Weinreich 1946, 291.
42. See e.g. Mansikka's Russian and Southern Slavic examples from epic and common demon-evading incantations: Mansikka 1909, 75–8.
43. Brummer 1908, 6–7, 36, 41, 47, 48, 54, 91.
44. Erdélyi 1976, 124.
45. Csoma 1994, 258. For similar Serbian examples see: Conrad 1983, 112, 117; for Slovenian examples: Möderndorfer 1964, 348, 395.
46. Dobrossy and Fügedy 1978–79, 257. (from pages 86–7 of the spellbook, text No. 39.).
47. Albert 1995, 19. On the motif see Jung 1992, 111–12.
48. T. V., Gyimesközéplok, Rumania, 2003.
49. For a summary on the *lidérc* see: Pócs 1980.
50. Erdélyi, 1999, 181; Tokaj, Zemplén county, Hungary.
51. From a spell for healing cut wounds, from a manuscript of unknown origin: Hampp 1961, 209. For a similar example, ibid. 173.
52. Tura, Pest county, Hungary, Pócs 1985–86. II, 386. Similar examples, with the content of 'no one is greater/older than Jesus,' see ibid. 386–7.
53. Vajkai 1947, 119. Berhida, Zala county, Hungary, from a manuscript spellbook. In this article Vajkai includes several variants of the text and devotes attention to the appearance of the incantation in 18th century spell-books, as well as questions of its origin. For relevant variants see: Pócs 1985–86. II, 387–9. An 18th century manuscript that has come to light since that date is available in: Dobrossy and Fügedy 1978–79, 257.
54. See the above quoted places in the spell for horses that have kicked a tendon.
55. Kretzenbacher 1972, 443–4. A 'negative' proof of my assertion of this legend's existence can be found on page 446. This structure and its context in legend were brought to my attention by a conference paper given by Ilona Nagy on the miracle of the roast cockerel and her subsequent article 'The Roast Cock Crows: Apocryphal Writings (*Acts of Peter*, the Ethiopic *Book of the Cock*, Coptic Fragments, the *Gospel of Nicodemus*) and Folklore Texts', *Electronic Journal of Folklore* vol. 36 (2007), 7–40.
56. Hampp 1961, 164.
57. Hampp 1961, 157.
58. Kropp O. P. 1931. II, 242. (German translation of the original Coptic text cited in Volume I.).
59. Dömötz, Elba region, Hampp 1961, 157.
60. For a few examples among amulets against Lilith see Pócs 1990, for examples of the house possessed by a divinity: Pócs 2003.
61. Erdélyi 1976, 159–60, Kakasd, Tolna county, Hungary, spoken beside a dying person. For similar examples see ibid. 237; Tánczos 1995; in an incantation

from Marosvásárhely, Transylvania from 1620 (for successful outcome of law suit): Dézsi 1898, 249–50. (If someone should take the veil of the Virgin Mary ...)

62. Hampp 1961, 98–101; Mansikka 1909, 96–7, 307–8. Mansikka quotes from an orthodox spell-book but it was also popular in German spell-books. For further Central European or Balkanic, as well as more scattered Western European textual variants against pressing demons such as the *Alp* or *mora*, see Spamer 1958, 95–108.

63. Mansikka 1909, 195–7; text cited: 96–7. For similar Croatian texts from Dalmatia: Krauss 1908, 125, 150. On these texts and the *mora* demon, in the context of incantations against Lilith, see Pócs 1990, 125–7.

64. Spamer 1958, 167–218.

65. Spamer 1958, 192; Oberlausitz.

66. Erdélyi 1999, 604.

67. See Pócs 1985–86. I, 107–10. Róheim also did work on rites and texts of this kind and emphasised the derivation of 'impossibility spells' from rites (Róheim 1920, 246.) His conclusion is certainly valid for these cases but cannot be generalised for the whole of the textual wealth here under discussion. This kind of averting rite is present in European folk lore as a motif of *magic escape*, cf. e.g. the tales of type ATU 313, The Magic Flight.

68. From a sheet of lead found in a cemetery in Oxrrhynchus: Naveh and Shaked 1985, 83. (Translated by the publishing author.)

69. Bolte 1906, 90–1; as a fable in a sermon from 1732 see Moser-Rath 1964, 412–13. As a folk song from the time of "Des Knaben Wunderhorn" see: Grißebach 1806, 772–73.

70. Kretzenbacher 1972. He also offers a brief history of the literary and folklore research of the topic.

Bibliography

Aarne, Antti, *Vergleichende Rätselforschungen III*, Folklore Fellows' Communications 28, Hamina: Suomalainen Tiedeakatemia, 1920.

Albert, Jenő, *Boszorkányos dógok. Gyimesi csángó hiedelemmondák, hiedelmek* [Of Witches and Magic. Chango Beliefs and Belief Legends from Gyimes], Sepsiszentgyörgy: Bon Ami Kiadó, 1995.

Bolte, Johannes, 'Die Legende von Augustinus und dem Knäblein am Meere', *Zeitschrift des Vereins für Volkskunde*, XVI, 1906, pp. 90–5.

Brummer, O., *Über die Bannungsorte der finnischen Zauberlieder*, Akademische Abhandlung, Helsinki: Finnische Literaturgesellschaft, 1908.

Conrad, Joseph L., 'Magic Charms and Healing Rituals in Contemporary Yugoslavia', *Southeastern Europe/L'Europe du Sud-Est*, 10, 1983, No. 2, pp. 99–120.

Csoma Gergely, 'A somoskai ráolvasófüzet' [Spellbook from Somoska], *Néprajzi Látóhatár*, III, 1994, Nos 1–2, pp. 253–9.

Dézsi, Lajos, 'Babona a tizenhetedik században' [Superstition in the 17th Century]. *Irodalomtörténeti Közlemények*, VIII, 1898, pp. 249–50.

Dobrossy, István and Fügedy, Márta, 'Ráolvasások egy 18. századi gyógyítókönyvből' [Incantations from a 18th Century Spell Book], *Herman Ottó Múzeum Évkönyve*, XVII–XVIII, 1978–79, pp. 245–60.

Eis, Gerhard, 'Das Rätsel vom "Vogel federlos"', in *Altdeutsche Zaubersprüche*, Berlin: Walter de Gruyter & Co., 1964, pp. 67–76.

Erdélyi, Zsuzsanna, *Hegyet hágék, lőtőt lépék. Archaikus népi imádságok [Archaic Folk Prayers]*, Budapest: Magvető Könyvkiadó, 1976.

Erdélyi, Zsuzsanna, *Hegyet hágék, lőtőt lépék. Archaikus népi imádságok [Archaic Folk Prayers]*, (3rd edn) Pozsony: Kalligram, 1999.

Fabó, Bertalan, 'Magyar ráolvasások', *Ethnographia*, XVIII, 1905, pp. 125–6.

Faraone, Christopher A., 'The Agonistic Context of Early Greek Binding Spells', in Christopher A. Faraone, in Dirk, Obbink, eds, *Magika Hiera. Ancient Greek Magic and Religion*. New York – Oxford: Oxford University Press, 1991, pp. 3–32.

Grißebach, Eduard (Hrsg), *Des Knaben Wunderhorn. Alte deutsche Lieder*, gesammelt von L. A. von Arnim und Clemens Brentano, Leipzig: Max Heßes Verlag, 1806.

Hampp, Irmgard, *Beschwörung, Segen, Gebet. Untersuchungen zum Zauberspruch aus dem Bereich der Volksheilkunde*. Stuttgart: Silberburg-Verlag, Werner Jäckh, 1961.

Haug, Walter and Benedikt Konrad Vollmann (Hrsgs), *Frühe deutsche Literatur und Lateinische Literatur in Deutschland 800–1150*, Frankfurt/Main: Deutscher Klassiker Verlag, 1991.

Hästesko, F. A., *Motivverzeichnis westfinnischer Zaubersprüche, nebst Aufzählung der bis 1908 gesammelten Varianten*, Folklore Fellows' Communications 19, Hamina: Suomalainen Tiedeakatemia, 1914.

Heim, Ricardus, 'Incantamenta Magica Graeca Latina', *Jahrbuch für classische Philologie 46*, Supplementsband 19, 1893, pp. 3–576.

Jankovics, József, *Archaikus betegségelhárító imádságok* [Archaic Prayers for Averting Disease], A Lymbus füzetei 13, Szeged, 1990.

Jung, Károly, 'Folklóradatok egy középkori pillérfő értelmezéséhez' [Folklore Data for Interpreting a Mediaeval Pillar-Head. Contribution to the Question of Averting the Evil Eye], in id., *Köznapok és legendák. Tanulmányok a népi kultúra köréből*, Újvidék: Forum Könyvkiadó, 1992, pp. 104–21, 241–2.

Katona, Imre, ' "Amikor egy búza száz keresztet terem." Lehetetlenségi formulák a magyar népdalokban' ['When One Grain of Wheat Yields a Hundred Sheaves.' Impossibility Formulas in Hungarian Folk songs], in Mihály Hoppál – Márton Istvánovits, eds, *Mítosz és történelem*. Előmunkálatok a Magyarság Néprajzához 3, Budapest: MTA Néprajzi Kutatócsoport, 1978, pp. 186–96.

Kelemina, Jakob, *Bajke in pripovedke slovenskego ljudstva, z mitološkim uvodom*, Celje, 1930.

Krauss, Friedrich S., *Slavische Volksforschungen*, Leipzig, 1908.

Kretzenbacher, Leopold, 'Zeugnis der stummen Kreatur. Zur Ikonographie eines Mirakels der Nikolaus von Tolentino-Legende', in *Festschrift Matthias Zender. Studien zur Volkskultur, Sprache und Landesgeschichte*, Edith Ennen – Günter Wiegelmann, Hrsgs., (Separatabdruck), 1972.

Krohn, Kaarle, 'Wo und wann entstanden die finnischen Zauberlieder? I-III', *Finnisch-Ugrische Forschungen* I (1901), Heft 3.

Kropp O. P., P. Angelicus, *Ausgewählte koptische Zaubertexte II. Übersetzungen und Anmerkungen*, Bruxelles: Édition de la Fondation Égyptologique Reine Élisabeth, 1931.

Mansikka, V. J., *Über russische Zauberformeln mit Berücksichtigung der Blut- und Verrenkungssegen*, Helsinki: Finnische Literaturgesellschaft, 1909.

Mansikka, V. J., *Litauische Zaubersprüche*, Folklore Fellows' Communications 87, Helsinki: Suomalainen Tiedeakatemia, 1929.

Marót, Károly, 'A varázsdaltól az eposzig' [From the magic song to the epic poem], *Ethnographia*, LXIX, 1958, pp. 505–36.

Mészöly, Gedeon, 'A Szelestei-féle ráolvasás 1516-18-ból' [Szelestei's incantation from 1516-18], *Magyar Nyelv XIII* (1917), 271–6.

Möderndorfer, Vinko, *Ljudska medicina pri Slovencich*, Ljubjana, 1964.

Moser-Rath, Elfriede (Hrsg), *Predigtmärlein der Barockzeit. Exempel, Sage, Schwank und Fabel in geistlichen Quellen des oberdeutschen Raumes*, Berlin: Walter de Gruyter & Co. 1964.

Munkácsy, Bernát, 'Keleti típusú magyar varázsige', *Ethnographia*, XVI, 1905, pp. 57–97.

Naveh, Joseph and Shaked, Shaul, *Amulets and Magic Bowls. Aramaic Incantations of Late Antiquity*, The Magnes Press, Jerusalem: The Hebrew University – Leiden: E. J. Brill, 1985.

O. Nagy, Gábor, *Mi fán terem? Magyar szólásmondások eredete ['What Tree Did This Grow on?' The Origin of Hungarian Proverbs]*, (3rd edn.), Budapest: Gondolat Kiadó, 1979.

Ohrt, Ferdinand, ' "Tumbo" mit dem Kinde', *Hessische Blätter für Volkskunde*, 26, 1927, pp. 1–9.

Ohrt, Ferdinand, 'Über Alter und Ursprung der Begegnungssegen', *Hessische Blätter für Volkskunde*, 35, 1936, 49–58.

Polívka, Georg, 'Die Entstehung eines dienstbaren Kobolds aus einem Ei', *Zeitschrift des Vereins für Volkskunde*, 28, 1918, pp. 41–56.

Pócs, Éva, 'Lidérc', in Gyula Ortutay, ed., *Magyar Néprajzi Lexikon III*, Budapest: Akadémiai Kiadó, 1980, pp. 452–4.

Pócs, Éva, *Magyar ráolvasások I–II* [Hungarian Incantations I-II], Budapest: MTA Könyvtára, 1985–86.

Pócs, Éva, 'Ráolvasás' [Incantation], in *Magyar néprajz V. Folklór 1. Magyar népköltészet*, Lajos Vargyas ed., Budapest: Akadémiai Kiadó, 1988, pp. 633–91.

Pócs, Éva, ' "Lilith és kísérete". Gyermekágyas-démonoktól védő ráolvasások DK-Európában és a Közelkeleten' ['Lilith and her train': Incantations protecting from childbed demons in Southeastern Europe and the Near East], in Ildikó Kríza, (ed.), *A hagyomány kötelékében. Tanulmányok a magyarországi zsidó folklór köréből*, Budapest: Akadémiai Kiadó, 1990, pp. 110–30.

Pócs, Éva, ' "Nyers és főtt": halál és élet. A kulturális vívmányok helye az euró-pai parasztság archaikus világképében' ['Raw and Cooked,' Death and Life: The Place of Cultural Achievements in the Archaic Worldview of European Peas-antry], in Viga Gyula (ed.), *Kultúra és tradíció 1–2. Tanulmányok Ujváry Zoltán tiszteletére*, Miskolc: Hermann Ottó Múzeum, 1992, vol. 1, pp. 11–24.

Pócs, Éva, 'Az isteni megszállottság motívumai az archaikus népi imádságokban és ráolvasásokban' [Motives of Divine Possession in the Hungarian Popular Prayers], in Judit Czövek, ed., *Imádságos asszony. Tanulmányok Erdélyi Zsuzsanna tiszteletére*, Budapest: Gondolat – Európai Folklór Intézet, 2003, pp. 113–37.

Radvánszky, Béla, *Magyar családélet és háztartás a XVI. és XVII. században III* [*Hungarian Family Life and Households in the 16th and 17th centuries III]* Budapest, 1879.

Róheim, Géza, 'Lucaszék' [Saint Lucy's stool], in id., *Adalékok a magyar néphithez II*, Budapest, 1920, pp. 29–227.

Schulz, Monika, *Beschwörungen im Mittelalter. Einführung und Überblick*, Heidelberg: Universitätsverlag C. Winter, 2003.

Sebeok, Thomas A. 'Grammatikai paralelizmus egy cseremisz áldásban' [Grammatical parallelism in a Cheremis charm], in János Gulya, ed., *A vízimadarak népe. Tanulmányok a finnugor népek élete és műveltsége köréből*, Budapest: Európa Kiadó, 1975, pp. 311–24.

Sebeok, Th. and F. J. Ingeman, *Studies in Cheremis: The Supernatural*, New York: Wenner–Gren Foundation, 1956.

Spamer, Adolf, *Romanusbüchlein. Historisch-philologischer Kommentar zu einem deutschen Zauberbuch. Aus seinem Nachlaß*, bearbeitet von Johanna Nickel, Berlin: Akademie-Verlag, 1958.

Szendrey, Zsigmond, 'Találós meséink és külföldi megfeleléseik' [Our riddle tales and their foreign equivalents], *Ethnographia*, XXXII, 1921, pp. 79–81.

Taylor, Archer, ' "Vogel federlos" Once More', in *Festschrift für Hugo Hepding zum 80. Geburtstag 7. September 1958* (=*Hessische Blätter für Volkskunde*, 49/50, 1958), pp. 277–94.

Tánczos, Vilmos, *Gyöngyökkel gyökereztél. Gyimesi és moldvai archaikus népi imádságok* [Archaic folk prayers from Gyimes and Moldova], Csíkszereda: Pro-Print Kiadó, 1995.

Tomasek, Tomas, *Das deutsche Rätsel im Mittelalter*. Tübingen, Max Niemeyer Verlag, 1994.

Vajkai, Aurél, 'A lovak betegségéről való orvosságok ', ['Cures for the Maladies of Horses'], *Ethnographia*, LVIII, 1947, pp. 55–68.

Vargyas, Lajos, *A magyar népballada és Európa I–II* [Hungarian folkballad and Europe I–II]. Budapest: Zeneműkiadó, 1976.

Vargyas, Lajos, 'Honfoglalás előtti keleti elemek a magyar folklórban' [Pre-Christian Oriental Elements in Hungarian Folklore], *Történelmi Szemle*, XX, 1977, no. 1, 107–21.

Veltri, Giuseppe, *Magie und Halakha. Ansätze zu einem empirischen Wissenschaftsbegriff im spätantiken und frühmittelalterlichen Judentum*, Tübingen: J. C. B. Mohr (Paul Siebeck), 1997.

Versnel, H. S., 'The Poetics of Magical Charms: An Essay on the Power of Words', in Paul Mirecki and Marvin Meyer (eds.), *Magic and Ritual in the Ancient World*, Religions in the Graeco-Roman World, 141, Leiden – Boston – Köln: Brill, 2002, pp. 105–58.

Weinreich, Otto, *Unheilbannung im volkstümlichen Gebet, Segen und Zauberspruch*. Schmiedel, Stuttgart. Universitas: Zeitschrift für Wissenschaft, Kunst und Literatur 1, no 3, 1946, 275–99. (Separatabdruck).

4
Swedish Snakebite Charms from a Gender Perspective

Ritwa Herjulfsdotter

For some time now, I have been engaged in research on magical medicine and charming in Sweden and Swedish-speaking Finland. Part of this research, a survey of a wide variety sources, including folklore archives, museum archives and published materials, succeeded in locating over 500 Swedish snake charms. The bulk of the charms were recorded at the turn of the century, between 1880 and 1930. More than half of the corpus contain the Virgin Mary as a meaningful gestalt. Analysing the motifs in these charms, reveals the following broad groups: *Virgin Mary cures snakebites, Snake on a tuft of grass, Jesus meets a snake, Adam and Eve meet a snake, Snakes and roots*, and finally, a group of miscellaneous charms. Here I will focus on the users and informants of the first of these types, *Virgin Mary cures snakebite* type Swedish snake charms from a gender perspective. The analysed charm-type consists of a total of 246 records from folklore archives in Sweden and Finland.

In the Swedish folklore archives, there is often no record of the user of the charm (i.e. of the person who is expressly declared to have used the snake charm); in those cases, the informant (i.e. the person who has told the charm to the correspondent) is assumed to be the user. (An informant might be a user who uses the snake charm for healing purposes but *user* and *informant* do not necessarily denote the same person; one can not assume that they are the same.) In short, the archives are dominated by records featuring male users and male correspondents; this gives an unbalanced picture from a gender perspective, namely the false impression that most users of snake charms were men. The contextual records can fill out our picture, e.g. in cases where a user is not explicitly described, a closer look at the material can uncover further information. However, there is a problem when the name or gender of the user is not provided in the material. Where a named informant has described both charm and procedure thoroughly, I have made a judgement of how the record should be interpreted. In particularly uncertain cases, I have chosen not to include the material. My primary research question is whether snake charms of the *Virgin Mary cures snakebite* type be related to a specific gender. To answer this I chose to take the four largest charm variations from the group the *Virgin Mary cures snakebite* and analyse them from a gender perspective. The four variants have been named and categorized according to the significant motives that appear in the texts: *The Virgin Mary walked in the grass*, *The Virgin Mary walked on the road*, *The Virgin Mary gave me a cloth*, and *Snake on a tuft of grass*.

The Virgin Mary walked in the grass

Let us begin with an example of this variant:

Jungfru Marja gångar sig i gräset	*The Virgin Mary walked in the grass*
Där hörde hon ormen väsa	*Where she heard the snake hiss*
Jag skall dig binda	*I shall tie you*
Och tvinga	*And force you*
Med mina fem fingrar	*With my five fingers*
I Guds den heliges namn[1]	*In the name of the Holy Father*

In my research, I have found 33 records of this variant. For the charm-texts that can be linked to a certain recorder, the gender balance is 19 male and 11 female recorders who have contributed to collection and documentation of this charm-type. When we analyse the number of informants we see 14 male and 6 female informants. Consequently, there is clear male dominance both of recorders and of informants. However, a closer look at the records shows an equal number of male and female *users* related to this variant. Six texts can be connected to male users and twelve texts to female users. I also looked at the categories of users related to this variant. The female user categories that can be related to using and handing down this charm-type are as follows: a shepherd girl (1 record), a person supported by the parish (1 record) and eight 'old women', possibly female healers.[2] The male user categories that can be related to using and handing down this charm-type are three male healers, three so-called 'nature healers',[3] and two simply called 'father' (2 records).[4] Thus, while there is a male dominance in both users and informants of the *Virgin Mary walked in the grass* variant, we see that that there are an equal number of female and male users, and more female than male healers.

The Virgin Mary walked on the road

Jungfru Maria gick vägen fram,	*The Virgin Mary walked on the road,*
Mötte hon ormen	*She met the snake*
Då tog hon ett band	*She took a rope*
Och band ormen	*And tied the snake*
Hon band hans lever	*She tied his liver*
Hon band hans lunga	*She tied his lung*
Hon band hans etter i hans tunga	*She tied the venom in his tongue*
I Fadrens, Sonens och den helige Andes namn.[5]	*In the name of the Father, the Son and the Holy Ghost*

The *Virgin Mary walked on the road* variant is represented by 17 texts. Texts that related to recorders documenting this charm type can be divided into 9 male recorders and 4 female recorders with 7 male and 3 female informants. Two *Virgin Mary walked on the road* charms can be related to male users, six to female users. The female user categories are two 'aunts', one 'old woman who cures a 12-year old girl' and one healer. The male user is a building contractor who taught the charm to the male informant. Male recorders and male informants dominate documentation of the *Virgin Mary walked on the road* variants. However, once again, a closer look at the material shows that there is a dominance of female users.

The Virgin Mary gave me a cloth

Jungfru Maria gav mig en linda	*The Virgin Mary gave me a cloth*
Och med den skall jag binda	*And with this cloth I will tie*
Lever och longer	*Liver and lungs*
Etter och blod	*Venom and tongue*
I dessa tre namn	*In the name of these three*
Faderns, sonens och den helige Andes[6]	*The Father, Son and the Holy Ghost*

This third variant, *Virgin Mary gave me a cloth*, has the largest number of records (57 in total) and is the most difficult to analyse since much of the contextual information is missing. The texts related to a specific recorder are divided among 17 male recorders and 2 female recorders. There are 9 male and 5 female informants, and 6 male and 7 female users. A male or female user can be determined for seven of the *Virgin Mary gave me a cloth* texts. Five of these can be associated with a female user and two with a male user, while one charm was found in a written charm collection. The female user-categories are healers,[7] the written charm from charm-collection of a named woman[8] and an informant.[9] Male user-categories are a named man[10] and a written charm from charm-collection.[11] Male recorders and male informants are dominant for this variant, however, as before, a closer look at the written material shows that female users dominate the number of records.

Snake on a tuft of grass

Svarta snuva	*Black snake*
Låg på tuva	*Lay on tuft*
Med sin långa ettertann	*With his long venom tooth*
Fram kom jungfru Maria	*The Virgin Mary appeared*
Med sitt rödaste gullbann	*With her reddest gold band*
Nu svider och värker det inte mer[12]	*Now the stinging and aching are gone*

In my corpus, there are 28 records of this charm-type. The recorders that have documented the variant are divided among eleven men and ten women, while there are eight identified female informants and seven male informants. A closer look at the number of users reveals eight women and seven men.[13] In general, female informants have reported more female users and male informants have reported more male users. The female users of the charm are described as 'healer',[14] 'mother'[15] and 'the farm mistress who was tending the cows',[16] while the male users of the charm are described as 'healer',[17] 'father'[18] and 'a man called Bäng-Matts who taught me it while I was tending cattle'.[19] So, we can see that while the recorders of this variant consist of an equal number of males and females, and while the majority of informants are males, the majority of the users are female.

The transmission of charms

You see, it wasn't good for an old lady to teach another lady, so she had to teach a man and then he could teach a woman or a girl. It had to be the opposite sex, the one you passed it on to ... [20]

There were several records of the popular belief that the efficacy of a snake charm would be damaged if it was passed on to should not to be passed on to an incorrect category of person.[21] In some of the records, it is apparent that a woman handed the charm over to a man or vice versa. As elsewhere, contra-sexual transmission seems here to have been the desired norm. However, the ethnographic record is also full of contradictory evidence as well: in several cases, it seems as if the charms have been handed over between two women in a row and then to a man. Or again, in several other records, 'an old woman'[22] has handed over the charm to others, both men and women. There are more records of women passing the snake charms on, especially older women transmitting their medical knowledge to a younger person. However, I have not found any record of older men having transmitted their charms to younger women.

As far as the 246 *Virgin Mary cures snakebite* texts in my corpus are concerned, there are 19 cases of them being transmitted from an older woman to a younger person, and six cases in which a man handed down this knowledge. The majority of the records show an older woman handing over the charm to a younger woman. Consequently, there is a difference between the number of records for female and male transmission of snake charms. Another difference is the fact that more women seem to have been able to transmit the snake charm to both men and women, whereas men frequently seem to have handed over their knowledge to other men, often from father to son.

Snake charms have been transmitted from a variety of reasons – for example, they were taught for preventive reasons. However, there are also records in the material that indicate at least two other contexts: that of indoor textile work and that of animal tending. These are specifically female work environments, where women played an active, dominant role. One interesting factor is that snake charms are not only recited over snakebites, there are also indications that snake charms could also be read over other illnesses.[23] Magic medical charms, especially snake charms, might be considered as an expression of a specific female environment and knowledge in an ethno-medical context. This knowledge, inherited and handed down for generations, shared by both women and men, was mostly used by women in actual situations.

Who read the snake charms professionally? Who used them in the household?

The purpose of this analysis of the four most numerous varieties of snake-charms, *Virgin Mary walked in the grass*, *Virgin Mary gave me a cloth*, *Virgin Mary walked on the road* and *Snake on tuft of grass*, was to see who used these charms and for what reasons. In 16 cases, a family member treated snake bites with a snake charm of the type *Virgin Mary cures snakebite.* These records are divided among 12 men and 4 women. In 21 cases, a folklore practitioner read this type of snake charm. These records are divided among 5 men and 17 women. In some of the records, it is clearly stated that a female healer used the charm. There is suggestive evidence that women who were mentioned by names such as *Ängs-Anna (Meadow-Anna)*, *Britta Ersdotter* and *Käcka-Mor*, were also female healers, but we cannot be certain on this point. Fewer male healers are named, but they also occur in the records: *Varg-gubben (Wolf-man)* and *Pussen-gubben*. As far as the named male healers are concerned, the archival record state that these charms were handed down in *written* form. This is seldom the case with female healers. In some of the texts, it is stated that mother and father have handed down the charm. In the present research material, however, I have found no evidence that brothers or sisters, friends of the same age or younger people have handed down or used snake charms.

Conclusions

Only a few of the texts can be associated with a specific user. The variants I analysed are consistently evenly divided between male and female users. However, there is a small yet noticeable majority of female users. This is interesting considering the imbalance between male and female informants that exists in the records, the problem of insufficient contextual data and women's general invisibility in the archives. Given the research material's contextual weaknesses, all we can conclude here is that while female users are in the majority, all texts types were used by both men and women. There is a pattern that men relate that other men such as fathers or neighbours, handed the charms down to them, whereas women described receiving the charm from a female practitioner of folk magic. This indicates that, when it comes to snakebites, men did not turn to a folk-magical practitioner to the same extent that women did. This may also indicate that verbal magic had a stronger connection to female folk-magical practitioners.

My research material shows results similar to Swedish historian Linda Oja's discussions from the seventeenth and eighteenth centuries.[24] More women can be related to use of snake charms than men. It is evident from a life-cycle perspective that snake charms have been perceived differently depending on gender and position. Young girls have been handed the snake charms at a certain age, but there is no evidence of a similar age relation for young boys. While the contextual evidence considering snakebites and snake charms shows a preponderance of males,

due to the fact the material has been collected primarily by male informants and recorders, a closer reading and analysis of the material paints
a somewhat different picture: an outline of female superiority and a
male subordination. Maybe we should also consider snake charms as
an expression of a specific female environment and knowledge in an
ethno-medical context. This knowledge, inherited and handed over for
generations, was shared by both women and men but used primarily by
women in actual situations.

Notes

1. LUF 482,59. If you met a snake in the wood it could be tied with the charm
   that mother C. learnt from her mother. Informant Lovisa 'parish constable',
   75 years old. Recorder Birger Andersson, S:t Olof sn. Albo hd (county), Skåne
   (Scania) 1927.
2. Mrf. NM 1897,23 the female informant have heard the charm from the practitioner *Stina in Karshult*, Småland. ULMA 2894:2,2 *an old woman*, ULMA
   4888,59 *an old woman in Hölö*, ULMA 14830,209 *Wise mother in Näsdala*,
   ULMA 4470,4 *an old woman*, ULMA 8042,26 *an old woman here in Flänga*,
   ULMA 7041,8 *an old woman in Högfors in Skinnskatteberg.* ULMA 27505,37
   (Meadow) Ängs-Anna in Bollsbro.
3. ULMA 2894:8,5 *that old man.* IFGH 982,25 *The charm belongs to Varg-
   gubben (Wolf-man)*, Mfr.NM 1897,23. *From the type of book that Petter in
   Häradsskogen had.*
4. ULMA 6042,26 female informant. ULMA 8864,2 male recorder.
5. ULMA 5930,18 from Pelle Schenells' recordings. Recorder P. Bogren, 1932,
   Gnarp, Hälsingland.
6. IFGH 981,4. 'It was Anders Hök on Kopparudden south of here that taught
   it to me. I have tried it, when one of my boys was snake-bitten.' Informant
   Olov E. Olsson, Rämmen, Värmland, 69 years old. Rec. John Granlund, 1927.
7. ULMA 160:19,181 nature-healer, 'Hilla-Greta'. IFGH 3787,32 old woman
   from Rämen, ULMA 2542:1,44 Kuckelaktig old woman.
8. IFGH 982,24 The informant is the user and has learnt the charm from Klara
   Jacobsson in Kullerberget, Dalarna, ULMA 23364:2,24 the male informant
   owns several written snake charms.
9. ULMA 5751,25 Maria Forssgren f. 1851 I Dalarna.
10. IFGH 981,4 male informant.
11. ULMA 291:3.
12. ULMA 10923,233. Old woman (Lillbrommagumman) cured snakebites. She
    moved her left ring-finger counter clock-wise and read the charm. Informant
    Gustav Ersson, Floda, Södermanland, 92 yrs old. Recorder Imber Nordin-Grip,
    1937.
13. As far as the *Snake on a tuft of grass* variant is concerned, 23 texts can be
    associated with five female and four male users. If we include texts where the
    informant is named and where the charm and the treatment ritual are clearly

described, we find an additional two female users and one male user which makes a total of five male users and seven female users of this charm variant.

14. NM ELL 2894 Asserydsgumman, ULMA 10923,233 Lillbrommagumman, ULMA 10955,6 *an old woman who did that kind of thing*.
15. ULMA 8042,27 female informant.
16. ULMA 2173:8,55 female informant.
17. The archive of the Museum of Dalarna 7432. Lång-pelle. Female informant.
18. ULMA 6442,40 male informant, IFGH 982,23 male informant.
19. IFGH 982,18 male informant.
20. ULMA 2894:2, s.2. recorder S. Thornell.
21. See, for example, Lundgren 1927 IFGH 1020:27.
22. I interpret *an old woman* as an older woman not related to the person she choose to hand over the charm to.
23. Herjulfsdotter, Ritwa, *Swedish Virgin Mary Charms against Snakebite. Folk-religious practices in a reproductive sphere* (University of Göteborg doctoral dissertation, 2008).
24. Oja 1994: 52.

References

Published source

Oja, Linda, 'Kvinnligt, manligt, magiskt. Genusperspektiv på folklig magi i 1600-och 1700-talets Sverige', *Kyrkohistorisk årsskrift*, vol. 94 (1994), 43–55.

Unpublished sources

LUF Lunds universitet, Traditionsuppteckningar
NM Nordiska Museet, Folkminnessamlingen
NM EU Nordiska Museet, Etnologiska undersökningen
ULMA Dialekt och folkminnesarkivet i Uppsala

5
Charms as a Means of Coping
Ulrika Wolf-Knuts

In her 1965 overview of Nordic folklore, *Folklig diktning*, Anna Birgitta Rooth stated that the function of charms is magical, for their aim is to fulfil the wishes and needs of the person who pronounces them.[1] Obviously, Anna Birgitta Rooth was inspired by the classical Frazerian perspective which holds religion to be the opposite of magic. Magic was said to express man's will and power, whereas religion was said to be performed as an expression of man's submission to supernatural powers.[2] But consider the following:

Mot modstulenhet:

J[ungfru] Maria gick sigh uth på en grönan lööth, mötte hon sin wälsignade son så sööth. 'Huad leethe I, min wälsignadhe moor?' – 'Jag leetar min miöhumbla, ty min koo ähr blifuin miölkstulin och mostulin, lefuerstulin, lungstulin, hiärttstulin och all illa fahrin.' J[esus och?] Maria mille mor ginge bådhe om rådh: 'Will wij botha henne bådhe tuå. Will wij taga malt och salt och lätha i hennes munn, thet skall blifua booth i samma stundh.' ... [Fader vår.]

The Virgin Mary went out into a green meadow, and met her blessed sweet son. 'What are you looking for, my blessed mother?' – 'I look for my honey bumble-bee, for my cow has become milk-stolen and courage-stolen, liver-stolen, lung-stolen, heart-stolen and all over in bad condition.' Jesus and Mild Mother Mary looked for a way out: 'We will cure her together. We will take malt and salt and put into her mouth, there will be a cure at the same time.' ... [Our Father.].[3]

This charm, collected in Ångermanland in Sweden in the year 1674, relates the dramatic experience of the Virgin Mary looking for a bumble-bee, because her cow had lost its strength. On meeting her son, Jesus, they decided to help the animal by giving it malt and salt, remedies would cure it immediately. I would prefer to regard this text, along with other similar texts, as religious. It is not only the texts and rituals (or other products and performances), but also the believing person making use of them that is part of the encounter between man and the supernatural world.[4] Believers want their actions to be effective, no matter whether or not the formulated text or fabricated object needed is accepted by the religious authorities. From a functional perspective the classical difference between magic and religion can thus be dissolved.

This way of thinking can be adapted to a charm situation as well. The person who, in a certain situation, finds it necessary to utter a charm would occupy the central role on the dramatic stage which is, in this case, also populated by a sick cow, Jesus, the Holy Virgin, a bumble-bee, and God, not to mention the curing factors, the salt and the malt. This unhappy help-seeking person wanted the charm to be effective, in other words, to make the cow healthy again. No doubt we have here some central Christian figures, and the text moreover ends with hints to Our Father and maybe even to the Holy Ghost. But nevertheless, we also meet figures who have nothing whatsoever to do with the Christian tradition, and we see Jesus and Mary acting in a way that is not described in Christian codices. Obviously, the content of the charm was constructed in order to correspond to the needs of a certain situation in human life and the components were taken from several spheres, culturally inherited as well as self-experienced.

We must assume that charms were used in critical existentially important situations where the person who utilised the text referred to his or her own environment. We cannot know this for sure, of course. Today, in the Nordic countries, we know that the texts at our disposal are the results of more or less systematic collection conducted either by folklorists to save the supernatural tradition, or by priests or judges who wanted to erase superstition. Very seldom do we know anything of a more 'natural', immediate performance situation. One of the solutions to this constant problem of the historical study of folklore, the lack of context, is to presume that the reaction of modern man to a critical situation might to a certain degree also give clues as to how people in distress reacted some centuries ago. This is a risky path to take and it calls for caution and care. On the other hand, within the study of the psychology of religion several thorough empirical studies have been made of man's ways of handling crises. I will try to use some of the information we have in my analysis of the charm I mentioned as a document of a coping strategy.

If we agree that charms are religious texts, we also have to accept that they can be studied by the same methods as other religious texts. Exegesis and philology are good examples of methods utilised in the study of charms.[5] Thanks to the work done by students of political, economic and cultural history, we know quite a lot about Nordic society in the seventeenth to the twentieth centuries. This makes it possible for us to trace the historical prerequisites for understanding the society to which the texts applied.[6] Performance studies would meet our needs, provided we can accurately demonstrate how people behaved when performing the charm. There must, however, be some solution to the problem of the missing human. Just as students of religion try to reconstruct man's role in bygone cults and societies, it should be possible to reconstruct the context around charms and charming.

Such considerations have led me to the view that the psychology of religion might give us some good ideas on how to interpret the charm texts. By using the psychology of religion we can perhaps interpret charms by cautiously maintaining that man's psychological needs in critical situations have not changed much over the centuries. In any case, in a rural household, the crisis incurred severe economic and, consequently, existential risks. Man might adjust himself to the difficult situation; he might give in, and no charm would be needed. On the other hand, he might counteract it, both physically and mentally. Then, more or less consciously, he would decide to oppose the powers that caused the crisis and try to thwart them. Saying a charm would be one of several ways of coping with the dangerous situation.

Kenneth I. Pargament has developed a coping theory on how man handles his fate in order to create significance and coherence in life.[7] Coping is a cultural, socially anchored, repetitive activity that opens a person's eyes to new opportunities in times of distress. This sounds very optimistic – there are always new opportunities – but the opportunities need not be positive; they can also be negative; man can decide to give in. The main thing is that he has decided how to react to what happens. Man creates a system of orientation along which he conducts his coping process. The system of orientation is a general world view made up of customs, values, relationships, beliefs and personal characteristics. This system is not stable or unchangeable. On the contrary, it changes with life so that some factors that once were central may later become ephemeral.[8] The system of orientation is certainly grounded in culture, such as in folklore, and it is therefore understandable that a farmer with a sick cow might take to charms and turn to the Virgin Mary and Jesus in his need for help.

When the cow grew weak, the farmer had to decide what to do with her. Should he let her languish away or should he take her to a sorcerer, who might be able to cure her? Let us assume that in our case he decided in favour of approaching the sorcerer. This person, in turn, in his own coping process has utilised his knowledge about and memories of folklore and the Christian religion and hit upon a suitable charm populated with people and other beings that were said to have had dealings with a sick cow and who knew how to cure the animal. We have here two coping processes, that of the farmer and that of the sorcerer. In other cases, if the owner of the cow himself were able to charm, the farmer and the sorcerer would coincide and there would be only one process of coping connected to the charm.

Of significance here is the factor that creates self-conscience in man, meaning in life and feelings of belonging. 'The search for significance is the overarching guiding force in life, one that directs people along very different paths.'[9] In time of distress, man has to choose between various options, picking the one that gives him significance, so that he can accept his choice and acknowledge it as the best in that particular situation. 'Significance [. . . refers] to what is important to the individual, institution, or culture – those things we care about.'[10] Significance is the goal, and the way to it is what we call coping.

When the farmer chose to visit or to call upon a specific sorcerer, he coped in such a way that he could be happy when the cow recovered and he consequently got a good milk yield and other products for consumption and for sale. If the animal did not recover, the farmer would have to find some explanation for this, and that explanation would give him significance in the new situation. He would start a process of attribution, i.e. a process of creating meaning in the critical situation.[11] He would find some person, being or circumstance to blame for his failure. He would find an explanation to fill his need for significance and for meaningful reasons for this unsuccessful outcome, so that it would seem logical and open up a new perspective on life and new ways of living. In my view, attribution is one of the means by which man copes with life occurrences. However, unsuccessful charms are seldom found in the collections, simply because there is no mention of the real effect of charming.

Man can cope both positively and negatively. In our example the farmer was able to ask somebody, such as the Holy Virgin or God, for help, but he could also have decided never to breed animals again and take to drinking. In coping with the situation, the sorcerer, too, could choose between several options. He could, for instance, make a selection of several charms and pick out the one which he thought was most likely to cure the cow. If he succeeded, he would derive significance from the successful cure; if he failed, he would find some explanation which would leave him more or less satisfied. A visible token of a successful cure was a thriving cow, and perhaps a better status for him as an effective sorcerer.

Coping is a common human activity. I do not think I am mistaken when I extrapolate my interpretation from research in contemporary experiences of critical situations to a situation a couple of centuries ago. However, I am very well aware of the risks of over-interpretation. Coping is also a culture-specific process. And furthermore, it is also a very personal process that is influenced by the individual's personal experiences and characteristic traits. We know something about life in a Nordic peasant society of the seventeenth century, but we do not know anything about our farmer himself.

The text of a charm is also key. We know that the text in my example was repeated several times, because we have a large number of variants on the theme of Jesus and the Virgin Mary curing a sick cow. Notions about their particular skills in medical matters was well-known in contemporary society. People knew that Jesus and the Holy Virgin and all the other figures in the charms were able to help, and they had acquired this knowledge through socialisation, through learning and experience, 'through norms and patterns of behaviour (roles)', as Nils G. Holm says.[12] Roles are there as models for behaviour. When the cow is sick, the peasant or the sorcerer assumes the role of the holy persons; they actualise the curing with the help of the charm text.[13] In this way it is also possible to maintain that the charm gives the person in need of help a language in which to express his needs. Owe Wikström presents a theory that is valid for fictive literary texts, namely that the reading of novels can be regarded as a reading act for understanding and interpreting life.[14] Charms mentioning mythical beings and supernatural actors can function as fictive texts and provide the distressed with the same mechanism for understanding his or her life situation. This understanding is brought about with the help of a culture-specific text containing roles and wordings that suit the actual state. The charms are ready-formulated; they provide the person in need of help with efficient words, roles for behaviour and hope for a good solution.

The study of coping can help us to understand how charms functioned in times of distress, but only to a very general degree. But can we try to analyse the relationship between a charm and a charming situation in more detail? What, for instance, are the mechanisms behind the choice of a certain charm in a certain situation? In forming a response to this question, I have allowed myself to be inspired by Peter Seitel's analysis of proverbs.[15] Seitel regards proverbs as metaphors, and he shows how the situation described in a proverb and a 'real' situation can be connected. He gives us the example is an African proverb: 'If one finger brought oil it soiled the others', which in his case refers to a boy who has fallen into bad company.[16] The scholarly problem to be solved is why the father referred precisely to this proverb when he wanted to warn his son. What have oil and fingers got to do with bad company? Seitel's answer to this involves stressing the correlation between three situations connected to the mentioning of the proverb: the interaction situation, the text situation and the context situation. Let us try to apply this theoretical frame on the charm we have been considering.

In the interaction situation of the proverb we find the person who makes use of the proverb text and the person(s) to whom he speaks. In the charm these two actors are, on the one hand, the distressed party (the farmer) and the helper (the sorcerer) (sometimes these two roles coincide), and, on the other hand, the damaging actor. As in the proverb, what we have is a relationship between the harmed and the harmer. In the proverbs it is characterised by differences and similarities in age, sex or status, whereas in the charms the relationship is more complicated. The actor to which the charm is addressed may be another human, but it can also be an animal, an elemental force, an illness or a supernatural being. In the example we are considering, we do not know much about the original situation. However, the main precondition for Seitel's interaction situation remains in both genres: there are two partners, a speaker and a listener. And yet the charm differs from the proverb in one important respect. Unlike in the proverb, we find a supernaturally founded competence ascribed to the sorcerer. This trait supplies Seitel's scheme with a second dimension because it creates a relationship between the human world and the other world.

In the text situation of the proverb we find the finger dipped in oil and the hand as a whole getting dirty in due course. In the charm we meet Jesus and the Virgin Mary, other Christian persons, a cow, a bumble-bee, salt and malt. Most of the Christian personages and the bee constitute one category providing the cure for the illness together with the concrete remedies of salt and malt, whereas the cow, who is the victim in need of help, and by extension the Holy Virgin, who owns the cow, make up another category. The relationship between these two groups is the crisis, the need for help. The Holy Virgin plays a double role, for she is both in need of help and one of the helpers. I think that this ambiguous role must be explained by her role as a mediator or pleader between God and man.

The context situation tells about the situation in which the text is actualised. In the case of the proverb, this happened when the father wanted to warn his son. In the charm it is made up of a person who has a problem with his cow and, therefore, needs help. There is an analogy between the text situation and the context situation. Somebody needs help with his cow, and there is a charm that tells about a corresponding situation. However, this explicit correspondence is not necessarily always there. Some charms seem to be about things quite different from the situation in which they were needed.[17] This peculiarity might be explained by the fact that man tries to create significance and meaning along both cultural and fundamentally individual paths. It may be difficult to understand what analogies and associations a sorcerer might create in his choice of charms from archived material many centuries old with no context or personal information on the individuals connected to it. Seitel also speaks of 'correlation'. The person who utilises the proverb adjusts his way of doing so according to recent needs. This goes for charms as well. In the absence of variants, this aspect of charming cannot be studied using the Nordic charms as material. But, we should at any rate note that some charmers do refer to themselves within the texts, whereas others stick to a third person epic form.

Finally Seitel mentions the concept of 'strategy', i.e. recommendations on how to handle a situation. One can either resign oneself or do something about it. In charms, intervention must be seen as the only way out. Many charms include recipes for how to use the remedies, such as salt or malt. Most of them also contain descriptions of relevant rituals or gestures. The habit of sealing the effect of the charm by reference to Our Father or the Holy Trinity is also an expression of strategy. Drawing on Seitel's model and the ideas about coping and attribution, it becomes clear that the persons in the interaction situation build up a relationship between themselves and the persons in the charm text. Thinking by analogy seems to dominate. The charms appear to be regarded as models for solving a problem. They not only provide models for how to act in a critical situation; they also provide a language in which man can express himself in situations of fear and distress in order to cope with his situation. In this respect they remind us of prayers as culture-specific but individually utilised and varied formulas for creating contact with beings more powerful than man.

Notes

1. Rooth, *Folklig diktning*, p. 113.
2. Ringgren, *Religionens form och funktion*, p. 14.
3. Ytterlännäs, Ångermanland 1674. Signelser number 925.
4. Cf. Ringgren, op.cit., pp. 15–16.
5. For example, Ohrt, *Danmarks Tryllefomler*, Ohrt, *Trylleord*, Ohrt, *Da signed Krist*, Ohrt, *Fluchtafel*, Hampp, *Beschwörung, Segen, Gebet*, and Roper, *English Verbal Charms*
6. See for instance, Oja, *Varken Gud eller natur*, Bringéus, '"Ben mot ben, led mot led"', or Wall, *Hon var en gång tagen under jorden*.
7. Pargament, *The Psychology of Religion and Coping*.
8. Pargament, op.cit., pp. 99–105.
9. Pargament , op.cit., p. 95.
10. Pargament, op.cit., p. 31.
11. Spilka, Shaver & Kirkpatrick, 'A general attribution theory'.
12. Holm, *Människans symboliska verklighetsbygge*, pp. 20–1.
13. Holm, *Människans symboliska verklighetsbygge*, pp. 24–9.
14. Cf. Wikström, *Aljosjas leende*, p. 21.
15. Seitel, 'Proverbs', pp. 125–43.
16. Seitel, op.cit., p. 130.
17. See, for instance, Forsblom, *Finlands svenska folkdiktning VII.5*, no. 512 against pain: Stäm Kirji fors/Håll Nurjan bäck/Blodsdroppan skall stå/Ej mera rinna/I namn Fadrens och Sons o.d.H.A. (*Stop Kirji rapids/Stop Nurjan brook/the blood drops shall stand/not run any more/in the name of the Father and Son a.t.H.G.*).

Bibliography

Bringéus, Nils-Arvid, ' "Ben mot ben, led mot led". 25 gotländska signelser. *'Sæt ikke vantro i min overtroes stæd.' Studier i folktro og folkelig religiøsitet. Festskrift till Ørnulf Hodne på 60-årsdagen 28. september 1995*. Oslo, Novus forlag 1995. pp. 60–80.

Forsblom, Valter W., *Finlands svenska folkdiktning VII.5 (Folktro och trolldom, Magisk folkmedicin)*. Helsingfors, Svenska litteratursällskapet i Finland, 1927. P. (Skrifter utgivna av Svenska litteratursällskapet i Finland 195.)

Hampp, Irmgard, *Beschwörung, Segen, Gebet. Untersuchungen zum Zauberspruch aus dem Bereich der Volksheilkunde*. Stuttgart, Silberburg-Verlag, 1961.

Holm, Nils G., *Människans symboliska verklighetsnygge. En psykofenomenologisk studie*. Åbo, Åbo Akademi, 1997. (Religionsvetenskapliga skrifter 40.)

Ohrt, Ferdinand, *Da signed Krist. Tolkning af det religiøse indhold i Danmarks signelser og besværgelser*. København, Gyldendalske boghandel, 1927.

Ohrt, Ferdinand, *Danmarks trylleformler*. vol.l., 1917.

Ohrt, Ferdinand, *Fluchtafel und Wettersegen*. Helsinki, Suomen tiedeakatemia, 1929. (FF Communications 86.)

Ohrt, Ferdinand, *Trylleord, fremmede og danske*. København, Schønberg, 1922. (Danmarks Folkeminder 25.)

Oja, Linda, *Varken Gud eller natur. Synen på magi i 1600- och 1700-talets Sverige*. Stockholm/Stehag, Symposion, 1999.

Pargament, Kenneth I., *The Psychology of Religion and Coping*. New York & London, 1997.

Ringgren, Helmer, *Religionens form och funktion*. Lund, Gleerups, 1968.

Rooth, Anna Birgitta, *Folklig diktning. Form och teknik*. Stockholm, Almqvist and Wiksell, 1965.

Roper, Jonathan, *English Verbal Charms*. Helsinki, Suomalainen Tiedeakatemia, 2005.

Seitel, Peter, 'Proverbs, a Social Use of Metaphor' in Dan Ben-Amos (ed.) *Folklore genres*. Austin & London, University of Texas Press 1976. pp. 125–43. (Publications of the American Folklore Society. Bibliographical and special series 26.)

Signelser ock besvärjelser från medeltid och nytid. *Svenska landsmål ock svenskt folkliv* B 41.

Spilka, Bernard, Shaver, Phillip & Kirkpatrick, Lee A., 'A General Attribution Theory for the Psychology of Religion.' *Journal for the Scientific Study of Religion* 24.

Wall, Jan-Inge. *Hon var en gång tagen under jorden . . . Visionsdikt och sjukdomsbot I gorländska trolldomsprocesser*. Uppsala, Dialekt- och folkminnesarkivet i Uppsala, 1989. (Skrifter utgivna genom Dialekt- och folkminnesarkivet i Uppsala B. 19.)

Wikström, Owe, *Aljosjas leende. Om gudsfrånvaron, mystik och skönlitteratur. Religionspsykologiska perspektiv*. Stockholm, Natur och Kultur, 1997.

6

On Systematizing the Narrative Elements of Slavic Charms

Vladimir Klyaus

Charms represent a unique genre of folklore: in contrast to other folkloric genres, the narrativity of charms is not exhausted by the texts themselves. The 'charm' is not only expressed by words but also exists outside their bounds. P. Maranda and E. Köngas-Maranda have written that 'charms and ritual [texts], as opposed to other more or less self-sufficient narratives, do not supply enough information for analysis when presented in normal textual transcription. One may indicate the following distinction between narratives such as Märchen, Sage, ballads and various epic songs and charms: the first group may be called "historical," "objective", and convey a dramatic event without demanding the active involvement of either the narrator or audience; while the second group, that may be called "actual" and "subjective," requires that both take part in a dramatic action, the performer in an active way, the audience at least passively' (Маранда 1985: 228). This important insight alerts us to the fact that in the case of charms, the information required for analysis lies not only within the immediate text itself (as with 'epic' type narratives) but is also contained in the ritual context in which it is performed, and in the sphere of religious and mythological ideas that condition its performance.

We may examine, as an example, some very simple charms that literally consist of but a few words: '*Дума, притки вон. Аминь*' ('Thought, misfortune [*or* illness, *or* evil eye] away! Amen'). The person who pronounces these four words is supposed to wash herself, and thus rid herself of influence of the evil eye (P33 1998. No. 2105). The given text merely consists of two nouns addressed to the malady, *дума, притки*, an adverb, *вон*, and the formulaic word, *аминь*. It has no verb to indicate action. Nevertheless, an action is more or less explicitly implied in the text, as the maladies are ordered to leave the person. Moreover, the maladies are made to leave with the help of the water, to be washed away, and this also underscores the charm as an action. The charm text, structured in the form of an imperative exclamation, as well as the performers' actions, exist within the context of belief in the evil eye, the idea that it may be purposefully brought down upon a person, or washed away with water, that it may be gotten rid of by means of magic words and actions, that the water has magic power, etc.

Here is another short text, one that is pronounced when curing boils: ' *Чирей в сук чирей в сук*' ('Boil into the branch, boil into the branch'). While saying these words, the performer of the charm must 'twirl' the boil with the ring finger and point at bough (Адоньева, Овчинникова 1993. No. 492). In this text, consisting of a repeated imperative address to the malady, there are again no verbs, and, as in the preceding case, the action is simply understood (the address to the boil – *чирей*, and the noun *сук* in the accusative case), the action being that the boils must depart or dry out. In this case the text's narrative information, or more precisely, its quasi-narrative content, exists within the context of the action of the charm, and the presumption that boils may be produced or removed by incantation, be made to appear or dry up, etc.

These examples are sufficient to illustrate that narrativity is a fundamental characteristic of charms, even if the narration is absent in the text proper, but rather is a function of the charm's broader performative or objective nature. The performance combines with the words in one single incantatory action, so that the words, so to speak, are pooled with the beliefs and ideas that create and condition the existence of charm rituals. The short forms of incantatory folklore, which are sometimes referred to simply as phrases or formulas, demonstrate quite clearly that the most important narrative element in magical texts is the *action,* and this independent of whether or not it is expressed in any kind of verb since the short forms, together with other incantatory texts, serve as 'a magical means to achieve the desired ends, in curative, protective, and other rituals' (Толстая 1999: 239).

But an action does not exist in and of itself; it is carried out by a particular subject, has a defined goal, condition, and character. And therefore in any charm-text there exists, if only in highly curtailed form, a given narrative *plot structure* consisting of at minimum the following elements: the action; subject of the action (what we call the *personage*), and place of action in the broadest sense. These may be reconstructed if only in part from the known repertoire of ritual actions, beliefs, and other known data. In the first charm text we cited, the narrative fabric, understood within this larger context of ritual action, consists of the following plot elements (those words present in the text itself are italicized here): the *дума, притки* [bad, grave thoughts and maladies] that affected a person are sent by evil people. The *дума, притки* go away [*вон*] from a person. Water cleans away the *думы* and *притки* (or they are washed away by water). The *дума, притки* disappear forever or depart for a place from which they cannot return (*Аминь*).

In the second text (against boils) more attention is paid to the localization of the disease: *Чирей* affect a person (the narrative structure includes reasons for the boils' appearance, although in the given instance they did not happen to be included in the recording). *Чирей* leaves the person and goes into the *сук*, remains in it, dries up and never returns. The abbreviated nature of charms' plot structure allows for variativity in its reconstruction, a variativity that is lessened in proportion to the amount of detail collected about the incantatory ritual, with all its component parts; it is desirable that the participants be interviewed about the various ideas and beliefs that condition the charm's performance.

Among the active charming traditions, there are charm texts far more complex in the narrative respect than those we have examined. Their complexity involves a greater number of characters taking part and the nature of their actions, and may be more or less fully expressed in the text, that is, without reference to the extra-textual context of the ritual action. Hence we may speak of a qualitative difference in charms' narrative and plot structure – either abbreviated, expressed in the text in only a fragmentary way; or fully expressed, when the text is a self-sufficient narrative, that itself reflects religious ideas and beliefs, and exists as it were in parallel to the performative aspect of the ritual act. In the latter case, a fully expressed narrative may be of two types – detailed and less detailed. The difference between them is somewhat relative, but still empirically tangible. For example, here is a Russian charm against insomnia from the Yenisei Region, recorded in mid-nineteenth century:

Кочеток серый, кочеток пестый, кочеток красный, возьми крик у рабы Божией (имя рек)

(Кривошапкин 1865, 2: 3).

Grey cock, multi-coloured cock, red cock, take away the crying of servant of God (name of the sleepless person).

Here the bird (whether there is one *кочетка* or three is not entirely clear) asks that the malady (*крик*, insomnia) be removed from the child. This charm has much in common with those cited earlier: from various ethnographic sources we know that insomnia affecting a child at night may be personified as a bird that comes to him, especially a chicken, which may steal him, peck him, and destroy him, so that the narrative also transcends the bounds of the text. But unlike the charms analysed above, we need not 'reconstruct' the entire narrative structure, as the text itself is sufficient, with its clearly expressed plot describing the personage (*кочеток*), the action (*берет*), the object of the action (*крик*), and its place (*у раба Божьего*).[1]

In all of the texts we have cited so far, there has been one personage (or rather, identical ones or doubles of one another), who performs a single action, and this single action *correlates with the functional purpose of the charm text*. In Slavic charm traditions there exist a significant number of texts in which there are more than one personage, and these personages perform more than one action. Works of this type have more developed narratives, as in epic folkloric genres. We will cite just one example, from the Bulgarian tradition:

> *Оздол иде чуден човек и носи чудна секира, та ойде у чудна гора, да отсече чудно дрьво, да го отнесе на чудна нъива, па направи чудна бачийа, та збра чудно стадо, та измлъзе чудно стадо, подсири чудно сиренье. Павезе чуден човек чудното сиренье, та го отнесе на чуден пазар, та везе чудни пари от чуден пазар. От чуден пазар отиде у пуста гора, дека секира не сече, дека петел не пьейе и дека пиле не лети, дека колач не меса, дека турта не меса, дека на чрьква не ида. От там везе чудните пари, отнесе ги чуден човек, отнесе га у чудна меана и купил ie чудно вино чрьвено, та ie испил чуден човек чудно вино чрьвено, та ie оздравел чуден човек от чудни почудишта.*

(Стойков 1890: 142–3, No. 3)

A wonderful man walked along and he carried a wonderful axe, then he came to a wonderful forest and cut down a wonderful tree, and he carried it to a wonderful meadow and made a wonderful sheep-fold and gathered a wonderful flock, and he milked the wonderful flock and made a wonderful *brinza* cheese. The wonderful man took the wonderful cheese and carried it to the wonderful market, and he got wonderful money there and he took the wonderful money from the wonderful market. From the wonderful market he went to the bleak forest where the axe did not cut, the cock did not crow, where the chicken did not fly, where the bread is not kneaded, where he did not go to church. He took the wonderful money there, up to a wonderful tavern bought some wonderful red wine, and the wonderful man drank the wonderful red wine and the wonderful man was cured of his wonderful wonder.

Here there are several personages – the wonderful (literally *full of marvels*) person, who walks in the forest, carries an axe, builds a sheepfold, gathers the flock, milks and prepares cheese, etc.; the rooster, who does not sing in the empty forest; the bird who doesn't fly; the people who (it is understood) do not knead bread or go to church. Besides this, there is the wonderful forest, where the wonderful herd is located, the market, where they buy *brinza* cheese, and so on. We need not list everything, but simply note that besides the personages, their actions, and places of habitation, we also find that the instruments of the action and objects acted upon are also mentioned. It is characteristic that, for all the diversity of personages here, it is relatively easy to single out the one who carries out a given action, that correlates – as in the charms already cited – with the functional purpose of the ritual act. Hence in this Bulgarian *baianija* we associate the 'wonderful person' with drinking the wine, which was purchased with the money received from the sale of the *brinza*, prepared from the 'wonderful milk.' In this narrative it is precisely the drinking of the wine that leads to curing the malady (*чудни почудишта*). We may consider this action as being the basic one.

In our research we have analysed a significant number of charms from various Slavic traditions, and discovered that for all the variety of the personages' actions, there are relatively few basic plot actions. These are present in works with very different plots, and are performed by various – at times surprisingly remote – personages. For example, we can compare the Bulgarian charm above to a Serbian *basme* against evil eye (Раденкович 1982. No. 536) and to a Russian charm against 'collar', i.e. a disease caused by the evil eye (Логиновскии 1903: 92–3, No. 4). In the Bulgarian charm the 'marvelous person' drinks wine and therefore is cured, in the Serbian charm the 'urok' and 'urochitsa' lick the 'uroki', and in the Russian charm the pike chews through the 'khomut' (*collar*). In each case the personages destroy the maladies by eating and swallowing them. The basic actions in the plots of all three charm texts are similar.

The concepts of plot and plot structure developed in Russian folklore studies over more than a hundred years have still not been completely and unequivocally defined, although as T. V. Zueva has correctly noted, a series of scholars – V. Ia. Propp, A. F. Losev, B. N. Putilov, V. P. Anikin – 'have come to similar conclusions about correspondences in the structure of *complex* folkloric plots' (Зуева 1995: 6; my italics). The reference to complex plots here is important as it indicates that the material under discussion here are the long genres, such as the *skazka* (folktale), the epic poem, etc. And as a matter of fact, theoretical works on folkloric plots and narrative hardly mention the problem in reference to short genres such as verbal charms.

Nevertheless, the plots of 'long' and 'short' folkloric genres have much in common. The studies of the Lithuanian scholar B. Kerbelite have demonstrated this convincingly. [Кербелите 1991: 23–8]. Her analysis of oral traditions, mythological and aetiological tales, and fairytales, has shown that the narrative structure of folk prose consists of simple, elementary plots that come together in various combinations, forming the basis for independent works. In Kerbelite's opinion, the simplest plots 'begin with the description of a certain situation, further describe the circumstances of the action, then the action of the personage itself that changes the initial situation, and finally communicates the changed situation'. At the same time, 'compressed oral plots only contain one action by the personage plus an indication of its result' (Кербелите 1991: 24). Generalizing on the personages' actions, Kerbelite describes the supreme importance of one single action in the elementary plot, or, as she puts it, the hero's action, which she calls 'the main action of the elementary plot' (Кербелите 1991: 69), that corresponds to what we have described as the basic action in charm plots.

Among research on charm narrative, B. N. Putilov's position seems to us important methodologically. Putilov argues that in folklore, 'The notion of "plot (*sjuzhet*)" represents a known scholarly convention, but only in the sense that it is not the same as the idea of "text" and is formulated as the result of a special analysis of a group of texts' [Путилов 1988: 137]. We have done exactly this: after analysing several thousand Slavic charm texts, we have concluded that the *charm plot* may be understood as the presence in the text of *several groups of interconnected narrative elements – the personage, his actions, the place of the action, and the object of the action* (as in the example of the Bulgarian *baianija* against 'evil eye', cited above). In cases where *one group* of these elements is present in the text (as in the Russian charms against insomnia discussed earlier) we may speak of a *charm plot situation*. Any *pair of narrative elements* in a charm text amount to a *charm motif* (on this see Кляус 1994: 9–12).

This scheme of charm plot [narrative] construction is not consistent with that of (for example) V. N. Anikin, who holds that a motif is structurally made up of a subject (the active personage), the predicate (the action), the object (personage at whom the action is directed) and the conditions or situation of the action (Аникин 1996: 261–62). But in our opinion the difference between charm plots and those of other folkloric narrative genres which Anikin analyses lies in the fact that charm plots frequently are not limited to the text alone (and indeed, the shorter the charm, the more significant its extra-textual content).

The exposition of charm text narratives as self-sufficient in plot, based on a wide spectrum of incantatory material from the eastern and southern Slavs (Russian, Belarusian, Bulgarian and Serbian); and the description of these plots, their basic actions, and formal analysis of their separate predicates, as well as their common semantics and 'themes'; have allowed us to describe charm plot structure as a single system for the first time: see my book, *Указателе сюжетов и сюжетных ситуаций заговорных текстов восточных и южных славян* ('Guide to plots and plot situations in charm texts of Eastern and Southern Slavs'), published in 1997 (Кляус 1997).

In the structural system I have devised there, plots and plot situations that have similar basic actions are grouped together into 'plot themes' (ST – sjuzhetnye temy), which in turn are divided into two groups, A and B. This division of charm texts into groups A and B is a broad generalization, significantly abstracted from the texts themselves, but from our perspective nevertheless reflects important structural and semantic differences within incantatory traditions.

The ST's (plot themes) that make up set A and B are grouped according to formal criteria of predicates that denote basic plot actions that relate to this or that plot theme. For example, ST A1 includes: Вынимают. Унимают. Отнимают. Вытаскивают. Берут. Забиют. Отбирают. Уничтожают. Относят. Отвозят (*They take out. They remove. They take from. They take out. They collect. They take away. They destroy. They carry off (on foot). They carry off [by vehicle]*). Predicates, presented in third person plural forms, indicate that in the ST, the personage (or to be more specific, the plot's hero) accomplishes the main action that is connected with taking something away from another personage or object. The semantic differences among various predicates in this and other ST groups that may at first seem glaring, recede upon closer inspection of the plots.

Here follows a complete list of STs in my Groups A and B. After the ST number are given the generalized description of the given plot theme and the number of plots here grouped; then comes a list of the predicates that we include as relating to this basic ST action:

Group A.
ST A1. Destruction by means of taking out (55 plots).
ST A2. Destruction by means of blowing or sweeping out (28 plots).

ST A3. Destruction by means of water (26 plots).
ST A4. Destruction by means of eating (75 plots).
ST A5. Destruction with the help of a cutting or stabbing instrument, the absence of pain when using the cutting ot stabbing instrument (76 plots).
ST A6. Destruction by means of shooting (with a bow or other instrument), by beating, by expulsion (101 plots).
ST A7. Destruction in battle (20 plots).
ST A8. Destruction with the help of words, the recitation of words (32 plots).
ST A9. Existence (birth) – disappearance, metamorphosis (19 plots).
ST A10. Destruction of barriers (17 plots).
ST A11. Destruction of barriers for water (5 plots).
ST A12. Destruction of an object that comprises some sort of whole by breaking or beating it into parts (41 plots).
ST A13. Destruction of diseases with a plant, destruction (collection, plucking up) of plants (29 plots).
ST A14. Destruction of fire (17 plots).
ST A15. Absence of friendly relations or attachment of one to another (14 plots).
ST A16. Forced subjugation (14 plots).

It is clear from this listing that the basic actions of Group A are of one type, as all are directed at the *destruction* of something or someone. To some degree the semantics of the basic action of Group A is opposed to that of those in Group B:

Group B.

ST B1. Return, passing on of something to the object of the action, the creation (recreation) of a larger multiplicity by means of this return or passing on of its parts (65 plots).
ST B2. Attraction of objects by promises to satisfy their desires and needs; creation of a new multiplicity by attracting objects by promises to satisfy their desires and needs (22 plots).
ST B3. Bringing close, transposition of the object, creation of a new multiplicity by bringing close, transposition of the object (34 plots).
ST B4. Impossibility of destroying the object (21 plots).
ST B5. Preservation by sewing on, tying; creation (recreation) of a single whole by means of sewing on, tying (37 plots).

ST B6. Creation of defense, preservation by means of locking up, closing, protection (72 plots).
ST B7. Preservation of the object in an immobile state (18 plots).
ST B8. Restoration of something broken, displaced (14 plots).
ST B9. Preservation of the form (6 plots).
ST B10. Impossibility of fulfilling defined actions (6 plots).
ST B11. Impossibility of growth (9 plots).
ST B12. Setting on fire, use of fire, light (54 plots).
ST B13. Voluntary subjugation, desire for beauty and happiness (14 plots).
ST B14. Romantic, friendly relations (19 plots).
ST B15. Unification, impossibility of transfer, movement, life without something (25 plots).

In our opinion, one may speak of a basic opposition between the two groups, although this opposition is not absolute. In Group A, as we have noted, action is directed toward what we may in general terms refer to as 'destruction', while in Group B action is generally oriented toward 'creation, preservation, usage'.

Opposition is one of the typical characteristics of charm poetry, and may be observed on various levels – functional and occasional, and on the textual level, in motifs, plots and plot situations, as well as in other narrative elements. The opposition of plot themes that we have described also serves as an example of this. When we compare them to the usual division of charm texts into 'black' and 'white' (referring to the nature of the magic they summon), one can't say that this accords to an opposition between those that 'cause evil' and those that 'prevent evil'. Charm texts may be divided into many thematic oppositions that include both categories. For example, one may 'close' or 'shut' a wound, so as to stop the bleeding, but one can also 'close' or 'shut' bodily organs that are necessary to life. Mythological creatures or animals may 'eat up diseases', but they may also attack people, 'eat' them, and make them suffer.

The STs express only very general actions by the charm-text personages, for example, to 'take away', 'take out', or 'eat up'. These descriptions reflect one aspect of the action, and are abstracted to a degree. Their more concrete meaning that more accurately reflects the functional purpose of the charms becomes clearer when the object of the action is specified.

Let us examine the problem of opposition on the level of STs (plot themes). The themes A1 and A2 are opposed to B1 (we repeat that after the generalized semantic meaning of the basic action, which is given in italics, are given the predicates – verbs that express the basic action in the actual charm texts, here given in third person plural form):

ST A1. Destruction by means of taking out.
ST A2. Destruction by means of blowing or sweeping out.

ST B1. Return, passing on of something to the object of the action, the creation (recreation) of a larger multiplicity by means of this return or passing on of its parts.

Other ST groups also include oppositions:

ST A6. Destruction by means of shooting (with a bow or other instrument), by beating, by expulsion.

ST B3. Bringing close, transposition of the object, creation of a new multiplicity by bringing close, transposition of the object.

ST A14. Destruction of fire.

ST B12. Setting on fire, use of fire, light.

Similarly, A10 is opposed to B6, B7; A12 to B8, B5; A7, A15, A16 to B13, B14, B15 and so on.

The opposition of plot themes is dependent on the opposition between the discrete charm plots that make up the charm as a whole. Here are several representative examples.

Cases when the same personages carry out opposite actions[2]

In Russian love charms, the plot in which the charmer meets the *wind* and asks it *to put, carry in, or bring* (*вложить, внести, пустить*) 'longing' or 'desire' (*toska*) on another person is very widespread [Кляус 1997: 242–5]. For an example see Иванова 1994. No. 220. Similarly, in a Serbian *basma*, the blowing wind blows sleep onto a child (see Раденкович 1982. No. 435, for an example). However, the wind may not only give something to a person, it can also take things away. In Belorusssian tradition there is a charm in which holy saints meet the wind and ask it to remove disease from a person (Кляус 1997: 56), see Романов 1891: 4. No. 9, for an example. To give another example, in a Russian charm against wasting disease, holy saints drive 'pritoshnitsa' and other diseases out of a person's house and into the field (Майков 1869. No. 222). So in the examples we have cited, we can see that the wind carries out opposing actions – sometimes bringing, sometimes taking.

Holy people can also perform the opposite action – banish beasts and birds to the one charmed:

> ... *Подступлю я к престолу господню со огненным ружьем, раб божий (имя рек), стрелец, попрошу и помолю Егория храброго и Михаила архангела, чтобы мне сослал разного зверя, и разнаго копыта и разную лемучую птицу* ...

(Толмачев 1911–12. No. 3: 145)

> ... I shall approach the altar of the Lord with a fiery gun, servant of God [name], a marksman, I shall beg and pray to St. George the Brave and Michael the Archangel to send me all kinds of wild beasts and all kinds of hoofed beasts and all kinds of birds ...

While one and the same personage can perform opposite actions, these actions may sometimes even be found in one and the same plot (Кляус 1997: 236, 242–4, 251, 332). For example, in eastern and south Slavic charms plots in which a bird takes away, carries off, or pecks out a person's or livestock's illness are widespread:

> *На сіянь-моры стаіць дуб, на том дубі дванаццаць сукоў на мых суках па дванаццаць кокамаў, на мых кокатах па дванаццаць варвновых гняздоў -- кокци жалезныя, а дзюбы сярэбряныя. Вараны, злятайця, боль жалезнымя выдзірайця, головы вынімайця, сярэбраным дзюбамі боль із скаціны вынімаіця, амін*

(Романов 1891: 133. No. 46).

> On the ocean-sea there stands an oak, on the oak there are twelve boughs, on each of these boughs there are twelve branches, on each of the branches there are twelve ravens' nests – iron claws and silver teeth. Ravens fly away, take out the pain with your silver claws, open your heads, with your silver teeth take out the pain from the cattle, Amen.

This special power of birds is also encountered in love charms, where they not only may bring sadness upon a person, but may also take it away and send it onto someone else:

> ... *Попрошу из чиста поля четырех братьев, – четыре птицы востроносы и долгоносы, окованы носы. Лети из чиста поля белый кречет, неси кречет вострый нож и востро копье, садись белый кречет рабу Божию (имя рек) на белы груду, на ретиво сердце. Режсь...*,

*вынимай из его ретива сердца ... тоску и кручину. Полети белый кре-
чет, ... донеси всю тоску и кручину ... до раба Бажия (имя рек), ...
клади в его белые груди, в ретиво сердце ... всю тоску кручину ...*

(Ефименко 1878. No. 17).

I beg from the pure meadowland four brothers – four birds with sharp
beaks and long beaks, ironclad beaks. Fly, white falcon, from the pure
meadowland, bring, falcon, a sharp knife and a sharp lance, alight, white
falcon, on the white breast of servant of God [name], on the eager heart,
Cut ... take from his eager heart ... grief and woe. Fly, white falcon, ...
take all the grief and woe ... to servant of God [name], place in his white
breast, in his eager heart, all the woe and grief ...

Cases when opposed personages perform diametrically opposed actions

The tsar-fire burns – the ice tsar freezes

*Батюшка ты, царь огонь ... как ты жгешь и палишь в чистом поле
травы и муравы, ... жги и спали с раба Божуя (имя рек) всяки скорби
и болезни ...*

(Майков 1869, No. 239).

Father, Tsar Fire ... just as you burn and bake the grasses and plants
in the clean field, burn and bake from servant of God [name] all griefs
and illnesses ...

*... Стоит в подсеверной стороне ледяной остров, на ледяном
острове ледяная камора ... и сам сидит царь ледяной. ... Ай же
ты царь ледяной, не студи не морозь ни рек, ну озер ... Застуди,
заморозь ретиво сердце у раба Божия (имя рек) ...*

(Виноградов 1908. No. 32).

There stands in the north an icy island, on the icy island is an icy
chamber ... and the icy tsar himself sits there. Oh you icy tsar, do not
ice, do not freeze either rivers or lakes... Freeze, ice the eager heart of
servant of God [name] ...

The diabolical force harms – the divine force helps

*... Сатана-батюшка, сослужи мне служду ... Освободи ты одного из
грешников, сними ты с него железные цепи, и свей из них железные
обручи и заставь ты моего злодея (такого-то) веки помучиться!
Надень ты ему одруч туда-то ... Отвечает на это покровитель.*

Твоя просьба исполнена ... На тебе ключ и замок, замкни у всех хомутов зубы и губы ...

(Логиновский 1903: 85. No. 1).

Father Satan, perform a service for me ... free one of the sinners, take from him the iron chains and bend them into iron hoops and make my enemy [name] suffer for ages. Place a hoop on him there on him ... The protector answers to this. Your request is granted. Here is a key and lock for you, lock up the teeth and lips of all the horse-collars ...

Ішоў Гасподзь Бог Сус Хрыстос з нябес, за ім Прачыстая матка ішла, у правой руцэ залатыя ключы нясла ... Куды ты, маць Прачыстая ідзешь? -- Іду я парадніцу адведаці і младзенца з жсываата выпускаці ...

(Романов 1891:57–8, No. 21).

Lord God Jesus Christ came down from heaven, behind him came the Most Pure mother, she held golden keys in her right hand ... – Where are you going Most Pure mother? – I am going to visit the woman in childbirth and let the child out of the belly...

In this system not every action has a clearly opposed counterpart, that is, the second half of the pair may be missing. It seems to us that this may be explained on the one hand by the complex functioning of charm poetry, and at the same time by the fact that we only have a limited quantity of texts at our disposal. The absence of certain actions as members of paired oppositions may also be explained by the fact that in folk magic (a category which encompasses charms) a primary role may be accorded to ritual action, and this may be accompanied by words, or sometimes have its own, separate, independent status. All the same, in magic rituals, word and action have equal rights and value, so that a search for the missing halves of opposed pairs not listed in charm plot guidebooks may meet with success, and their hypothetical existence should be taken into account in carrying out research on ritual actions.

One may go so far as to propose that if we had at our disposal the record of all charm texts that ever existed, then each charm plot (and consequently, each action by the personage) would correspond to another, opposing charm plot, with an opposite action. Support for this idea, and of the systematic bi-polar character of charm traditions, may be found in 'mirrored' pairs of texts – such as the following one – which correspond completely in structure and imagery, and differing only in their personages' opposite actions and functional purpose:

> a) *Как висит колокол, так виси у раба NN сором на рабу NN отныне до веку. Аминь, Как висим мохор, так виси у раба NN сором на рабу NN отныне до веку. Аминь*
>
> (Киреевский 1983. Т. 1, No. 215).

Just as the bell hangs, so may my penis hang over servant [female name] henceforth till eternity, Amen; just as the fringe hangs, so may my penis hang over servant [female name] henceforth till eternity, Amen.

> b) *Как стоим стержень, так стой у раба NN сором на рабу NN отныне до веку. Аминь*
>
> (Киреевский 1983. Т. 1, No. 215).

Just as the rod stands up, so may my penis stand up on servant [female name] henceforth till eternity, Amen.

A more extended example of this is provided by the charms collected during fieldwork by Moscow State University (МГУ 1960, ФЭ 03, 9777–9779 and МГУ 1960, ФЭ 03, 9779–9780). These two charms are virtually mirror-images of one another – the former has the charmer speaking of going to a white field, the latter of the charmer going to a black field, the former travelling on a wide white road, the latter travelling on a narrow black road, in the former meeting a young couple who love one another, in the latter meeting a couple who dislike one another. Further instances of 'mirrored' pairs have also been cited by scholars (см Афанасьев 1997: 545; Иванова 1994a. No. 489 633).

Each such mirrored pair apparently belonged to one performer (which is definitely the case for A. A. Ivanova's material). On the one hand, this doubling may be explained by the fact that each performer of charms has at his or her disposal a discrete selection of verbal formulas (Кляус, 1990). On the other hand, it has been observed in folk practice that a healer who knows a certain kind of text may also have mastered (or be said to have mastered) charms of a totally opposite type. While on an expedition in the Nerchinsk-Zavodskii Region of the Chita Oblast' in 1992, I managed to get a woman to agree to record charms against 'collar'. When I approached her house at the designated hour, I met a passing neighbour, who on the day before had recorded folk songs and tales. We began to talk, and in my naiveté I mentioned to her the goal of my outing. The middle-aged woman looked me over carefully, and said: 'Кто хомут снимает, тот его и надевает' (*The one who removes 'collar' is the one who brings it on.*). Moreover, in order to protect me, she pronounced in proverbial form one of those folk observations about the tradition of charms that suggested its systemic character.

More specific information about the systematizing of charm plots and plot situations, as well as further conclusions to which this leads, may be found in my monograph *Сюжетика заговорных текстов славян в сравнительном изучении. К постановке проблемы* ('Slavic Charm Plots in Comparative Perspective') (Кляус 2000).

The analysis of charm plots of the eastern and southern Slavs permits us to conclude that the basic plot elements of this genre are the personages' actions, the personages themselves, the place of action, artifacts and objects of the charm-world, and the constants and attributes of these characters and objects. Their correspondence and role in the plot are not uncomplicated. The basic, plot-forming, element, as in other genres of folklore, is the action. Next in significance are the personages taking part and the place of their habitation, and the world of everyday objects. Constants and attributes also play a definite role in the narrative system. This analysis, taking account of all of the narrative elements of charms, allows us to posit a generalized model for the world of the charm, one that surprisingly recalls that of the folk tale. This once again confirms that narrativity is a supremely important category for charm texts.

(Translation: Marcus Levitt)

Notes

1. This kind of narrative structure, although also conditioned by the ritual situation (and from the majority of descriptions of this kind of text it is clear that they were to be recited out loud while bringing the child to the chickens), does not depend on that situation, and is pronounced as an *independent, self-sufficient* speech act, so that while the chickens are addressed, it is not necessary to bring the child out to the chicken coop.
2. This phenomenon has been noted in reference to Slavic beliefs about snakes (Гура 1997: 290–1).

Bibliography

Адоньева, Овчинникова 1993. *Традиционная русская магия в записях конца XX века* (Сост. С.Б.Адоньева, О.А.Овчинникова). СПб., 1993.

Аникин, В.Н. 1996, *Теория Фольклора*. М., 1996.

Афанасьев 1997. *Народные русские сказки не для печати, заветные пословицы и поговорки, собранные и обработанные А.Н. АФанасьевым 1857–1862.* М., 1997.

Виноградов, Н.Н. 1907–09. 'Заговоры, обереги, спасительные молитвы и прочее', *Живая старина.* 1907. Вьш.1–4. 1908. Вьш.1–4. 1909. Вьш. 4. Отд. изд.: В 2 т. СПб., 1909.

Ефименко, П.С 1878. 'Материалы по этнографии русского населения Архангельской гуоернии', *Известия общества лобителей естествознания, антропологии и этнографии.* М., 1878. Т.5. Бьш. ½. С.139–222.

Зуева, Т.В. 1995. *Восточнославянская волшебная сказка в аспекте исторического развития.* Адд. М., 1995.

Гура, А.В. Символика животных в славянской народной традиции. М., Индрик, 1997.

Иванова, А.А. 1994. *Заговоры и заклинания Пинежья.* (Составитель А.А.Иванова). Карпогоры, 1994.

Иванова, А.А. 1994а. *Вятский Фольклор. Заговорное искусство* (Сост. А.А.Иванова). Котельнич, 1994.

Киреевский, В.Л. 1983. *Собрание народных песен П.В.Киреевского. Записи П.И.Якушкина: Памятники русского Фольклора. (Подготовка текстов, сост. и коммент. З.И.Власовой, А. Лобановой):* В2. т. Л., 1983–86. 2 т.

Кляус, В.Л. 1990. 'Повторяемость мотивов в заговорах', *Русский Фольклор Сибири. Элементы архитектоники.* Новосибирск, 1990, С. 105–12.

Кляус, В.Л. 1994. *Заговоры восточных и южных славян: Опыт систематизации повествовательных элементов.* Акд. М., 1994.

Кляус, В.Л. 1997. *Указатель сюжетов и сюжетных ситуаций заговорных текстов восточных и южных славян.* М., 1997. 464 с.

Кляус, В.Л 2002. *Сюжетика заговорных текстов славян в сравнительном изучении. Кпостановке проблемы.* М., 2000 191 с.

Кербелите, Б.П. 1991. *Историческое развитие структур и семантики сказок: на материале литовских волшебных сказок.* Вильнюс, 1991.

Логиновский, К. Д. 1903. 'Материалы к этнографии Забайкальских казаков', *Записки общества изучения Амурского края Владивостокского отделения Приамурского отдела РГО.* 1903. Т. 9. Вып. 1. С. 1–135.

МГУ – Фольклорный архив кафедры фольклора МГУ.

Майков, Л.Н.1869. 'Великорусские заклинания', *Записки РГО по отделению этнографии.* СПб, 1869. Т. 2. С. 419–580.

Маранда, П. 1985. Э.Кенгас-Маранда. 'Структурные модели в Фольклоре', *Зарубежные исследования по семиотике Фольклора.* М., 1985. С.194–260.

Путилов, Б.Н. 1988. *Героический эпос и действительность.* Л., 1988. 224 с.

Раденкович, Љ. 1982. *Народне басме и бајања.* Ниш-Приштина-Крагујевап, 1982.

Романов, Е.Р. 1891. *Белорусский сборник.* Киев, 1891. Вып. 5.

РЗЗ 1998 – *Русские заговоры и заклинания.* (Составители Т.Б.Дианова, Н.Ф.Злобина, А.А.Иванова, С.В.Алпатов, В.П.Аникин, А.В.Кулагина. Под ред. В.П.Аникина). М., 1988. 479 с.

Стойков, Д. 1890. 'От Софийско', *СбНУ.* 1890. Т.3. С.142–4.

Толмачев, П.М. 1911–12. 'Заговоры и поверья в Забайкалье', *Сибирский архив* 1911. No. 2 С. 63–75. 1912. No. 3. С. 136–52.

Толстая, С.М. 1999. 'Заговоры', *Славянские древности.* Т.2. М., 1999.

7
Conformity and Originality in Middle English Charms

T.M. Smallwood

When compared with the use of charms in various other cultures, charming in late medieval England might well seem to have offered little scope for originality. Whereas in some other European language-communities the expert 'charmer' has often been a person apart, perhaps somewhat shady, and his or her reciting of the verbal element of a charm has been an individual performance of a variable version of the inherited words and ideas, in late medieval Western Europe – north of the Alps and Pyrenees at least – the use of verbal charms was evidently quite different. In England in particular, in the fourteenth, fifteenth and early sixteenth centuries, charms were not the arcane material of personal performance, but rather something to be shared, often in writing. Within the literate stratum of the population written charms circulated in manuscripts that survive in their hundreds (the charms of course only one part of their content), with particular charms surviving in scores, sometimes many scores, of copies. Altogether, far from being the preserve of the 'cunning' man or woman, the white or off-white witch, late medieval healing and protective charms in England seem usually to have been openly disseminated and perfectly respectable – socially, medically and doctrinally.

As Lea Olsan has recently described, certain handbooks of practical medicine produced in England between the thirteenth and fifteenth centuries by 'four medical writers with academic credentials' include enough charms to show that these authorities could take them seriously, whether readily or as a last resort.[1] On a far larger scale, the innumerable collections of brief remedies produced in the same period in England show without any doubt that highly literate men (if they *were* all men) regarded charms as being, potentially, as useful as the physical or pseudo-pharmaceutical prescriptions and treatments among which they were collected. As a prime example, the manuscript from which two of the charms quoted below are taken, MS British Library Royal 12.G.iv, was owned and at least partly produced in the priory of St. Mary in Coventry, one of the richest and most important religious houses in the English Midlands.[2] Part of it, consisting of one or more collections of remedies, was written by a certain John of Greenborough, who says that he was *'infirmarius'* of the priory for over thirty years, and boasts of his expertise and wide medical learning; his compilation, like various others in the codex, contains charms.[3] Other codices containing collections of remedies are usually less handsome in form and less sophisticated in their overall content, but they, and the charms that most of them contain, still represent the professional or semi-professional knowledge of men who could usually move easily between English and Latin and, up to the early fifteenth century, Anglo-Norman French. Altogether, the late Middle Ages were, in Western Europe, the period when charming was the closest that it has ever been to mainstream medicine as practised by men trained, to some extent, in universities or other communities of the educated.

The respectability of these charms extended to their content. Late medieval charms in England were, as a rule, devoutly Christian. The typical healing charm consists of a brief sacred narrative (usually taken from the life of Christ, much less commonly from a saint's legend) or some statement of sacred truth, followed by words saying or implying 'as surely as this is true ...' or 'in the same way ...' and an appeal for help or cure. This makes them close to set prayers, which by long Christian tradition can also contain charm-like invocation of familiar sacred truth; indeed some charms are labelled in the surviving copies with the Middle English forms of the words 'prayer' or 'orison'. A few begin by directly addressing God; others, like example 7 below, end with fulsome supplication. Surviving pagan elements are slight compared with, for example, those in the best-known charms in Old English. What might once have been pagan has been Christianised or, in the case of obscure or meaningless verbal formulae, made as harmlessly inscrutable as the pious names or words with which they are mixed. Any copy of any charm in Middle English was very likely to end with 'Amen', accompanied by the instruction to say so many Pater Nosters and Aves and often a Creed.

Given, then, that late medieval charms in England were thoroughly Christian, were treated as intellectually and professionally respectable, and were freely shared in writing by the literate, they could hardly be expected to display the originality and boldness of imagination of charms that were personal and constantly re-invented. They represent charming that was respectful of precedent, done by the book. At the same time various factors in this late medieval period made it easy for charms, especially their verbal component, to be shared across language-frontiers,[4] reinforcing the impression that there was a canon of widely-accepted charm-motifs (or 'types' or formulae) dominating the whole practice of charming. Consequently the study of late medieval charms, whether within one language or across several, has tended to focus on what is shared or commonplace, on the recognition of similarity and continuity. And this approach has indeed been satisfying and valuable.[5]

However, even when dominated by convention and propriety, charms are an unregulated form of belief, and in so large a body of material as that of late medieval charms in England some originality or inventiveness is bound to appear. What follows tries to point out the forms of originality that this could take in Middle English. It will not include the narrative by-forms of a clear-cut motif (or 'type') when that motif remains the backbone of the charm, as for example in the distinct variant versions of the **Flum Jordan** blood-staunching charm;[6] nor the many examples of the combining of normally separate motifs in one charm. Both of these could indeed be considered forms of originality, but of a variety that is easily achieved and easily recognized. The intention is to sketch less predictable and less obvious examples of inventiveness which nevertheless are characteristic of a considerable part of the corpus of Middle English charms.

First, however, must come something exceptional. Probably the most exotic of surviving Middle English charms is one found in a composite codex, MS Cambridge University Library Kk.6.33, in a distinctly personal collection of receipts or remedies:[7]

1. A charm for brennyng and scaldyng. Aske leue at oure lady Seynt Marie and her swete sone, þat I mote hele N[omen] þat is forbrend and forscald.

> Þe fowle lay in þe leme,
> The flessh lay in the grounde.
> Holy Criste cam ageyn;
> With Cristendom he was befonge.
> 5   He helde up his holi honde;
> He blessed N[omen] þat is forbrend or forscalde,
> His body and his bone,
> Þat it ne frete, ne oute breke,
> Ne aboute go the hole place.
> 10   Þe Cristendome is hole;
> So be N[omen] þat is forbrend and scalde,

His body *and* his bone.
The heuen is playn, the myst is colde,
So be N[omen] þat is forbrend and forscalde,
15 His body and his bone.

As holy and also stedefast be þes wordes as is þe holy Pater
Noster Goddis, þat God hymselfe spak when he stye into
heuen. Amen.

(f. 4v)

Unusual for Middle English in its form, being apparently written in
unrhymed free verse, it is even stranger in its ideas. The word *leme* in the
first line probably means 'daylight', setting up an opposition of light and
dark, and perhaps suggesting one of hot and cold. Whereas line 4 might
initially seem inscrutable, when the idea of Christendom as a source of
well-being is taken up in line 10 it has a certain strange rationality. What
playn means in line 13 is a mystery, though the coldness of mist seems a
felicitous image to bring in. Despite the overall incoherence of the ideas
(which others may be able to explain better than I) the charm must stand
as a quite exceptional example of personal inventiveness.[8]

A different type of exercise of imagination is seen in the proem to a
veterinary charm for farcy, *'rankel'* and *'all wormes'* found in MS British
Library Sloane 962. It was first printed by Douglas Gray over thirty years
ago,[9] and runs:

2.   Michael, in þe Hel,
        Cam to his brother Raphael,
            the archangele, *and* seyde to hi*m*,
        'Raphael, wher astou ben
5   Þat I ne mith þe þis day sen?'
        'I haue ben in þe land of wormes.'
        'Turne ageyn, Raphael, and sle þe wormes ...'

(f. 135r)

This then becomes a conventional counting-up and counting-down
charm. Assuming that what is printed here as the third line is an inter-
polation, we have a neat enough little fragment of verse, evidently
meant to be an example of the 'Two Characters Meeting' broad type
of historiola (or *Begegnungstyp*) particularly associated with the French
charm-tradition.[10] Aiming to be naturalistic, it succeeds merely in being
ludicrous. Not surprisingly, it does not seem to be found elsewhere in
surviving Middle English.

Almost no other evidence of originality in Middle English charms can be said to spring from uninhibited or frivolous imagination.[11] Inventiveness normally falls within the bounds of conventional Christian doctrine – in fact it is in a way made easier by shared belief. Since the narrative element of a charm normally consisted of a familiar fact about the life of Christ, another such fact could easily be used. For example, in an intelligently composed and presented collection of remedies in MS Bodleian Library Laud Misc. 553 there appears:

3. Forto take an adder oþ*er* a snake in þyn hond and do þe non harme ...

    Ich coniure þe, adder, þ*at* þu be unmevable as was Iudas þ*at* bytrayed God, and aft*er*ward anheng hym ...

    (f. 54v)

Judas is presumably chosen as an archetype of slipperiness and venom, his death being the conquest of these. Anyone could have used the familiar Christian truths in the same way, but apparently no-one else did.[12] (Incidentally, it is to be hoped that no-one tried to use this charm.)

Incorporating fragments of narrative into a conjuration or adjuration in this way was a fertile means of multiplying sacred references in a charm. In one of the sequences of remedies in the codex from St. Mary's Priory in Coventry already referred to, MS British Library Royal 12.g.iv, a charm against bleeding runs:

4.   In þe nome of I*esu* þat suffred wou*n*des on þe mou*n*te of Calu*er*ie for me *and* not for hym, ȝif me, mon, myght *and* grace þat I stau*n*che þy[s] wound; in þat nome þat he kept his blod from þe erthe til þe aungeles kepten hit; in þat
5   worship of þat self wou*n*des *and* of þe self blod *and* of þe self nome, stanche þis blod in N[omen].

    (f.197r)

Line 3, MS *þy*.

Two separate ideas that are unusual in charms, one doctrinal (that Christ's suffering was for 'my' sins and not for His) and one narrative, (that the angels caught and preserved the blood) are thus incorporated into more familiar ones, the whole being almost certainly distinct from any other known charm.

On a less sophisticated level, charms could display originality simply in the wealth of invocations that they used, without any real narrative. For example, the well-known toothache charm in the Thornton Manuscript, *'I conjoure the, laythely beste ...'*,[13] conjures away the *'wikkyde worme'* by invoking Longinus' spear, Christ's *'hatte of thorne'*, *'alle þe wordis mare & lesse'*, the Mass, Christ and his twelve apostles, Our Lady and her ten maidens, Saint Margaret and Saint Katherine. In MS Sloane 962, in the sequence of remedies for horses already quoted, *'A charme for þe Feloun'* invokes even more:

> 5.   I coniure þe, wikked feloun, in þe name of God alweldyng
>   of heuen, erthe *and* Hell, and of þo sonne *and* of þo mone
>   *and* of þo vii steres *and* of all creatures *and* of all aungeles and
>   of all þo confessoures, bisschopes *and* of all hundred abbotes
> 5   redy to syng on mydwyntur nyght, þat þu ne entre ne no
>   lenger dwell; in þo name of þo Fader *and* of þe Sonne *and* of
>   þe Holy Gost.
>
>   (f.137v)

This is in fact a fairly close translation of a charm *'Pur tuz felunz tuer'* in Anglo-Norman French recorded about sixty years earlier in a notable manuscript from the Ludlow area, MS British Library Harley 273.[14] This earlier version was slightly fuller, invoking not just singing abbots but a hundred singing bishops too, and the straw in which the Christ-child was wrapped; and it is likely that this is the form in which the charm was originally composed. The translation into English would, for a literate charm-user or remedy-book compiler of the late fourteenth or early fifteenth century, have been done with scarcely a thought. Apparent originality in Middle English, therefore, is better seen as a reflection of Anglo-Norman originality in charm-composition a little earlier.

The relevance of this becomes clearer in the case of a very widely copied charm which invokes sacred truths on a far larger scale, that supposedly brought by the angel Gabriel to either Saint Susannah or Saint William, according to copy or to language.[15] Directed against various forms of *'goute'* and other indeterminate forms of festering and suppuration, in its fullest version it asks that 'as truly as God is, and was, and shall be, and as truly as what he said he said truly, and as truly as what he did he did well ...' and so forth with fully sixteen further truths about the life, death and resurrection of Christ, up to the Last Judgement, so, 'as verily as all that is true', may this man be cured. This is charm-building

on a monumental scale, and while that in itself does not constitute originality in Middle English, the history of the charm, progressing through
two languages and over more than a century, does happen to illustrate
how it came about that by the early fifteenth century certain Middle
English charms had come into use which were distinctively or uniquely
English.

The earliest three copies of the charm known to me, earliest in fact by
a considerable margin, are all in Anglo-Norman French.[16] In the absence
of clear evidence from before the early fourteenth century of the same
charm in continental French or other languages it is fair to assume that
it was composed in England, or only flourished here at so early a date.
However, it only appears in copies in the English language from about
the end of the fourteenth century; when it does so appear copies soon
multiply.[17] At the same time another similar charm directed against the
festering of wounds, this time attributed exclusively to Saint Susannah
and found only in Middle English, which is even more massive and
laborious in its invocation of familiar events or truths ('as truly as the
Jews took a crown of thorns . . .', etcetera, running to over eight hundred
words) appears in an almost equally large number of copies.[18] This can
indeed be considered original, known apparently in no other language;
but it is surely reasonable to think that the earlier Susannah charm, once
Englished, suggested and prepared the way for the later.

This is representative of the record of Middle English charms at large.
Very few copies of charms in Middle English survive from before the last
third of the fourteenth century,[19] and this is not likely to be simply a
matter of chance. Of course various charms in Middle English must have
been in oral circulation far earlier among exclusively English-speaking
people, though we cannot know which they were (beyond a handful),
nor when they first appeared. What we do know is that, despite the fact
that by the 1360s a great deal of Middle English literature in various
genres had been written down, those who could accept their charms,
together with most of their medical lore, in Latin and French preferred
to do so.[20] It was only with the advent of English as the first language
of the literate and socially privileged that the written record of Middle
English charms rapidly expands. It is hard not to suspect that it was also
only when compendia of practical medicine were at last written chiefly
in English that much of the translation and re-working of established
charm-formulae took place. The same people, that is, who compiled the
remedy-books from the late fourteenth century onwards, and the literate
people around them, could well have shaped, and in some cases virtually
invented, the charms in Middle English that the books contain.

This would account for the obvious 'literary' nature of many of these Middle English charms. Whether longwindedly rhetorical, like the Saint Susannah charms or others with manifold invocations, or simply put into a careful verse form, they often seem to be crafted with as much interest in eloquence as content. This 'literariness' can itself be tantamount to originality: when an inherited motif or 'type' was given a distinctive verse-form, besides perhaps some incidental elaboration of ideas, the resultant charm could have a fresh identity of its own. For example, the already long-established and widely distributed theme of The Uncorrupted Wounds of Christ[21] was given a particular form in six couplets (with a brief prose interruption) which obviously stood apart. To quote from a copy in British Library MS Additional 33996:[22]

6.   I coniure þe, wounde, blyue,
          By þe vertu of þe woundes fyue
          Of Iesu Cryst boþe God *and* man –
          Wyþ ryȝt he vs from Helle w[a]nne –
5   And by þe pappes of Seynt Marye,
          Clene mayde wyþoute folye,
þat þe wounde ne ake ne swelle, ne rancle, ne festre, ne blede
          No more ne dede þe woundes gode
          Of Iesu when he heng on þe Rode;
10   But fro þe grounde upward be as hole
          As weren Iesu woundes euery dol.
          In þe name of þe Fader of myȝtes most,
          Of þe Sone *and* of þe Holy Gost.

(f. 109v)

Line 4, MS *wonne*; 6, MS *mayde* written twice.

The addition of supporting ideas to the essential Wounds-Healing motif (the reference to *five* wounds and a substantial invocation of the Virgin Mary being just what one might expect in late medieval England), together with the efficiency of the versification, evidently made this appealing and convincing as a charm with its own identity: at least twenty-four copies survive in diverse contexts,[23] not quite uniform word-for-word, but recognizably the same composition.

A charm 'invented' in this way could have actual literary merit, coming close to the sort of Middle English devotional lyric verse which was produced, and survives, in considerable quantity. This is perhaps true of a charm in the compendium from St. Mary's Priory in Coventry already quoted, in a collection of remedies added probably soon after 1400.[24] Directed against *'Hache and swellyng'*, it reads:

7.   God hat lant to prest[es] pouwer god
                In bred to maken flesh and blode;
                And hys pouwer euer y[s] on
                In word *and* gras and in ston.
   5   Vpon þe Gode Fryday at none
                God w[as] on þe Rode done.
                On þe Rode he was lent;
                Þe brey[þ] out of hys body we[n]t.
                Long*ius* to þe hert him stong;
  10   Hour leuedy her greuet [þeramong?].
                Þe same wond hyt neu*er* hachet ne swall,
                No [þ]ys neu*er* more schal.
                God þ*at* sit in Trinite,
                Wy[þ] holy *pater* [?] *noster* [?] I pray to þe,
  15   As þu art sauiour of alle sores,
                Þat [þ]ys ake no swel no more.

                                        (f.216v)

Line 1, MS *prest*[-], rest obscured; 3, y[s] on, MS (apparently) *ycono*; 6, MS *w*[-]; 8, MS *brey*[-]; MS, *wet*; 10, [þeramong?], conjectured, no gap in MS; 12, MS *ȝys*; 14, MS *wyl*; *pater* [?] *noster* [?], MS unclear and obscured; 16, MS *ȝys*.

This is obviously a very imperfect copy, even omitting a rhyme-word and fumbling another, while a few letters are lost in the binding. Nevertheless, we can still glimpse what must have been competent versification, and can see the author's relish for ideas, even if rather rambling ones. The theme of The Uncorrupted Wounds has been subordinated to a wish to describe the Crucifixion, to bring in at least two further points of belief,[25] and to address God directly. It seems confident, fresh composition. No doubt caviar to the general, it does not seem to survive anywhere else.

Also apparently surviving in only one imperfect copy is a charm found in the collection of remedies in MS Laud Misc. 553 already quoted which seems essentially literary or rhetorical, based on no recognized motif or 'type' other than an awareness of the threefold nature of the Trinity. It is labelled *'A charme to do away a felon'* (here meaning a boil, swelling or scab in humans):

8.   In no*mine* pa*t*ris yc haue ysou3t þe;
            In no*mine* filii yc haue yfounde þe;
            In no*mine* sp*iritus* sa*n*cti yc schal do awey þe.
            God Fader [go] aboute þe;
5   Sone God [go] aboute þe;
            Holy Gost go aboute [þe].
            God Fader do þe away;
            God Sone do þe away;
            Þorw ve*r*tu of þe Holy Gost. Amen.

Lines 4, 5 and 6: missing words supplied, no gaps in MS.

Really this is simply an imprecation against the disease, with incantatory repetition in figures of three of the obvious ideas of seeking, finding (or circling) and destroying the *felon*; but it is neatly composed and easily recited. Whether or not it was ever freely circulated and used, it constitutes a good example of the willingness of certain educated Englishmen of this period to devise well-turned charms out of familiar doctrine.

Notes

1. Lea T. Olsan, 'Charms and Prayers in Medieval Medical Theory and Practice', *Social History of Medicine*, 16:3 (2003), 343–66. To the four authors chiefly covered (Gilbertus Anglicus, John Gaddesden, John Arderne and Thomas Fayreford) could perhaps be added John of Mirfield, comparable in many respects, including the acceptance of charms.
2. See George F. Warner and Julius P. Gilson, *Catalogue of Western Manuscripts in the Old Royal and King's Collections in the British Museum* (London: 1921), II. 69–71, particularly p. 71, col. 1.
3. For a valuable discussion of Greenborough see Tony Hunt, *Popular Medicine in Thirteenth-Century England* (Cambridge: D.S. Brewer, 1990), pp. 33–5.
4. For some suggestions as to how the ideas used in late medieval charms spread throughout western Christendom, see T. M. Smallwood, 'The Transmission of Charms in English, Medieval and Modern', in Jonathan Roper, ed., *Charms and Charming in Europe* (Basingstoke: Palgrave Macmillan, 2004), pp. 16–17.
5. The most thorough description and analysis of 'universal' or pervasive ideas and motifs in charms (including medieval ones) is found in Hanns Bächtold-Stäubli, *Handwörterbuch des Deutschen Aberglaubens* (Berlin and Leipzig: de Gruyter, 1927–42), which throughout ten large volumes traces particular themes or formulae across language-frontiers and through many centuries.

A recent proposal for a comprehensive 'typology' of charms in England, or in all European languages (using the term 'type' in a sense close to German folklorist *Typ*) is found in Jonathan Roper, 'Typologising English Charms', in Roper, ed., *Charms and Charming*, pp. 128–44; this cites various earlier surveys or collections of charms made according to *Typ* or *Motiv*.

6. In this case, and others, the variations can be simply the result of a quest for new rhymes. See Smallwood, 'Transmission of Charms', in Roper, ed., *Charms and Charming*, pp. 18–19.

7. This collection is foliated 1–113 in the third sequence in the codex. The hand of this section is probably datable close to the middle of the 15th century. The text given here, like all those which follow, preserves the original spelling but adds editorial punctuation, capitalisation and lay-out, with slight modernisation of word-division.

8. On the same page as this charm in MS Kk.6.33 is *A charme for a breste* in about fifty words which, though mostly using conventional charm-material, seems at two points to become simply nonsensical, without necessarily being corrupt. One has to trust that some features of the charm just quoted cannot be similarly dismissed as mere nonsense.

9. Douglas Gray, 'Notes on Some Middle English Charms', in Beryl Rowland, ed., *Chaucer and Middle English Studies in Honour of Rossell Hope Robbins* (London: Allen and Unwin, 1974), pp. 56–71; see p. 64.

10. Examples of charms of this form or genre in French, from the sixteenth century (if not earlier) onward, are so numerous that it would be pointless to cite examples. In late medieval England they are almost confined to copies of the **Tres Boni Fratres** or Three Good Brothers charm for wounds, quite common in Latin and Middle English. Beyond that, the only clear example in Middle English is probably a charm against farcy in horses in MS Cambridge University Library Dd.4.44, at f. 19r (apparently a sole copy), in which St. Firmin meets Sts Peter and Martin, who instruct him how to perform a cure. It is in fact tempting to count this as an example of original composition in English, but the use of a northern French saint, besides St. Martin, does suggest the possibility that it is a translation from a lost charm in continental French.

11. This is not to deny that a few unique Middle English charms survive which are, in part at least, so obscure and surprising that it is hard to separate imagination from nonsense. An example is the charm *'To binde a house agynste theffes'* in MS Bodleian Ashmole 1378, p. 73, published (rather inaccurately) in J. M. McBryde, 'Charms for Thieves', *Modern Language Notes* 22 (1907): 170. See also note 8 above.

12. Bächtold-Stäubli, *Handwörterbuch*, refers to no such association under *Judas Ischariot in den Segen* or *Schlangen-Segen*.

13. *Religious Pieces in Prose and Verse*, ed. George G. Perry, *Early English Text Society Original Series* 26 (London, edn of 1914 only), p. 119.

14. At f.213r. A slightly normalised printing of this piece is given in Hunt, *Popular Medicine*, p. 89, among various quotations from MS Harley 273. I respectfully disagree with Dr Hunt's implied opinion about the handwriting of certain parts of the manuscript, notably that including f.112v, in so far as it affects the point made in note 20 below.

15. Copies in Middle English normally have the attribution to St. William, presumably of York. One such copy is given in Gray, 'Notes on ME Charms' in Rowland, *Chaucer and ME Studies*, p. 68; another in F. Holthausen, 'Rezepte, Segen und Zaubersprüche ...', *Anglia* 19 (1897): 82.

16. In apparent chronological order, all gauged chiefly by handwriting, they are found in MSS Trinity College, Cambridge, B.15.36, f.41r (early 13th c.?); British Library Sloane 146, ff.67r–68r (very early 14th c.?); and Trinity College, Cambridge, 0.7.37, f.145v (early 14th c.?).

17. See George R. Keiser, *Works of Science and Information* (Vol. 10 of *A Manual of the Writings in Middle English 1050–1500*, ed. Albert E. Hartung, New Haven, 1998), p. 3872, where the charm (item 345) is headed 'Charm of St. William (Eustace) ...'. In fact the attribution to Eustace is a relatively rare and probably late variation. To the seven manuscript copies that Keiser lists can be added those in MSS British Library Harley 3383, f.20r; Sloane 2187, f.51r; Cambridge University Library Dd.5.76, f.68v; St. John's College, Cambridge, B.15, f.23r; Durham University Library Cosin V.3.11, f.95r; and Glasgow University Library Hunterian 117, f.28r. None of these thirteen copies can be dated earlier than the last quarter of the fourteenth century.

18. See Keiser, *Works of Science*, p.3872, item 344, 'Charm of St. Susan'. To the ten manuscript copies listed by Keiser one can add that in MS Cambridge University Library Addit. 9308, ff.62v–65v.

19. None can be confidently dated before c1300 (the well-known *Wen Charm*, known from a copy of c1150, being unquestionably an Old English charm in its ideas, its verse-form and most features of its language). The few from before c1360 known to me are printed in T.M. Smallwood, ' "God Was Born in Bethlehem ...": the Tradition of a Middle English Charm', *Medium Ævum* 58 (1989): 206–7; and Smallwood, 'Transmission of Charms', in Roper, ed., *Charms and Charming*, pp. 23–4. To these could be added the fragment of a **Longinus** charm in MS Harley 273 described in the following note, very probably set down close to 1340–5.

20. This is perhaps nicely illustrated by a sequence of charms found in a manuscript already cited, MS Harley 273 (note 14, etc.), at f.112v. The compiler quotes six lines of an acephalous and perhaps incomplete *Longinus* blood-staunching charm in English, then runs straight on into the first of three charms in Anglo-Norman French and one in Latin (see Hunt, *Popular Medicine*, pp. 88–9), offering no charms in English at any other point. Yet this is very probably in the hand of the scribe, also widely assumed to be the compiler, of the celebrated collection of Middle English lyrics in MS British Library Harley 2253, that is, someone obviously appreciative of the merits of verse in Middle English.

21. This has also been called *Schwellen und Schwären, zwellen en zweren, Sie quellen nicht* and **Neque doluit neque tumuit**. Its essential *historiola* is simply that when Christ was wounded with spear and nails on the Cross, his wounds did not fester. It happens that it is not fully described in Bächtold-Stäubli, *Handwörterbuch*.

22. Though not a holograph, this is probably the closest of surviving copies to the charm as originally written in this Middle English version. In line 1 the word *'blyue'* (*blive*) means 'promptly', 'at once' or conceivably 'heartily'. As

regards line 10, I confess to not understanding what is implied by *'fro þe grounde upward'*.

23. Keiser, *Works of Science*, p. 3871, section 342, 'Five Wounds of Christ Charm', lists nineteen copies (two under no. 13), to which can be added copies in MSS British Library Sloane 433, f.31r; Sloane 2135, f.74r; Cambridge University Library Addit. 9308, f.62r; Bodleian Addit.A.106 (also at) f.240r; and Longleat House 332, f.21v (second sequence).

24. MS British Library Royal 12.G.iv, ff.212r–216v, but conceivably continuous from f.203r.

25. The allusion in lines 3 and 4 to a mysterious power found in 'word', 'grass' and 'stone' (elsewhere usually accompanied by 'tree') is quite common in Middle English charms. See, e.g. the charm beginning (in various Middle English forms) 'Lord God in Trinity' quoted in Curt F. Bühler, 'Middle English Verses Against Thieves', *Speculum* 33 (1958): 372, and J. Daniel Vann, 'Middle English Verses Against Thieves: A Postscript', *Speculum* 34 (1959): 637, in lines 14 and 16 respectively.

8
The Nightmare Charm in *King Lear*

Jacqueline Simpson

In Act II scene iv of Shakespeare's *King Lear* (1605) there occurs a jingle which can be recognised as a version of a charm against the nightmare current in late medieval and Tudor times. Before discussing it in detail, it is as well to explain its context within the play, which is rather complex. In *Lear* there are two tightly interwoven plots, one concerning the king and his daughters, and the other dealing with the Duke of Gloucester and his two sons, the virtuous Edgar and the villainous Edmund. By a series of vicious lies, Edmund causes such mistrust between his father and Edgar that the latter flees from home, convinced that his beloved father wants to have him murdered. He then disguises himself as a mad half-naked beggar, Poor Tom, and hides in a hovel on the heath, where Lear and his Fool accidentally find him. They do not recognise him, and indeed the transformation in his appearance and mode of speech is so complete that, from the point of view of a theatre audience, the identity of Edgar is rapidly obliterated by the powerful persona of the sinister madman Tom. The shock of the encounter terrifies the Fool, and tips Lear himself, whose mind is already cracking, into complete madness.

The chief subject in Tom's ravings is the foul fiend that torments and tempts him. He cries out that it leads him through fire and flame, through whirlpools and bogs, tempting him to suicide, and filling him with sinful thoughts. While Tom is ranting, the Duke of Gloucester arrives at the hovel, seeking Lear, but never guesses that this madman is really his own son. Nor does Shakespeare at this point give 'Tom' any lines which would reveal the true feelings of 'Edgar' at this appalling situation. Instead, on catching sight of Gloucester, Tom immediately reacts by a further outburst of craziness, denouncing him as yet another demon and then bursting into verse:

> This is the foul Flibbertigibbet; he begins at curfew, and walks till the
> first cock; he gives the web and the pin, squinnies the eye, and makes

the hare-lip; mildews the white wheat, and hurts the poor creature of earth.

> Swithold footed thrice the old;
> He met the night-mare, and her nine-fold;
> Bid her alight,
> And her troth plight,
> And aroint thee, witch, aroint thee![1]

Throughout the eighteenth and nineteenth centuries, editors made no comment on these lines, apparently accepting them as simply one among many examples of 'nonsense' talk which Shakespeare gives to mad characters and professional fools. The first scholar to identify them as a charm was the American G. L. Kittredge in 1929 in his *Witchcraft in Old and New England*;[2] he repeated the identification in 1946 in his *Sixteen Plays of Shakespeare*. It is now accepted in standard editions of the *Lear*.

Kittredge based his interpretation on the similarity between Shakespeare's lines and a small group of late medieval and Tudor charms against the nightmare, citing first one which is found in Thomas Blundevill's *Fower Chiefyst Offices of Horsemanshippe* (1566). In a section on 'Horse Diseases', Blundevill describes how the nightmare oppresses either men or beasts at night, so that they cannot breathe, and is called Incubus in Latin. He goes on to say that 'an old English writer' recommends 'a fonde foolishe charme' to cure it in horses. Speaking from a Protestant point of view, he says he only included it 'bicause it may perhappes make you gentle reader to laugh, as well it did me'; he claims that it was invented by 'the false Fryers in times past' to get money from the gullible. He then quotes the charm as follows:

> Take a Flynt Stone that hath a hole of hys owne kynde [a natural hole] and hang it ouer hym [the horse] and wryte in a bille: *In nomine patris* &c
>> Saint George our Ladyes Knight,
>> He walked day so did he night,
>> Untill he hir found,
>> He hir beate and he hir bounde
>> Till truly hir trouth she him plyght
>> That she woulde not come within the night
>> There as Saint George our Ladyes Knight
>> Named was three tymes. Saint George.
> And hang this Scripture ouer him, and let him alone.[3]

The text in Blundevill's unnamed 'old English writer' must have been very similar to that in a manuscript dating from about 1425 to 1450 which is now in the Bodleian Library, which contains the following recipe for use with a horse:

> Ffor the nygthe-mare. Take a flynt stone that hath an hole thorow of hys owne growing, & hange ouer the stabill dore, or ell ouer horse, and ell writhe this charme: Seynt Iorge, our lady knygth, he walked day, he walked nygth, till þat he fownde þat fowle wygth; and whan þat he here fownde, he here bete & he here bownde, till trewly þer here trowthe sche plygth þat sche sholde not come be nygthe, With-Inne vij rode of londe space þer as Seynt Ieorge i-namyd was. St. Ieorge. St. Ieorge. St. [Ieorge.] In nomine patris &c. & wryte this in a bille and hange it in the hors' mane.[4]

A third pre-Shakesperean example is to be found in Reginald Scot's *The Discoverie of Witchcraft* (1584). Interestingly, Scot is not concerned with horses but with human beings; he gives a vivid and accurate account of the phenomenon now called 'sleep-paralysis', describing the 'nightmare or Incubus' as 'a bodilie disease . . . although it extend unto the trouble of the mind: which of some is called the Mare, oppressing manie in their sleepe so sore, as they are not able to call for helpe, or stir themselves under the burthen of that heavie humour.' There are, Scot continues, various magical cures, one of which is the verse:

> S. George, S. George, our ladies knight,
> He walkt by daie, so did he by night:
> Untill such time as he hir found,
> He hir beat and he hir bound,
> Untill hir troth she to him plight,
> She would not come to hir that night
> Whereas S. George our ladies knight was named three times. *S. George.*[5]

Scot does not say that the words should be written down or hung up over the sufferer's bed, so it would seem that he knew the charm purely as a verbal one.

Kittredge notes that 'the same charm' occurs in a Jacobean play by John Fletcher, *Monsieur Thomas* (1639), Act IV scene vi. Here, however, the purpose seems to be mockery, since the final line is given a twist which turns it into a sexual joke:

St George, St. George, Our Ladies Knight,
He walks by day, so does he by night,
And when he had her found,
He her beat and he her bound,
Until to him her troth she plight
She would not stir from him that night.[6]

There are variants from Shetland in which St. George does not appear –
possibly he had been discarded as too English and too Catholic (especially when called 'Our Lady's knight'). In one he has been replaced by
an anonymous 'man of might'. It was published in the late nineteenth
century by Mrs J. M. E. Saxby, who recalled it from her childhood and
gave an interesting indication of the accompanying ritual gestures used
by her nurse as she charmed away a nightmare:

Pulling from my head the longest hair it possessed, and then going
through the pantomime of binding a refractory animal, she slowly
chanted this spell:
De man o' meicht
He rode a' neicht,
We nedder swird
Nor faerd ne leicht.
He socht da mare,
He fand da Mare,
He band da Mare
Wi' his ain hair,
An' made her swear
By midder's meicht
Dat shö wad never bide a neicht
Whar he had rod, dat man o' meicht.
. . . There are different versions of this incantation, and I forget which
it was that the old nurse used on the occasion mentioned. Therefore
I have given the one most familiar to me.[7]

One of these other versions is given (alongside Mrs Saxby's) in
G. F. Black's *County Folklore: Orkney and Shetland Islands* (1903), being
taken from a paper by Karl Blind (1879), and here the hero is Arthur:

Arthur Knight
He rade a' night

Wi' open swird
An' candle light.
He sought da mare;
He fan' da mare;
He bund da mare
Wi' her ain hair.
And made da mare
Ta swear:
'At she should never
Bide a' night
Whar ever she heard
O' Arthur Knight.[8]

Other such texts may also have been recorded in this area.[9] The 'Arthur' version must be as old as the English St. George charm, since its opening lines occur (in isolation) in an anonymous political pamphlet, *The Compleynt of Scotland* (c.1550). This lists a considerable number of medieval romances, ballads, songs, and folktales supposedly performed by shepherds as entertainment, among which is one simply identified by the couplet: 'Arthour knycht he raid on nycht vith gyltin spur and candil lycht'.[10]

In the Shetlands, as in Shakespeare, the nightmare is identified as the target in the actual words of the charm, whereas in the English medieval manuscript, in Blundevill, and in Reginald Scot, it is only named in the accompanying instructions, while the verse itself talks more vaguely of 'she' and 'her' or of a 'foul wight'. A vivid detail not found elsewhere in this British series, is that the Nightmare is bound with hair, and that in one instance this action was mimicked by the charmer while reciting the charm. In Mrs Saxby's nurse's version the hero-figure uses his own hair, but in Karl Blind's the Mare is bound with her own hair.

Underlying all versions of the charm is an international pattern, the 'Encounter with Evil', common in ancient Mediterranean and Near Eastern cultures, and in the folk religion of Eastern Europe.[11] In this, the historiola tells how an angel, prophet, saint, or other holy figure on his or her travels meets a female demon personifying a disease or the evil eye, and either banishes it or makes it swear to do no harm. Repetition or display of the charm is a defence against the particular evil mentioned in it, and the name either of the holy figure or of the demon is often the focus of this apotropaic power. For example, in eighteenth- and nineteenth-century Jewish communities protective amulets displayed in the room of a woman in childbirth commonly included the story of how the prophet

Elijah once met the she-demon Lilith on her way to the house of a woman in labour, 'to give her the sleep of death, to take her son and suck the marrow of his bones'. Elijah excommunicated Lilith and/or bound her in chains, whereupon she promised never to harm women in childbirth in any place where she saw or heard her own name.[12]

In his study of Russian magic, Professor Will Ryan cites several instances of the same pattern in prayer-spells:

St Moses meets twelve maidens who are naked, barefoot, with wild loose hair, who are travelling the world spreading misery. They beg St. Moses not to beat them, and promise not to afflict those who repeat the prayer. A (?Siberian) spell invokes St. Simon who meets twelve misshapen women who say they are going to Holy Russia to drink the blood of the people. Another has St. Nicholas meeting Herod's three sisters who are going into the world to break bones and suck out the marrow. The idea of the meeting of the deity/angel/saint with the evil force causing illness or unhappiness and vanquishing or banishing it is a commonplace of spells and amulet inscriptions both Christian and pagan.[13]

In Hungary, the encounter may be between the Virgin Mary and multiple demons personifying the Evil Eye:

The Blessed Virgin Mary set off
With her blessed holy Son.
She met seventy-seven kinds of Evil Eyes...

Or, in another charm:

... she met the Evil Eye
With its seventy-seven sons and daughters...[14]

Returning to Shakespeare, we can see how this pattern serves to clarify the puzzling words 'and her nine-fold' in Poor Tom's verse. Some editors emend this to 'and her nine foals', explaining it as 'her nine offspring' or 'her nine imps or familiars', and presumably thinking that 'foals' became 'fold' to fit the rhyme. However, it is also possible that the nightmare herself is to be understood as multiplied nine times. Either way, the multiplicity of hostile figures is comparable to the twelve misshapen women and the three sisters of Herod in the Russian spells, and to the seventy-seven sons and daughters of the Evil Eye in the Hungarian ones. In Shakespeare's verse the beating and binding is lacking, but when Swithold 'Bid her alight/ And her troth plight...' he is extorting a pledge of future good conduct, as the other holy figures do.

More problematic is the conclusion of Tom's verse. The St George charm and its analogues normally end with an assurance that the demon is defeated, and all future users of the charm will be protected. This is absent in Shakespeare, where Tom appears to break off abruptly:

> Bid her alight,
> And her troth plight,
> And aroint thee, witch, aroint thee!

Is this final cry ('Begone, witch!') part of the charm, or an interruption? Is it to be understood as a formula of exorcism, or a shriek of panic?

There remains one more question: who is 'Swithold'? All editors agree that this word should be divided in two, as 'St Withold', but dictionaries of saints do not include any such person, even though Sir Walter Scott stole the name for use in his novel *Ivanhoe*. Thomas Tyrwhitt, an eighteenth-century editor of *Lear*, suggested that Withold is a corruption of the name of St Vitalis, an Italian martyr of the third century, and patron saint of Ravenna;[15] but there is no reason to think that an Elizabethan audience would have recognised that name, nor why he should have replaced the familiar English St. George – one of the very few non-Biblical saints whose popularity was allowed to survive the Reformation.

My own speculation is that Shakespeare is making a harsh and bawdy joke, intercutting horror with humour in a way quite typical of his technique. Poor Tom is supposedly a madman, Lear is on the verge of madness, and there is also present Lear's court Fool, whose profession involves the pretence of madness. Can it be a coincidence that 'Withold' sounds almost exactly like 'wittold', and that 'wittold' in Elizabethan English means both 'half-wit' and 'complaisant cuckold'? At that period, madness could be a subject for laughter, and on stage the nonsense speech of mad characters and fools was full of bawdy double meanings, while cuckolds were a perennial target for humour.

King Lear is a play full of cruelty and nightmarish evil, and it is set in a world where Christian saints have no place. So when Poor Tom attempts a protective spell, the distorted version that emerges does not invoke the gallant St. George, but the ludicrous 'St Wittold' – 'St cuckolded half-wit'. There was, I think, a brief but loud guffaw from the groundlings.

Notes

1. William Shakespeare, *King Lear*, ed. Kenneth Muir (The Arden Shakespeare, London: Methuen & Co., 1952), pp. 123–4.

2. G. L. Kittredge, *Witchcraft in Old and New England* (Harvard: Harvard University Press, 1929; facsimile paperback reprint, New York: Athenaeum Publishers, 1972), pp. 219–20.

3. Thomas Blundevill, *Fower Chiefyst Offices of Horsemanshippe* (1566), p.17; cited in Iona Opie and Moira Tatem, *A Dictionary of Superstitions* (Oxford: Oxford University Press, 1989), p. 378.

4. MS Bodleian Rawlinson C 506 f. 297, cited in Opie and Tatem, *A Dictionary of Superstitions*, p. 378.

5. Reginald Scot, *The Discoverie of Witchcraft* (1584), ed. Montague Summers. (London, 1930), p. 49.

6. Cited by Jennifer Chandler, 'St George and Horses', *FLS News* 35 (November 2001), p. 17

7. B. Edmondston and J. M. E. Saxby, *The Home of a Naturalist* (2nd edn, 1889), pp. 186–7; cited in G. F. Black, *County Folk-Lore Printed Extracts III: Orkney and Shetland Islands* (London: David Nutt for the Folk-Lore Society, 1903), p. 145.

8. Karl Blind, 'Discovery of Odinic Songs in Shetland', *Nineteenth Century* (1879), p.1106; cited in Black, *County Folk-Lore III: Orkney and Shetland Islands*, p.145.

9. Robert Graves, in *The White Goddess* (2nd edn, paperback, London: Faber, 1961), p.26, gives what he calls 'the North Country charm against the Night Mare':

> Tha mon o' micht, he rade o' nicht
> Wi' neider swerd ne ferd ne licht.
> He socht tha Mare, he fond tha Mare,
> He bond tha Mare wi' her ain hair,
> Ond gared her swar by midder-micht
> She wolde nae mair rid o' nicht
> Whar aince he rade, that mon o' micht.

As he does not name his source, it is unclear whether he is conflating the two versions given by Black, or whether he had seen some third Shetland text.

10. A. M. Stewart (ed.), *The Compleynt of Scotland* (Edinburgh: Scottish Texts Society, 1979), p. 50.

11. See, among others, Moses Gaster, 'Two Thousand Years of a Charm against the Child-Stealing Witch', *Folklore* 11 (1900), 129–62; W. F. Ryan, 'Ancient Demons and Russian Fevers' in Charles Burnett and W. F. Ryan (eds), *Magic and the Classical Tradition* (Warburg Colloquia no. 7; London: Warburg Institute, 2005), pp.37–58.

12. Gerschom Scholem, *Kabbalah* (Jerusalem: Keter, 1974), p. 359.

13. W. F. Ryan, *The Bathhouse at Midnight: An Historical Survey of Magic and Divination in Russia* (Stroud: Sutton, 1999), p. 249.

14. Eva Pócs, 'Evil Eye in Hungary: Belief, Ritual, Incantation', in Jonathan Roper (ed.), *Charms and Charming in Europe* (Basingstoke: Palgrave Macmillan, 2004), 208.

15. Jennifer Chandler, 'St George and Horses,' p. 17.

9

Expressions of Impossibility and Inevitability in Mari Charms

Natalia Glukhova and Vladimir Glukhov

This chapter aims to show the linguistic means used in Mari verbal charms to denote those events, actions and processes which are either impossible or inevitable. The notions of **impossibility (improbability)** and **inevitability** are expressed with the help of folklore hyperboles and metaphoric similes. But their usage is of a distinct character, which reveals the intuitive folk understanding of several concepts also found in contemporary probability theory.

Mari charms are an integral part of Mari intangible culture, a constituent of its magic realm. Charming is still a living cultural phenomenon among the Mari. The Mari (approximately 605,000 people according to the 2002 census of population) are one of the two Volga–Finnic nations living in the centre of Russia, in both the Republic of Mari El as well as other nearby parts of the Russian Federation. Mari El is situated in the eastern part of the East European Plain in the middle reaches of the Volga basin. The territory of Mari El stretches for 275 km west to east and 150 km north to south and totals 23.3 thousand square kilometres in area.

According to the 2002 census, 728,000 people live in Mari El, the most numerous ethnic groups being Russians (47.5 per cent) and Mari (42.9 per cent). Despite strong Turkic and Russian influence, due to centuries of cultural contact, the Mari have succeeded in preserving their cultural traditions and rich folklore. Researchers especially remark upon the elaborate variety of folktales, songs, riddles, proverbs and sayings, and folk observations of nature among the Mari folklore repertoire. Of considerable interest too are the sacred and esoteric texts: Mari ethnic prayers and charms.

A Mari charm – *shüvedyme, shüvedyme mut* – is an oral text containing a wish, a will or a command, a rhythmically organized verbal

108

formula, which is employed in a ritual situation, and is believed to produce a desired effect under certain conditions because of the magic power both of the word and of the person who uses it with a definite pragmatic goal. Mari charms have already been a subject of linguistic analysis (Ivanov 1975; Sebeok, Ingemann 1956; Sebeok 1974). In these works, the authors presented a functional classification of some Mari charms, showed particular characteristics and singled out sporadic stylistic features at different textual levels. Although the description of some linguistic features has been one of the central research topics, recent text linguistic and pragma-linguistic studies provide new methodological techniques for a broader systemic approach to this folklore genre (Glukhova 1997).

Various specialists who possess supernatural powers (they are variously called *wizards, witches, sorcerers, seers, magicians*) can arrange and concentrate their magic might in order to achieve a desired goal. This is in addition to the actual magic power that is believed to be present in the texts themselves. In contemporary anthropological literature on the Mari, one can mainly read about folk healers known as *juzo* (Petrov 1993: 7–41). But taking a longer historical perspective, Mari ethnographers classified those people who were endowed with extraordinary abilities (allegedly they could receive bio-energy from nature and transform it into personal power to help people or to inflict evil upon them) into five categories. These categories were: (1) *muzhaŋche* (who could foresee and predict the future, could find thieves and stolen things); (2) *shinchanuzhsho* or *uzhsho-kolsho* (who were also considered to be clairvoyant, and could also diagnose illness and tell the cause of diseases); (3) *shüvedyshe*, or healers, (who manifested their powers when reciting charms, enchanting different objects by spitting on and murmuring to them); (4) *juzo* (who were termed magicians or sorcerers; they could heal or harm people and animals, objects and places); (5) *loktyzo-puzhykcho* (who were called witches, as their main aim was to inflict evil upon people or animals and to spoil everything) (Yakovlev 1877; Vasiliev 1915). Successful charming was deemed to have come from the magical practitioner strictly following the correct order of action and from the practitioner's exact knowledge of the charm text.

Mari esoteric texts have clear-cut pragmatic goals. According to these goals, we can classify Mari charms under six headings (and numerous sub-headings): (1) *Charms for healing:* (a) people, (b) animals; (2) *Charms protecting from witchcraft aimed at:* (a) people, (b) animals, (c) plants and objects; (3) *Counter charms* and *charms for unbewitching:* (a) people, (b) animals, (c) plants and objects; (4) *Charms changing interpersonal relationship among people, spoiling or changing them for the better;* (5) *Charms bringing good, benefit or profit to:* (a) people, (b) animals, (c) plants; and (6) *Charms inflicting evil on:* (a) people, (b) animals, (c) plants (Glukhova 1996:10).

There is some overlap, however. We can note that charms from groups 2, 3, and 5 may be thought of as belonging simultaneously to two groups: charms against witchcraft and charms annihilating bad effects and releasing from evil. Charms inflicting evil are connected with the texts from group 1 as they lead to changes in people's and animals' health. Healing charms have the notion of *'freeing from witchcraft'*, *'dissolution of evil'* or *'annihilation of evil'*. The general aim of all six of the groups of texts is twofold: either to prevent from an undesired destructive (harmful) effect (which could be seemed as *inevitable* and *certain* but should be turned into *impossible* or *improbable*) or to achieve an intended result (whether it be positive or negative).

The compositional structure of the esoteric text, its sound form, lexical and syntactic stylistic devices help to achieve these goals (Glukhova 1997). A specific role in the expression of inevitability and impossibility is played by simple and sustained types of hyperbole, as well as by situational (sustained) simile. Hyperbole is the deliberate overstatement of a feature essential to a particular object or phenomenon, which uses exaggeration for emphasis or effect (Galperin 1977: 176–7).

In Mari charms, folk hyperbole is used as an overstatement of different situations including events, actions and processes which lead to the impossibility of the desire fulfillment. The hyperboles in Mari charms can be divided into *simple* and *sustained.* Both simple and sustained hyperboles can be *numerical*: numerals such as one, seven, nine, eleven, forty-one and seventy-seven are frequently used in the texts. They are considered to be magical in Mari culture.

In the charms analysed here, hyperbole usually appears as part of the understanding of the apparent discrepancy between the normal flow of events and the imaginary situation depicted in the texts. The most typical circumstances for hyperbole in this material are those connected with the unreal character of events and situations, an exaggerated amount of conditions and the intentionally reduced time for certain actions to be completed.

In the following extract from *Poshartysh shörymö* ('Against witchcraft', Porkka 1895: 32), the **impossibility** is expressed by simple hyperbole containing only one unreal condition:

– Mündyr üzharam kunam posharen kertesh, tunam izhe posharen kertshe!	– *When s/he (the sorcerer) is able to bewitch a far-away dawn, only then let her/him be able to bewitch me!*
– Er kechym kunam posharen kertesh, tunam izhe posharen kertshe	– *When s/he (the sorcerer) is able to bewitch the morning sun, only then let her/him be able to bewitch me!*
– Küdyrchym kunam posharen kertesh, tunam izhe posharen kertshe	– *When s/he (the sorcerer) is able to bewitch the thunder, only then let her/him be able to bewitch me!*
– Volgenchym kunam posharen kertesh, tunam izhe posharen kertshe	– *When s/he (the sorcerer) is able to bewitch the lightning, only then let her/him be able to bewitch me!*
– Tylchym kunam posharen kertesh, tunam izhe posharen kertshe	– *When s/he (the sorcerer) is able to bewitch the moon, only then let her/him be able to bewitch me!*
– Shüdyrym kunam posharen kertesh, tunam izhe posharen kertshe!	– *When s/he (the sorcerer) is able to bewitch the stars, only then let her/him be able to bewitch me!*

There might be two joint **impossible** actions to provide the necessary effect in the text. The part of the charm *Iükshyshtaryme* ('Against love awakening', Gorskaya 1969) is aimed at prevention from establishing relationships. The sorcerer resorts to analogy of the improbable events still allowing a small chance (i.e. low probability) for their realization:

– Pyrys den pii kunam vash öndal malen kertesh, tunam izhe tudo [*name*] den tudo [*name*] pyrl'ya ilen kertysht!	– *When a cat and a dog, having embraced each other (1), can sleep together (2), only then let her [name] and him [name] live together!*

– Pire den maska kunam vash
öndal malen kertesh, tunam
izhe tudo den tudo pyrl'ya ilen
kertysht!

– *When a bear and a wolf,*
having embraced each other
(1), can sleep together (1),
only then let her and him
live together!

In the majority of texts against witchcraft, charmers enumerate several unreal events to secure the impossibility of evil to be inflicted on their 'clients'. Whole texts may be based upon sustained hyperboles, as can be seen in the following extract from the charm *Loktysh dech* ('Against witchcraft', Petrov 1993: 48–9):

– Shii üshtym üshtalynat, shii
tovarym chykenat, shii meŋgym
ruenat, shii meŋgym kerynat,
shii pidyshym pidynat, shii pechem
pechenat, shii imn'ym kychkenat,
shii omytam chiktenat, shii
örynchakym pyshtenat, shii pügym
rualynat, shii sapkeremym
pushtenat, shii shagavui dene
kuralynat, shii urlykkomdo dene
üdenat, shii tyrma dene tyrmalenat,
shii shurno shochyn, shii sorla dene
türedynat, shii kyltam yshtenat, shii
orvash opten naŋgayenat, shii
idymysh shii shagesh shii kavanym
yshtenat, shii idymymsh voltenat,
shii agunysh shyndenat, shii
idymysh luktyn, shii sapondo dene
kyrenat, shii üshtervoshtyr dene
üshtynat, shii kolmo dene pualtenat,
shii meshakysh optenat, shii vaksh
deke naŋgayenat, shii vakshküesh
shii lozhashym ioŋyshtenat, shii
shokte dene shoktynat, shii
ruashvochkesh shokte shii ruashym
lugenat, shii koŋgash shii kindym
küktenat, shii üstembake luktynat,
shii kümyzh-sovla dene kunam
pyrlya iüyn-kochkyn kertat tide

– *Only then you can bewitch*
me when, having put on a
silver belt, and having
stuck (into a silver belt) a
silver axe and having felt
a silver pole, and having
put up a silver pole, and
having fastened it by a
silver band and having
enclosed the space by a
silver fence and having
harnessed a silver horse,
and having put on a silver
horse's collar, and having
saddled it with a silver
saddle, and having put on
a shaft bow, and having
tied up silver reins, and
having ploughed with a
silver plough, and having
sown from a silver basket,
and having harrowed by a
silver harrow, and, after
the silver corn has been
ripened, having reaped by
a silver sickle, and having
bound a silver sheaf, and
having placed it on a silver
cart, and having made a

kindym yshten shukten, tunam
izhe myiym lokten kert!

*silver stack on the silver
perches on the silver
threshing ground, and
having lowered it on the
silver threshing ground,
and having placed it into
a silver barn for crops, and
having carried it out onto
the silver threshing ground,
and having thrashed it with
silver flails, and having
swept it with a silver broom,
and having raked it up with
a silver shovel, and having
filled silver sacks, and
having brought it to a
silver windmill, and having
ground it to silver flour by
the silver millstones, and
having screened it by a silver
sieve, and having kneaded
silver dough in a silver
trough, and having put silver
firewood into a silver oven,
and having baked silver
bread in the silver oven, and
having put it out onto a
silver table, together with me
you can eat the baked bread
from silver plates and dishes!*

The name of the metal – *silver* – is subsequently changed to *gold* and *copper* and the same events are enumerated.

In the following example, *Osalym pokten lukmo* ('Against witchcraft', Glukhova 1991), the **impossibility** of witchcraft is allegedly achieved by the multiplication of the exaggerated amount of unlikely actions (though thought as potential) with a deliberately minimized time, necessary for the action:

– Indesh chyra dene lümegozh,
  pyzle voshtyr, shuanvondo

*– I'll drive away the bewitchment,
  evil spirit, with the help of fire of*

voshtyr dene osalym pokten luktam.

nine splinters, with the help of the juniper twig, mountain ash twig, sweetbrier twig.

– Shörmychym nalyn (1), osh maskam (... osh pirym, osh ryvyzhym, osh meraŋym ...) chodyra gych kuchen konden (2), shogavuiym kychken (3), kunam möŋgeshla kural kertesh (4) tunam izhe osalym purten kertshe!

– *Let the sorcerer be able to cast spells when s/he is able, having taken the bridle, to bring a white bear (... a white wolf, a white fox, a white hare ...) from the forest, to harness it into the wooden plough, to plough the furrow back!*

– Shymlu-shym türlö oshmam kunam ik minut-sekundyshto pyrchyn-pyrchyn shotlen pytaren kertesh, tunam izhe myi dekem osalym purten kertshe!

– *Let the sorcerer be able to bewitch me, when s/he can count 77 different grains of sand one by one in a minute, in a second!*

The full text contains the enumeration with additional wild animals – a white wolf, a white fox, a white bear. So, the block of text beginning *Shörmychym nalyn* ... is spoken a further three times in order to secure the desired effect.

Thus we can see people expressing a complex event by the logical multiplication of simple actions and events. The probability of a complex event will be lower than that of a simple event. Thus complex events are considered more effective in charms in counteracting the possibility of highly improbable but still possible events.

Sustained hyperboles in the five hundred charms that have been ana-lyzed are mainly concerned with the exaggeration, displacement and enumeration of imaginable actions taking place in time and space. The use of hyperbole provides a chain of unlikely circumstances, impossible to realize, aimed at preventing an undesired effect. The enumeration of excessively difficult or sometimes absolutely unreal events independent of each other brings to naught the attempts to meet all the requirements, thus preventing (it is believed) a person from all probable evil doings of sorcerers.

If improbability is mainly expressed by hyperbole, inevitability is mainly shown by simile. Inevitable or certain events feature in charms aiming to change interpersonal relationships. The texts of such charms are composed on analogy, which is represented in linguistic terms by situational simile. This stylistic device is defined as intensification of a particular feature of the concept in question. Simile excludes all the properties of the two correlated (juxtaposed) objects, except the one which is common to them (Galperin 1977:167–8). In Mari charms, similes show analogy, but do not exhibit the contrast in the character of performed actions or ongoing processes. Similes in the analysed material can be subdivided into *simple* and *sustained (situational)*. The latter group is the more common. As hyperboles, similes can also contain numerals.

In the following extract from *Iükshyshtarymö* ('Spoiling a relationship', Gorskaya 1969), the charmer uses the following analogies:

– *Shoksho kürtnö kuze iüksha, tuge tudo tuddech iükshyzhö.* — As the burning hot steel gets cold, so let him/her cool off towards her/him.

– *Shoksho vüd kuze iüksha, tuge tudo tuddech iükshyzhö.* — As the boiling water gets cold, so let him/her cool off towards her/him.

– *Chodyra maska dech shümzhö kuze lüdesh, tudyn uzhyn, tudyn shümzhö lüdshyzhö, iükshyzhö.* — As his/her heart gets frightened having seen a forest bear, so let him/her get frightened and cool off towards her/him.

The following charm, *Symystaryme* ('Love awakening', Glukhova 1991), draws a parallel between the desire of the beloved's closeness with some articles of clothes, agricultural events and nature's phenomena:

– *Iydal kerem kuze iolesh pütyrnen kelshen shoga, tuge myi dekem tudyn chon-shüm mokshyzho pütyrnen kelshen shogyzho.* — As the bast sandals' ties twine nicely round my legs, so let him/her cling to me with all his/her heart–liver–soul.

– *Iümal üshtö kuze velenem kelshen pizhyn shoga, tuge myi dekem tudyn chon-shüm mokshyzho pütyrnen kelshen shogyzho.* — As the dress belt nicely girds me, so let him/her cling to me with all his/her heart–liver–soul.

– *Melgandyra kuze oiyrlydymyn vash pizhyn shoga, tuge myi dekem tudyn chon-shüm mokshyzho pütyrnen kelshen shogyzho.* — As the shirt laces are inseparable tied up, so let him/her cling to me with all his/her heart–liver–soul.

– *Umyla vachyrenge kuze varash pütyrnen shoga, tuge myi dekem tudyn chon-shüm mokshyzho pütyrnen kelshen shogyzho.*

– As the hops entwining with the pole rises upwards, so let him/her cling to me with all his/her heart–liver–soul.

– *Keche mlande iyr kuze pördyn savyrna, tuge myi dekem tudyn chon-shüm mokshyzho pütyrnen kelshen shogyzho.*

– As the sun goes round the earth, so let him/her cling to me with all his/her heart–liver–soul.

– *Tylze kuze pördyn savyrna, myi dekem tudyn chon-shüm mokshyzho pütyrnen kelshen shogyzho.*

– As the moon goes round, so let him/her cling to me with all his/her heart–liver–soul.

– *Shüdyr kuze pördyn savyrna, myi dekem tudyn chon-shüm mokshyzho pütyrnen kelshen shogyzho.*

– As the stars go round, so let him/her cling to me with all his/her heart–liver–soul.

In the next extract *Vash ushnash* ('Bewitchment [for love]', Gorskaya 1969), the potential beloved's feelings are compared with animals' instincts towards their offspring:

– *Choman vül'ö kuze chomazh dek kum pasu goch kudalyn tolesh, tuge myi dekem tudo, chonzho iülen, kurzhyn tolzho.*

– As a mare comes galloping to her foals through three fields, so let him/her with all his/her heart burning(from love) run up to me.

– *Prezan ushkal kuze prezyzhe dek kum pasu goch tolesh, tuge myi dekem tudo, chonzho iülen, kurzhyn tolzho.*

– As a cow gallops to her calves through three fields, so let him/her with all his/her heart burning (from love) run up to me.

– *Pachan shoryk kuze pachazh dek kum pasu goch kydal tolesh, tuge myi dekem tudo chonzho iülen, kurzhyn tolzho.*

– As a sheep gallops to her lambs through three fields, so let him/her with all his/her heart burning (from love) run up to me.

The similes in such texts help show a sort of balance between events and the desired goals. To guarantee the effectiveness of the charms, those who originally composed the texts metaphorically compared inevitable events from nature with the intended goals of their lives.

According to the *American Heritage Dictionary*, the probability of a particular event is 'a number expressing the likelihood that a specific event will occur, expressed as the ratio of the number of actual occurrences to the number of possible occurrences' (*The American Heritage Dictionary*, 2000: 1397). Sustained hyperboles and similes conveying the ideas of improbability and inevitability appear in Mari charms as expressions of the axioms of probability. Axioms (1) and (3) refer to hyperboles and axioms (1) and (2) apply to similes.

1. The probability (P) of an event (A) lies between *zero* (0) and *one* (1):

$$0 \le P(A) \le 1$$

2. The probability of an **inevitable** event is equal to one (1):

$$P(\Omega) = 1$$

3. The probability of an **impossible** event is equal to zero (0):

$$P(\emptyset) = 0$$

Events with a probability of close to zero are **improbable**. Events with a probability of close to one are **certain** (Kremer 2004: 18–52). One of the axioms of probability theory states that the ultimate probability of any event (P) is equal to the product of probabilities of independent events (A, B ...): $P(AB) = P(A)P(B)$. Thus, $P(AB)$ is far less probable than either $P(A)$ or $P(B)$ taken separately (Kremer 2004: 38–52). The majority of Mari charms aim at prevention of quite probable destructive events: illnesses, accidents, the loss of cattle or belongings, the deterioration of a relationship etc. According to the conditions expressed in the texts, these incidents can only occur if a string of unlikely or impossible events occur. Thus, the texts of charms are based on the opposition between possible and highly improbable events. By the logical multiplication of episodes, hyperbole in four types of Mari charms (2, 3, 4, 6) helps express improbability of the situations leading to a diminution or a dramatic reduction of the possibility of any undesirable negative effect to close to zero.

On the other hand, comparing a desired goal to an event which is bound to happen with 100% assurance, and sometimes by also multiplying this by further analogous and certain actions, the original composers of the charm thus secure the certainty of the positive pragmatic aim with the help of similes. The skilful employment of both of these stylistic devices in Mari charms suggests an (untaught) awareness of the rules and axioms of probability theory. Though the charms may lack the symbolic mathematical representation of probability theory, this does not devalue the role of the instinctive ethnic comprehension of the laws of nature, nor the intuitive wisdom of numerous generations of charm authors.

Bibliography

Galperin, I. R. 1977. *Stylistics*. (Moscow: Vyshaja shkola, 1977).

Glukhova, N. 1996. *Struktura i stil' tekstov mariiskih zagovorov* (Yoshkar-Ola: Mari State University, 1996).

Glukhova, N. 1997. *Structure and Style in Mari Charms* (Bibliotheca Ceremissica Tomus III). (Szombathely: Savaria University Press, 1997).

Ivanov, I.G. 1975. 'O yazyke odnogo iz zhanrov mariiskogo folklora', *Voprosy mariiskogo yazyka* (1975): 65–75.

Kremer, N. 2004. *Teoriya veroyatnostei i matematicheskaya statistika* (Moscow: Yuniti, 2004).

Petrov, V. N. 1993. *Marii you: Türlö loktymo, cher, muzho vashtaresh shüvedymash* (Yoshkar-Ola: Marii kniga savyktysh 1993).

Sebeok, T. and Ingemann, F. 1956. *Studies in Cheremis: The Supernatural* (Studies in Anthropology no 22). (New York: Wenner-Gren Foundation for Anthropological Research, 1956).

Sebeok, T. 1974. *Structure and Texture. Essays in Cheremis Verbal Art* (The Hague–Paris: Mouton, 1974).

Vasiliev, V. M. 1915. *Materialy dlya izucheniya verovanii i obryadov cheremis* (Kazan: Inorodcheskoje obozrenije, 1915).

Yakovlev, G. 1887. *Religioznyie obryady cheremis* (Kazan: Izdaniye pravoslavnogo missionerskogo obshestva, 1887).

The American Heritage Dictionary of the English Language. Fourth edition (Boston, New York: Houghton Mifflin, 2000).

Collections of charms

Glukhova, N. 1991. N. Glukhova's notes from field expeditions into New-Toryal region. Informants: Kolgasheva Anastasiya Ivanovna (1922), Shabalina Alevtina (1972).

Gorskaya, V.P. 1969. NRF MarNII, notes OP 1., N 942.

Petrov, V. N. 1993. *Marii you: Türlö loktymo, cher, muzho vashtaresh shüvedymash.* (Yoshkar-Ola: Marii kniga savyktysh, 1993), pp. 41–42.

Porkka, V. 1895. *Volmari Porkka's Tscheremissische Texte mit Übersetzung. Herausgegeben von Arvid Genetz* (Journal de la Société Finno-Ougrienne XIII: 1) (Helsingfors, 1895).

Part II
National Traditions

10
Russian Love Charms in a Comparative Light

Andrei Toporkov[1]

Problems of the comparative study of Russian charms

The comparative study of Russian charms [*zagovory*] has its own traditions, reaching back to the works of such famous scholars from the nineteenth and early twentieth centuries as Buslaev, Afanas'ev, Veselovskii,
Zelinskii, Mansikka, and Poznanskii. In recent years Russian charms
have been examined primarily in comparison with the charms of other
Slavic peoples (Agapkina, Toporkov 1990; Kharitonova 1991; Kliaus
2000; Agapkina 2002; Levkievskaia 2002; Toporkov 2002; Worobec
1995). There have also been attempts to compare Russian magical texts
with German and ancient Indian texts (Toporov 1969; Toporova 1996:
108–23).

Nonetheless, the possibilities of comparative (comparative–typological
and comparative–historical) study of Russian charms have been far from
exhaustively explored. Comparison of Russian charms with the charms
of other Slavic and non-Slavic peoples has traditionally come down to
the simple establishment of resemblances between separate texts, themes
and motifs. Such lists of similarities are useful in themselves, but as a
rule they have a selective character and present a somewhat accidental choice of materials. Besides this, the causes for these similarities
remain unclear: are they due to a genetic relationship, a typological
resemblance, or a mutual influence of various ethnic traditions? If we
wish to explain its nature and ancestry, rather than simply noting the
resemblance, we must consider the geography of textual dissemination,
the presence or absence of texts in the manuscript tradition (where
early evidence is particularly important), and their quantitative param-
eters, i.e. how many charms of a given type are known in a particular
tradition.

If Russian scholars do not take the magical traditions of other European peoples into account sufficiently, it is also true that western scholars know little about Russian charms. General works on the history of European magic have presented Russian material unsystematically and in insufficient quantity; as a rule, any Russian material is drawn from English-language works by Western philologists.

The comparative study of Russian charms may have two interconnected but nonetheless distinct goals: first, to reveal the resemblance between Russian charms and those of other traditions, and, second, to reveal the specific character of Russian charms in comparison with corresponding texts in other languages (formulae, themes, motifs). I would particularly like to underline the second aspect, since it often causes misunderstandings for western researchers. For Russian folklorists it is important in principle that a comparison should not only establish similarities, but also discover distinctions and particularities. Even if a text was borrowed from one ethnic group by another, complete study requires investigating the history of the text's adoption in its new cultural sphere. We observe that a text borrowed from elsewhere does not remain unchanged. Rather, it undergoes pressure from other texts and generic schemata; it 'grows into' the tradition, takes on new forms, changes its emphases of meaning, etc.

In Russian scholarship the task of comparative study of charms in recent decades has been connected primarily with reconstructing the old Slavic and even the Indo-European text (Toporov 1969; Agapkina, Toporkov 1990). The essential problem, however, is that we find one and the same texts and formulae in ethnic traditions that have no connection with one another from the point of view of language classification. Given their small format, the presence of a defined poetic structure, their presence in the written record, and their inclusion in sacred texts, it is easy for charms and charm-incantational formulae to migrate over time and space. They can pass from one ethno-linguistic tradition into another by way of oral contacts or translations of written texts (e.g., books of home cures and herbals). The task of re-establishing the history of magic texts in Europe from antiquity to the present and from the Atlantic to the Urals is, in any case, just as attractive as the reconstruction of ancient ancestral texts.

The comparison should be carried out on several parallel levels:

1. The contrast of various ethno-linguistic traditions of verbal magic from the point of view of their structure and patterns of function: the correspondence of various generic varieties (charms [*zagovory*],

incantations [*zaklinaniia*], non-canonical prayers, etc.), oral and written forms of textual function, and the presence or absence of certain functional or thematic groups of charms (medicinal, love, protective, and others).

2. Comparison of concrete charms from various traditions with the same purpose and similar themes, motifs and formulae.

3. The contrast of separate formulae that resemble one another in structure and lexical composition and appear in charms that have the same purpose.

Some characteristics of the Russian charm tradition

Before turning to our main topic, let us make a few general observations about the the Russian charm tradition.

Extent

First of all, it is extremely large and various, including many thousands of texts and dozens of themes. In recent decades, charms have been discovered in the Novgorodian birch-bark documents of the thirteenth to fifteenth centuries (Zalizniak 1993; Zalizniak 1995: 293 (No. 734), 428–9 (No. 715), 540 (No. 521); Zalizniak 2004: 694 (No, 930); Gippius 2005). The two earliest manuscript collections of charms, the so-called Olonetsky and Velikoustiuzhsky collections, date from the second quarter of the 17th century. Archival research by N. N. Pokrovsky, E. B. Smilianskaia, A. S. Lavrov, A. V. Pigin, A. A. Turilov, A. V. Chernetsov, and other scholars, has made available a whole series of formerly unknown collections of charms from the seventeenth and eighteenth centuries, and scholars have described the forms of social function of verbal magic (Lavrov 2000; Toporkov and Turilov, 2002; Smilianskaia 2003). As a result, it is now possible to survey the Russian charm tradition in the seventeenth and eighteenth centuries amid its historical dynamics and geographical and social stratification.

Charms circulated actively through geographical and social space (Bobrov and Finchenko 1986: 154–5; Lavrov 2000: 99–115). This resulted in the wide dissemination of texts and their variants and versions over the territory of Russia, not only in villages but also in urban centres. Charms were found in peasant and trading environments, though they were also known among church functionaries and nobles. They were written down on separate sheets of paper or in special notebooks, which were kept at home or carried about as amulets; they were included in medical manuals, in mixed-content collections; they were confessed at interrogations, sometimes under torture.

Oral/written dimension

In the seventeenth and eighteenth centuries there was no strict boundary between the oral and written functioning of charms: the oral text could easily be fixed in written form, and the manuscript version was accompanied by instructions in how to pronounce it, and which ritual actions should accompany it. There was also a tradition of using manuscripts as amulets. For example, illiterate people would take a little booklet with a military charm into battle, and it was supposed to protect them, even though they could not read it themselves (Sazonova and Toporkov 2002).

This half-oral and half-written kind of textual functioning led to a variety of consequences. On one hand, texts whose evolution was linked with local folklore traditions, once recorded on paper, became detached from ritual practice, moved into new social and geographical settings, and took on a more bookish and religiously-coloured character. On the other hand, canonical and non-canonical prayers began to function alongside folk charms, undergoing abbreviation and various kinds of revision. One and the same apocryphal prayers, translated from Greek, were found among all the Orthodox peoples, and to some extent in the Catholic countries as well. In the Russian tradition these prayers were not only recopied, but also re-written, brought closer to the oral charms. Our textological tradition has stressed the fact that during its existence and use, a prototypical text is not so much distorted as subjected to a purposeful and sensible correction with a creative character. In this sense, following the gradual evolution of the text during its recopying, inclusion in manuscripts of various contents, and replacement of the oral form of function by the written and vice versa – all this is a task no less important than the determination of its genesis.

Manuscript collections were often composed and preserved by people knowledgeable about liturgical literature but at the same time close to folk culture (in part, village and urban priests; Lavrov 2000:123–7; Mikhailova 2000; Smilianskaia 2003:119–41; Ryan 1999: 166–7).[2] In many collections and 'libraries,' confiscated by the authorities over the course of the seventeenth and eighteenth centuries, we encounter a combination of charms and apocryphal prayers (such as 'The Dream of the Virgin,' 'The Prayer of the Archangel Michael,' 'The Prayer of Cyprian,' 'The Prayer of the Apostle Paul against Snakes,' 'Sissinius's Prayer against Fever,' etc.). Charms and apocryphal (non-canonical) prayers were not clearly demarcated (Eleonskaia 1994; Levin 1997).

In manuscripts charms were often called 'prayers,' and it is more than likely that they were perceived in that way by their copiers.

Charms reside at the intersection of the Christian church and folkloric knowledge. The whole body of magical charm texts may be imagined as a kind of continuum. Canonical and non-canonical prayers are at one of its poles, with pagan folkloric and 'black' charms and incantational formulae at the other. Texts located at the extremes of this continuum are fundamentally distinct from each other in structure, lexicon, religious and moral goals, and so on. Nonetheless, the space between the extremes is continual in character, representing a series of gradual transitions between canonical prayers, on one hand, and folkloric–magical texts, correlated with notions of natural spirits and ways of interacting with them, on the other.

An innovative structure

No later than the second quarter of the seventeenth century, a distinctive type of charm developed, most characteristic of the Russian North and practically absent in Ukraine, Belarus, and the south of Russia. This kind of charm may begin with the formula 'I arise blessing myself, I go out crossing myself . . .' ['*Vstanu blagoslovias', vyidu perekrestias'*]. Further, these charms describe how the protagonist goes to the sea or into an open field, meets some mythical personage there and addresses a request to it (for example, to protect him or her against enemies or to inflict love on a person of the opposite sex). These charms are characterized by the presence of a subject, the motif of a 'mythological centre,' images of the protagonist, a mediating personage and an addressee, and a description of the location in space (Toporkov 1999; Agapkina 2005).

The appearance of such a structure had several consequences for the charm tradition. Texts of a single type were easy to memorize and pass on, and new texts were composed according to the set pattern. Typically, we encounter the same formulae in Russian charms as in analogous charms from other Slavic magical traditions, but at the same time the formulae are organized in a new way, included in configurations of subject and motif that are specific to the Russian tradition.

Issues in the study of love charms

A sizable literature has been devoted to love magic in Russia and the other Slavic and non-Slavic countries of Eurasia and interest in this topic has grown significantly in recent decades through a series of factors: removal of the taboo on formerly forbidden or dangerous themes, the growth of gender and historical–anthropological scholarship, the spread of contemporary neo-pagan movements, and the publication of numerous handbooks on contemporary magic and occult sciences. Aspects of the contents and functional existence of love charms have attracted the attention of collectors, publishers and scholars of Russian folklore (Toporov 1969; Kharitonova 1991; Kliaus 1994; Minyonok 1994; Kis' 1994; Toporkov 1999; Pushkareva 1999; Kiseleva 2001; Ryan 1999: 179–83).

Russian ethnographers and folklorists have studied young women's love and marriage charms, noted the many parallels between the formulae of love charms and ritual wedding songs, and analyzed the folkloric magical repertoire of the sorcerer and the *druzhok* at weddings. These works rely on material from local traditions, such as Zaonezh'e and the Perm' region (Zyrianov 1975; Lipatov 1983; Loginov 1988; Kuznetsova 1992; Kuznetsova 2000; Kalashnikova 2000). Love charms have also been studied from the structural point of view (Klagstad 1958; Chernov 1965; Peskov 1977; Carus 1977; Conrad 1989; Kiseleva 1992; Kiseleva 1998; Toporkov 1999).

E. B. Smilianskaia and A. S. Lavrov have cast light on the social functioning of love charms using materials from eighteenth-century trials involving sorcery (Smilianskaia 1996: 15–19; Lavrov 2000: 89–132; Smilianskaia 2001). I would note in particular Smilianskaia's article from 2001, the title of which can be translated as ' "Your love causes me great wounds..."': Sentiments and passions according to judicial materials from the eighteenth century', and the chapter 'Magic and Love' in her 2003 book: 172–86). Valerie Kivelson has examined the gender aspects of the functioning of charms in Russia in the seventeenth century in a series of articles (Kivelson 1991; Kivelson 1995). From the literature published in other Slavic countries, I would mention first and foremost the collection of Serbian love charms of M. Mijusković (1985), with a substantial introduction by L. Radenković. A fundamental edition of Romanian charms was prepared by Sanda Golopentia (Golopentia 1998; see also: Golopentia 1996; Golopentia 2004).

In recent decades, scholars from Western Europe and the United States have often turned to the love magic of medieval and Renaissance European traditions (Kieckhefer 1976: 56–61; Flint 1991: 231–53; Wilson 2000: 142–7). Richard Kieckhefer's splendid article 'Erotic Magic in Medieval Europe' (Kieckhefer 1991) provides a general introduction to the topic. Another series of works investigates the love magic of a particular country (for example, Italy, Spain, and the Spanish colonies of the New World) or even city (for example, Renaissance Florence and Venice,

Modena at the end of the 16th century; Brucker 1963; Brucker 1971: 266–8; Couliano 1987; Martin 1989; O'Neil 1987; Ortega 1991; Ruggiero 1993: 88–129; Scully 1995; Stephens 2002). These works offer rich collections of materials as well as valuable observations about the social and gender aspects of the function of love magic.

John Winkler's book *The Anthropology of Sex and Gender in Ancient Greece* includes a chapter on love charms (Winkler 1990: 71–98). Christopher Faraone has also devoted many articles to ancient Greek love charms (Faraone 1991; Faraone 1993a; Faraone 1993b), as well as his more general book *Ancient Greek Love Magic* (1999). Many of Faraone's observations apply with certain reservations to Russian love charms, too, although the Russian charms are completely unfamiliar to him and he does not take them into account. There are special studies of specific formulae from antique love spells, in particular the formula of sending fire (Kuhnert 1894; Tavenner 1942) and the formula 'let the maiden/woman be unable either to drink or eat (until she comes to me)' (Martinez 1995).

In this way, Russian and worldwide scholarship has accumulated broad experience in the study of love charms from various ethno-linguistic traditions. This creates preconditions for a study of Russian love charms that examines them in comparison with analogous love spells of other peoples of Eurasia.

Evolution of the formula 'let her neither eat nor drink'

Here we will examine in detail one formula from love charms – 'Let the maiden/woman not eat and not drink (until she has come to me).'[3] This formula is the topic of a special article by D. Martinez, from which we will take comparative material (Martinez 1995); Faraone's book also offers some valuable observations (Faraone 1999: 53–4).

Martinez examines two basic modifications of the formula: one found in oaths and vows, the other from love charms. Among the earliest fixed forms of the formula, he notes the oath of Achilles not to eat or drink until he has killed Hector (*Iliad* 19. 204–10), the vow of Saul not to eat until he has taken revenge on the Philistines (1 Kings 14.34), and the promise of some of the Judeans 'not to eat and not to drink until they have killed Paul' (Acts 23.12). In pre-Islamic Arabia, 'a man who had decided to take revenge for the death of a member of his family would vow that he would not drink wine, eat meat, rub himself with fragrant unguents, approach a woman, or wash the dirt from his hair until he had carried out his intention' (Rezvan 1988: 41). Among the early fixed forms of the formula in love spells is the Greek text on a lead tablet from the

4th century AD from Egypt, in which a certain Ailurion asks the spirits of the underworld to cause his beloved Kopria to be unable to eat or to drink until she has come to him and fulfilled all his wishes (Martinez 1995: 335).

According to Martinez's observations, when a person made a vow he took upon himself the obligation to refrain from eating and drinking until he had done what was promised. In Greek erotic magic of the Roman and Byzantine eras, a man was trying to force restraint not on himself, but on another, the woman he hoped to win, and moreover was trying to force her to adopt this behaviour against her will (Martinez 1995: 352).

The magical texts containing the formula of interest to us date primarily from the third and fourth centuries A.D. However, it is also found in two early magical papyri (one from the era of Augustus, the other from the first century A.D.). The second of these reads, 'If she is sleeping, let her not sleep; if she is eating, let her not eat; if she is drinking, let her not drink until she has come to me' (Martinez 1995: 353). Thus the sources testify that the formula was already known at the beginning of the first millennium of our era.[4]

The wish for a woman to be unable to drink and eat may arise independently, and it may be combined with the wish that she be unable to sleep, that she break off relations with her parents and other relatives, that she behave as if possessed or mad. The basis of these motifs is a conception of lovesickness characteristic of the ancient Greeks, reflected not only in magic,[5] but also in love lyrics (e.g., Sappho), and later adopted by medical literature (Galen) and the love novel (*Daphnis and Chloe*). Love charms happened to follow many of the same rules as charms employed to send spoiling [*porcha*] and sickness.

Refusing food and drink and inability to sleep are characteristic symptoms of lovesickness. For example, Galen writes about those 'who have grown thin, or grown pale, or lost their sleep, or even fallen ill of fever because of love' (Martinez 1995: 354). One of the love charms of the Paris papyrus from the fourth century A.D. described the desired result of the magical action this way: 'she is distressed and wants to talk with you... she is distressed or even dying' (PGM IV: 132–37).[6] In another charm, the state so-and-so wishes to call up in his beloved recalls a clinical description of illness and greatly resembles Galen's description (PGM XXXVI: 356–60; Betz 1996: 278). We can also note that in Longinos' novel *Daphnis and Chloe* the trials of the heroes are at times described in complete correspondence with love charms and medical literature.[7]

The formula in European charms (from the Renaissance until the modern era)

As Faraone rightly observes, love charms with the formula 'let her not eat, or drink, or sleep' remained popular in Europe for centuries (Faraone 1999: 54, note 63). Similar wishes occur in magical manuscripts compiled in Holland and Germany in the fifteenth century (Kieckhefer 1991: 40–1), and in Italian and Spanish love charms from the sixteenth and seventeenth centuries, preserved in the archives of the Inquisition (Ruggiero 1993: 45, 88–9, 167–8; Ortega 1991: 71–4).

In an Italian charm from Modena in 1597 a woman, addressing St. Martha, expressed the wish 'that he should fall in love with me, take *drink, food,* sleep, strength away from him, that he should be unable to leave or to remain in one place, nor ride a horse, nor gallop, nor stroll, nor have relations with other women, until he comes to me, to fulfill all my wishes and do all that I ask him' (O'Neil 1987: 102).[8] One of the earliest recorded Spanish charms, preserved in the archives of the Inquisition, dates from 1499. A woman addresses nine stars and asks them to ensure '. . . that he be *unable to eat or drink,* Until he has come to love me well/And receive pleasure with me' ('. . . que no pueda *comer ní beber*/hasta que a mi venga a bien querer/e a aver plaçer' (Ortega 1991: 74).

In another love charm from Spain, a woman asks Satan and all the devils: '. . . And do not permit him/to rest *or eat* or sleep, / He may not rest in his bed,/without thinking of me' ('. . . Y no le dejaréis/reposar, *ni comer,* ni dormir/ni en la cama reposar/sino conmigo pensar' (Ortega 1991: 71). Love charms in the form of prayers to St. Onofrius and St. Martha also included the formula 'let him not eat and not drink' ('que no pueda comer, ni beber') (Ortega 1991: 78). Also close to our formula, although not coinciding in every detail, is one of the wish-curses addressed to Gerd, daughter of the giant Gümir, from the so-called 'Potion of Skirnir' (included in the song 'The Journey of Skirnir' [strophe 27] from the Elder Edda): 'Fouler to you shall food look/ Than the snake seems to warriors.'[9]

To supplement materials collected by scholars of European sorcery, we may add a series of examples referring to Southeastern and Eastern Europe (Poland, Bohemia, Serbia, Romania, Ukraine and Russia). Records of a judicial proceeding from 1544 have preserved a Polish love charm which begins with an address to the dawn: 'Witajże zorze, idź-żesz mi do tego Filipa, roztargniej-że mu jego serce, iżby nie mógl ni pić ni jeźdź bez niej, iżby nie miał woli ni do dziwki ni do wdowy, ni do żadnego stworzenia, jedno do samej Łucyi ...' ('Welcome, morning star. Go to

Philip and break his heart, so that he be unable either to eat or to drink, be sexually attracted to neither maiden nor widow, nor to any other creature, except *Lucia* . . .') (Kolberg 1962: 241).[10]

E. V. Vel'mezova, compiler of the most complete collection of Czech charms, notes that there are not many love charms in Czech culture (Vel'mezova 2004: 22). She cites a single text of the kind, recorded at the end of the nineteenth century in eastern Moravia (Valasko). The charm is pronounced as follows. Three times a day (in the morning at sunrise, at noon, and in the evening at dusk), the wise woman goes out with a maiden to an open space; the woman pronounces the charm, and the maiden repeats it after her. The text includes the following fragment (here in translated form), addressed to the sun:

> You, clear sun, you shine for us, you see him [the intended], so inflame him and warm his heart, his lungs, his three hundred parts and joints, so that this intended one of mine, intended for me by God, so that *he can neither eat, nor drink, nor smoke tobacco, nor sleep, nor be cheerful*, but only think about me, the maiden christened (so-and-so), run to me, so that an hour will not be an hour for him, nor his family a family, his sister a sister, his brother a brother, his mother a mother, his father a father, so that none of that will be dear to him, only I, his intended, with God's help would stand before his eyes, so that it drips onto the crown of his head, onto his shoulder, onto his heart, into his lungs, into his three hundred parts and joints, so that *he can neither eat...*, but only run to the one christened (so-and-so), until he runs to her and says a word to her, and enters into marriage with her . . .
>
> (Vel'mezova 2004: 84).

In a collection of Serbian love charms compiled by M. Mijusković, the formula that interests us occurs only once: 'Dobro jutro bel pelenće! Ja te zovem omajniće, rasporniće, razbolniće, da mi omajesh dragog, da ga rasporish i ubodesh u srce, u dzigericu, za mene, u oci, u usta, ruke, noge, za mene; s dushom se rastavio, sa mnom se sastavio.... Pa da se ukhvatish za zemlju pa da kazhesh: Ne vadzam se za zemlju, no za Dzavola da dovede dragog kod mene, *da nema mira ni da ide, ni da jede, ni da spava...*' ('Good morning, white wormwood! I call you, exhauster, tearer, infector, to sweep over my darling, to rip him open and pierce him in the heart, in the kidneys, for me, in the eyes, lips, arms, legs for me; so he will part with his soul and come together with me.... Then you touch the ground and say: I hold not to the earth, but to the devil, so he will bring my darling to me, *so he will have no peace to walk, nor to eat, nor to sleep.'* Mijuskovic 1985: 53, No. 77).

In Romanian charms, a girl expresses the wish for a young man to be unable to eat or drink without her: 'Fără mine n-au putinţă, nici a bea, nici a mânca, până nu m-or săruta, nici să beie nici să mânce, pân ce-n braţă nu m-or strange' ('Without me they can neither drink nor eat until they kiss me, nor drink nor eat until they take me in their arms') (Golopentia 1998: 67–8. No. 6; see also: 217, No. 72.) A girl sends the devil to a young man and conjures him: 'Şi de l-ei găsi mâncând nu-l da a mânca, iar da l-ei găsi bând nu-l da a be' ('And if you find him eating don't let him eat, and if you find him drinking don't let him drink') (Golopentia 1998: 242–3, No. 86). In other texts, the girl wants her beloved to eat and drink together with her: 'Aşa să nu poată până cu mine nu s-o ogoi, si nu s-o odihni, pană cu mine în pat nu s-o culca si dintr-o bucată n-o mânca! Să mă visez cu dânsul la masă şezând, dintr-o bucată de pâne muşcând şi din pahar plin bând' ('So may he not find solace till he takes comfort in me, till he rests, till he goes to bed with me and eats of the same food as I. Let me dream of myself with him sitting at the table, eating from the same piece of bread and drinking from a full glass.' Golopentia 1998: 223, No. 76; see also 248, No. 87).

In Ukrainian charms recorded in the second half of the nineteenth century and the early twentieth century, our formula occurs more than once, with two basic modifications. In the first variety a girl addresses three star-sisters, the wind, or the moon with the request that they let the young man neither eat nor drink; for example: 'Vy zori-zirnytsi, vas na nebi tri sestrytsi: odna nudna, druga pryvitna, a tretia pechal'na. Berit' holky i shpyl'ky, hordove kaminnja; bijte joho i pechit', palit' i nudit'; ne dajte jomu ni spat', ni lezhat', ni jisti, ni pyt' – drugykh ljubyt' ('You dawn-stars, you three sisters in the sky: one dull, the second welcoming, and the third sorrowful. Take needles and pins, stones, beat and bake, burn and urge him; do not let him either sleep, or lie down, or eat, or drink – or love others.' Vasilenko and Shevchuk 1991: 218; see also SMU 1998: 76 [No. 221]; 80 [No. 229]; 84 [No. 246]; Bondarenko 1992: 23).

In the second modification, a girl asks for her young man to be unable to eat or drink his fill (that is, be unable to forget her while eating or drinking), for example: 'Shchob ty i izheju ne zaiv, i vodoju ne zapyv, i snom ne zasnuv, ta vse dumav pro mene ...' ('That you be unable to eat me away with food, and to drink away with water, and to fall asleep, but always think about me ...' Vasilenko and Shevchuk 1991: 234; see also ibid. 218–19, and SMU 1991: 78 [No. 226]).

Parallels between Greek and Russian charms

In Russian charms the formula appears dozens of times in three basic modifications, and each of these modifications has a corresponding number in the Greek charms from the Egyptian papyri. For clarity, we cite in parallel the fragments of the Greek with the Russian texts; naturally, we could add many more examples:

1. 'So-and-so asks for the person of the opposite sex to be unable to drink or eat.'

PGM IV: 1510–1520; IV cent. A.D.

If she is sitting, let her not keep sitting; if she is chatting with someone, let her not keep chatting; if she is gazing at someone, let her not keep gazing; if she is going to someone, let her not keep going; if she is strolling about, let her not keep strolling; *if she is drinking, let her not keep drinking; if she is eating, let her not keep eating;* if she is kissing someone, let her not keep kissing him; if she is enjoying some pleasure, let her not keep enjoying it; if she is sleeping, let her not keep sleeping. (Betz 1996: 67).[11]

Pokrovskii 1987: 261; dated 1734

... pokamest menia, raba imiarek, ne uvidit i ne osmotrit i ne obozrit i so mnoiu vmeste ne prebudet, po ta mes"[ta] by ei ne vmestimo bylo *ni jasti, ni piti*, ni s mater'iu, ni s gosti, ni s ynymi ljud'mi ni s kakimi.

['So long as she does not see and observe me, [God's] slave so-and-so, and is not together with me, then may she be unable *to eat, or to drink*, neither with her mother, or with guests, or with any other kinds of people.']

Vinogradov 1908/I: 30, No. 37. Middle of the nineteenth century

... chtoby ne mog onyi rab Bozhij (imiarek) bez raby Bozhiei (imiarek) ne zhit', ne byt', *ne s"is', ne ispit'*, ni chasu schasovat', ni veku svekovat', ni maloi minuty minovat'.

['... so that this (male) slave of God (so-and-so) be unable to live, or to be, *or to eat up, or to drink up*, or to spend an hour, or to spend a whole life, nor to spend a little minute without God's (female) slave (so-and-so)].'

2. 'So-and-so asks that a person of opposite sex think of him or her while eating.'

PGM XVIIa, 7–15; IV cent. C. E.

Make her cease from her arrogance, calculation, and her shamefulness, and attract her to me, beneath my feet, melting with passionate desire at every hour of the day and night, *always remembering me while she is eating, drinking,* working, conversing, sleeping, dreaming, having an orgasm in her dreams ... (Betz 1996: 253).

Lipatov 1983: 104; XIX cent

Gde by on ne khodil, gde by ne gulial, khot' by on v torgu torgoval ili *v piru piroval,* ili v besede besedoval, vse by on menia, rabu Bozhiiu, na ume na razume derzhal pri dne, pri krasnom solntse, pri temnoi noche, pri svetlom mesiatse.

['Wherever he may go, wherever he may stroll, even if he be trading at trade or *feasting at a feast,* may he always have me, God's servant, in mind and in thought by day, by the red sun, by dark night, by the bright moon.']

3. 'So-and-so asks that a person of the opposite sex feel hunger and thirst (be unable to eat or drink his fill).'

PGM XXXVI: 110–113; IV cent. A.D.

Attract to me, NN, her, NN, aflame, on fire, flying through the air, *hungry, thirsty, not finding sleep,* loving me, NN, whom NN bore, until she come and glue her female pudenda to my male one, immediately, immediately; quickly, quickly (Betz 1996: 271).

OR NBU, f. 301, unit 455, sheet 5 verso; end of 17th or beg. of 18th cent.

... ne mogla b ona toi toski po mne, [rbi] krov'iu, lezhankoi (?) ne otlezhatts, snom ne otospatts, khozhankoi ne otkhoditts, besedoi ne otsidetts, bogomoleniem ne otmolitts, krestom ne otkrestitts, dut'eiu ne otduttse, *pit'em ne otpitts, estvami ne otistittse,* ni travami ni koren'iami ne otgrysts ...

['... let her not be able [to bear] that longing for me, [so-and-so] with blood, not lie her fill of lying down (?), in sleep not sleep her fill, in walking not walk her fill, not sit her fill in conversation, not pray in prayer to God, not cross herself in crossing, not breathe her fill of breathing, *not drink her fill of drink, not eat her fill of eating,* not bite her fill of the herbs or roots ...']

Vinogradov 1908/I: 47–8, No. 60; undated ms

S toi by ei toski i velikiia pechali – *edoi by ei ne est' i pit'em by ne zapit'*,
gul'boi by ne otguliat', v plat'e by ei ne otnosit'; gde by ne zaslyshala
zychnyi golos, tak by ona bezhala i v sakharnyia usta tselovala.

['From that longing and great sorrow *let her be unable to eat of food,
and drink her fill of drink*, not stroll her fill of strolling, let her be unable
to wear her dress; wherever she may hear a loud voice, then let her
run and kiss my sweet lips.']

Various modifications of the formula differ from one another somewhat in meaning. In one case it is a matter of depriving a person of
the opposite sex entirely of food and drink (either taking them away, or
else bringing her to such a state that she herself is unable to eat anything ['kusok v gorlo ne polezet,' 'the piece sticks in the throat']). In the
second case, the person may take part in a meal, but in so doing must
think about the performer of the charm. The third case stresses that the
woman should be tormented by hunger and thirst and be unable to eat
or drink her fill. In Russian versions of the third modification of the formula one may see an echo of the Old Testament curse on dishonorable
ones: 'They shall eat – and will not be sated, they shall sin carnally – and
not multiply . . .' (Hosea 4: 10).

The semantics of the formula 'let her not eat or drink'

Regardless of its apparent simplicity, the formula allows differing interpretations. It contains them in compact form, and they can be actualized
depending on the context.

1. Deprivation of food, drink and sleep: this is in essence torture, supposed to force a person to do something that he himself is not inclined
   to do, to move him to agree to everything in order to end the suffering.
2. Each of the actions declared taboo for a maiden or a woman, when
   they are addressees of the charm (eating a meal with others, sleeping at
   night, etc.), is meant not only for satisfaction of physiological needs,
   but also for social communication. A person who does not eat in the
   family circle and does not sleep at night not only has a more difficult
   life, but also falls out of the conditions of normal interactions, winds
   up in an isolated condition.
3. Food, drink and sleep are basic physiological needs, essential for life.
   Considering the 'death-bearing' context of the love charms and how

close they are to curses, one may see a concealed threat: the woman may expect to die of hunger and thirst if she does not give herself to the man.

4. Insofar as hunger and restraint in general (among other things, during a religious fast) are a means of purifying and preparing oneself to encounter the sacral world, we might see the wish that someone not eat or drink as a way of bringing that person into a special elevated condition, close to ecstasy, in order to intensify his feelings and open him to new emotional experiences.

5. The charms say that a maiden should be hungry and tormented with thirst and insomnia until she gives in to the man; however, it nowhere says that after she gives in she will get something to eat and drink and be put to bed. This may be understood as follows: love itself will ease her hunger and thirst and allow her to relax and forget herself in sleep – or else in the sense that after her 'fall' she will be doing all this along with her new master.

The multitude of meanings of the formulae and the possibility of variant interpretations are characteristic of the whole poetics of charms.

Interpreting similarity

It is no accident that the formula 'let her not eat nor drink' in Greek charms from the Egyptian papyri of the first through fourth centuries and in Russian manuscript collections from the seventeenth and eighteenth centuries appears so similar. It should be understood as part of a more general system of relationships and connections among love charms across Eurasia.

In principle, the resemblance may be explained either typologically or else as a result of historical and cultural connections. In the first case, we see the general mechanisms of the origin and functioning of magical texts, and in the second that the Greek texts could have influenced the Slavs in one way or another (in translations directly from Greek, or else through some intermediate links). At the same time, the typological resemblance does not argue against genetic links: they may mutually reinforce and support each other. The inheritance of the antique world led in certain circumstances to new sprouts on different ethnic soil. We may also not exclude *a priori* the possibility that both Greek and Russian charms descended from some common, third sources (for example, the traditions of the ancient Middle East).

The magical texts preserved in Greek papyri of the first to the fourth centuries and in Russian manuscripts, have common typological characteristics. To a large extent, they may be considered as written traditions, 'male' and 'educated' in distinction to the oral, 'female' and 'the simple people's' traditions. For all the differences between Egyptian Mages and Russian sorcerers (*kolduny*), priests or other copiers of the charm letters in the seventeenth and eighteenth centuries, it seems probable that both groups did not merely record the texts of everyday magic, but approached the act in a creative way. They carried out a selection of texts, they reworked them in part, completed their composition, brought in charms from various regional and even ethnolinguistic traditions, etc.

Let us note that in Ukrainian, Serbian and Bulgarian love magic we also see individual formulae known in the Russian and Greek charms, although on the whole the love charms of these peoples have a completely different character. In these traditions only oral magical texts are known, not written ones; they were pronounced mainly by girls or women, not by men; the performers of the charms had the goal of marriage or strengthening the family, not sexual subordination of a person of the opposite sex.

From the point of view of gender, both the Greek and the Russian love charms we have been discussing are mostly men's texts, directed towards taking mastery of a maiden or a woman (though there are exceptions). Along with the men's magic, both Greeks and Russians also had maidens' and women's magic, which was distinct from the men's. As among other peoples, this aimed at marriage or retaining a husband, inspiring him to behave better towards his wife or increase his sexual activity. This women's tradition left considerably less trace in manuscripts than the men's tradition.

Greek and Russian love charms share the concept of the fiery nature of love (a flame seizes the heart, the liver, and other internal organs of the victim), of lovesickness, its causes and symptoms (refusing food and drink, insomnia, heat and fever, social isolation, breaking with parents and other relations, madness or possession by evil spirits, being struck in the heart with an arrow or some other sharp weapon), the association of the emotion of love with melancholy (in part, leading to suicide), and also that love may be imposed on a person from outside, and that gods and demons (for the Greeks) or natural elements and demons (for the Slavs) may be helpers in this matter.

These typological resemblances suggest a few ideas of cultural-historical and social-psychological character. In many cultures, love and magic are tightly interconnected. Attempts to act on a person of the opposite sex by magical means, and likewise to explain suddenly inflamed feelings as a result of sorcery, were known among the earliest peoples. Love charms serve in identical everyday situations and are called upon to resolve social–psychological collisions that arise completely independently and spontaneously in various societies (the impossibility for whatever reason of union with the beloved, sexual betrayal, love triangles, and so on). To these cultural universalia we may add the link of sexual relations to the problems of power and violence. Both Greek and Russian charms speak not only of taking mastery over some person, but also of subordinating her to oneself, depriving her of her own will, forcing her to act as the performer of the charm desires. This is linked to the aggressiveness of love charms and the traits of cruelty and even sadism we find in them.

Furthermore, the incantational formulae of love charms not only accompany magical actions, based on the universal principles of magic; they also describe these actions. Therefore, one and the same formula, or in any case extremely similar formulae, may arise completely independently in different cultures, where the magical actions arose just as independently. For example, the formula of sending fire, of the type 'As fire burns in a stove, so let the heart of N. burn,' could arise in any place where myrrh or wood were ritually burned in order to inflame the heart and other internal organs of a man or woman.

Finally, to a significant extent the picturesque quality of the charms grows out of linguistic metaphors. The metaphorization of love as fire is known in many languages, including, e.g., ancient Greek, Russian and English (Kövecses 1988; Kövecses 1991). If some language describes love as a fire (*the flame of love, the heart burns, to set a man on fire, fiery feelings, fiery glances*, etc.), then naturally in magical rituals and charms a person will attempt to ignite the flame of love in his victim by the means available. Given that similar linguistic metaphors are widespread in various languages, it is not surprising that charm formulae too may arise completely independently in a variety of traditions, suggested by the language.

Some further hypotheses

In this way, the correspondences we have shown between ancient Greek and Russian charms may be explained by the fact that they serve in identical, or at least very similar, everyday situations, and by their link with magic and the language of metaphor. Yet, nonetheless, the number and variety of the coincidences and their systematic, motivated and multi-levelled character suggest that Greek and Russian charms are most probably linked not only by typology, but also by borrowing.

The very fact of the closeness of Greek and Slavic charms is neither strange nor surprising. As we know, the Church Slavic language arose in the process of translation from Greek, and old Slavic literacy initially formed as a result of intentional transplantation of the Byzantine tradition into Slavic soil. A large number of prayers close to charms were included in liturgical books translated into the Church Slavic language. We also cannot dismiss the possibility of direct inheritance between the Greek and Slavic traditions of verbal magic in the Balkans.

We cannot establish direct links between Greek and Russian love charms at this time, although we can indicate one probable direction for further research. It is possible that Greek love charms reached Slavic soil among the erotic charms ascribed to the holy martyr Cyprian of Antioch. Let us recall that Cyprian (third century) was, according to tradition, a considerable philosopher and sorcerer. His *vita* is preserved in various versions in Greek and Latin. According to one version, Justina (in the Russian texts, Ustin'ia) was the daughter of a pagan priest in Antioch; she converted to Christianity along with her parents and made a vow of virginity. The upper-class youth Aglaid fell in love with Justina and appealed for help to the pagan Mage Cyprian. Cyprian sent demons to tempt Justina, but each time Justina drove away her tempters. In the end, Cyrprian became convinced of the uselessness of his sorcery, began to believe in Christ, was christened, and burned his magical books (Loparev 1993). In another ancient version of the vita, Cyprian is not the helper of Aglaid but his rival: having seen Justina, he himself began to burn with passion for her and wanted to win her love with the help of the devil (see Zhirmunskii 1978: 263).

Some versions of the confession of Cyprian include a wide-ranging erotic charm, which Cyprian employed as he tried to make Justina pine for love. One extant eleventh-century Coptic text of the 'Confession' includes the formula, 'let her not eat and not drink,' and all the basic formulae of Greek love charms in general (Meyer and Smith 1999: 153–8, No. 73). There is an extensive literature devoted to the legends of Cyprian, but their history in Russia has not yet been studied (e.g. Beletskii 1911–12: 62–3; Bezobrazov 1917: 223–6; Zhirmunskii 1978: 263; Bagno 1985: 369). While in the *Great Reading Menaion* of Metropolitan Makarii, the entry for October 2 includes several versions of the legend of Cyprian and Ustin'ia: 'Cyprian's Repentance,' 'The Life of the Holy Maiden Ustina,' 'The Torments of Saint Cyprian and the Maiden Ustina'

(*Velikiia Minei-Chet'i* ['The Great Menaion for Reading'] 1870: 45–80), these works do not include any retelling of the love charms.

While further research is needed to confirm or refute our hypothesis, the question of the intermediate links between the Greek and Slavic traditions of verbal magic deserves special investigation by specialists in Byzantine studies.[12]

Notes

1. This chapter was written with the support of the Historic-philological Department of the Russian Academy of Sciences under the programme 'Russian Culture in World History' and the project 'Russian Folklore in the Nearest Ethnic Surroundings'.
2. On analogous phenomena in England in the 16th and 17th centuries, and in continental Europe, see Thomas 1991: 55–56, 78–80, 326–27; Arnautova 2004: 274–79.
3. A comparative analysis of other formulae of Russian love charms is made in our book Заговоры в русской рукописной традиции XV-XIX вв.: История, символика, поэтика ('Charms in the Russian manuscript tradition of the 18th and 19th centuries: History, Symbolism, Poetics'), (Moscow: Indrik, 2005).
4. For a bibliography of magical texts, including the formula 'let her not eat and not drink, until . . .' see Martinez 1995: 353, note 61.
5. Many texts include madness in one list with other symptoms of illness, while in others it is the central idea (Martinez 1995: 354, note 64).
6. English translation: Betz 1996: 40.
7. On similar formulae in the antique love novel see Likht 1995: 194.
8. In O'Neil's article the text is published in English translation (ALT).
9. From the translation of W.H. Auden and P.B. Taylor, found at http://eljudnir. hit.bg/skirnismol.htm, accessed 19 May 2007.
10. For the English translation see Brzozowska-Krajka 1994: 79.
11. See also ibid 45.
12. For some information on love charms in Byzantium see: Greenfield 1988: 246–48.

Bibliography

Agapkina, Tat'iana A. 2002 'Siuzhetika vostochnoslavianskikh zagovorov v sopostavitel'nom aspekte.' *Literatura, kul'tura i fol'klor slavianskikh narodov* (Moscow): 237–49.

Agapkina, Tat'iana A. 2005 'Siuzhetnyi sostav vostochnoslavianskikh zagovorov (Motiv mifologicheskogo tsentra).' *Zagovornyi tekst: Genezis i struktura* (Moscow): 247–91.

Agapkina, Tat'iana A. and Toporkov, Andrei L. 1990 'K rekonstruktsii praslavian-skikh zagovorov.' *Fol'klor i etnografiia: Problemy rekonstruktsii faktov traditsionnoi kul'tury* (Leningrad): 68–75.

Arnautova, Iu. E. 2004 *Kolduny i sviatye: Antropologiia bolezni v srednie veka* (St. Petersburg).

Bagno, V. E. 1985 'Dogovor cheloveka s d'iavolom v 'Povesti o Savve Grudtsyne' i v evropeiskoi literaturnoi traditsii.' *Trudy Otdela drevnerusskoi literatury*, vol. XL (Leningrad): 364–72.

Betz, H. D. (ed.) 1996 *The Greek Magical Papyri in Translation*. 2d edn. (Chicago and London: The University of Chicago Press).

Bezobrazov, P. 1917 *Vizantiiskie skazaniia*. Part I. *Rasskazy o muchenikakh*. Iur'ev.

Beletskii, A. I. 1911–12 'Legenda o Fauste v sviazi s istoriei demonologii,' *Zapiski Neofilologicheskogo obshchestva pri S.-Peterburgskom universitete*, vyp. 5(1911): 59–193; vyp. 6 (1912): 67–84.

Bobrov, A. G. and Finchenko, A. E. 1986 'Rukopisnij "otpusk" v pastush-eskoj obrjadnosti Russkogo Severa (konets XVIII–nachalo XX v.),' *Russkij Sever.* (Leningrad): 135–64.

Bondarenko, G. B. (ed.) 1992 *Taiemnaia sila slova (Zahovory, zamovliania, zakli-naniia)*. (Kyiv).

Brucker, G. A. 1963. 'Sorcery in Early Renaissance Florence.' *Studies in the Renaissance*. Vol. 10.

Brucker, G. A. 1971 *The Society of Renaissance Florence* (New York).

Carus, A. B. 1977 'The Affective "Grammar" and Structure of Great Russian Charms.' *Forum at Iowa on Russian Literature*, vol. 2: 3–19.

Chernov, I. 1965 'O strukture russkogo liubovnogo zagovora.' *Trudy po znakovym sistemam*, vyp. 2 (Tartu): 159–72.

Conrad, J. L. 1989 'Russian Ritual Incantations: Tradition, Diversity, and Conti-nuity.' *Slavic and East European Journal*, vol. 33, no. 3: 422–44.

Couliano, I. P 1987 *Eros and Magic in the Renaissance*. Trans. M. Cook. Chicago.

Eleonskaia, E. N. 1994 'K izucheniiu zagovora i koldovstva v Rossii.' *Skazka, zagovor i koldovstvo v Rossii* (Moscow): 99–143.

Faraone, C. A. 1991, 'The Agonistic Context of Early Greek Binding Spells.' *Magika Hiera: Ancient Greek Magic and Religion*, Ed. C. A. Faraone, D. Obbink. New York, Oxford: Oxford University Press, 1991: 3–32.

Faraone, C. A. 1993a 'The Wheel, the Whip and Other Implements of Torture: Erotic Magic in Pindar *Pythian* 4:213–19.' *Classical Journal*, vol. 89 (1993): 1–19.

Faraone, C. A. 1993b 'Molten Wax, Spilt Wine and Mutilated Animals: Sym-pathetic Magic in Early Greek and Near Eastern Oath Ceremonies.' *Journal of Hellenic Studies*, vol. 113 (1993): 60–80.

Faraone, C. A. 1999, *Ancient Greek Love Magic*. Cambridge, MA and London: Harvard University Press, 1999.

Flint, Valerie I. J. 1991, *The Rise of Magic in Early Medieval Europe*. Princeton, NJ: 1991.

Gippius, A. A. 2005 ' "Sisinieva legenda" v novgorodskoi berestianoi gramote.' *Zagovornyi tekst: Genezis i struktura* (Moscow, 2005): 136–42.

Golopentia, S. 1996 'Love Charms in Cornova, Bassarabia.' *Studies in Moldovan: the History, Culture, Language and Contemporary Politics of the People of Moldova*, Ed. L. D. Donald. New York, 1996: 145–205.

Golopentia, S. 1998 *Desire Machines: a Romanian Love Charms Database*. Bucharest, 1998.

Golopentia, S. 2004 'Towards a Typology of Romanian Love Charms.' *Charms and Charming in Europe*. Ed. J. Roper. New York, 2004: 145–87.

Greenfield, R. 1988 *Traditions of Belief in Late Byzantine Demonology*. Amsterdam: Adolf M. Hakkert, 1988.

Kalashnikova, R. B. 2000 'Svadebnoe soderzhanie i "prisushivatel'naia" simvolika zaonezhskikh besiodnykh pesen vtoroi poloviny XIX veka.' *Kizhskii vestnik*, no. 5 (Petrozavodsk, 2000): 72–94.

Kharitonova, V. I. 1991 'Liubovna mahiia slov'ian (serbs'ko-rosiis'ki paraleli).' *Problemy slov'ianoznavstva* (L'viv, 1991): 59–66.

Kieckhefer, Richard 1976 *European Witch Trials: Their Foundations in Popular and Learned Culture, 1300–1500*. Berkeley and Los Angeles: University of California Press, 1976.

Kieckhefer, Richard 1991 'Erotic Magic in Medieval Europe.' *Sex in the Middle Ages*. Ed. J.E. Salisbury (New York, 1991): 30–55.

Kiseleva, Iu. M. 1998 'Smyslovye komponenty zagovora kak deistvuiushchego slova.' Konferentsiia 'Slovo kak deistvie.' Tez. dokl. (Moscow, 1998): 32–7.

Kiseleva, M. 2001 *Smyslovaia organizatsiia russkikh lechebnykh i liubovnykh zagovorov*. AKD. Moscow, 2001.

Kis', R. 1994 'Eros i vodna styhiia (Pervisna semiotichnist' shljubnoi mahii).' *Suchastnist'* (Kyiv, 1994), No. 1: 83–98.

Kivelson, Valerie A. 1991 'Through the Prism of Witchcraft: Gender and Social Change in Seventeenth-Century Muscovy.' *Russia's Women: Accommodation, Resistance, Transformation*. Ed. Barbara E. Clements, Barbara A. Engel, Christine D. Worobec. Berkeley and Los Angeles, 1991: 74–94.

Kivelson, Valerie A. 1995 'Patrolling the Boundaries: Witchcraft Accusations and Household Strife in Seventeenth-Century Muscovy.' *Harvard Ukrainian Studies*, vol. 19 (1995): 302–23.

Klagstad, H. L. 1958 'Great Russian Charm Structure.' *Indiana Slavic Studies*, vol. 2 (1958): 135–44.

Kliaus, V. L. 1994 'Vzaimootnosheniia polov v slavianskikh zagovorakh (na materiale iuzhnykh i vostochnykh slavian).' *Zhenshchina i svoboda: Puti vybora v mire traditsii i peremen* (Moscow, 1994): 369–73.

Kliaus, V. L. 2000 *Siuzhetika zagovornykh tekstov slavian v sravnitel'nom izuchenii*. Moscow, 2000.

Kolberg, O. 1962 *Dzieła wszystkie*, vol. 15. Wielke Księstwo Poznańskie. Cz. 7. Wrocław; Poznań, 1962.

Korablev, L. 2003 *Runicheskie zagovory i apokrificheskie molitvy islandtsev*. Moscow, 2000.

Kövecses, Z. 1988 *The Language of Love: The Semantics of Passion in Conversational English*. Lewisburg, PA: Bucknell University Press; London and Toronto: Associated University Presses, 1988.

Kövecses, Z. 1991 'A linguist's quest for love.' *Journal of Social and Personal Relationships*, vol. 8 (1991): 77–97.

Kuhnert, E. 1894 'Feuerzauber.' *Rheinisches Museum*, vol. 49 (1894): 37–54.

Kuznetsova, V. P. 1992 'O funktsiiakh kolduna v russkom svadebnom obriade Zaonezh'ia.' *Zaonezh'e* (Petrozavodsk, 1992): 117–31.

Kuznetsova, V. P. 2000 'Druzhka i ego rol' v russkoi svad'be Zaonezh'ia.' *Kizhskii vestnik*, no. 5 (2000): 95–104.

Lavrov, A. S. 2000 *Koldovstvo i religiia v Rossii: 1700–1740 gg*. Moscow, 2000.

Levin, *Eve* 1997 'Supplicatory Prayers as a Source for Popular Religious Culture in Muscovite Russia.' *Religion and Culture in Early Modern Russia and Ukraine* (De Kalb: Northern Illinois University Press, 1997): 96–114 (In Russian: Levin Iv. *Dvoeverie i narodnaia religiia v istorii Rossii*, trans. A. L. Toporkov and Z. N. Isidorova (Moscow, 2004): 84–109).

Levkievskaia, E. E. 2002 *Slavianskii obereg: Semantika i struktura*. Moscow, 2002.

Likht, G. 1995 *Seksual'naia zhizn' v Drevnei Gretsii*. Trans. from English by V. V. Fedorin. Moscow, 1995.

Lipatov, V. A. 1983 'K probleme regional'noi spetsifiki fol'klora: O variativnosti zagovorov.' *P. I. Chaikovskii i Ural* (Izhevsk, 1983): 99–108.

Loginov, K. K. 1988 'Devich'ia obriadnost' russkikh Zaonezh'ia.' *Obriady i verovaniia narodov Karelii* (Petrozavodsk, 1988): 64–76.

Loparev, Kh. M. 1993 'Kiprian.' *Khristianstvo. Entsiklopedicheskii slovar'*, vol. 1 (Moscow, 1993): 736–7.

Martin, R. 1989 *Witchcraft and the Inquisition in Venice, 1550–1650*. Oxford: Blackwell, 1989.

Martinez, D.G. 1995 ' "May She Neither Eat nor Drink. . ."': Love Magic and Vows of Abstinence.' *Ritual Power in the Ancient World*. Ed. M. Meyer, P. Mirecki (Leiden, 1995): 335–60.

Meyer, Smith 1999 *Ancient Christian Magic: Coptic Texts of Ritual Power*. Ed. M. Meyer and R. Smith. Princeton, NJ, 1994.

Mijusković, M. 1981 *Ljubavne čini*. Belgrade, 1985.

Mikhailova, T. V. 2000 'Predstaviteli dukhovkogo sosloviia v koldovskikh protsessakh vtoroi poloviny XVIII v.' *Vestnik molodykh uchenykh. Istoricheskie nauki* (St. Petersburg, 2000): 31–40.

Mineyonok, E. V. 1994 'Rol' zhenshchin v zagovornoi traditsii.' *Zhenshchina i svoboda: Puti vybora v mire traditsii i peremen* (Moscow, 1994): 362–8.

O'Neil, Mary 1987. 'Magical Healing, Love Magic and the Inquisition in Late Sixteenth-Century Modena.' *Inquisition and Society in Early Modern Europe*. Ed. and trans. S. Halizer (London, 1987): 88–114.

Ortega, M.H.S. 1991 'Sorcery and Eroticism in Love Magic.' *Cultural Encounters: The Impact of the Inquisition in Spain and the New World*. Ed. by M.E. Perry, A.J. Cruz (Berkeley, 1991): 58–92.

PGM *Papyri Graecae Magicae. Die Griechischen Zauberpapyri*. Herausg. von K. Preisendanz et al. 2. Aufl., vol. 2. Stuttgart: Teubner, 1973–74.

Peskov, A. M. 1977 'Ob ustoichivykh poeticheskikh elementakh russkogo zagovora.' *Filologiia*, vyp. 5 (Moscow, 1977): 26–39.

Pokrovskii, N. N. 1987 'Tetrad' zagovorov 1734 goda.' *Nauchnyi ateizm, religiia i sovremennost'*. Novosibirsk, 1987: 239–66.

Pushkareva, N. L. 1999 ' "Kako sia razgore serdtse moe i telo moe do tebe. . .": Liubov' v chastnoi zhizni cheloveka srednevekovoi Rusi po nenormativnym istochnikam.' *'A se grekhi zlye, smertnye. . .' Liubov', erotika i seksual'naia utika v doindustrial'noi Rossii (X-pervaia polovina XIX v.)*. Ed. N. L. Pushkareva (Moscow, 1999): 507–15.

Rezvan, E. A. 1988 'Eticheskie predstavleniia v Korane.' *Ѐtiket u narodov Perednei azii* (Moscow, 1988): 38–59.

Ruggiero, C. 1993 *Binding Passions: Tales of Magic, Marriage and Power at the End of the Renaissance.* New York, Oxford: Oxford University Press, 1993.

Ryan, William F. 1999 *The Bathhouse at Midnight. An Historical Survey of Magic and Divination in Russia.* University Park, PA: The Pennsylvania State University Press, 1999.

Sazonova, Toporkov 2002 'Zagovory ot vrazheskogo oruzhiia v sbornike XVIII v.' *Otrechennoe chtenie v Rossii XVII–XVIII vekov.* Ed. A. L. Toporkov, A. A. Turilov. (Moscow, 2002): 267–89.

Scully, S. 1995 'Marriage or a Career? Witchcraft as an Alternative in Seventeenth-Century Venice.' *Journal of Social History,* vol. 28 (1995): 857–76.

Segal, C. 1974, 'Eros and Incantation: Sappho and Oral Poetry.' *Arethusa,* vol. 7 (1974): 139–60.

Smilianskaia, Elena B. 1996 'Sledstvennye dela 'o sueveriiakh' v Rossii pervoi poloviny XVIII v. v svete problem istorii obshchestvennogo soznaniia.' *Rossica,* no. 1 (1996): 3–20.

Smilianskaia, Elena B. 2001 ' "Liubov' tvoia rany mne velikie daet..." (Chuvstva i strasti po sledstvennym delam XVII v.).' *Mifologiia i povsednevnost': Gendernyi podkhod v antropologicheskikh distsiplinakh* (Saint Petersburg, 2001): 26–40.

Smilianskaia, Elena B. 2003 *Volshebniki. Bogokhul'niki. Eretiki. Narodnaia religioznost' i 'dukhovnye prestupleniia' v Rossii XVIII v.* Moscow, 2003.

SMU 1998 *Slovesna mahiia ukranntsiv.* Kyiv, 1998.

Stephens, W. 2002 *Demon Lovers: Witchcraft, Sex, and the Crisis of Belief.* Chicago and London: The University of Chicago Press, 2002.

Tavenner, 1942 E. 'The Use of Fire in Greek and Roman Love Magic.' *Studies in Honor of F.W. Shipley* (St. Louis, 1942): 17–37.

Toporkov, Andrei L. 1999 'Russkie liubovnye zagovory XIX veka.' *Eros i pornografiia v russkoi kul'ture.* Ed. Marcus Levitt and Andrei L. Toporkov. Moscow, 1999: 54–71.

Toporkov, Andrei L. 2002 'Zagovorno-zaklinatel'naia poeziia v rukopisnykh traditsiiakh vostochnykh i iuzhnykh slavian.' *Literatura, Kul'tura i fol'klor slavianskikh narodov: XIII Mezhdunarodnyi s'ezd slavistov (Liubliana, avgust 2003). Doklady rossiiskoi delegatsii* (Moscow, 2002): 351–61.

Toporkov, Torilov 2002 *Otrechennoe chtenie v Rossii XVII–XVIII vekov.* Ed. Andrei L. Toporkov, A. A. Turilov. Moscow: Indrik, 2002.

Toporov, V. N. 1969, 'K rekonstruktsii indoevropeiskogo rituala i ritual'no-poeticheskikh formul (na materiale zagovorov).' *Trudy po znakovym sistemam,* vyp. 4 (Tartu, 1969): 9–43. (Uchen. zap. Tart. god. uni-ta; vyp. 236.)

Toporova, T. V. 1996 *Iazyk i stil' drevnegermanskikh zagovorov.* Moscow, 1996.

Vasilenko, Shevchuk 1991 *Vy, zori-zorytsi... Ukrannska narodna magichna poeziia (Zamovliannia).* Ed. M. G. Vasilenko, T. M. Shevchuk. Kyiv, 1991.

Velikiia Minei-Chetii 1870 *Velikiia Minei-Chetii, sobrannyia Vserossiiskim mitropolitom Makariem.* October, days 1–3. St. Petersburg, 1870.

Vel'mezova, E. V. 2004 *Cheshskie zagovory: Issledovaniia i teksty.* Moscow, 2004.

Vinogradov, N. 1908/I–II *Zagovory, oberegi, spasitel'nye molitvy i proch. (Po starinnym rukopisiam i sovremennym zapisiam).* St. Petersburg, 1908, vyp. 1; 1909, vyp. 2.

Wilson, St. 2000 *Magical Universe: Everyday Ritual and Magic in Pre-Modern Europe.* London and New York, 2000.

Winkler, J. J. 1990 *The Constraints of Desire: The Anthropology of Sex and Gender in Ancient Greece.* New York, 1990.

Worobec, Chg D. 1995 'Witchcraft Beliefs and Practices in Prerevolutionary Russian and Ukrainian Villages' *The Russian Review*, vol 54:2 (1995), 165–87.

Zalizniak, Andrei A. 1993 'Drevneishii vostochnoslavianskii zagovornyi tekst.' *Issledovaniia v oblasti balto-slavianskoi dukhovnoi kul'tury: Zagovor* (Moscow, 1993): 104–7.

Zalizniak, Andrei A. 1995 *Drevnenovgorodskii dialect*. Moscow, 1995.

Zalizniak, Andrei A. 2004 *Drevnenovgorodskii dialect*. 2nd edn Moscow, 2004.

Zhirmunskii, V. M. 1978 'Istoriia legendy o Fauste.' *Legenda o doktore Fauste*. Ed. V. M. Zhirmunskii. 2nd ed., corrected (Moscow, 1978): 257–362.

Zyrianov, I. V. 1975 'Zagovor i svadebnaia poeziia.' *Fol'klor i literature Urala*, vyp. 2 (Perm', 1975): 49–81.

OR NBU – Otdel rukopisei Nacional'noi biblioteki Ukrainy im. V. I. Vernadskogo (The Manuscript division of the V. I. Vernadsky National Library of Ukraine) (Kiev)

(Translated by Sibelan E.S. Forrester).

11

Slovenian Charms Between South Slavic and Central European Tradition

Monika Kropej

As the title of this chapter suggests, parallels to Slovene charms can be found in the South Slavic oral tradition, and in the cultures of Central Europe, especially in the Friuli, Romanic, Austrian, and Swiss Alpine heritages. In Slovenia, charming typically consists of several elements, all of which aim at restoring an original state of order. Incantation procedures are a system of communication between the conjurer and impure forces, representing a fight between the good and the evil. It is necessary to know folk magic and symbolism as well as a specific model of the world, because these are namely the elements that provide the key to correct understanding of the act of charming. Of special importance is the right time of performing the ritual of incantation: the phases of the moon can greatly affect the outcome of the ritual, hastening or impeding the healing process. Friday, for instance, is the day most suited for this kind of work. Night is an especially appropriate time, but so are noon, early morning before sunrise, and early evening after sunset. People also believed that magic was potent on St. George's Day, on the night before Pentecost Sunday, on Midsummer Day, or during Ember Week. Of equal importance is also the right – the sacred – location. Sacral incantational rites could take place by a hearth; at a threshold; in a courtyard; by a well (in myths the well represents the boundary between that which belongs to oneself and the foreign, between this world and the one beyond); at crossroads; by a fence or a brook, etc. Nowadays incantation rites are usually performed at home.

A charm contains a series of lexemes, among which the following are typical: the crag, the forest, the mountain, the river, the sea, the path, the field, the yard, the house, the village, etc.; a text or a prayer that follows a charm and which has to be repeated a certain number of times: three, five, seven, nine, and so forth; this odd number, which can also be termed a 'fairy number', therefore possesses a symbolic value. The same can be said for colors: the most frequent colors that occur in charms are white, red, and black. The evil is addressed by name: the underworld worm, evil blood, spell, etc. The true power of invocation, however, is contained in charm itself, in saying the words that supposedly have a magic power. As in hypnosis, in which a hypnotic state can provoke certain conditional reflexes, a word can cause organic changes in a patient. Thus charms can be said to operate by the power of suggestion or autosuggestion. The strength of words and thoughts in formulas such as the charms, supplications, oaths, prayers, exorcist formulas, etc. is obvious. Charms represent one of the oldest forms of struggle against disease.

In contemporary Slovenia, charming is generally performed at home. Healers usually use different herbal concoctions and 'transfers', like objects such as bread, knife, kerchief or a towel, for instance, which is placed on the sore part of the body; the patient continues putting the towel on the sore place at home.

Verbal charms in the village of Windish Bleiberg/ Slovenji Plajberg

Most of my own field research was undertaken in Windish Bleiberg/Slovenji Plajberg – a small mountainous village in Carinthia on the border between Austria and Slovenia, inhabited mostly by Slovene-speakers. Several hundred people still live in the vicinity, cultivate the land, breeding cattle, and (ever since the lead-mine was closed down in 1904) working in nearby towns.

Marija Wieser, who was born in the year 1923 in Windish Bleiberg, was my main informant. She uses charms to heal people and animals, to drive away thunderstorms, hail, and strong winds. Like many other healers, she possesses divinatory and a gift of premonition. In her dreams she can foresee future event. She can also predict danger or recognize signs predicting an accident, death, etc. Ever since her childhood, she has felt that she has possessed a gift for performing this kind of work. Marija has learned her magic skills from when she was a young girl, firstly from her grandmother, then from her elders – mostly women – to whom she had delivered the post (in her youth she used to be a postwoman).

In time, she married and had five children. Her husband's (Milan's) grandfather, Klančnik, knew a lot about such things and was considered to be a very wise man. He cured animals. She owned a manuscript book of folk medicine called the *Kolomon Book of Charms* that was the most commonly used book of this sort in Slovenia. Marija, who had received the manuscript from an old woman who was also a charmer, learned several charms from it, along with some apocryphal prayers. In Carinthia, mothers and wives copied out the charm against bullets and shots from the *Kolomon Book of Charms* and sewed it into shirts or undershirts of their soldiering sons and husbands to protect them during battles. When performing magic, Marija sometimes read from the *Kolomon Book of Charms*, or copied magic formulas from it.

When charming, Marija often uses a kerchief. She twists it into a belt, places it on a sore spot, puts both hands upon it, and utters a relevant charm over it. The kerchief is then given to the patient who wraps it around the sore spot when needed. Often she also uses a towel brought by her customers. Folding it and placing it upon the sore spot, she repeats the charm three times. The afflicted person should not thank her at the end of the ritual, but should remain silent. A kerchief is very often used for healing afflicted animals as well because Marija does not heal them by placing her hands upon them. If cattle have swollen legs, for instance, Marija utters her charm while placing her hands upon the kerchief. The kerchief is then wound around the swollen leg in such a way that that part of it her hands had touched lies directly on the afflicted part of the leg. She also cures cattle by cooking certain household items such as the skin of an Easter ham, to which she added salt and pepper.

When warding off thunderstorms, or other weather calamities, Marija uses a small two-hundred-year-old bell that had been blessed at Višarje in the church of pilgrimage, and has been in her family's possession for years. When chasing away storms she occasionally uses a napkin which had been blessed in church on Easter Saturday – but it should not be washed – hanging it over a fence. Other objects used magically include ashes, which have been blessed in church on Ash Wednesday (these would be scattered against the wind to drive strong winds away), and rakes, forks and scythes, which could be placed under the eaves to help prevent hail.

At times she drove off thunderstorms by ringing a bell, sprinkling holy water, making a fire, pouring a spoonful of holy water over it, and by throwing flowers into the fire. Hail or thunderstorms would not damage a field if holy water had been buried into the ground in three corners of the field – as the rhyme has it: '*Blessed churchbells, ring, fetch the water from three parishes!*'. It is necessary to ensure that the plough does not come into contact with this holy water and that the holes in which the water was put were sufficiently deep.

Marija's charm to ward off a thunderstorm

Tam gor je na megla,	*Up there is a fog,*
tam gor je na meglica,	*Up there is a mist*
med njim je pa sveta trojica.	*And in between the Holy Trinity.*
Kdor je pa hujš,	*Whoever is tougher*
naj se gre pa skušat z nami.	*Should try their luck with us.*

She then made the sign of a cross in front of herself and said 'God the Father, help; God the Son, help; God the Holy Ghost, help.'

She could also chase away a thunderstorm if she was quick enough and managed to say the proper charm as soon as mists started to gather over the Vranca and the Žingarca Mountains, by saying:

Vsi žegnani zvonovi zazvonite,	*All the blessed churchbells ring,*
zaženite,	*ring,*
ta ti črne megle,	*And chase away that black fog,*
ta ti v sive peči,	*To the grey cliffs,*
čer se nobena reč ne veseli,	*In which no thing can be merry,*
nobena roža ne cveti.	*And no flower blooms.*

Than she made the sign of the cross in all four directions: *God the Father, help, God the Son, help; God the Holy Ghost, help.*

Marija also used the following charm to cure sprain or broken bone, meniscus, backpain, and for sick cattle:

Buh pa svetə Petər	*God and St. Peter*
sta črez ano brv šwa.	*Were walking across a footbridge*
Swet Petər se je pa noho zgənu	*When St. Peter sprained his foot.*
in Ježəš Krištuš je pa te besede	*Jesus Christ then spoke*
zgovoru:	*the following words:*
'Prim se kri kərvi,	*'Blood stick to blood,*
žiwa žiwe,	*vein to vein,*
čita čite,	*sinew to sinew,*
ust usti,	*bone to bone,*
məso məsa,	*flesh to flesh,*
ožaože.'	*Skin to skin.'*

Then she crossed herself three times: *God the Father, help. God the Son, help. God the Holy Ghost, help.* Then she said the Lord's Prayer, repeating the whole procedure three times. The sick person is forbidden from thanking her because Jesus Christ has also given of his own free will. Marija Wieser adds that it also helps if sore joints are smeared with ordinary oil. (Another variant of this charm collected from the same woman can be found in group 4 below.)

Charm against rheumatism, gout, sore joints

V imenu Boga očeta in sina Jezusa Kristusa, v imenu Svetega duha, amen.
    In the name of the Father, the Son, and the Holy Spirit! Amen.

Ti proti skrmini,	*You, who are against rheumatism,*
ki sušiš kri in meso!	*Who dry up blood and flesh!*
Jaz te zapovem	*I command you*

v imenu Boga očeta, Sina in Svetega duha,
    In the name of the Father, the Son and the Holy Spirit,

v imenu (visoke) Svete Trojice,	*In the name of the Holy Trinity,*
da moraš ven s teh kosti,	*To leave these bones,*
ven s teh sklepov,	*To leave these joints,*

ven s tega žegnanga, krščenga, birmanega trupla,
    To leave this blessed, baptized, confirmed body,

na visoko goro,	*And go to high mountains,*
globoke grabne,	*To deep gorges,*
kamor noben žegn ne doseže,	*Where no blessing can reach you,*
nobeni zvonovi ne odzvonijo,	*Where no bell tolls,*
noben petelin ne odpoje.	*Where no rooster crows,*
Tam ti vse zrij in skoplji!	*Go and dig and rout around!*

Pomagaj Boh oče, Boh sin in Sveti duh,
    Help me, Father, Son, and the Holy Spirit,

(Sveta Trojica,) ljuba roža devica Marija,
    The Holy Trinity, Virgin Mary, you white blossom,

sveta krstna patronja,	*The holy baptizing patroness,*
svetih pet krvavih ran	*The five holy, bleeding wounds of*
Jezusovih in sveti Valentin.	*Christ, and St. Valentine.*

(Then say the Lord's Prayer three times.)

Charm against cramp

Jezusova desna stran,	*The right side of Jesus,*
katera je bila prebodena,	*Which had been pierced,*

tam je tekla kri in voda.	*There bled blood and ran water.*
Prosim te operi vse te bolečine	*Please cleanse all this pain,*
in skrij v svoje svete rane.	*Hide it within your holy wounds!*
Pomagaj Buh oče, Buh sin in	*Help us, Father, Son and the*
Buh Sveti duh!	*Holy Spirit,*
Pomagaj še ljuba roža	*Help us, Virgin Mary, our dear flower.*
Devica Marija.	

(Make the sign of the cross 3 times.)

Classification of the Slovenian healing- and weather charms[1]

Charms are narrated magic formulas containing elements of exorcism, different kinds of magic practices,[2] subtraction, repetition, as well as elements or parts of the myths and parables. Slovenian charms can be by their formal features classified into the following main groups:

1. Formulas driving affliction or a culprit away to an inaccessible place
2. Formulas with God or a Saint prohibiting a culprit from causing harm
3. Formulas ordering a culprit to take back poison,
4. Formulas of supplication to heal afflicted tissue,
5. Narrations of analogous acts (including formulas of cessation,
6. Formulas of subtraction,
7. Formulas asking for relief from pain for holy wounds,
8. Narrations of parables,
9. Formulas asking for Saints' help.

1 Formulas driving affliction or a culprit away to an inaccessible place

I Charms against rheumatism, gout, sore joints

V imenu Boga Očeta	*In the name of the Father,*
in sina Jezusa Kristusa,	*And the son Jesus Christ,*
v imenu sv. Duha.	*And in the name of the Holy Spirit.*
Amen.	*Amen.*
Ti proti skrmini,	*You, who are against rheumatism,*
ki sušiš kri in meso!	*Who dry up blood and flesh!*
Jaz ti zapovem	*I command you*
v imenu Boga Očeta, Sina,	
sv. Duha,	

In the name of the Father, the Son and the Holy Spirit

v imenu sv. Trojice,	*In the name of the Holy Trinity,*
da moraš ven s teh kosti,	*To leave these bones,*
ven s teh sklepov,	*To leave these joints,*
ven s tega žegnanega, krščenega,	*To leave this blessed, baptized,*
birmanega trupla,	*confirmed body,*
na te visoke gore,	*And go to high mountains,*
globoke grabne,	*To deep gorges,*
kamor noben žegen ne doseže,	*Where no blessing can reach you,*
nobeni zvonovi ne odzvonijo,	*Where no bell tolls,*
noben petelin ne odpoje,	*Where no rooster crows,*
tam ti vse zrij in skoplji!	*Go and dig and rout around!*
Pomagaj Bog Oče, Bog Sin	*Help me, Father, Son, and*
in sv. Duh,	*the Holy Spirit,*
sv. Trojica, bela roža	*The Holy Trinity, Virgin Mary,*
devica Marija,	*you white blossom,*
sv. krstna patronja,	*The holy baptizing patroness,*
sv. pet krvavih ran Jezusovih in	*The five holy, bleeding wounds*
sv. Valentin.	*of Christ, and St. Valentine.*

Say the Lord's Prayer 3 times,
Repeat 3 times.
(collected from Marija Wieser).

II   Charms against bone tuberculosis

Bodi ramar ali ramarka,	*Be you he-tuberculosis or she-tuberculosis,*
pojdi na javor,	*Go to a maple tree,*
čez javor na list,	*From the maple to a leaf,*
čez list na planino,	*From the leaf to a mountain,*
kjer nobeden zvon ne zvoni,	*Where no bell tolls,*
noben stol ne stoji,	*No chair stands,*
nobena rit ne sedi,	*No behind sits,*
nobeden ogenj ne kuha,	*No fire cooks,*
nobena usta ne jedo.	*No mouth eats.*
Tam ti prebivaj, tu nimaš kaj iskati!	*There you stay, this is not where you belong!*

Jaz ti zagovorim v imenu Boga Očeta, Boga Sina in sv. Duha.
I beseech you in the name of the Father, the Son and the Holy Spirit.
(Košir and Möderndorfer, 1926, 90).

2   Formulas with God or a Saint prohibiting a culprit from causing harm

I   Charms against gout, rheumatism

Throw a pebble from a brook into a pot, pour scalding water over it, place the pot on the afflicted area and say:

Jezus je na Veliko noč zjutraj zgodaj vstal,	*On Easter morning Jesus Christ rose early,*
vzel zlato palico in šel po svetu.	*Took a golden stick and left to roam the world.*
Srečali so ga protini in skrmine,	*He met gouts and rheumatisms,*
in Jezus jih vpraša: 'Kam pa greste?'	*And asked them: 'Where are you headed?'*

Pa so odgovorili: 'Mi gremo N.-ove kosti ven metat, ude krijat, truplo v črno zemljo polagat.'

They replied: 'We're off to dig out N's bones, to twist his limbs, to put his body into the blackened sod.'

Jezus jim odgovori: *Jesus said:*

'Vi nimate pravice N-ove kosti ven metat, ude zvijat, truplo v črno zemljo polagat.

'You have no right to dig out N's bones, to twist his limbs, to put his body into the blackened sod.

Ampak pojdite na visoke planine,	*Off you go to high mountains,*
kjer noben črv ne prebiva,	*Where no worm lives,*
noben petelin ne zapoje,	*Where no rooster crows,*
tam naj vas požrejo črne megle.'	*And be devoured by black fog.'*
Pomagaj Bog Oče, Bog Sin in sv. Duh.	*Help me, Father, Son and the Holy Spirit.*
	(Košir and Möderndorfer, 1926, 98).

We can also consider an old charm against poison from snakebite recorded in Rezia in 1967.[3]

3   Formulas ordering a culprit to take back poison

I   Charms against poison

Strup jaz te zagovorim u tem djani,	*Poison, I beseech you in this act,*
ko prosim na pomoč sv. Urha in	*Ask help from St. Ulrich and*
sv. Marjeto.	*St. Margaret.*

Te zagovorim pred živim Bogom,	*Beseeching you in front of the living God*
da moraš ti strup nazaja uzet vse strupne živali.	*To take back the poison of all poisonous animals.*
Ako ti nisi živ, naj ga vzame tvoj žlahtnik.	*If you are no longer alive, your kin has to take it back for you.*

Make the sign of the cross, blow onto bread, 3 times stab it
with a knife.
Say the Lord's Prayer, Hail Mary.

(Križnik).

II   Charms against poison

Tam stoji ena sv. gora, tam stoji en sv. stol.	*There is a holy mountain, there is a holy chair.*
Na tem stolu sedi sv. Šempas,	*St. Shempas is sitting on the chair,*
v rokah drži en sv. meč.	*Holding a holy sword in his hands.*
Prišla je k njemu devica Marija,	*The Virgin Mary comes to him,*

prinesla na rokah vsmiljenega Jezusa in mu je rekla:
> *Holding the merciful Jesus in her hands, and says:*

'Zakaj ne prеženeš tega strupa in to žival, od katere je prišel?
> *'Why do you not drive away this poison and the animal from which it had come?*

Ti prеženi ta strup na to žival od katere je prišel'
> *Chase away the poison back into the animal from which it had come!'*

Say the Lord's Prayer in the honor of St. Shempas for 3 times over a
piece of bread, give the bread to the animal.

(Dolenc, 1999, 159).

4   Formulas of supplication to heal afflicted tissue

I   Charm against sprain or broken bone

Ježuš pa svet Peter	*Jesus and St. Peter*
sta čez eno brv šla,	*were crossing a footbridge.*
svet Peter si je pa eno nogo zganu.	*When St. Peter broke his leg*
Ježuš je pa te besede zgovoru:	*Jesus spoke these words:*
"Prim se kri krvi,	*'Blood to blood,*
žila žile,	*Vein to vein,*
kita kite,	*Sinew to sinew,*
kost kosti,	*Bone to bone,*

meso mesa,	*Flesh to flesh,*
koža kože.	*Skin to skin.'*

This last phrase is uttered while making the sign of the cross. Then the Lord's Prayer is repeated three times. (Collected from Marija Wieser).

5   Narrations of an analogous act

I   Charm against fire

Ta voda ta vogn pogasi,	*This water shall put out this fire*
kakor je ob potoku Jordan	*Just as by the Jordan brook*
Jovanez Jezusa krstil.	*John the Baptist baptized Jesus,*
Je velik vogn pogasu.	*Putting out a big fire.*

(Križnik).

II   Charm against fire

Sv. Neža, sv. Boštjan pa sv. Florjan,	*St. Agnes, St. Sebastian and St. Florian,*
nesite vodo,	*Carry the water,*
pogasite ogenj!	*Extinguish the fire!*
V imenu Očeta in Sina in sv. Duha.	*In the name of the Father, the Son and the Holy Spirit.*

(Dolenc, 1999, 55).

III   Charm against bleeding

Nenek (dedek) mlinar, oče mlinar, sin mlinar.
             Grandpa a miller, father a miller, son a miller.
Kakor se bodo ti trije mlinarji ustavili pri nebeških vratih,
             Just as these three millers shall stop at the heavenly gate,
tako naj se ti ustavi kri!   *You shall stop bleeding!*
Pomagaj Bog Oče, Bog Sin in sv. Duh.   *Help us, Father, Son and the Holy Spirit.*

(Košir and Möderndorfer, 1926, 104).

6   Formulas of subtraction

I   Charm against swelling

Koliko je uredov?	*How many swellings are there?*
Jih je devet,	*Are there nine,*
ni jih devet, jih je osem,	*Not nine, but eight,*
ni jih osem, jih je sedem ...	*Not eight, but seven...*

(Košir and Möderndorfer, 1926, 101).

7 Formulas asking for relief from pain for holy wounds

I   Charm against cramp

Jezusova desna stran,	*The right side of Jesus,*
katera je bila prebodena,	*Which had been pierced,*
tam je tekla kri in voda.	*Bled blood and water.*
Prosim te, operi vse te bolečine	*Please cleanse all this pain,*
in skij v svoje svete rane!	*Hide it within your holy wounds!*

Make the sign of the cross 3 times: Help us, Father, Son
and the Holy Spirit,
Help us, Virgin Mary, our dear flower.
(collected from Marija Wieser).

8   Narrations of parable

I   Charm for Healing a Broken Bone or a Sprain

Sv. Florijan je konjiče pasu,	*While St. Florian was grazing his horse*
je črez skalco padu,	*He fell over a rock,*
nogco si je zvinu.	*Spraining his ankle.*
Klicov je Boga Očeta, Sina	*He called to the Father, the Son and the*
in sv. Duha:	*Holy Spirit:*
'Pomagajte, da bo moja	*'Please help heal my poor leg!'*
nogca zdrava!'	
Viš, je vstav, skoču je,	*Lo and behold, he jumped up,*
nogca je bla zdrava.	*And his leg was healed.*
	(Košir and Möderndorfer, 1926, 109).

9   Formulas asking for Saints' help

In this group is we have the oldest surviving Slovenian charm, which is
against snakebite, and was written about 1641:

I   Charm against snakebite

Stoi ena slata Gora,	*There stands a golden Mountain,*
Na gori stoy ena sueta Zerku,	*On top of which is a sacred church,*
V zerkui lessi Gospud Sueti Jobst,	*In the church lies Saint Job,*
K nemu je preshla luba	*To whom fled our dear*
Diuiza Maria,	*Virgin Mary,*
Ti lesshis inui trdu spish.	*You lie fast asleep.*
Vsatani gori inui pomagi N.N.	*Wake up and help N.N.*

Od tega hudiga Zerua	*To get rid of this evil*
Ka zeuiedi ne,	*Worm not to bite,*
De bode tako sdrau,	*So he can get as well,*
Koker ie od suiga ozheta inui	*As he was when he was born of*
matere royen,	*his father and mother,*
Na to zerno semlo (črno zemljo)	*On this black soil and blue skies,*
patu Synu Nebu,	
In nomine Paris et Filius et	
Spiritus Sancti. Amen.[4]	

II   Charms against gout

Vsi božji svetniki,	*All the Lord's saints,*
vas prosim za pomoč za tega človeka,	*I beg you to help this man,*
v imenu sv. Florijana, sv. Boštjana,	*In the name of St. Florian,*
sv. Urha,	*St. Sebastian, St. Ulrich,*
ko tdno verujem, da je Bog	*I firmly believe that God is*
vsemogočen,	*almighty,*
da bo ta moja prošnja pomagala.	*That my plea shall help.*
Ker vi prti, vas zagovorim,	*I beseech you, gout,*
v imenu Boga Očeta, Boga Sina in	*In the name of the Father, the*
sv. Duha.	*Son and the Holy Spirit.*
	(Križnik).

Slovenian charms within Central and Southeast Europe

Verbal charms, at least as far at their structure and concept are concerned, often differ little from nation to nation. The reason for this would seem to be the common origin of charms deriving from the common sources and archetypes. Even Egyptian Hermetic writings, and Kabbalistic magic contained charms. Similar charms were later written in other magic books such as the *Kolomon Book of Charms* (Kolomon is the patron saint of cattle); the *Defence of the Spirit*, the *Book of Elizabeth*, *The First and the Second Book of Moses*, *The Book on the Suffering of Christ*, the *Apocryphal Book*, the *Tobias Book of Charms*, the *Household Book of Charms* ('Hišni žegen'), the *Egyptian Book of Dreams*, *Die Sieben Himmelsriegel*, *Schlüssel des Salomonis*, manuscripts of charms, and other books on magic. Since different cultures possessed different perceptions of the world however, there are some differences to be found despite kindred sources and the remarkable age of invocation formulas. It is clear that different social and cultural groups understandably infused these formulas with local elements. Analysing these formulas we can notice that there is a definite connection between the local myths and cosmological perceptions and the local charms.

The tradition of charms was also influenced by the Catholic – and in some Balkan regions the Muslim – religion which was spreading in the Middle Ages. In Slovenia, the Christian religion was disseminated mostly by Irish monks and, to a lesser degree, by Ss. Cyril and Methodius. To this day, Slovenia and Croatia are mostly Catholic while the prevalent religion in Serbia is Orthodox. Central European/Romanic/Germanic cultural circles on one side, and the Byzantine/Islamic/Oriental on the other, have tightly intermingled with each other. The saints, who have replaced older deities and demi-gods, are therefore locally determined. Beside the Virgin Mary, Jesus Christ, God the Father, and the Holy Ghost the most frequent deities in Slovene invocations are St. Peter, St. Paul, St. Margaret, St. Ulrich ('Urh'), St. Pelagius, etc.

In Macedonian charms the impure forces are exorcised into green mountains, into a cool spot by a brook, or to Đurđa (*Georgia*) the shepherd-girl of illness. In the mid-nineteenth century, many charms were collected by Marko Cepenkov. The still-preserved Serbian invocations are similar to those in Macedonia and Bulgaria, often addressing St. Evrem. Many Serbian charms had been collected already by Vuk Karađić. It is interesting that John Miles Foley who has been doing comparison between Old English and Serbian charms has found many similarities between them.[5] In Bosnia, the oldest layer of charms has been affected by Islam; the third layer has developed under the influence of the Catholic Church. The latter has also affected Croatian charms which, due to its influence, resemble those in Slovenia. Many Croatian charms, which were collected by Mijat Stojanović in the 19th century, were published in *Arkiva za povjesnitnicu jugoslovensku u Zagrebu*. St. Anne has an important role in them, along with the Virgin Mary and Jesus Christ. Slovene charms, published by Karel Štrekelj in *Slovenske narodne pesmi III* (1895–1923 nos 5163–5180), cure snakebite, sprain, harmful spells, stye, swelling, gout, and thunderstorm. The book also features two charms that work against a hunter who wants to shoot an animal. By far the most frequent charms in Slovenia are the ones against snakebite. The oldest record of a Slovene charm, a charm against toothache, was written in Latin in the second half of the twelfth century. The oldest one in Slovene, which worked against snakebite, was written down around 1641 (see group 9 of my classification). It was found in the library of the Lord of Turjak manor in Lower Carniola/Dolenjska. It had been copied by the parish priest in Dolenjske Toplice and was found by Fran Levstik several centuries later.

Slovenian charms are very close to both Austrian and Italian charms. Similarities can be found especially in charms in which the charmer orders an illness or an injury such as bleeding, for instance, to leave the body: *'Stop, blood, stay as still as the Red Sea, only so little blood may flow from your wounds as from the Red Sea. Stop, blood, stop, blood.'* Or: *'Just as St. John baptized Christ in the Red Sea that stood still; N.N., your blood should stand still, stop, blood, stop, blood...'* (Grabner, 1985, 219). Similarities can also be found in charms with which an charmer exorcises impure forces, for instance from leg to flesh, from flesh to skin, from skin to lightning or arrow, etc. (Imfeld, 1994, 128). And charms similar to Slovenian examples of charms against thunderstorms can be found in northern Italy and Switzerland, some of which were identified by Milko Matičetov. An example of such a charm comes from Ter in Italy:

Bejži bejži mahla,	*Run away fog,*
ku je oća tu travi,	*because the father is in the grass,*
u ma sakiru ta na lavi,	*he has an axe on his head,*
rita, rita, podkorita,	*ger, ger, manger,*
u će ti noe podrobiti.[6]	*he will tear your legs off.*

Similar parallels between Slavic – especially the ones from Carniola and Carinthia – and Romanic/Germanic charms against snakebite were identified by Ivan Grafenauer.[7] He sought their origin in Old Saxon and Old Bavarian charms from the ninth century.

Cosmological elements in Slovenian charms

Local narrative tradition reflects people's notions about the triple character of the world, and this can be perceived also in folk charms. They speak of the underground world with its snakes, dragons and devils, with the wild chase (*divja jaga*) which comes under the ground, and rages around in wintertime, specially during the twelve sacred nights around Christmas. It rushes through the fields with the barking of dogs, the howling of cows, horses, cats, dogs, dragons and other beasts, making a terrible racket.

The sphere, which is usually invisible to people but is still surrounding the earth, is the home of numerous creatures: fairies, wild men and wild women, nightmares or incubuses, poor souls or enchanted souls, water sprites, giants and heathen, gnomes, goblins and dwarfs, and many more. All of these creatures either help people, giving them advice on how to live with nature, teaching them different skills and showing them hidden treasures, or attack people, frighten them, avenge themselves upon them, etc.

The celestial world is populated with angels. Old pagan deities, however, have long ago been replaced by Mother Mary, Jesus Christ, God the Father, and the Holy Spirit, and the saints, and they are addressed even in invocations. Women especially seek help from the Virgin Mary. This tripartite cosmological conception of the world can be seen in charms. In Slovenian charms we often find the old scheme of the cosmical mountain or the tree of life. In a linear image we often find the following sequence in the charms: *you evil, go from the land, over the water, in to the tree, on the mountain!. . . .* The vertical conception of the cosmos is here represented in linear terms.

In the charms this type of cosmological perception of the world occupies an important role. The tree and the mountain are frequent allegories found in the charms. The mountain, as an inaccessible and sacred place, is located behind the land, the water and the tree. The high unattainable mountain cliffs and tops are considered to be the other world where bad spirits and the evil can be banished. The second, equally obvious parallel between the cosmological perceptions which are recognizable in charms as well as in folk tales, is the basic myth about the Dragon Slayer. The very concept of the charms is namely in the battle between the good and the evil (for more on this, see: Toporov, 1993).

Notes

1. This classification was first presented in my article (Kropej, 2003: 67–72).
2. Sympathetic magic, antipathetic magic, transferential magic, magic involving amulets, magic involving herbs, verbal magic, written magic etc. (Roper, 2003: 31).
3. Matičetov, 1972, p. 186:

Gospobuk nu svete Sampjere nu svete Sampawle	*God and St. Peter and St. Paul!*
ni so šle po ne pote	*The Lord walked along a path,*
anu so srëtle no invalanjano kačo.	*And he met a poisonous snake.*
Anu wony so reklë ta w nju:	*Whereupon he said to the snake:*
'Da ti, invalanjana kača,	*'Hey, you poisonous snake,*
ko-baj te dilaš?'	*What are you doing?'*
'Ja' – na rekla – 'ja mən trikradwysti valenj:	*'My poison,' said the snake, 'Is three times two hundred strong,*
wse to, ke ja pyknen,	*So that everything I bite*

to ma wmrit anu krapet!'	*Shall die and perish!'*
Anu Gospobuk nu svete Sampjere nu	*God and St. Peter and St. Paul!*
svete Sampawle	
wony so reklë:	*The Lord said:*
'Mi mamo trikradwyjste nu dno	*'Our medicine is three times two*
medežino,	*hundred strong,*
ke wsë to, ke me namažemo,	*So that everything we anoint*
nu wsë to, ke me dimo,	*And everything that we do*
to ma wošćapet anu prejet	*Shall vanish and shall pass –*
an ti, invalanjana kača, te məš krapet!'	*And you, poisonous snake,*
	are to die!'

4. Dolenc, 1999, 158.
5. Foley, 1980, p.80.
6. Matičetov, 1961: 160.
7. Grafenauer, 1961, 148–52.

Bibliography

Conrad, J. L. 1983. Magic Charms and Healing Rituals in Contemporary Yugoslavia. *Southeastern Europe* 10:2, 99–120.

Dapit, R. 2001. Moč besede, moč prednikov. Zagovorni obrazci v Reziji in drugje [Power of the Word, Power of the Ancestors. Incantations in Resia and Elswhere]. *Studia mythologica Slavica* 4: 141–58.

Davies, O. 1996. Healing Charms in Use in England and Wales 1700–1950. *Folklore* 107: 19–32.

Dolenc, M. 1999. *Zagovori v slovenski ljudski medicini [Charms in Slovenian Folk Medicine]*. Ed. By Z. Zupanič Slavec and M. Makarovič, Ljubljana: DZS.

Foley, J. 1980. Epic and Charm in Old English and Serbo-Croatian Oral Tradition. *Comparative Criticism: a Yearbook* 2. Cambridge: Cambridge University Press, pp. 71–92.

Grabner, E. 1967. *Volksmedizin – Probleme und Forschungsgeschichte*. Darmstadt: Wissenschaftliche Buchgesellschaft.

Grabner, E. 1985. *Grundzüge einer ostalpinen Volksmedizin*. Wien: Verlag der Oesterreichischen Akademie der Wissenschaften.

Grafenauer, I. 1907. O 'Duhovni brambi' in nje postanku [On 'Spiritual Defence']. *Časopis za zgodovino in narodopisje* 4: 1–70.

Grafenauer, I. 1937. Najstarejši slovenski zagovori [The Oldest Slovene Incantations], *Časopis za zgodovino in narodopisje* 32: 275–293.

Grafenauer, I. 1943. 'Duhovna bramba' in 'Kolomonov žegen' ['Spiritual Defence' and the 'Kolomon Book of Charms']. *Razprave/Dissertationes* 1, št. 4, Ljubljana, pp. 201–339.

Grafenauer, I., 1961. Ein altpflanzerisch-chtonischer Wurmsegen in der Schweiz und in Slovenien. *Alpes Orientales* III, Basel, pp. 148–52.

Hampp, I., 1961. *Beschwoerung, Segen und Gebet. Untersuchungen zum Zauberspruch aus dem Bereich der Volksheilkunde*. Stuttgart.

Imfeld, K. 1994. Alpine Bann- und Segensbraeuche. *Alpenbraeuche – Riten und Tradition in den Alpen*. Wien: Edition Tau, pp. 125–42.

Ivanov, V. V. & Toporov, V. N. 1974. *Issledovanija v oblasti slavjanskih drevnostej: Leksičeskie i frazeologičeskie voprosi rekonstrukcii tekstov* [*Research in the field of Slavonic antiquities: Lexical and phraseological contributions towards a reconstruction of texts*]. Moskva.

Košir, P. 1922. Ljudska medicina na Koroškem [Folk Medicine in Carinthia]. *Časopis za zgodovino in narodopisje* 17: 20–32.

Košir, P. & Möderndorfer, V. 1926. Ljudska medicina med Koroškimi Slovenci [Folk Medicine Among the Carinthian Slovenes]. *Časopis za zgodovino in narodopisje* 21: 85–112.

Koštial, I. 1911. Sieben Beschwörungsformeln aus dem slowenischen Teile des Küstenlandes. *Zeitschrift für österreichische Volkskunde* 17: 171–3.

Kropej, M. 2000. Magija in magično zdravljenje v pripovednem izročilu in ljudsko zdravilstvo danes [Magic as Reflected in Folk Traditions and in Contemporary Folk Medicine]. *Etnolog* 10: 75–85.

Kropej, M. 2003. Charms in the Context of Magic Practice. The Case of Slovenia. *Electronic Journal of Folklore* 24: 62–77.

Matičetov, M. 1961. Uno scongiuro sloveno contro la nebbia e i suoi corrispondenti svizzeri, *Alpes Orientales* 3: 160–3.

Matičetov, M. 1972. Rezijanski zagovor proti kačjemu strupu [A Resian Charm against Snake Venom]. *Traditiones* (Ljubljana) 1: 186.

Möderndorfer, V. 1964. *Ljudska medicina pri Slovencih* [*Folk Medicine in Slovenia*]. Ljubljana: SAZU.

Mrkun, A. 1934. Narodopisno blago iz Dobrepoljske doline [Ethnographic Materials from Dobrepoljska dolina]. *Etnolog* 7: 1–37.

Omersa, N. 1922. Zagovorna kniga Antona Petriča. *Časopis za zgodovino in narodopisje* 17, Maribor.

Pócs, E. 1999. *Between the Living and the Dead*. Budapest: Central European University Press.

Radenković, L. 1996. *Narodna bajanja kod južnih Slovena* [*Folk Charms Among the South Slavs*]. Beograd: Prosveta.

Roper, J. 2003. Towards a Poetics, Rhetorics and Proxemics of Verbal Charms. *Electronic Journal of Folklore* 24: 7–49.

Šašel, J. & Ramovš, F. 1936. *Narodno blago iz Roža* [Folklore from Rož], Maribor: Arhiv Zgodovinskega društva.

Šindin, S. G. 1999. Ob odnom vozmožnom vostočnoslavjanskom 'protorituale' (na materiale zagovornoj tradicii) [On the Possible East Slavic 'Protoritual'. Based on the Tradition of Invocation]. *Studia mythologica Slavica* 2: 245–58.

Štrekelj, K. 1895–1923. *Slovenske narodne pesmi* [Slovenian Folk Songs] I–IV, Ljubljana: Slovenska matica.

Toporov, V. N. 1993. *Ob indoevropejskoj zagovornoj tradicii. Issledovanija v oblasti baltoslavjanskoj duhovnoj kulturi : Zagovor* [*On the Indoeuropean Incantations. Research on Balto-Slavic Folklore: The Charm*]. Moskva 1993.

Zablatnik, P. 1972. Iz ljudske medicine pri koroških Slovencih [From Folk Medicine in the Carinthian Slovenes], *Traditiones* (Ljubljana) 1: 181–5.

Other sources

Križnik, Gašpar – (unpaginated) manuscript in the Archive of the Institute of Slovenian Ethnology, Scientific Research Centre of the Slovenian Academy of

Sciences and Arts, Ljubljana: ŠZ 1/25. Printed: Monika Kropej, Karel Štrekelj. Iz vrelcev besedne ustvarjalnosti (Karel Štrekelj. From the Springs of Poetics), Ljubljana 2001.

Wieser, Marija – Tape recordings of Maria Wieser by Monika Kropej, Carinthia, 1996–2001. Archive of the Institute of Slovenian Ethnology, Scientific Research Centre of the Slovenian Academy of Sciences and Arts, Ljubljana.

12
Finnish Snake Charms

Henni Ilomäki

The snake as a magical character

The order of reptiles contains about 2,500 species of snakes. Due to biological and physical variation, popular interpretations of the qualities of snakes differ greatly between cultures. But generally facets emerge, due to its appearance, way of motion and (supposed) dangerousness, the snake has frequently been seen as an anomalous, and often also mythical, animal. Due to this a rich snake-lore exists. Despite contradictory elements in oral traditions worldwide, it would be foolhardy to assume that the variety found in the interpretations of and attitudes taken towards snakes is solely due to its multiplicity of species. The differences between local species have been both recognised and disregarded by people in illiterate cultures.

Besides mythical interpretations of the snake as an active creature, magical power has generally been attributed to it at a purely physical level, usually concerning healing. In many cultures, snake-skin was used to cure illnesses and snake-blood was believed have a relieving effect. According to folk beliefs, pricking a live snake with needles would strengthen its healing power (Wilson 2000, 357–9). In order to use parts of the body of the snake for healing, the animal had to be killed. An alternative to this was to make an appeal to a live snake. Because of their real or assumed dangerousness snakes have been prevented from injuring man by different methods, including charms.

Charms directed against dangerous snakes are known from cultures worldwide. Sometimes the zoological definition of this animal seems to be somewhat superficial. In an archaic Egyptian *Incantation against noxious animals*, the snake is equated with the crocodile. The lines do not actually describe the snake, instead they testify to its status as a not only a highly dangerous but also a highly honoured creature:

> *Come to me, O Lord of Gods!*
> *Drive far from me the lions coming from the earth,*
> *the crocodiles issuing from the river,*
> *the mouth of all biting reptiles coming out of their holes*
> *Stop, crocodile Mako, son of Set!*
> *Do not wave your tail;*
> *Do not work thy two arms:*
> *Do not open thy mouth.*
> *May water become as burning fire before thee!*
> *The spear of the twenty-seven gods is on thine eyes:*
> *The arm of the twenty-seven gods is on thine eye:*
> *Thou who wast fastened with metal claws to the bark of Ra,*
> *Stop, crocodile Mako, son of Set!*
>
> Egyptian magic tablet (Wedeck 1961, 21)

In Europe, ritual expulsion or exorcism has been a general feature of popular charms. Incantations are reported to have been used for instance to treat unusual swellings. In such cases, something was believed to have penetrated a person's body. Creatures most likely to intrude themselves were the creeping ones: snakes, lizards and worms. These creatures were believed to enter a victim's mouth while the person was asleep. The intruder then had to be removed (Wilson 2000, 361–2). According to a Finnish folk belief, a snake that had crawled inside a person could be persuaded to leave the human body in order to drink some milk placed on a bowl in front of a person standing on his or her head (Hästesko 1918, 64).

Belief in the curative property of the snake's body may not only derive from the animal's anomalous character, but also from the acknowledged poisonous quality of its bite. The poison was supposed to have a duplex influence: poisoning and curative. Once a poisonous snake had managed to bite a person, the wound required healing. As well as the physical removal of the poison, the healing required magical confirmation. According to a Carpathian charm, the influence of the poison was to be removed step by step.

> *From the heart you are called out into the blood,*
> *From the blood into the veins,*
> *From the veins to the flesh,*

From the flesh into the lining [of the skin],
From the lining into the skin,
From the skin into the hair.

Wilson 2000, 350

Types of Finnish snake-charms

According to Finnish folk belief as well as transmitting magical power the snake was believed to be able to cause danger not just by its bite, but also by being a bad omen. In certain charms, a special relationship between seer and snake can be recognised. According to archaic beliefs a snake could be *raised* to cause either material harm or mental disturbance. In order to make a snake attack an enemy one simply had to tell it: 'Olipa isälläsikin ennen hampaat, mihin sinun on joutunut!' (*Your father used to have teeth, where are yours?*). However, most of the oral snake-texts collected and preserved in the archives of the Finnish Literature Society in the nineteenth century or recorded in court transcripts from the seventeenth century were for healing a snakebite.

As is common for an oral folklore genre, Finnish snake-charms vary a great deal at the verbal level. Nevertheless, two main kinds of attitude may be discerned. The snake may be prevented from causing damage by a brief command: 'Maa pidä matoa, pyhä pelto perkelettä, niin kauan että ma aseen saan!' (*Earth keep the snake, holy field keep the devil, until I get a weapon!*), 'Pidätä piru hevoses, että mä suitset suuhun saan!' (*Devil keep your horse, so that I can bridle it.*) These short curses are not addressed to the snake itself, but to the sacred earth or to the Devil, both referring to a context of magical power involving a close relationship with the snake. According to Jouko Hautala, a curse (a brief command, a strict denial) is the most primitive type of charm (Hautala 1960, 31). Charms for healing a snakebite may also be of cursing character, as the snake is addressed directly and cursed to obey.

Mäne sinne, jonne kässen:	*Move where I tell you to go:*
liikkumattoman kiven alla.	*under an immobile stone*
kus ei päivä piällä paissa,	*where the sun does not shine*
kuudama kohti kuumota	*where the moon does not shine*
siit ilmossa igänä!	*not to the end of eternity*
SKVR VII:3, 1056	

Katkee paha kaheks,	*Break, evil, in two pieces,*
konna kolomeks repii!	*villain, tear in three pieces!*
SKVR VII:3, 1097	

Ihe tuivu tuskihisi,   *Suffer in pain yourself,*
paisu pakkopäivihisi   *Swell under aching pressure*
(SKVR VII:3, 1047)

The snake may also be simply told to 'bite wood, gnaw stones and stocks, not a man's meat' or not to 'rise your head upright, to stretch your throat' Salminen, *SKVR* VII:3, 1051, 1047.

Another possibility is to persuade the snake to heal the wound caused by it:

Mato musta maan alainen	*Black worm under ground*
koikero kulon sekainen	*wriggler in the grass*
riukuma risuin sekanen	*rod among brushwood*
uiku aitaen alanen	*snake under fences*
kirjava kiven alainen	*bright under the rock*
mytty mättähän alanen	*coiled under the knoll*
raukka raudan karvanen	*iron-hued wretch, thin*
ruika ruosten alainen	*under the steel-grass*
hyvin teit ettäs panit	*you did well to strike*
vielä paremmin jos parannat:	*better if you make better:*
tuo mettä metulast	*bring honey from the hive, mead*
sima simalastas	*from your meadery*
laske mettä kielestäs	*drip honey from your tongue, pour*
sima suustas valota	*mead out of your mouth*
ensimmäiseks eriks	*for the time being*
parahiksi voitehiksi	*for the best ointment*

(Honko 1993, 545; collected from Kerttu, daughter of Eerik in Halikko or Paimio, in 1666 trial records).

Here the snake is supposed to co-operate, and no threats nor hostile allusions are included. Besides the persuasive attitude of this text, the wording is also characteristic: instead of directly naming the animal, a euphemistic description is used and the snake is described as a part of nature. Similar practice is known all over the world, for instance in India a snake could be described as 'the creeper by night' (Clodd 1920, 90). The euphemistic description of the opponent – the snake – is somewhat ambiguous. When told to be humble like a twig in the grass the snake is demythologised and made ordinary, it is treated as an equal with or even inferior to the charmer. First of all, in the spiritual situation the charmer needs to get the upper hand by defining it, and in this case by using a nature-bound description. Only then the animal is told how to compensate the damage caused by it.

In order for the charmer to succeeding in dominating the opponent, Finnish charms often include a section on the opponent's origin, describing alternative backgrounds, all of which are negative. According to some charm-texts, the snake is constructed from ridiculous natural pieces or some village oddments. Other charms claim that the snake was created by an ethnic supernatural being, or by Christ, who presented the animal with its eyes. The origin may also be connected with some other church legends and saints. Yet another variant relates a narrative describing the original healing act with a Biblical background. According to a Finnish popular charm, the snake originated when an ethnic supernatural character (*lempo*, or *syöjätär*, or even in a Christian variant *Judah*!) spat on waves[1] or a rock. In these charms the wound caused by a snakebite is afterwards healed by St. Peter or by Christ himself.[2] In any event, by stating several possible origins for the snake, the charmer succeeds in dominating it.

A snake-charm may also communicate with a third party. In this case the text is not addressed to the snake, but to one or more supernatural beings. Most often this is the Virgin Mary:

Neitsyt Maaria emoni,	*Saint Mary dear lady,*
pyhä piika pikkarani,	*Sacred little maid,*
rakas äiti armollini,	*Dear tender mother*
käessä kipu vakkani,	*With a basket of pains in your hand*
tule tänne kipuja keriämäh,	*Come here to gather the pains.*
kunne kivut kiistellähe,	*Where is the pain stuffed,*
kunne vammat valittavi,	*Where the wounds gathered?*
kivut kiistele kirjavan	*Stuff the pains beside a*
kiven sivulla,	*colourful stone,*
kahen kallion rakoh!	*Between two rocks!*

(SKVR VII:3, 1068)

The helping character may also be an ethnic supernatural spirit, for instance the 'girl of pains, maiden of Hades, sitting on the hill of pains, on the rock of aches' (Niemi, *SKVR* VII:3, 1079). The pain is then sent to the hole of her stone or she may also be asked to fetch some ointment.

On the background of Finnish charms

The differences in the words and performance of the charms cited above are clear enough. But in addition to this variation, there is also heterogeneity in the ideological background of the texts, reflecting fundamentally opposed worldviews. Firstly, we can note that according to the archaic religious concepts of Finno-Ugric peoples' worldview (and indeed the worldview of many other peoples) no emphatic distinction was made between man and nature, nor between the living and the dead. The border between this existence and the world beyond was seen as vague. Man was not believed to be superior in relationship to the creatures of nature (Loorits 1949, 364; Kuusi 1963, 212–14). In ritual texts a balanced coexistence between human beings and animals was a natural starting point, and communication between them was based on this assumption. As a consequence a snake that had caused a problem had to be approached using persuasion. Accordingly, the healing act was interpreted as a process of negotiation. A charmer's aim was to communicate with the opponent, in order to make a deal.

The picture was altered, little by little, by the Christian ideology of duality. The change was slow, but the mental processes introduced in the twelfth century gradually made progress. But their success was never quite complete nor secure. In Matti Kuusi's words, the struggle between the priest and the shaman resulted, due to popular rational doubt, towards the end of the nineteenth century in a defeat for them both. The beneficiary of this was the third party: the religiously indifferent, conservative or passively adaptive peasantry. Characteristically enough, folk poetry ridicules the charmer: 'Lumooja lumelle kuoli, noita nevan notkelmalle' (*the charmer died at the snow, the witch at the hollow bog*) and correspondingly the priest 'Lukkari lumelle kuoli, pappi paskoitantereelle' (*the parish clerk died on the snow, the priest at the dungfield*) (Kuusi 1963, 273–4). Charms as ritual texts reflect people's traditional mental ideas. It seems likely that they kept to the customary worldview more conservatively than other oral texts, which may have been more apt to change. Eventually, the representatives of the Catholic Church succeeded in reinterpreting such data in the popular mind – archaic truths told by and practised by shamans came to be condemned as questionable. The binary of good and evil, embedded in Christian doctrine, led to a dualistic interpretation of reality, reorganising man's relationship to the supernatural. Not only new verbal material but also new ideas merged into the archaic texts.

The original conception of the snake as a representative of common nature changed gradually towards the snake being seen as a negative symbol of Evil, a rejected expression of sin, whose elimination was beneficial for the community. It was supposed that a permanent state of war existed between man and snake, and that a snake should be killed whenever seen, otherwise one would be forced to kill snakes by hand eternally in the post-mortal existence. A snake-killer's nine sins would be forgiven, it was believed. According to a church legend, the snake originally had feet, but lost them when cursed by Christ. This motif is quoted also in charms (e.g. Niemi, *SKVR* VII:3, 1081). It was also claimed that an attacking snake could be stopped by a cross drawn in the mud or formed by a couple of branches (Hästesko 1918, 61–5). The problems caused by a snakebite could be combined with Christian explanations in folk belief and legends. Alongside Christian elements, a negative attitude toward snakes was expressed in charms. The popular formula 'black worm under the ground, death-coloured maggot' originally referred to the snake's possible different colours (several other natural variants were usually added). Latterly, its black colour was interpreted to refer to Satan (Niemi, *SKVR* VII:3, 1075).

A parallel overlapping of archaic and Christian attitudes of snake-lore was known in the Baltic countries, which formed a region where elements of pre-Christian snake-beliefs prevailed for longer than elsewhere in Europe. In these countries, an archaic cult of the positively determined domestic snake was maintained and honoured (Gimbutas 1989). However, at the same time, a negative characterisation of the snake spread in those countries too. Although obviously Christian elements cannot be found in Baltic texts, Baltic folklore has been influenced by church teachings (Luven 2001, 97–100). The character of the snake is never unambiguous, however,

Contradictory ideas

Contradictory conceptual elements may be reflected even in a single Finnish snake-charm. An archaic variant would address the snake asking it to heal the injury. Often the text begins with a euphemistic description of the animal. This is done in order to create a situation in which the opponent and the charmer are at the same level of authority, and can recognise one another. At the same time, by revealing the outlook and the origin of the snake, the charmer dominates it. This is how the charmer is capable of making the snake obey, and to force it to heal (or in some cases, to attack) according to the will of the charmer. The persuasive lines may be followed by an invocation of a cursing character, or a negative description of the snake's origin, or an aetiological description featuring Christian elements (the order of these elements is flexible). In none of these phases is any suggestion of a consultative approach to the snake expressed. The original 'agreement' between man and (super-)natural forces has been replaced by a Christian attitude with a conjuring approach.

When the charmer relies on texts with Christian influence, he obviously needs an outsider's power. He refers to Christian personages, such as Christ, St. Mary, Saint Peter etc. This may also mean that a part of the authority is forwarded to a Christian agent. This leads to the problem of a supposed difference between saints and ethnic supernatural beings: are they to be considered as equal or contradictory? Does appealing to saints introduce a religious element to the charms? How do the seemingly contradictory ideologies fit together in the human mind? Were charmers aware of this duality or did different charmers possess different worldviews? Are there obvious differences between Christian and pagan charmers? All of these questions share a common focus.

The charms referred to above were interpreted as a vehicle to be used when acting in the realm of supernatural. While most theories of magic are based on two differing assumptions – magic is seen either as a mode of social practice, or as that of a mental view of reality – when it comes to charms, both elements seem to be present. Reciting charms in order to promote practical aims is a socially controlled action. It is, however, based on an assumption of potential influence in a special situation dependent on worldview. As has been shown above, charm-texts may include several Christian names or concepts and religious allusions as well as seemingly religious attitudes alongside magical elements. According to Matti Kuusi, prayer-like charms added no basically new elements to this ritual genre (Kuusi 1963, 272). Instead, only in terms of attitude is there any substantial deviation from the earlier norm.

Researchers of religion have argued that religions consist of patterns of manifestations concerning the sacred. This is why religion appears to us as a power of quite another order than that of the forces of nature. According to Mircea Eliade, it is 'the Wholly Other' that is encountered in religious experience (quoted by Pyysiäinen 2004, 4). From a hermeneutical point of perspective, religion is based on subjectively reasoned meaning. Religion is said to aim at general welfare, whereas magic usually has specific and quite concrete goals (Pyysiäinen 2004, 4–5). A religious appeal is founded on a supplicatory attitude, whereas as a magical approach is manipulative. Further features distinguishing magic from religion have been outlined as well (see Goode 1949). According to a magical worldview, supernatural forces and agents have a specified effect in a known situation, whereas religion operates by natural actions aiming at having an effect in a supernatural reality. Thus magic can be characterised as a specific kind of attitude toward religious representation

(Hill 1987, 90). However, it is not necessary to see magic as completely contradictory to religion, instead magico-religious complexes may be outlined. It is evident that magic and religion share the use of supernatural processes. It may even be claimed that a balance between magical and religious elements is necessary for the cultural success of these complexes. The main distinction should perhaps be seen in the direction that people of an ethnic culture believe causality to operate (Pyysiäinen 2004, 90–3, 96–7). This is simply a theoretical definition however, in the mind of a layman the rules are shaped according to experience.

Above it has been shown that features of an archaic ethnic religion and later Christian elements are mingled together in Finnish snake charms, albeit sometimes with apparent contradiction. According to a field note recorded in 1924 in Ingria, a man was bitten by a snake, but God saw what happened and taught the man a snake-charm in order to heal the bite (Salminen, *SKVR* III:3, 4404). Furthermore, Marina Takalo, a person with a rich folklore repertoire, claimed that 'the nature spirits are created by God' (Pentikäinen 1971, 288). According to some Christian practice, saints can be prayed to for help. This kind of thinking was combined with earlier magical attitudes, meaning that saints could be equated with ethnic supernatural beings. As a result they become objects of verbal manipulation. This kind of analogy is far from rare in folklore texts, and the phenomena has been interpreted as systematic syncretism. Corresponding religiously mingled elements appear also for instance in Seto folksongs (Arukask 1999). In this kind of worldview, archaic ethnic as well as Christian agents are sacred beings and may represent the otherworld (Stark-Arola 1999, 112–16). All of the beings are invisible spirits, whose existence is based on supposition and who should be approached spiritually.

The bricolage of worldview

In peasant societies, learning by listening was an important and practically inseparable part of getting information. Everyday life was accompanied by oral tradition, but even Christian information was transmitted mainly by audition. The compulsory confirmation class organised by the Lutheran Church after the Reformation in the sixteenth century guaranteed people's ability to read, but continuous reading was not an essential part of peasants' everyday life. During church services priests read extracts from the Finnish language Bible and obviously at special occasions some extracts were read at home, too. In both cases people *listened* to religious texts as they were used to listen to pieces of folk-lore. According to church legends, Christian agents proved powerful: they caused miracles and forced their opponents to obey. When the ethnic belief system gradually lost credence, it was natural to replace the roles of supernatural beings with saints. The power of the word was still present, and was related to their names. The new characters seemed to resemble the previous ethnic supernatural beings. Gradually, through information gained by audition, Christian characters were equated in the mind of the people with the forces of nature, the supernatural beings and with the very magic that the Church interpreted as negative. The power of the word (*väki*) was anyway secret, independent of its spiritual background.

As far as the (assumed) influence of a charm is concerned, the connection between the expression and the concept it refers to is the most essential factor. Thus both Christian and ethnic supernatural beings are magically charged referents. Differing mental systems do not exclude each other, but preserve and add to the magical power needed in a healing session. In principle, a greater change happened non-verbally, at the level of worldview, when the dualistic opposition between good and evil was adopted. Sometimes the verbalisation shows some confusion. In certain charm texts the most archaic attitude, the original equality between man and nature is still reflected as a relic. The overwhelming Christian influence is also twofold. When the snake's dangerousness is connected to Christian symbolism, the animal is personified and as a result is sometimes equated with the charmer's ethnic supernatural opponents. Only then can it be dominated by reciting its origin. But according to Christian belief, the charmer relies not on his own magical strength, but by appeals to helping characters. Parallels to Christ, St. Mary or other saints may, however, still be characters from the ethnic religion. Thus we see the presence magical thinking in the Christianised charms as well.

Notes

1. The snake's connection to water and the rain goddess may loom in the background (cf. Gimbutas 1989, 113).
2. The question of the seeming contradiction between the norms of the Finnish Lutheran church and the frequent occurrence of Catholic saints in such texts has been addressed by Ulrika Wolf-Knuts (1999, 65–78). It should however been underlined that most Finnish charms were collected from the eastern part of Finland, where the Orthodox Church was dominant. Its attitude towards folk traditions was remarkably more tolerant than that of the Lutheran church.

Bibliography

Abbreviation

SKVR = Suomen Kansan Vanhat Runot, e.g. Niemi (1931) and Salminen (1924).

Arukask, Madis 'Religious Syncretism in Setu Runo Songs', *Studies in Folklore and Popular Religion* 2 (1999), 79–92.

Clodd, Edward, *Magic in Names and in Other Things*. London: Chapman and Hall, 1920.

Gimbutas, Marija, *The Language of the Goddess, Unearthing the Hidden Symbols of Western Civilisation*. San Francisco: Harper Row, 1989.

Goode, William J., 'Magic and religion. A continuum', *Ethnos* 14 (1949), 172–82.

Hautala, Jouko, 'Sanan mahti' in *Jumin keko. Tutkielmia kansanrunoustieteen alalta*. Helsinki: Suomalaisen Kirjallisuuden Seura, 1960, 7–42. (Tietolipas, 17).

Hill, Donald R., 'Magic in primitive societies' in *The Encyclopedia of Religion*. Vol. 9. New York & London: Macmillan, 1987.

Honko, Lauri, Timonen, Senni & Branch, Michael, *The Great Bear. A Thematic Anthology of Oral Poetry in the Finno-Ugrian Languages*. Helsinki: Suomalaisen Kirjallisuuden Seura, 1993.

Hästesko, F. A., *Länsisuomalainen loitsurunous*. Helsinki: Suomalaisen Kirjallisuuden Seura, 1918. (SKS toimituksia, 161).

Kuusi, Matti, 'Keskiajan kalevalainen runous' in *Suomen kirjallisuus 1*. Helsinki: Otava, 1963, pp. 273–397.

Loorits, Oskar, *Grundzüge des estnischen Volksglaubens 1*. Uppsala: 1949. (Skrifter utgivna av Kungliga Gustav Adolfs Akademien, 18:1)

Luven, Yvonne, *Der Kult der Hausschlange. Ein Studie zur Religionsgeschichte der Letten und Litauer*. Köln, Weimar & Wien: Böhlau Verlag, 2001. (Quellen und Studien zur Baltischen Geschchte, 17).

Niemi, A.R. ed., *Suomen Kansan Vanhat Runot VII: 3: Raja- ja Pohjois-Karjalan runot 3. Lyyrillisiä. Toisinnot 3812–4627. Loitsuja. Toisinnot 1–1549*. Helsinki: Suomalaisen Kirjallisuuden Seura, 1931.

Pentikäinen, Juha, *Marina Takalon uskonto. Uskontoantropologinen tutkimus*. Helsinki: Suomalaisen Kirjallisuuden Seura, 1971.

Pyysiäinen, Ilkka, *Magic, Miracles and Religion. A Scientist's Perspective*. Walnut Creek: Altamira Press, 2004.

Salminen, V., ed., *Suomen Kansan Vanhat Runot III: 3: Länsi-Inkerin runot 3. Toisinnot 2581–4634*. Helsinki: Suomalaisen Kirjallisuuden Seura, 1924.

Stark-Arola, Laura, 'Christianity and wilderness: Syncretism in Orthodox Karelian magic as culture-specific strategies', *Studies in folklore and popular religion* 2 (1999), 93–120.

Wedeck, Harry E., *A Treasury of Witchcraft*. London: Vision, 1961.

Wilson, Stephen, *The Magical Universe: Everyday Ritual and Magic in Pre-Modern Europe*. London: Hambledon and London, 2000.

Wolf-Knuts, Ulrika, 'The Virgin Mary in Ostrobothnian Magic Spells', *Studies in Folklore and Popular Religion* 2 (1999), 65–78.

13

Estonian Narrative Charms in European Context[1]

Jonathan Roper

The Estonian Folklore Archives in Tartu have been described as 'a cultural marvel',[2] and for charms-scholars at least this statement is not hyperbole. The card indexes there hold the texts of at least 10,000 verbal charms. In fact, the total figure maybe substantially larger.[3] But, in any event, the holdings are still one of the largest collections of charms in Europe. The overwhelmingly most common form of charm to be found in the Estonian archives is the direct address, something which is also the case in the even larger charms holdings of the Finnish Folklore Archives in Helsinki.[4] Narrative charms and comparison charms, on the other hand, form less than ten per cent of both corpora, whereas in other parts of Europe, we might expect narrative charms and comparison charms to represent something more like 25–50 per cent of the corpus. For example, in the English charms corpus I put together (Roper 2005), 35 per cent of the texts were narrative charms. Nevertheless, as the Estonian corpus is so large, although narrative charms may be a fractional presence, the absolute size of that fraction is still quite substantial – I identified just short of eight hundred such texts in the archive.[5] The following discussion is intended to provide an overview of these Estonian-language narrative charms, which form an interesting set in that they are found in a Baltic Finnic culture, which has also experienced significant and prolonged contacts with Swedes, Finns, Russians, Latvians and Germans.

In its lateness, the Estonian narrative charms corpus differs again from some of the other European corpora, such as the English and the German. The vast majority of the Estonian narrative charms were recorded during the century between 1860 and 1960; only a trickle of narrative charms are recorded before that date, e.g. in the records of witch trials, or in the work of early folklorists. As elsewhere, some of these early folklorists, such as Friedrich Reinhold Kreutzwald, 'improved' their texts, which can make their material problematic. But it seems that the later nation-wide efforts to collect folklore were very fortunate in their timing, at least as far as charms were concerned, in that many verbal charms were still current, but, additionally, in that belief in the efficacy of charm-ing was beginning to fade, which in many cases must have enabled the elicitation of texts which might have a generation earlier been kept secret for fear of losing their power, or which might, a generation later, have already been forgotten. My own minor experience of collecting charms in the far south-eastern Seto corner of Estonia tends to bear this out. In August 1995, two elderly women in the village of Tsütski, Nati Lillestik and Olga Kalasaar, each told us the charm they knew and did not believe in (incidentally these charms, one for snakebite, the other for sprains, were both direct addresses).[6] In July 1996 however, a third woman, Anne Rebane of Lädina (which is on the Russian side of the bor-der), who told us that she knew a written charm for erysipelas, informed us that she could not tell us the words she used because she would then lose their power. So in the first instance we came just at the right time to collect the charms, but in the second case we were in the unusual situation for folklorists of arriving too early, while the belief system was still intact.

A few general remarks about the Estonian charms and charming might be appropriate here. In common with the situation in the rest of Europe (and indeed with that in large parts of Asia), three is an important num-ber in Estonian charming, either as the threshold number of the charm itself, or the number of repetitions of the ratifying word 'Amen' at the end of the charm, or the number of repetitions of the ratifying action of making the sign of the cross at the end of the charm. And the number three is also evident in the personages and objects found in the histori-olas of the narrative charms – three men, three angels, three roses, three flowers, three crosses, etc. Indeed, the historiolas themselves are often tripartite (sometimes we find a more elaborate tripartite form which also has a three-part clause nested inside its final part). The *In Nomine* for-mula ('In the name of the Father, the Son and the Holy Spirit', and its close variants) is also a popular ratification, which is itself very often concluded with 'Amen'. While much effort has been expended by cul-tural activists to delineate a pre-Christian and supposedly *echt* Estonian (or Baltic-Finnic, or Finno-Ugric, depending on one's ideology) element in verbal folklore, Estonian charms, at least as much as they are reflected in the relatively recent records we have of them, have much in common with charms in other countries, and one, if not the, key reason for this is that they are shot through with vernacular Christianity.

We should note the undoubtedly important role of written and printed sources in establishing at least part of the corpus of Estonian charms. As elsewhere, printed spellbooks were well-known in recent centuries. The majority of these were in German: *Sechstes und siebentes Buch der Mosis, Das wahrhaftige feuerige Drache, Romanusbüchlein, Geheime Kunst-Schule magischer WunderKräfte*, etc.[7] An Estonian magical chapbook seems to have been a late and solitary example,[8] although Estophone charms did crop up in print from time to time in almanacs and newspapers.[9] Handwritten charmers' books were also distributed between interested parties. As well as such items, there was, with the development of the study of folklore, also some leakage from the study back to the folk – for example, a scholarly work on the Sixth and Seventh Books of Moses by the Estonian folklorist, Mattias Eisen, seems to have been the source of charms for some early twentieth century Estonian charmers.[10] This type of leakage back to the folk is no doubt typical of other countries too.[11] We can also find examples of *genre shift*. For example, religious songs were sometimes used as (or should we say 'sometimes became') charms. For example, songs from Schtal's *Hand und Hauszbuch* (1632–8) were found as charms in nineteenth and twentieth century folk tradition.[12] Similarly, 'Maarja otsib poega', a charm with five variants in the archive which was intended to treat vaginal discharge (*valgevoolus*), derives from the words of a hymn.

As for narrative charms, they first appear in the early eighteenth century, not very long after the date of the earliest of the surviving written records of Estonian charms, and in the same contexts: the records of witchcraft trials. The absence of earlier records makes the question of whether narrative charms in Estonian substantially predate the early modern period a matter of conjecture. From one point of view, we might imagine that they did, given that narrative charms appear earlier in Europe, for example in the records of charms found in the eastern Mediterranean in late antiquity (e.g. the fifth century), and in the earliest (tenth century) records of Germanic charms. And yet, the fact that narrative charms make up certainly less than 10 per cent, and perhaps less than 5 per cent of the total number of recorded charms in both Estonia and Finland, gives us pause for thought. Given the preponderance of direct addresses among the recorded Baltic Finnic charms, we might well assume that such charms, and particularly that highly characteristic form which involves the listing of the origins of the evil that is to be dispelled (what Krohn termed *Ursprungsrunen*),[13] were the original Baltic Finnic form of charms. Such an assumption is complicated somewhat by the fact that origin charms are not a uniquely Baltic

Finnic phenomenon. Indeed what is perhaps the earliest of all English charms, the so-called 'Wen charm', can be seen as an origins charm. However, as we shall see, the large number of German-language parallels that exist for the Estonian-language narrative charms, suggests that our most plausible working hypothesis is that narrative charms as a folk magical device in Estonia are a relatively recent cultural loan largely derived from German-speakers and German texts.

The predominance of a limited number of types

One of most striking characteristics of the corpus of Estonian narrative charms is that it is dominated by just two types. Both of them, **Bone to bone** and **Three Roses**, are known widely elsewhere in Europe. Together, examples of these two charm-types make up more than 59 per cent of the total number of narrative charms. At first, this would seem to be an unusually high figure. But when we look for example at the English narrative charms corpus, again on the basis of the corpus used in Roper (2005), we see that the most two numerous narrative charm-types there make up a substantial 40 per cent of the total corpus of narrative charms. Indeed, in both corpora approximately two-thirds (68 per cent in the English case, 67 per cent in the Estonian) of the narrative charms are represented by just four types.[14] Whether such a preponderance of a limited number of narrative charm-types is typical more broadly is an interesting question, answerable when we have more descriptions of the narrative charm-stock of other linguistic and national groupings.

The other narrative charm-types represented by more than half a dozen examples in the Estonian archive are (in order of popularity): **Flum Jordan, Tres angeli, Christ's Garden, The Snake bit and Christ spoke, Neque doluit neque tumuit, Jesus and the fiery torch, Vita Christi, Stans sanguis in te, Thieves and the Holy Child, Tres boni fratres,** and **Jerusalem you town of pain.**[15] The presence of Biblical names (with the characteristic long Estonian vowels) such as 'Jeesus' (or 'Kristus'), 'Maarja', and 'Peetrus', alerts us to the fact that many of these narrative charms are part and parcel of vernacular Christianity. As well as their predominantly New Testament personnel, we can also find occasional Old Testament figures such as 'Aadam' and 'Mooses'.[16]

But let us begin our discussion of the charm-types by turning to the most popular charm-type (I found 286 examples in the archive), used for sprains in animals and humans: *Bone to bone*.[17] As well as being the most popular charm-type, it is also the earliest documented narrative charm-type in Estonia, the following example having been recorded in an early eighteenth-century witch trial:

Jesus Kärko minnike,	*Jesus went to church,*
Lohhe Musta modusse.	*The black snake (?dragon),*
Kalla karva karvaselle,	*Attacked the hairy one,*
nikkotas Hebbose jalgo,	*Sprained the horse's leg.*
Jesu täus mahh rattalt,	*Jesus dismounted the wagon*
isto sys Kiwwike pähle,	*Then sat on a stone*
panni Sonet soonte wasta,	*Put veins to veins,*
jässemit, jässemite wasta,	*Limbs to limbs,*
Likemet Likemette wasta.[18]	*Joints to joints.*

This, the first witness of this charm-type (here in Kalevala metre), is also a good example of how this type's historiola shows rather distinctive features in the Baltic Finnic area. Those recomposing the charm here seemed to be at pains to provide motivation for the horse's (or in some cases Peter's) sprain. In this case (although the language of the court clerk is not entirely clear), a snake appears to have attacked the horse causing it to sprain its leg.[19] In other cases, the cause of the fall is put down to the actions of a grouse, a dove, a gun, a tree, thunder, or to the trembling of the earth. As far as I am aware, historiolas elsewhere do not focus in upon this detail.

The longest discussion of an Estonian narrative charm-type made to date came from the pen of the Norwegian researcher Reidar Christiansen and focussed on **Bone to bone**. On the basis of the 123 examples that had found their way into the archives prior to 1908, he presents a sixteen page discussion.[20] While he notes that the 43 examples in Kalevala metre show affinities with the Finnish examples, he finds German influence at work in Estonian examples of this charm-type. One of his arguments for this is the presence of the ratification in Estonian examples (otherwise absent in Finnish examples). But surely the ratification (whether the *In Nomine* formula, or words to the effect of *as that was, so may this be*) are signs of German influence (or, perhaps more broadly speaking, Christian influence) on the vocabulary of Estonian charming in general, rather than specifically upon this charm-type. There may well have been *some* German influence, but for this charm-type at least, given the extensively-documented existence of a large number of Baltic Finnic representatives of this type, which are highly variable in content, I am still inclined to at least entertain the possibility that this may be one of the few narrative charm-types which originates in northern Europe.[21]

But, this exception, if that is what it is, is the exception that proves the general rule that narrative charm-types seem to have sprung from the near east, and from southern or central Europe.[22]

The other main charm-type represented in the Tartu archive is **Three roses**, a type that has its heartland in Teutophone Central Europe – German examples date from the 1500s onwards, and the type later appeared in the popular German book of charms, *Romanusbüchlein*. In terms of the countries close to Estonia, it is known in Scandinavia[23] (though not in Finland, according to Christiansen) and in Latvia, Lithuania and Russia. It does not seem to have been popular in Romance areas – although the first witness is in French, it is from French-speaking Switzerland, and may be the only text in that language. (No Latin examples have come to light either, hence my choice of the non-Latin type-name **Three Roses**, rather than 'Tres Rosae'.)[24]

An example of the Estonian form can be found in an eight-page Estonian magical chapbook published in 1910 by one Jaan Pill:

> Meie Issand Jeesus Kristus. Reisis üle mere ja maa. Kolm roosi oli tema käes. Üks oli walge, teine sinine, kolmas punane. Üks lendas ära, teine kuiwas ära, kolmas kadus ka selle roosiga. See Isa Poja ja Püha waimu nimel.[25]

> *Our Lord Jesus Christ travelled over sea and land. Three roses were in his hand. One was white, the second blue, the third red. One flew off, the second dried up, and the third disappeared as with this rose. In the Name of the Father, Son and Holy Spirit.*

'Jaan Pill' printed this charm without any word as to what it should be used for. If we consult the ethnographic record however, we can see that most of the 236 Estonian examples were used for healing erysipelas (the 'rose disease', *roosihaigus*, in Estonian), although a minority (about one in ten of the archive examples) are recorded as having been intended for use in staunching blood, and there are also solitary examples of the type having been used for a cow's swollen udders, as a thief charm, or for colic. Some of the Estonian examples betray their German origins by the inclusion of German words such as 'Gemüth' in otherwise Estonian texts.[26]

In terms of the treatment of the historiola in the Estonian examples, the main variables as usual are protagonists, location and action, which can be cashed out in this case as – *what* are there three of, *where* are they located, and *how* do they disappear. The central 'protagonists', if we can call them that, are most often roses in the Estonian examples, though we do also find lilies, or simply flowers, as in the German examples. The locations where these roses are found to grow are generally Jesus' heart, or sometimes his grave, a location which appears to correlate with the presence of lilies or flowers rather than roses in the German examples according to Ohrt.[27] In the example quoted above, where Jesus is a protagonist and we appear to have some 'contamination' from a fire charm we will refer to below. Other examples of sacred protagonists include Mary, Jesus and Mary, Jesus and Peter, Three Virgins, and Three Angels. Mare Kõiva in her discussions of this charm-type has identified sixty-six different sets of three verbs each (e.g. burns, dies, sinks down; burns, dies, disappears; sweeps, smokes, throws; etc.), but this is really only micro-variation, in that all of these sixty-six sets express the same notion, that of the roses' disappearance.[28] Overall, although there is a great deal of micro-variability, the Estonian examples are not so different from the common European variants. Certainly the extent of variability that we found with the previous charm-type is in no way echoed here.

I shall turn now to discuss two of the other charm-types. Although relatively well-represented with 23 and 14 examples respectively, they are nowhere nearly as widespread as the two types we have just discussed. The first is an example of a charm-type to deal with snake-bite, which I have titled **The Snake bit and Christ Spoke:**

Siusõnad.	*Snake Charm*
Siug pistse ja Marja ütel,	*The snake bit and Mary spoke,*
Jeesus ütel:	*Jesus spoke:*
See nõgel mingu välla	*This needle go out!*
Jumala see Isa ning Poja ja	*In the name of the Father,*
Püha Vaimu nimel.	*Son and Holy Spirit*
Aamen.[29]	*Amen.*

This short charm was to be said three times. It is notable that this example features Mary as well as Christ, for when we look at the historiolas of snake charms more broadly, we find that Mary was often a protagonist, as Ritwa Herjulfsdotter discusses in her chapter in this book with regards to the Swedish material. The text above is a representative of a type is found in Germany, Denmark, Sweden and France.[30] German examples typically open 'Die Schlange sticht, Christus spricht'. On what we might call *the principle of the priority of rhyme*, in other words, the idea that it is more plausible that rhymed versions are prior to prose versions, we might suggest that this was a German charm before it was an Estonian one. (But of course, just because a text is prior does not mean it is the original.)

We can apply this principle in another case, that of another charm-type, **Jesus and the fiery torch**. This is a type popular in central and eastern Europe. Harmjanz in his monograph on charms for 'fire' notes German, Danish, Norwegian and Estonian examples, along with some close analogues in Latvian and Finnish. A typical Estonian version runs:

> Jeesus läts üle liiva ja maa nink löüs sääl üte tule tungla ja ütel: Sa olet palanu nink ei pala enamb.[31]

> *Jesus went over sand and land and found there a fiery torch and said: you are burnt out and no longer burn.*

That Jesus should go over land seems standard enough, but that he should also go over sand as well seems less well-motivated, until we invoke the priniciple of the priority of rhyme again. If we translate this charm into German we would find the rhyming words *Sand, Land, Feuer-brand* and *Gebrannt*. Indeed in other German versions we also find *Hand*. This should suggest that we consider that German examples (or more broadly perhaps, examples in the Germanic languages) are prior to the Estonian examples, a view that the fact that the earliest surviving representative of the charm-type was recorded in Swabia around 1400 also reinforces.[32]

Overall, we find German parallels to all of the fifteen most popular narrative charm-types (as opposed to, for example, English parallels for just four of them). For the historical folklorist, the corpus has a frustrating lateness, which prevents one from making entirely secure conclusions. Nevertheless, the ultimate path that the vast majority of these narrative charm-types trod is clear – most of them entered Estonian via the medium of German. We should nuance this by noting that in certain border areas Russian, Latvian or Swedish could be influential, as could Latin, at an earlier date, e.g. via the Dominicans and their educational establishments.

Role of innovative composers and prolific translators in 'unbalancing' a corpus

In the archives we find two examples of a charm of a type we might call **Three Snakes from the Field**. Upon closer examination, both of these examples turn out to have been collected at different times from the same woman, Anna Kuusik. It is perfectly possible that we are dealing with independent creation based on a Biblical text (what, in more favourable circumstances, might have amounted to the birth of a charm-type), although it is much more likely that this is an example of translation of a charm-type from a foreign language, especially given that we know that Kuusik was a woman who, in addition to lending out her own charm books, actively sought out fresh charms from foreign-language magic books. She is also the sole (or most significant) source for other putative charm-types (many of which might only be found within a single parish). This raises the whole question of the individual versus the national (or the parish versus the nation). If only one person, here an Estonian, knew a particular charm (and quite possibly never even had cause to use it) can that charm-type truly be said to be an Estonian charm, with all the national representativity that would seem to suggest?[33]

Instead of answering that question, I should like to close by recalling a conversation I had with a folklorist in Eastern Canada. In it, he compared our scattered samplings of the ocean of culture to the infrequent surveys of fish populations made by Government agencies. In both cases, the fact that the researchers' samples are so few and far-between in comparison with the vastness of the potential material may mean that the catch we haul up for analysis could well lead us into making unfounded conclusions. Whatever a true picture of life in the past, or below the waves, might amount to, it could well differ considerably from the pictures that we draw. Even when working with a corpus as large as the Estonian one, we still only have a set of samples, rather than a complete picture. And in many other cases we will have far less data to go on. As we build our much-desired charm typologies, one factor we should always be aware of is that even in cases with an apparent wealth of data, we are still dealing with a partial sample, and we should always keep in mind the question of how typical are our types.

Notes

1. I am grateful to both the British Academy and the Estonian Academy of Sciences for enabling me to make an individual research visit to the Estonian Folklore Archives in Tartu in May 2006 to undertake research there. Everyone who undertakes research on Estonian verbal charms is indebted to Mare Kõiva both for her studies and assistance, and that I am no exception. And I should also say that I am indebted to Jaan Puhvel and Laura Stark for assistance in putting this chapter together.

2. Puhvel, Jaan, 'The mythical element in Estonian poetry', *Journal of Baltic Studies*, 5:2 (1974), 87–99: 96.
3. The exact number may be substantially higher (20,000 or more) but the precise total is currently obscured by the existence of duplicate records of particular charms, the knowledge that some other cards have gone missing, and a general degree of disorder in the drawers containing the index cards at present. The situation should become clearer when the corpus is digitised in due course.
4. I owe this observation to Laura Stark (personal communication, 2004). For a brief discussion of direct addresses see Roper, Jonathan, *English Verbal Charms* (Helsinki: Academia Scientiarum Fennica, 2005) (Folklore Fellows' Communications 288), pp. 131–3.
5. To be precise, I identified 783 relevant texts. Again, this figure is subject to revision due to the current situation of missing, disordered and duplicate index cards. A thorough examination that addresses all the potential types (which would include thirty possible narrative charm-types with between two and five examples in the archives, and the sixty putative charm-types with but a single representative) will be possible when the archive is eventually digitised (Roper, Jonathan, *English Verbal Charms* (Helsinki: Academic Scientiarum Fennica, 2005) (Folklore Fellows' Communications 288).
6. Roper, Jonathan, 'Two recently-recorded South Estonian verbal charms and some analogues', *Lore and Language* 14:2 (1996), 165–73.
7. Mare Kõiva notes in 'Palindromes and Letter Formulae: Some Reconsiderations', *The Electronic Journal of Folklore*, vol. 8 (1988), 21–50: 41 that 'many copies show signs of heavy use, i.e. underlinings and exclamation marks in the margins, etc.'.
8. Pill, Jaan, *Sõnadega arstimise õpetus* (Viljandi: A. Rennit, [1910]). This booklet is only eight pages in length.
9. For example, one regional newspaper published a series of charms in December 1929: *Põltsamaa Teataja* 32: 2, (21 Dec. 1929).
10. Eisen, Mattias, *Seitse Moosese raamatut. Katse kuuenda ja seitsmenda Moosese raamatu seletuseks* (Tallinn: Busch, 1896). Mare Kõiva has shown how it was subsequently used as a source by the Saaremaa folk-healer Tiitsu Seiu: Kõiva (1988), 41–2. See also her article about him: 'Aleksei Lesest ehk Tiitsu Seiust', *Paar sammukest essti kirjanduse uurimise teed*, vol. 12 (1989), 80–100. The south Estonian healer Laine Roht told me on 11 September 1996 that she had learnt charms from an anthology of Estonian folk poetry, namely Tedre, Ülo, *Eesti Rahvalaulud* (Tallinn: Eesti Raamat, 1974).
11. For example, cheap nineteenth-century editions of Reginald Scot's *Discoverie of Witchcraft* (a seventeenth century deflation of belief in charms) seem to have been the source for some of the repertoire of some nineteenth-century charmers in England.
12. Examples include 'Kui Jeesus risti naeliti', 'Herodes, miks sa ehmatud', 'O Adam sinno essitus', 'Kui Jeesuse armoga Jordan jõele', Kõiva, Mare, *Estonskije zagovory – klassifikatsija i genrovyje osobennosti* (Tallinn: unpublished dissertation, 1990), p. 87.
13. Krohn, Kaarle, *Magische Ursprungsrunen der Finnen* (Folklore Fellows' Communications 52) (Helsinki: Academia Scientiarum Fennica, 1924). Henni Ilomäki touches on such origins charms in the course of her chapter in this book.

14. The four most popular English narrative charm-types are **Flum Jordan, Neque doluit neque tumuit, Out Fire in Frost**, and **Super petram**.

15. Examples and discussions of many of these types can be found in entries by Ferdinand Ohrt in Hoffmann-Krayer, Eduard, and Bächtold-Stäubli, Hanns, eds, *Handwörterbuch des deutschen Aberglaubens* (Berlin: de Gruyter, 1927–42), *s.vv.* 'Jordansegen' (for **Flum Jordan**), 'Dreiengelsegen' (for **Tres angeli**), 'Schlangensegen' §2a (for **The Snake bit and Christ spoke**), 'Brandsegen' §1a (for **Jesus and the fiery torch**), 'glückselige Stunden' §1a (for **Vita Christi**), 'Blutsegen' §1b (for **Stans sanguis in te**), 'Diebsegen' §1 (for **Thieves and the Holy Child**), 'Dreibrüdersegen' (for **Tres boni fratres**), 'Jerusalem in den Segen' §3 (for **Jerusalem you town of pain**). As far as the two types not referred to in this list are concerned, for **Christ's Garden** see Ebermann, Oskar, *Blut- und Wundsegen in ihrer Entwickelung dargestellt* (Berlin: Mayer und Möller, 1903), chapter twelve: 'Ein Baum', and for **Neque doluit neque tumuit**, see the entry under that name in chapter 3 of Roper (2005).

16. In a few cases however, such as 'Valge mees tõuseb meresta' (*A white man rose from the sea*) or 'Must mees käib maate kaudu' (*A black man went along the paths*), such a Christian connection is not evident.

17. A solitary example of **Bone to bone** was said to be for *haigus*, or general illness.

18. Recorded from 'Wielo Ado' at his trial in Tartu in 1723: MS Tartu Maakohtu arhiiv 182, f.30.

19. The confused language at the opening of this charm is open to alternative interpretation: 'Jesus went to church, a fish-coloured hairy wyrm from the black side sprained his horse's leg'; or even: 'Jesus went to church, on a dragon-black mount, on a fish-coloured shaggy creature. The horse sprained its leg'.

20. Christiansen, Reidar, *Die finnischen und nordischen Varianten des Zweiten Merseburgerspruches. Eine vergleichende Studie* (Folklore Fellows' Communications 18) (Hamina: Suomalaisen Kirjallisuuden Seura, 1915), pp. 163–78. See also the discussion in Koiva (1990), p. 94.

21. I first suggested this in Roper, Jonathan, *Traditional Verbal Charms with particular reference to the Estonian and English charm-traditions* (unpublished University of Sheffield MA dissertation, 1997), pp. 61–2.

22. Even the existence of numerous Kalevala metric examples, which can certainly be taken as suggesting that the charm-type was known in Estonia at a date when alliterative verse was still an active tradition, do not help us here. In practice, it need not mean that these translations and adaptations (if that is what they are) were made any earlier than the first quarter of the nineteenth century, whereas this is a date that this text already antedates by another century.

23. See for example, Ohrt, Ferdinand, *Danmarks Trylleformler 1–2* (København, Kristiania: F[olklore] F[ellows] publications, northern series 3, 1917, 1921) no. 146 (vol. 1, p. 168).

24. Ohrt referred to this type as 'Dreiblumensegen': see *Hoffmann-Krayer* and Bächtold-Stäubli (1927–42), *s.v.* 'Dreiblumensegen'.

25. Pill (1910), p. 2.

26. MS Tartu Estonian Literary Museum ERA II 202, 36 (71), recorded from Anna Kuusik on Kihnu island in 1938.

27. Hoffmann-Krayer and Bächtold-Stäubli (1927–42), *s.v.* 'Dreiblumensegen'.
28. Kõiva, Mare, 'On Some Common Elements in Baltic-Finnish and Baltic Incantations' in Skrobenis, S., ed., *Professor August Robert Niemi and Comparative Folklore Investigations of Balts and Baltic Finns* (Vilnius: Institute of Lithuanian Literature and Folklore, 1996), pp. 58–69 (discussion pp. 64–5); see also Kõiva (1990), pp. 94–5.
29. MS Tartu Estonian Literary Museum RKM II 27, 236 (13), recorded from Anna Lindvere in Kodavere parish in 1948.
30. See Hoffmann-Krayer and Bächtold-Stäubli (1927–42), 'Schlangensegen' §2a. Laura Stark (personal communication May 2007) has told me that she knows of no example of this type among the Finnish charms, an observation which tends to suggest that the type originates from outside the Baltic Finnic orbit.
31. Harmjanz, Heinrich, *Die deutschen Feuersegen und ihre Varianten in Nord- und Osteuropa. Ein Beitrag zur vergleichenden Segenforschung* (Folklore Fellows' Communications 102) (Helsinki: Academia Scientiarum Fennica, 1932), p.118.
32. Hoffmann-Krayer and Bächtold-Stäubli (1927–1942), *s.v.* 'Brandsegen': '1. Der Heilige und der Brand'.
33. Similarly, as we have seen above, while the earliest text of **Three Roses** is in French, we would be unwise if from that fact we drew the conclusion that it is a predominantly Romance charm.

14

Lithuanian and Latvian Charms: Searching for Parallels

Daiva Vaitkevičienė

The Lithuanian and Latvian languages, both representatives of the same Baltic branch of Indo-European languages, are very similar. The folklores of the two nations, however, are different: not all the phenomena of Lithuanian and Latvian folklore are comparable. For example, the Lithuanian and Latvian song structure, subjects, and performance characteristics are dissimilar, providing almost no possibilities for comparison. But comparison of Lithuanian and Latvian folk narratives demonstrates that their subjects are fairly close, which is also the case as regards riddles and proverbs. In this comparative context, it is of great interest to look into the tradition of Lithuanian and Latvian charms: what is the relationship between their national characteristics, shared Baltic roots, and international characteristics? Which common subjects can we identify, and how many of these are there?

In doing the research, I focussed on healing charms, because the other charm corpora (e.g. those of social, agricultural, meteorological, etc. charms) are not yet ample enough to yield comparison and generalisations. This chapter draws its examples from 'Lietuvių užkalbėjimų: šaltiniai: elektroninis sąvadas' ('Sources of the Lithuanian Verbal Charms: Electronic Database'),[1] also by the author of this article.

The current Lithuanian corpus of healing charms consists of around 1, 300 texts. In organising the material into a system, various charm-types have been identified, i.e. groups of texts related by common motifs, and usually by similar syntactical structure as well. Classification into types has yielded 345 types of Lithuanian healing charms. Latvian charms are by far more numerous than Lithuanian ones: according to data provided by the Archive of Latvian Folklore (LFK), this one institution alone holds around 54,262 items.[2] Latvian charms have been little investigated both in typological and textual aspects. It is known that they used to spread in (hand-made) copies (LFK possesses a number of note-books with charms used by enchanters), so the exact number of variants has not yet been ascertained. But the material published by K. Straubergs alone shows that Latvia has a much more numerous and varied corpus of charms than that found in Lithuania.

Published Latvian material[3] has been used for the comparisons drawn here. We can state straightaway that only a few types correlate: the article discusses 28 parallels. The material recorded at the edge of Latvia and Lithuania has been excluded and will not be analysed (this are primarily the texts from Matas Slančiauskas' folklore collection *Juodoji knyga*[4]) because the charms in those areas were often translated out of on language into another when they were written down, and thus do not provide us with a reliable sample of data.

The examples of the correlating Lithuanian–Latvian charm-types will be presented in groups shaped according to formal criteria, which, while enabling us to structure the article, has had no impact on the analysis itself. We shall begin with the short texts dominated by invocations and comparisons, then move on to texts with dialogue structures, and finally turn to narrative charms.

Invocations and comparison charms

Only a few Lithuanian–Latvian parallels are found among the direct invocation. The most common charm of this type (well-known both in Europe and outside its territory)[5] is the following invocation used by children (here in a Lithuanian example):

Pele, pele, te tau dantį kaulinį – duok man geležinį![6]

Mouse, mouse, here you are a bone tooth – give me an iron one!

The charm is uttered when a child tosses his/her milk tooth behind the stove, so that the new tooth is healthy and strong. A mouse is usu-ally invoked, less commonly a wolf (2 variants), or a rat (1 variant), i.e. the animals whose teeth are undoubtedly strong. The Latvian variant published by Straubergs mentions a cricket rather than a mouse:

Še tev, circen, kaula zobs, dod man dzelzs [tērauda, zelta] zobu.[7]

Here, cricket, a bone tooth for you and you give me an iron [steel, golden] one.

One Lithuanian variant invoking a cricket has been recorded in the northern Lithuania in the vicinity of the Latvian border. The overall number of this charm as recorded in Lithuania is at least 31 variants (from 1890 up to 1999),[8] although it is likely that this number could be far larger as children are still jokingly reminded of this charm when their milk teeth fall out, i.e. it was a case in which a formula was so common that people recording folklore did not pay much attention to it.[9] The three early recordings (in 1890, 1918, and 1926) made in completely different regions of Lithuania, invoked God. The archaic nature of this invocation is supported by Russian folklore, namely one of the 24 variants published by Anikin invokes a home deity *domovoj*:

> Dedushka domovoi! Na tebe repianoi, a mne dai kostianoi.

> Dedushka domovoi! *Take this turnip tooth and give me a bone one.*[10]

Variants addressing God are known in English folk tradition as well.[11]

Another invocation is associated with the zoomorphic encoding of an illness where a mote in the eye is called a wolf or a bear:

> Vilke, vilke, išlįsk iš akių, aš tau duosiu maišą pinigų ir maišą rugių![12]
> [Lithuanian]

> *Wolf, wolf, get out of my eyes and I will give you a sack of money and a sack of rye!*

There are only 2 variants with this theme in Lithuania, the second being recorded in 1970 and unlike the variant recorded by Mansikka, it was found in the north of Lithuania and not in the south; the syntactical structure of the texts is identical, only the second charm invokes a bear with a promise of a jug of honey.

The Latvian parallel has the same objects as Mansikka's variant, i.e. *a wolf* and *an eye*, but there is no invocation here and the charm structure is based on inversion (in the eye – in the wood):

> Vilks acī, gruzis mežā![13]

> *A wolf in the eye, a mote in the wood!*

One more analogue of Lithuanian–Latvian charms is an interesting example of a juncture between non-narrative and narrative texts. The seven Lithuanian variants[14] are intended to cure herpes by saluting it in the following way:

> *In the morning 'Good evening, herpes!'* ['Labs vakars, dedervine!'] *is said.*
> *In the evening 'Good morning, herpes!'* ['Labs ryts, dedervine!']*is said.*

It was thought that being 'it will disappear sooner by being teased'.[15]

In some variants the address has dropped out, only the greeting text remained, which could be inverted and 'impaired' in other ways, for instance, by adding a negation: 'Ne labas rytas, ne labas vakaras!'[16] [*No good morning, no good evening!*].

Thus, the Lithuanian variants are devoid of narrative elements. Meanwhile, in the Latvian variant published by Brīvzemnieks in 1881, the invocation is supplemented by a sentence, indicating a charm's potential for a narrative development. This text as well as the Lithuanian texts are intended to treat a herpes infection, only here not the illness is addressed but the mythological beings 'Svētās meitas', i.e. Holy Maidens,[17] who cause it:

The charm spoken in the morning:

'Labvakar, svētās meitas, māsiņas!'
'Good Evening, Holy Maidens, sisters!'

In the evening they used to say:

'Labrīt, svētās meitas, māsiņas! Trīs māsiņas pirti kūra triju kalnu stārpiņā.'[18]

'Good morning, Holy Maidens, sisters! Three sisters are heating sauna in the midst of three hills.'

In this case there is a small fragment of a narrative charm alluding to the belief legends where *Svētās meitas* are depicted as great lovers of sauna: they would come at night to sauna.[19] Furthermore, the room of sauna itself could be used to cure herpes; this is seen in other Latvian charms:

Svētās meitas, jumpraviņas, peṛas pirts palāvē visādiem zariņiem, puceņu, bērzu u. t. p. Pēršu (Anniņas) pumpulīšus projām.[21]

Holy Maidens, young ladies, take a steam bath on the wooden steps sauna with all kinds of branches – viburnum branches, birch branches and others. I shall beat Anniņas pimples away [with tree branches].

Svētās meitas, svētās meitas, uguṇu vātes, uguṇu vātes, liku vātes, liķu vātes iznīkst, iznīkst kā piertes dūmi, kā rijas ardi, kā pērnais pūpēdis![21]

Holy Maidens, Holy Maidens, fire blains, fire blains, blains of corpses, blains of corpses[22] go away, go away like smoke from sauna, like stacks of crop in a stackyard, like last year's smoke-ball.

It should be noted that the Latvian formula 'Trīs māsiņas pirti kūra triju kalnu stārpiņā' is, as we can tell from its rhythmical composition, half of a common Latvian quatrain (quatrains are the formal basis of all Latvian folk songs and some Latvian charms).[23] But this charm apparently lacks an ending.

There are more parallels where mythological beings are invoked (see the invocation of the new moon at the comparisons) or mythologized parts of the body, or illnesses. This is how a womb is mythologized:

[Lithuanian]

Močiute, močiute, gražioji mergele, nusiprausk, apsistok, atsigulk! Pilkieji akmenys, baltosios šaknys. Amen, amen, amen.

Old woman, old woman, beautiful maiden, wash yourself, settle, lie down! Grey stones, white roots. Amen, amen, amen.

Make the sign of the cross before charming and say it three times (for women's illnesses).[24]

[Latvian]

Dieva māte, ziedu māte, neej kā kaķe plēzdama, sēdi savā krēsliņā, guli savā gultiņā.[25]

Mother of God, mother of blossoms,[26] do not walk as a clawing cat, sit on your little chair, lie in your little bed.

This charm-type is relatively close to the Belorussian charms used for stomach-ache invoking a mythological part of the body, the 'zolotnik', by ordering it to 'Siadz' ty na mestechku, Na zolotom kreslechku' ['*Sit in your place, on a little golden chair*'.][27] The examples from Lithuania and Latvia are quite different from one another; it should be noted that we have only one Lithuanian variant and there are a few Russian variants recorded in Lithuania, e.g. the following childbirth charm:

Al'zhbeta, o matitsa, krasnaia devitsa! Umyisia, ustoisia u syroi kamen.[28]

Al'zhbeta [the name of a childbearing woman is then mentioned], oh, matitsa, beautiful maiden! Wash yourself and settle on a wet stone!

Out of the charms with a direct invocation, an example with an address to a thistle (*Carduus*) (in the Lithuanian variant) could be mentioned. When a wound gets infected with the worms, one should put a stone on a thistle saying the following words:

Dagi, dagi, aš tav slegiu, kad išbyretų (pamini gyvuli) margai karvei kirmeles! Jeigu išbarstysi, tave palaisiu, neišbarstysi – tu čia supūsi![29]

Thistle, thistle, I am pressing thee so that the worms fall out from the (mention an animal) rufous speckled cow! If you scatter the worms, I shall release thee, if you don't – you will rot here!

After the worms fall out, the thistle should be released, otherwise the medicine will not help.

This charm-type in Lithuania was recorded in the north and east regions, and there are fourteen known variants.[30]

In the Latvian tradition, a formula with a very similar structure is used in a different situation, namely treating a horse's leg:

Es turu tevi, es sienu tevi, es neatlaidīšu tevi, iekams būsi kāju dziedinājis un dzesinājis sāpes un slimās asinis.[31]

I am holding you, I am binding you, I will not let you go until you heal the leg and soothe pains and [make good] sick blood.

Even though the circumstances are not indicated, it can be inferred from the context that the charm was uttered while tying the leg with something, probably with a cord or a thread.

Turning now to comparisons, we should note that, irrespective of the fact that comparisons are one of the most productive charm-structures both in Lithuanian and (especially) Latvian charms, only a few parallels have been identified, and they are not particularly close matches either. The syntactical forms differ markedly, which could be explained by the fact that comparisons make improvisation (subsequent variation) easier. In some cases, a comparison structure in a charm is hardly visible but it is implied by the action where an object used is compared with or even identified as an illness. All such parallels are associated with curing of skin diseases, such as rashes, warts, blains, pimples. In all of the following examples, the Lithuanian example is cited first, followed by its Latvian parallel:

1. Rashes used to be healed in the following way: the infected spot would be rubbed with the dew collected in the moonlight and the words would be spoken:

   Dyla mėnuo, dyla baltas, dilk ir tu![32]

   The moon is waning, the white is waning, so you wane too!

   Iznīks, iznīks kā dilstošs mēness.[33]

   It will disappear, disappear like the waning moon.

2. A person who has warts and sees a new moon should say the words looking at the moon:

> Ką matau, tą rauk, ir ką gnybu, tas tur išdilti![34]

> *Tear away what I see and what I am pinching – it should wane!*

[For 'navikaulis', i.e. tumour]

> To, ko es redzu, tas spīd un dilst, un ko es redzu un trinu, tas dilst.[35]

> *The one I see is shining and waning, and the one I see and I am rubbing, is waning.*

3. One should count his/her warts, tie knots on a thread in a number of the warts and bury it in the ground under a threshold saying the following:

> Kai jie supus, kad ir karpos sunyktų![36]

> *When they rot, let the warts disappear!*

They used to tie knots on a thread in a number of the warts and bury it in the ground [saying]:

> Ar šo diedziņu lai satrūd manas kārpas
> *Let my warts rot with this thread.*

> *Or:* Sapūsti, diedziņ, noejat, kārpas[37]
> *Rot, thread, disappear, my warts.*

4. If blains keep appearing, one should go to the cemetery, find a bone of a dead person and say these words while rubbing the bone:

> Kaip anas numire, kad taip mana votys numirtų![38]

> *As that one died, so my warts will die!*

> Lai pazūd kā šis mirons.[39]

> *Let it disappear as this dead person.*

5. Jaunas mėnuli – tu švarus, kad ir mano kūnas būtų toks pat švarus![40]

> *New moon, you are clean, let my body be as clean as you!*

> Lai manas rokas ir tik tīras kā šis mēness.[41]

> *Let my hands be as clean as this moon.*

These charms were found only on a very small scale in Lithuania, for instance, two variants of no. 1, one variant of no. 2, one variant of no. 3,

and one variant of no. 4. Example no. 5 represents the most popular type
in Lithuania with 31 variants,[42] but the comparison structure is maintained only in one sub-type composed of four variants. Latvian types
and sub-types seem to be much more numerous, according to the work
of Straubergs. This charm also has Belorussian and Russian parallels.[43]

Dialogues

We could provide two parallels of dialogue nature, although it is likely
that their number is greater by far. The first charm-type is widespread
both in Lithuania and Latvia:

> In the evening on Thursday, after the sunset, a person with 'girgždėlė'
> [i.e. cracking joints[44]] should place his/her hand on the threshold and
> then either the oldest or the youngest child should slash with an axe
> near the hand. Then the patient will ask:

> Kon kerti? *What are you cutting?*

The other person answers:

> – Gėrgždielė kerto. *I am cutting the cracking.*
> – Kuol kėrsi? *How long will you be cutting?*

The other person replies:

> – Tuol kėrso, kuol nukėrso.[45] *I will be cutting until I cut it.*

This should be repeated three times for three evenings.

Over seventy variants of this charm-type were recorded in Lithuania
(from 1882 up to 2000).[46] In some variants, instead of the cutting with an
axe mentioned above, biting with teeth, pinching with fingers, jamming
with the door, grounding with an edgestone, baking in a stove (fireplace),
striking a spark with a striker, pouring hot wax on water, hammering
a stake in the ground, sweeping with a broom, and dragging on the
ground in a shoe[47] are mentioned. A similar variation of tools, actions
and charms is observed in the Latvian tradition and this variety can
already be seen from the published variants.[48] Some of the Latvian details
have not been found in Lithuania, for instance, cutting with scissors,
cutting with a scythe, trampling with feet, etc. This charm-type was
mainly used in Lithuania to help in case of the disease called 'grižas'
(cracking joints) and one of the most frequently used motifs is biting
with teeth. The biting motif is also popular in Slavonic parallels.[49]

The charm in question can sometimes be performed by one person and then it loses its dialogue structure, as in this Lithuanian example:

> Cracking of joints should be cut. Put your hand on a chopping-block and shout:
>
> > Kertu, kertu grižą! *I am cutting, cutting grižas!*
>
> Then you should slash the chopping-block close to your hand so that the illness is frightened.[50]

There are more such examples, some of them are relatively rare. For example, the following non-dialogic Lithuanian charm was recorded in Latvia with a dialogical structure, as seen in the second example.

In order for a child to start walking sooner, he/she should be taken out of the support and one should utter while cutting a cross with a sharp knife on the floor:

> Šitai perpjaunu pančius![51] *Here I am cutting his/her shackles!*

If a young child does not walk for a long time, one should pick up in a pasture lost shackles of a horse and tie the child with the shackles. Then one should cut the shackles with a knife. The other person asks:

> – Ko tu griez? *What are you cutting?*

The cutter should answer:

> – Pineklu griežu. *I am cutting the shackles.*

Then the first one should say:

> – Griez, griez, ka tu pārgriez.[52] *Keep cutting until you cut.*

In the Lithuanian tradition this charm can hardly be identified as the above-mentioned dialogue-type, but the Latvian parallels seem to show that it belongs exactly to the dialogue variants.

The quoted dialogue charms use wishing formulae, e.g. 'Slash so that you cut', 'Keep cutting until you cut', etc. Here is one more parallel with a dialogue structure, which is a charm performed when a sheep with lambs does not allow them to suckle:

> When a beggar comes along, one should take his stick and strike softly the sheep three times. One should ask it while striking:
>
> > – Ar kavosi vaiką? *Will you take care of your lamb?*

Then one should say to the beggar:

– Mūsų avis vaiką nekavoj! *Our sheep does not take care of its lamb!*

And he should answer:

– Kavos, kavos! *It will take care of it, it will!*

Then they say a sheep begins feeding its lamb.[53]

If a sheep does not love its lamb, the mistress of the house should say to a Jew when he enters their house:

> Izgrauz, žīdiņ, aita jēra nemīlē! *Damn you, Jew, the sheep does not love its lamb!*

The Jew answers:

> – Lai mīlē, lai mīlē! Lai Dievs dod, ka mīlētu! *Let it love, let it love! Let God allow it to love* [i.e., *the lamb*]!

The Jew gets a couple of gloves for that.[54]

Although the charm-type is not amply represented in Lithuania with a mere four variants,[55] but it was recorded in different regions of Lithuania, and its authenticity is beyond doubt. One of the variants is non-dialogic: only a wish is left, which is uttered when beating a sheep with a pair of man's trousers: Mylėk vaiką, mylėk vaiką . . .[56] *Love your youngster, love your youngster.*

Enumeration charms

Enumeration charms, as might be expected for a from which has widespread international parallels, are very common both in Lithuania and Latvia. In some cases they are only a supplement to narrative charms (counting is particularly frequent in tying knots), whereas in other cases enumeration is the main text. There are 73 solely enumerative charms in Lithuania,[57] and their Latvian parallels are found in the work of Straubergs.[58] In comparing the Lithuanian and Latvian enumeration charms it is possible to see that enumeration charms are directly integrated into a text in Latvia. Here are a couple of Latvian examples:

> Velns brauc pa smilkšu kalnu deviņiem melniem zirgiem, Velns brauc pa smilkšu kalnu astoņiem melniem zirgiem . . .[59]

A devil is riding on a sandy hill with nine black horses; a devil is riding on a sandy hill with eight black horses ... [and so on down to one]

Skrej, skrej grēmiens, atmet ļipu – tev viens, man viens, tev divi, man divi ...[60]

Run, run, waterbrash, unbend your tail – one for you, one for me, two for you, two for me ... [and so on up to ten]

The Lithuanian context provides a few examples only with enumerations integrated into a text. One of such charms is an international charm-type:

Turėjo Jobas devynias kirmėles, iš devynių aštuonios, iš aštuonių septynios ...

Job had nine worms, eight out of nine, seven out of eight ... etc.[61]

However, there are only 2 known variants of this type as well, both published by V. J. Mansikka.

Malicious wishes

This group of texts consists of short wishes or curses when they are used in a healing situation and function as a charm. Some of those formulae are designed to make an illness pass from one person to another, others to protect from evil intentions of another person. An illness is passed on using a charm, which is uttered when one sees two people riding on one horse:

Lithuanian:

When two brats are riding on one bay horse (a bay horse is a must here), one should take one's wart with two fingers, lift it with the skin and say:

– Du joja, paimkit ir trečią! *Two are riding, take a third one!*[62].

Latvian:

Warts are being pinched off and thrown after a bearded Jew, a horseman on a white horse, two horsemen or two people riding in a cart:

– Paņem man kārp.[63] *Take this wart from me.*

There are nine variants known in Lithuanian tradition,[64] which vary from the formula 'Take a third one' to a dialogue structure where the person saying charm would at first ask 'Are you riding in two?' and only after they answer, she/he could say 'Take my *norikaulis* [tumour; lump] as a third one!'.[65] There is no information about the distribution of Latvian variants. The charm-type is well-known in the tradition of Eastern Slavs, the reference can be made to Belorussian, Polish, and Bulgarian variants.[66]

Another (Lithuanian) charm designed to pass on an illness is as follows:

> One should tie a piece of red cloth in so many knots as one has warts, lose it on a crossroads and say:
>
> Buvo man, dabar tebus tau![67] *I had them, now you have them!*
>
> Warts will appear on a person who will touch the piece of cloth, and the one who threw it away will get rid of the warts.

The Latvian counterpart has the same syntactical structure of a wish:

> Saņem! Kas man, tas tev![68] *Here you are! What is mine, it is yours!*

The addressee of the wish may be specified, but in that case the formula is not necessary as it is enough to identify the addressee:

Lithuanian:

> Take a red thread from the first child's or the last child's clothing, tie so many knots as there are warts. When tying it is necessary to say to whom the warts should be given, e.g.:
>
> Vilkui! Šuniui! Katei! *To a wolf! To a dog! To a cat!*
>
> And so on and so forth. Then throw the thread to rot.[69]

Latvian:

> Vilkam, lāčam, ne manam bērnam.[70]
>
> *To a wolf, to a bear, but not to my child.* [for use when a child is frightened]
>
> Pie suņiem, pie kaķiem, pie vārnām, pie žagatām, pie visiem zvēriem, kas pa mežu skrien, lai tās sāpes piesitas.[71]
>
> *For dogs, for cats, for crows, for magpies, for all animals running in the woods, let them have these pains.* [for getting rid of a blain].

Curing a disease by sending it to birds and animals is also found in Slavic charms, cf. the Russian variant: '... Idite zh, ety liaky, Na sobaky, na koty, Na soroky, na vorony', i.e. *'Go away, scares, on dogs, on cats, on magpies, on crows.'*[72]

By the use of a similar wishing formulae, the illnesses caused by people could be returned back:

Lithuanian:

When a spot rises on the tongue, people throw a pinch of salt into a burning stove three times at the same time uttering three times:

Tegul tam išdygs, kas mani apkalbėja![73] *Let it rise on the person who was backbiting me!*

Latvian:

When the tongue swells, one should spit on the lap of a skirt and say:

Kā tu man aprunā, tā lai citi tevi aprunā.[74]

As you are backbiting me, let others backbite you.

Curse formulae are sometimes used for protection from sorcerers and the evil eye; such parallels are also found both in the Lithuanian and Latvian folklore:

Lithuanian:

Charm against bewitchment. One should take some salt into his/her hand, circle by it a whole person three times and say:
Druska tau akysna, nedėgulis dantysna![75] *Salt into your eyes, firebrand into your teeth!* This should be repeated three times.

Latvian:

Uguns caur tavu galvu, sāls tavās acīs; lai izput tavas dusmas un domas, kā dūmi izput pa skursteni.[76]

Fire on your head, salt into your eyes; let your anger and thoughts dissipate like smoke through a chimney. [charm used to appease a bad-tempered woman].[77]

The present charm-type has not been recorded amply (in general few curse-charms have been documented as people are unwilling to say them) with seven variants known in Lithuania.[78] The motif is more developed in Slavic parallels and sometimes the curse formula is integrated into a broader text, for instance, the charm from the evil published by Anikin used the formula in the end of the charm: '... sberegite mladenca Sashenku ... ot likhogo scheloveka. Kamen' – v zuby, sol' – v glaza', i.e. '... *protect baby Sashenka ... from an evil-minded person. A stone into the teeth, salt into the eyes'*.[79] However, formulae of such a nature are more frequently used autonomously for protection from harm or the evil eye.[80]

Narrative charms

Narrative charms could be subdivided into two groups according to their authenticity and approximate date of origin, i.e. separating texts of the Christian culture from archaic charms. Latvian charms contain a lot of mythological subjects, which frequently identify gods and mythological beings, e.g. *Laima* (the goddess of fate and fortune), *Pērkons* (the god of thunder), *Zemes māte* ('mother of earth'), *Veļu māte* ('mother of souls'), etc.[81] It is only natural that sometimes they are replaced with Christian characters, particularly frequently with the Virgin Mary and Christ. Meanwhile mythological narratives in the Lithuanian charms are relatively few; therefore, it is hard to identify common Baltic parallels. But here is one case (with the Lithunian examples first):

> Yra baltos marios, ant tų baltų marių stovi balta pana, ji turi baltą karūną. Tegul pasidarys toj rona kaip ta karūna!
>
> *There lies a white sea, and there at the white sea stands a white maiden with a white crown. Let this wound become such [white] as the crown!*

The words would be repeated three times and they say bleeding would stop.[82]
Or:

> Sėdžiu an baltų marių, siūvu baltų karūnų, kad šitoji rona taip pabalt, kaip toji karūna![83]
>
> *I am sitting at the white seas, sewing a white crown;*[84]*let this wound whiten as the crown!*

> Caur divpadsmit klintim, caur melno jūru, iekš tumšas ledus jūras. Amen. Svēta Marija, Dieva māte, sēdēdama uz baltas jūras tur rokā adatu ar baltu zīda diegu, aizšuj visas āderes.[85]
>
> *Across twelve rocks, across the black sea from the dark icy sea. Amen. Holy Mary, Mother of God, sitting at the white sea, has in her hand a needle with a white silk thread and sews up all the veins* [a charm for staunching blood].

The examples above show a common motif of sewing, although the text structure and images are quite different, for instance, the Lithuanian variants mention a crown instead of a thread;[86] meanwhile the Latvian variant shows a standard motif, very popular in Slavic folklore, compare: 'V chistom pole – sine more. V sinem morie – chiornyi kamen'. Na etom kameniu sidit devitsa i zashivajet kravavyje rany', i.e. *'There is a blue sea on an open field. There is a black stone in the blue sea. A maiden is sitting on that stone and is sewing up all the bleeding wounds'.*[87] However, it should be admitted that the Christian motifs are sometimes so fused with the mythological ones that it is difficult to tell which of them are the original motifs and which of them are secondary: the maiden sewing wounds, which is sometimes represented as the Virgin Mary in both Baltic and Slavic charms, according to Russian researchers can arise in the charms out of the images of icons or apocryphal literature.[88]

The remaining charms can hardly be attributed to the ancient Baltic heritage; these are the cases where the Christian charms are transmitted both in Lithuania and in Latvia. The Lithuanian charms comprise a few very productive Christian charm-types. The most popular theme is three roses, which is used to heal erysipelas:

Lithuanian:

Ėja Panela Švinčiausia par pievų. Rada tris rožes. Vienų raškė, kita puola, tračia suvis prapuola. Taip tegu ir šita rože prapuola![89]

Blessed Virgin Mary was walking across a meadow. She found three roses. She plucked one, the second fell, and the third disappeared at all. So let this 'rose'[90] disappear as well!

Latvian:

Mūsu Kungs Jēzus gāja pa ūdeni un pa zemi; tam bija trīs rozes labājā rokā. Tā viena novīta, otra izņīka, trešā pazuda.[91]

Our Lord Jesus walked on the water and ground, and he had three roses in his right hand. One of them withered, the second disappeared, and the third vanished.

In Lithuanian tradition, this is one of the most widespread charms having 86 variants.[92] According to Straubergs' published data, this charm type was also recorded numerous times in Latvia and exhibited great variety.[93] The Lithuanian texts nearly always use the journey motif: Jesus (less frequently the Virgin Mary, three maidens, or three kings) is travelling along the road (across a meadow, forest, sands, water) and carrying in his hand (or sees) three roses (lilies). Only three variants mention roses growing in a meadow,[94] in Mary's garden,[95] or simply travelling somewhere.[96] Meanwhile in Latvia this theme varies more substantially and Biblical images are more numerous (the Red Sea, Garden of Eden, Jerusalem) and the Christian symbols of the Middle Ages;[97] the following are a few variants, which are still close to the medieval European legends:[98]

Stāv trīs rozes uz mūsu Kunga sirds. Tā pirmā ir laipnība, tā otrā – žēlsirdība, tā trešā – labprātība.[99]

Three roses stand on the heart of our Lord. The first is love, the second is mercy and the third is benefaction.

Trīs rozes auga uz mūsu Kunga Jēzus Kristus kapa. To vienu sauc Dievs tas Tēvs, to otru Dievs tas Dēls; to trešo sauc Dievs tas cienīgais sv. Gars.[100]

Three roses grew on the grave of our Lord Jesus Christ. One was called God the Father, the second was called God the Son, and the third was called honourable Holy Spirit.

Uz mūsu Kunga Jēzus Kristus kapa ir 3 rozes. Tā viena plauka, tā otra auga, tā trešā vīta.[101]

There are three roses on the grave of our Lord Jesus Christ. The first blossomed, the second grew, and the third withered.

Although the charm about three roses is known in Slavic regions, i.e. Belarus, Ukraine, southern part of Russia, and Poland,[102] it has a special place in the Lithuanian tradition in terms of quantity, as charms of this type account for around 6 per cent of total charm variants. Since the charm-type has been recorded only few times in Poland and a number of Polish variants have been recorded in Lithuania,[103] Maria Zavjalova suggests that it may not have entered Lithuania from Poland, but rather from Latvia, where it had, in its turn, been imported from Germany.[104] It is a most interesting assumption, yet it should be noted that, due to historical circumstances, Polish culture had a strong influence on the Lithuanian culture rather than vice versa. And after all, only one standard version of the charm with little variation is popular in Lithuania, while the Latvian variants exhibit a high degree of variation.

The next most popular Christian charm in the Lithuanian tradition (with 44 variants)[105] is the international charm-type called, according to the Latin analogy, **Flum Jordan**.[106] The Lithuanian variants, though short and simple, are subject to substantial variation. The standard variant is binary, i.e. as water stopped (other variants: as Christ stopped walking/as he stood on a stone), so the blood stops flowing:

Ėjo Ponas Jezusas Nazaranskas per Jordano upę. Susturėjo upė ir prasiskyrė unduo. Taip suturėk ir praskirk tą kraują, kurį aš matau savo akimis![107]

Lord Jesus from Nazareth went across the River Jordan. The river stopped and its water separated. So let stop and separate the blood that I see with my own eyes!

Such brief and simple variants are dominating and only 15 variants associate the stopping of the water with the birth, baptism or crucifixion of Jesus. There are also several autonomous charm-types, though partly related with the subject in question, e.g.:

Ėjo Jėzus per Cedrono upę ir tris kartus upėn nusispjovė (tai sakant reikia spjaut ant sergančios vietos). Kaip susiturėjo vanduo upėj, kad susiturėtų visos piktybės ant svieto![108]

Jesus walked across the river Kidron and spat into the river three times (here one should spit on the spot affected by an illness). As the water of the river stopped, let all the bad things stop in the world!

Apart from the standard Latvian variants,[109] there are only a few rather distant variations, for instance:

Joja kungs Jezus Christus uz sorkona zyrga par Jordana upeiti, par ašņotu ezeriņu. Aizašyun ezeriņ ar šolka dēdzeņu ar sudobra adatiņu![110]

Our Lord Jesus Christ rode a red horse across the River Jordan, across a lake of bloods. Sew the lake with a silk thread, with a silver needle!

The other parallel is a Christian charm-type widespread in Lithuania, which mentions Christ who fending off dogs in his travels:

Ėjo Viešpats per mišką, susitiko šunį. Šuo jo nelietė. Ir manęs teneliečia šunys, kaip tavęs, Viešpatie, nelietė![111]

Our Lord walked in the forest and met a dog. The dog did not touch him. Let dogs not touch me as they did not touch you, my Lord!

Eighteen variants were recorded in Lithuania,[112] all relatively similar to each other. For example, the charm character may vary (Christ, Christ with the apostles, Mary, the charmer himself/herself), the charm may sometimes supplemented with a formula to the effect that 'a dog was born blind and it will die blind' (this is interference from another charm), onomatopoeic words may be inserted (calling a dog *'siu-siu-siu'* or teasing it with sounds imitative of barking: *'am-am-am'*). The Latvian equivalent is very similar to the cited Lithuanian charm (Straubergs provided only a single variant):

Pestītājs iet pa ceļu, suņi viņu nerej. Es iešu pa Pestītāja pēdām, suņi mani neries.[113]

Our Saviour walks a road and dogs do not attack him. I shall walk the footsteps of the Saviour and dogs will not attack me.

A similar Latvian charm is used to protect from a snake.[114] A couple of Byelorussian and Polish variants of this charm-type can be found in the publication *Polesskije zagavory*,[115] 3 Polish variants are recorded in Lithuania.[116] According to Zavjalova this charm is not found in Poland; therefore its area of distribution would be limited to Belarus and Eastern Lithuania.[117] However the area of the charm type is in fact larger as three variants from central Lithuania exist,[118] as do Latvian parallels.

Another charm-type known both in Lithuania and Latvia is the story of five wounds of Christ:

Lithuanian blain charm:

Mūsų Jezus Kristus Išganytojas turėjo daug žeizdų ir skaudulių (ronų ir sopulių), bet jos visos jam nekenkė (neškadija). Taip ir šis neaugs, nekils, netins ir nedidės! Pranyk, pranyk, pranyk, Janošius![119]

Our Saviour Jesus Christ had many wounds and sores but none of them affected him. Let this [here one should say a blain or a sore] stop growing, rising, swelling and increasing! Vanish, vanish, vanish, Janošius!

Latvian blood-staunching charm:

Stāv, asins! Tā mūsu Kunga Kristus asins stāvējusi pie krusta koka. Tev nebūs uztūkt, ne ar sāpēt, tā kā viņa piecas vātis ne ir uztūkušas, ne ar sāpējušas, bet ir pie krusta koka bez sāpēm palikušas. Amen.[120]

Stop, blood, as the blood of our Lord Christ stopped on the wooden cross. Do not swell, do not ache as his five wounds did not swell, did not ache, but remained at the wooden cross without pain.

Up to now, only two variants of this type have come to light in Lithuania, whereas many more where recorded in Latvia, e.g. Straubergs cites 13 different variants of the charm.[121] A few Polish-language variants were also recorded in Lithuania.[122] Quite a large number of variants were documented in Russia; unlike the Lithuanian example designed to charm wounds or blains, the Russian variants are primarily intended to alleviate pains.[123] The charm type was popular in England too: ' "Our Saviour was fastened to the Cross with nails and thorns, which neither rats nor rankles, no more shan't thy finger" (For a thorn three times)'.[124]

One more relatively numerous Christian parallel in Lithuania and Latvia is a charm for chasing of a snake in the name of Christ:

Lithuanian:

Pikta gyvate inkunda. Matina Dieva ištara, Viešpats Jezus prižadieja, kad piktas gyvatas gielo atpuls![125]

An evil snake bites. Mother of our Lord says 'Our Lord Jesus promised that the evil fang will disappear [won't harm]!'

Latvian:

Čūska dūra, Kristus saka, Marija zvērēja: Lai tā dzelone izņīkst! Dievs Tēvs, Dievs Dēls, Dievs Svētais Gars, stāvi tu klāt, nāc par paglābšanu![126]

A snake bit, Christ said, Mary swore: 'Let the fang vanish!' God the Father, God the Son, and the Holy Spirit, stay [with the patient], come to the rescue!

Some Latvian texts of this type emphasise driving of poison out of the body; therefore such texts are close to exorcist literature. Here are two examples, the first for snakebite, the latter for rabies:[127]

Čūska dūra, Jēzus runāja, Marija zvērēja, – lai tā gipte izgāja.[128]

A snake bit, Jesus said and Mary swore so that the poison would leave.

Marija sacīja, Kristus svētīja: 'Sātān, izej arā no tevis'.[129]

Mary said and Christ blessed: 'Satan, leave this person'.

Only three of the total of ten Lithuanian variants[130] feature such a banishment motif. The other charms feature attempts to make the poison disappear, to prevent it from doing harm, etc. Nonetheless, the focus of all variants is a word of God (the Virgin Mary, Saints, angels) (he/she/they *said, swore* and the like), which is treated as *užkalbėjimas* (a 'charm')[131] in two variants: 'Motina Švinčiausia užkalbėja, Viešpats Jėzus atžadėjo' (*Holy Mother charmed and Our Lord Jesus promised*),[132] 'Švinčiausia Motina užkalbėja, per poną Jezų prisieke' (*Holy Mother charmed and swore in the name of Our Lord Jesus*).[133] This charm is also known in the Polish-language tradition of Lithuania, e.g.: 'Zła gadzina kąsiła, Maryja Matka mówiła, sam Pan Jezus rzekł, aby złej gadziny jad odszedł.' (*An evil snake bit, Mother Mary said and Our Lord Jesus himself said that the poison of the evil snake would leave*).[134]

Some of the parallels of Christian charms in Lithuania and Latvia have been very sparsely documented. Only traces of the following charm have been found in Lithuania (there is but one fragmentary variant); but it is better known in Latvia:

Lithuanian example, for snakebite:

Arė Petras, arė Jonas, arė Jėzus, suarė tris lysvutes, išarė tris rubokėlius: vieną juodą, kitą raudoną ir margą. Tegul bus pagarbintas Jezus Kristus![135]

Peter ploughed, John ploughed, Jesus ploughed; they ploughed three beds and turned up three little worms: one black, one red and one speckled. Praised be Jesus Christ!

Latvian example, for intestinal worms:

Pēteris un Jēzus brauca uz tīrumu un ara četras vagas, ara uz trīsiem tārpiem: tas viens balts, tas otrs melns, tas trešais sārkans. Tie visi tārpi nost miruši. Iekš tā vārda ...'[136]

Peter and Jesus went to a field and ploughed four beds, they ploughed for three worms: one of them was white, the second was black and the third was red. All those worms died. In the name ...'

Several variants of this charm were recorded in Latvia, but only three published variants feature a ploughing motif; the variants where worms are carried in the hand are far more numerous.[137]

The charm-type, though represented by only one variant in Lithuania, is not the result of Latvian impact upon Lithuanians as the geographical spread of the charm is maximally wide: the charm was recorded in southern Lithuania, more than 250 km from Lithuania's borderzone with Latvia.

Another international subject moderately well-represented in both Lithuania and Latvia is the story about three Marys (*Tres virgines*) who help to staunch bleeding. As of now, we have but one example of each variant, but it is likely that more variants could be found among the unpublished Latvian charms. As before, the Lithuanian example is the first below:

Dzievo galybe, pono Dzievo pagelba turejo Magdalena tris dukteris. Viena kalbeja: 'Einam, keliaukem'. Antra kalbejo: 'Grįžkem ir apsistokem'. Ir tu, kraujas, turi čia apsistot per Viešpatį Jezusą, Sūnų Dievo Motinelės, Jo kūno garbingiausio ir Šventos traices, ir aniolų šventųjų ir Dvases šventos. Vardan Dievo Tevo ... Amen.[138]

Thanks to the might of Our Lord and with the help of Our Lord, Mary Magdalene had three daughters. One said: 'Let us go'. The second said: 'Let us come back and stay'. And you, blood, must stay in the name of our Lord Jesus, the Son of the Mother of God, his most venerable body and the Holy Trinity, and Holy Angels and Holy Spirit. In the name of God the Father ... Amen.

Trīs jumpravas gāja pa zemi; viņas turēja trīs asens piles savā labā rokā. Tā pirmā sacīja: 'Asini, stāvi!' Tā otrā sacīja: 'Asini, tev vajaga stāvēt!' Tā trešā sacīja: 'Asinīm vajaga nostāties!' Iekš tā vārda ...[139]

Three virgins were walking on the land; they had three drops of blood in their right hand. One said: 'Blood, stop!' The second said: 'Blood, you must stay!' The third said: 'Blood must be still [i.e. become calm], settle!' In the name ...'

Although the examples are rather different, they both are feature the same three travelling Maries (virgins, sisters, saints).[140] In Lithuanian tradition, the motif of three women can also be identified in the charms for erysipelas:

Ėja trys panos. Rada tris rožes. Viena sako: "Kad tu sudžiūtum!" Kita sako: "Kad tu supūtum!" Trečia sako: "Kad tu čia nebūtum!"[141]

Three virgins were walking. They found three roses. One says: 'Let you wither!' Another says: 'Let you rot!' The third says: 'Let you disappear from here!'

In Latvian charms for erysipelas, three Maries appear wearing clothes of different colours (white, blue, and red), and picking flowers of different colours.[142]

The last Christian parallel to be presented in this article features the impossibility formula so common in charms:

Lithuanian, charm for wounds:

Nesena yra ta žeizda. Diena ši yra gydoma ir palaiminta (blagaslovyta) ta adyna (valanda). Kad tau daugiau neskaudėtų, kad netvinktų ir tuoj pagytų, kad neatsidarytų votys lig to laiko, kolei Švinčiausia Marija pagimdys kitų sūnų. Amen.[143]

This wound is fresh. This day is healed and this hour is blessed. Let you suffer no more pain [touch a patient's wound with your hand], let it not swell and let it heal soon, so that blains do not appear until Holy Mary gives birth to another son. Amen. [Cross the wound three times].

Latvian, charm for fire:

Stāvi uguns, kamēr Marija otru dēlu dzemdēs.[144]

Stay, fire, until Mary gives birth to another son.

The impossibility formulae in Lithuanian charms are usually used in the context of archaic tradition, for instance, the following formula is characteristic of Lithuanian snake-bite charms: 'Akmuo ba šakniu, paukštis ba pieno, kirmela be kramslo'[145] (*A stone has no roots, a bird has no milk and a snake has no fang*). This tradition in some cases is intertwined with the Christian content: 'Bitelė be kraujų, ponas Jėzus be vaikų. Kaip sustojo vanduo ant Ardonios, kad taip sustotų kraujas kūne!'[146] (*A bee has no blood and Our Lord Jesus has no children. As water stopped in the River Jordan, let the blood stop in this body!*) This serves as a good example of syncretism between native Lithuanian and international Christian traditions.

Even though the Lithuanian and (especially) the Latvian traditions contain a number of Christian charm-types, only eight share types have been identified up to now; four of these are very popular and account for 11 per cent of the Lithuanian corpus. All the parallels are international, although their variants in some cases exhibit a number of local features and are contaminated with non-Christian charm-types.

It is evident from the examples provided in the article, that Baltic charms frequently have their Slavic counterparts: out of the 25 Lithuanian–Latvian parallels discussed herein, 14 parallels are correlating with Slavic charm types or motifs (nine of them are attributable to the local tradition, five are migratory Christian historiolas). Since some of the Baltic charms correlate with the Belorussian, Ukrainian, Polish, and southern Russian material, whereas the others correlate with the charms found in the north of Russia, we tend to the view that the Baltic and Slavic equivalences have not resulted from contacts at the border,[147] but are rather based on the older cultural traditions, in some cases probably dating back to the age of the separation of Baltic-Slavic culture. However, there is a possibility to identify traces of the Baltic assimilation process in the territory of Belarus and south-west Russia, which was took place from the sixth century in the area of the upper reaches of the Dnieper and upper reaches of the Oka (present-day territories of Belarus and south-west Russia)[148] to Lithuanian assimilation in the nineteenth and twentieth centuries at the western edges of Belarus.

As far as the Lithuanian and Latvian parallels are concerned, it should be acknowledged that the material discussed in the article show a relatively low degree of correlation among the Baltic charms; whereas in the Byelorussian and Russian folklore we would find more equivalents of Lithuanian charms than in the Latvian folklore. The publication *Polesskie zagovory* alone (it is the newest academic edition of Slavic charms) (comprising over 1,094 charms from the Polesje region in Belarus and Ukraine) yields more than 25 charm-types similar to Lithuanian ones, though only seven of these have Christian content. It is yet premature to decide if that could mean that the Lithuanian charm tradition as well as folk songs are closer to Belorussians than Latvians, but it can already be claimed that the Lithuanian charms in terms of a number of parallels correlate almost equally both with the Latvian and East Slavic (primarily Belorussian) tradition.

Notes

1. D. Vaitkevičienė, ed., *Lietuvių užkalbėjimų šaltiniai: elektroninis sąvadas.* [CD-ROM] (Vilnius: Lietuvių literatūros ir tautosakos institutas, 2005). Here the charms recorded by V. J. Mansikka (V. J. Mansikka, *Litauische Zaubersprüche* (FF Communications 87) (Helsinki: Suomalainen tiedeakatemia, 1929) is included.
2. *Latviešu folkloras krātuve* (Rīga: LFK, 2004), p. 6.
3. F. I. Treiland (Brīvzemnieks), ed., *Materialy po etnografii latyshskago plemeni* (Izvestia imperatorskago obshchestva liubitelei estestvoznanija, antropologii i etnografii 40, Trudy etnograficheskago otdela 6) (Moscow, 1881); K. Straubergs, *Latviešu buŗamie vārdi*, Volume 1 (Rīgā: Latviešu folkloras krātuve, 1939).
4. Kostas Aleksynas, ed., *Juodoji knyga.* Collected by Jonas Basanavičius (Jono Basanavičiaus tautosakos biblioteka 12) (Vilnius: Lietuvių literatūros ir tautosakos institutas, 2004).

5. Eduard Hoffmann-Krayer and Hanns Bächtold-Stäubli, eds, *Handwörterbuch des deutschen Aberglaubens* (Berlin: de Gruyter, 1927–1942) (hereafter HDA), Vol. 9, p. 880; J. G. Frazer. *The Golden Bough: A Study in Magic and Religion* (London: Papermac, 1987), pp. 38–9; Jacqueline Simpson and Steve Roud, *A Dictionary of English Folklore* (Oxford: New York: Oxford University Press, 2000), p. 354.
6. Vaitkevičienė, *Lietuvių užkalbėjimų šaltiniai*, No. 804. Nos 794–818, 1082–1085, 1102, 1291.
7. Straubergs, *Vārdi*, p. 234
8. Vaitkevičienė, *Lietuvių užkalbėjimų šaltiniai*, Nos 794–818, 1082–1085, 1102, 1291.
9. Having talked to the folklore researchers at the Institute of Lithuanian Literature and Language, it appeared that nearly all of them remembered this custom from their childhood and half of them still remembered the charm itself.
10. V. P. Anikin. *Russkie zagovory i zaklinaniia: Materialy fol'klornykh ekspeditsii 1953–1993 gg.* (Moscow: Izdatel'stvo Moskovskogo universiteta, 1998), No. 109.
11. Jacqueline Simpson and Steve Roud, *Dictionary*, p. 354.
12. Vaitkevičienė, *Lietuvių užkalbėjimų šaltiniai*, No. 1003 (cf. No. 1004); Mansikka, *Litauische*, No. 19.
13. Brīvzemnieks, *Materialy*, No. 123.
14. Vaitkevičienė, *Lietuvių užkalbėjimų šaltiniai*, Nos 700–703; 3 variants published in: Rita Balkutė, ed., Liaudies magija: užkalbėjimai, maldelės, pasakojimai XX a. pab. – XXI a. pr. Lietuvoje (Vilnius: Lietuvių liaudies kultūros centras, 2004 [CD-ROM]). One more fragment variant was recorded in Lithuania in Polish: the herpes infected spot is rubbed by hand after the sunset and the following words are pronounced 'Dzień dobry!', i.e. 'Good day!' (Vaitkevičienė, *Lietuvių užkalbėjimų šaltiniai*, No. 1194).
15. Ibid., No. 700.
16. Ibid., No. 703.
17. Girls tortured to death or those who spinned on Sunday were believed to become mythological beings, *Svētās meitas*, after their death (Brīvzemnieks, *Materialy*, No. 137); according to other sources suicide spinsters would turn into such beings (P. Šmits, ed., *Latviešu tautas ticējumi*, Vol. 4 (Rīgā: Latviešu folkloras krātuve, 1941), p. 1794). When offended, the mythological beings inflict diseases on people and cattle. It was thought that in a house *Svētās meitas* lived in the space between the fireplace (stove) and the wall, and if someone spilled some water there or spat, *Svētās meitas* would inflict the person with an illness, which is called *uguns vātis* 'fire blain' (*Herpes*) in Latvian.
18. Brīvzemnieks, *Materialy*, No. 215.
19. P. Šmits, ed., *Latviešu pasakas un teikas*, Vol. 13 (Rīgā: Valtera un Rapas akc. sab. apgāds, 1937), p. 303.
20. Šmits, *Ticējumi*, p. 1796.
21. Ibid.
22. *Ugunsvāts* or a 'fire blain' is the name given to herpes, *līķa vātis* a 'corpse's blain' is a boil appearing on a body if a person urinates on the place where the water used to wash a dead person was spilled, Kārlis

Mīlenbhs, *Latviešu valodas vārdnīca*, Vol. 4 (Rīga: Kultūras fonds, 1932), pp. 295, 512.

23. Some of the Latvian charms made of four or more rhythmical lines were published in P. Šmits, *Tautas dziesmas: Papildinājums Kr. Barona 'Latvju Dainām'* (Rīga: Latviešu folkloras krātuve, 1938), pp. 210–19.

24. Vaitkevičienė, *Lietuvių užkalbėjimų šaltiniai*, No. 691.

25. Straubergs, *Vārdi*, p. 346.

26. The Latvian *ziedi* means blossoms of flowers only figuratively as it stands for blood of periods or blood running during childbearing.

27. A similar motif is seen in the Lithuanian charm from the illness called 'gumbas': 'Gumbas turi savo dvarų. Išsikačiok, išsivaliok ir in daikto atsistok', i.e. 'Gumbas *has its own manor. Roll over, tumble and stand up on the ground'*, Vaitkevičienė, *Lietuvių užkalbėjimų šaltiniai*, No. 371; Mansikka, *Litauische*, No. 155.

28. Vaitkevičienė, *Lietuvių užkalbėjimų šaltiniai*, No. 1156. A womb is called '*matitsa*' which is a euphemistic name (*matitsa* is a diminutive form of a 'mother').

29. Ibid., 109.

30. Ibid., Nos 96–109; Mansikka, *Litauische*, Nos 2, 16, 83, 84, 85.

31. Straubergs, *Vārdi*, p. 239.

32. Vaitkevičienė, *Lietuvių užkalbėjimų šaltiniai*, No. 625 (cf. No. 620). There are only 2 known variants of this sub-type.

33. Straubergs, *Vārdi*, p. 242.

34. Vaitkevičienė, *Lietuvių užkalbėjimų šaltiniai*, No. 536.

35. Straubergs, *Vārdi*, p. 243.

36. Vaitkevičienė, *Lietuvių užkalbėjimų šaltiniai*, No. 611.

37. Straubergs, *Vārdi*, p. 241.

38. Vaitkevičienė, *Lietuvių užkalbėjimų šaltiniai*, No. 615.

39. Straubergs, *Vārdi*, p. 241.

40. Vaitkevičienė, *Lietuvių užkalbėjimų šaltiniai*, No. 422.

41. Straubergs, *Vārdi*, p. 241.

42. Vaitkevičienė, *Lietuvių užkalbėjimų šaltiniai*, Nos 404–26, 1296; Balkutė, *Liaudies magija* (7 variants).

43. T. A. Agapkina, E. E. Levkijevskaia, A. L. Toporkov, eds, *Polesskie zagovory (v zapisiakh 1970–1990 gg.)* (Moscow: Indrik, 2003), pp. 209–10; N. I. Tolstoi, ed., *Slavianskie drevnosti*, Vol. 1 (Moscow: Mezhdunarodnye otnoshenie, 1995), p. 235.

44. Lithuanian '*girgždėlė*' or '*grižas*', German '*Galenkknarre*'.

45. Vaitkevičienė, *Lietuvių užkalbėjimų šaltiniai*, No. 538.

46. Ibid., Nos 537–96, 908; Aleksynas, *Juodoji*, p. 236; Balkutė, *Liaudies magija* (12 variants).

47. Vaitkevičienė, *Lietuvių užkalbėjimų šaltiniai*, Nos 537, 541, 548, 560, 574, 576, 580, 587, 592, 593; Mansikka, *Litauische*, Nos. 125, 149.

48. Brīvzemnieks, *Materialy*, No. 234; Straubergs, *Vārdi*, p. 249.

49. G. A. Bartashevich, ed., *Zamovy* (Minsk: Navuka i tekhnika, 1992), No. 230; Anikin, *Russkie zagovory*, No. 250; V. L. Kliaus, *Ukazatel' siuzhetov i siuzhetnykh situatsij zagovornykh tekstov vostochnykh i juzhnykh slavian* (Moscow: Nasledie, 1997), p. 98. There are other well-known Slavic motifs traced in Lithuanian and Latvian examples such as boiling, baking, and banishment. See Agapkina, *Polesskie*, pp. 72, 81–2.

50. Vaitkevičienė, *Lietuvių užkalbėjimų šaltiniai*, No. 554.
51. Ibid., No. 908.
52. Straubergs, *Vārdi*, p. 248.
53. Vaitkevičienė, *Lietuvių užkalbėjimų šaltiniai*, No. 64.
54. Brīvzemnieks, *Materialy*, No. 451.
55. Vaitkevičienė, *Lietuvių užkalbėjimų šaltiniai*, No. 64; Aleksynas, *Juodoji*, pp. 225, 381; Balkutė, *Liaudies magija* (1 variant).
56. Aleksynas, *Juodoji*, p. 225.
57. Vaitkevičienė, *Lietuvių užkalbėjimų šaltiniai*, Nos 704–61; Aleksynas, *Juodoji*, pp. 262, 235, 365; Balkutė, *Liaudies magija* (12 variants).
58. Straubergs, *Vārdi*, p. 252.
59. Ibid., p. 253.
60. Ibid.
61. (Vaitkevičienė, *Lietuvių užkalbėjimų šaltiniai*, Nos 386–7; Mansikka, *Litauische*, Nos 87–8.
62. Vaitkevičienų, *Lietuvių užkalbėjimų šaltiniai*, No. 524)
63. Straubergs, *Vārdi*, p. 235.
64. Vaitkevičienė, *Lietuvių užkalbėjimų šaltiniai*, Nos 521–28; Balkutė, *Liaudies magija* (1 variant).
65. Ibid., No. 523.
66. N. I. Tolstoi, *Slavianskie drevnosti*, Vol. 1, p. 235; Agapkina, *Polesskie*, p. 209; Anikin, *Russkie zagovory*, No. 1924.
67. Vaitkevičienė, *Lietuvių užkalbėjimų šaltiniai*, No. 78.
68. Straubergs, *Vārdi*, p. 237.
69. Vaitkevičienė, *Lietuvių užkalbėjimų šaltiniai*, No. 1006.
70. Straubergs, *Vārdi*, p. 260.
71. Ibid., p. 234.
72. Agapkina, *Polesskie*, p. 111.
73. Ibid., No. 930.
74. Straubergs, *Vārdi*, p. 237.
75. Vaitkevičienė, *Lietuvių užkalbėjimų šaltiniai*, No. 124.
76. Straubergs, *Vārdi*, p. 268.
77. Latvians have a separate functional group of charms – the so-called *kungs vārdi*, which are the charms designed to prevent the lord's anger or a punishment.
78. Vaitkevičienė, *Lietuvių užkalbėjimų šaltiniai*, Nos 118–24
79. Anikin, *Russkie zagovory*, No. 344. Cf. 'Le gros sel dans l'oeil de l'envieux', N. Poznanskij, *Zagovory: opyt issledovanija proisxozhdenija i razvitija zagovornyx formul* (Moskva: Indrik, 1995), p. 145.
80. Agapkina, *Polesskie*, p. 451.
81. Straubergs, *Vārdi*, pp. 383–438.
82. Vaitkevičienė, *Lietuvių užkalbėjimų šaltiniai*, No. 884.
83. Ibid., No. 885.
84. The word 'crown' (in Lith. *karūna*) was used for a headband of cloth with ribbons worn by unmarried girls.
85. Brīvzemnieks, *Materialy*, No. 270.
86. There is one Lithuanian variant with a thread motif, but it was recorded in the contact area of Lithuania and Belarus (Ceikiniai, Ignalina Distr.) (Vaitkevičienė, *Lietuvių užkalbėjimų šaltiniai*, No. 886; Mansikka, *Litauische*,

212   *National Traditions*

No. 160), and the text structure shows that it is a translation of a charm of Belorussian or Russian Old Believers.
87. Anikin, *Russkie zagovory*, No. 1654. The subject is very common in the Eastern Slav charms; See Agapkina, *Polesskie*, pp. 179–80; Kliaus, *Ukazatel'*, pp. 282–8; Bartashevich, *Zamovy*, No. 472.
88. See Agapkina, *Polesskie*, p. 180.
89. Vaitkevičienė, *Lietuvių užkalbėjimų šaltiniai*, No. 265.
90. In Lithuanian the word 'rožė' has two meanings – 'rose' and 'erysipelas'.
91. Brivzemnieks *Materialy*, No. 168.
92. Vaitkevičienė, *Lietuvių užkalbėjimų šaltiniai*, Nos 233–307, 1143, 1287, 1605; Balkutė, *Liaudies magija* (8 variants).
93. Straubergs, *Vārdi*, pp. 331–8.
94. Mansikka, *Litauische*, no 110.
95. Vaitkevičienė, *Lietuvių užkalbėjimų šaltiniai*, No. 264.
96. Ibid., 233.
97. Straubergs, *Vārdi*, p. 331.
98. 'Sur lai fosse nostre seigneur Ilia trois fleurs: l'une de grace, l'autre se volunté et l'autre por li sanc guarir'; 'Die Blumen sind Gott Vater, Sohn und Hl. Geist', HDA, Vol. 2, pp. 422–3.
99. Straubergs, *Vārdi*, p. 331.
100. Ibid.
101. Ibid.
102. Agapkina, *Polesskie*, pp. 190–1; Bartashevich, *Zamovy*, Nos 719–20; Anikin, *Russkie zagovory*, No. 1777; Kliaus, *Ukazatel'*, pp. 337–8.
103. The collection of Lithuanian Folklore Archive stores at least 21 polish variants, see Vaitkevičienė, *Lietuvių užkalbėjimų šaltiniai*; a few variants were published by Magdalena Zowczak, 'Mitologia zamawiana i mistyka zamów na podstawie współczesnych materiałów z Wileńszczyzny', *Literatura ludowa*, 4–6/XXXVIII (1994), pp. 19–21.
104. M. V. Zavjalova, 'Problema migracij zagovornykh siuzhetov epicheskogo tipa' in *Zagovornyj tekst: Genezis i struktura* (Moskva: Indrik, 2005), pp. 361–3.
105. Vaitkevičienė, *Lietuvių užkalbėjimų šaltiniai*, Nos 186–228, 1218; Mansikka, *Litauische*, Nos 20, 23, 26–7, 29–34, 117, 129.
106. Jonathan Roper, 'Typologising English Charms', in Jonathan Roper, ed., *Charms and Charming in Europe* (Basingstoke: Palgrave Macmillan: 2004), p. 133.
107. Vaitkevičienė, *Lietuvių užkalbėjimų šaltiniai*, No. 218.
108. Ibid., Nos 229–31; Mansikka, *Litauische*, p. 77. Cf. Kliaus, *Ukazatel'*, p. 330 (No. 1/X.1.1/B7).
109. Straubergs, *Vārdi*, p. 296.
110. Ibid.
111. Vaitkevičienė, *Lietuvių užkalbėjimų šaltiniai*, No. 167.
112. Ibid., Nos 167–83, 1630; Mansikka, *Litauische*, Nos 93–5.
113. Straubergs, *Vārdi*, p. 337.
114. Ibid., p. 420.
115. Agapkina, *Polesskie*, Nos 706–7.
116. Vaitkevičienė, *Lietuvių užkalbėjimų šaltiniai*, Nos 1278, 1441, 1464.
117. M. V. Zavjalova, *Problema*, p. 360.

118. Žasliai (Kaišiadoriai Distr.), Vadokliai (Panevėžys Distr.), Ukmergė (Ukmergė Distr.). Vaitkevičienė, *Lietuvių užkalbėjimų šaltiniai*, Nos 169–70, 180.
119. Ibid, Nos. 618 (cf. 617); Mansikka, *Litauische*, No. 36.
120. Brīvzemnieks, *Materialy*, No. 293.
121. Straubergs, *Vārdi*, pp. 299–300.
122. Vaitkevičienė, *Lietuvių užkalbėjimų šaltiniai*, No. 1475.
123. Žr. Kliaus, *Ukazatel'*, p. 127.
124. Roper, *English Charms*, p. 137.
125. Vaitkevičienė, *Lietuvių užkalbėjimų šaltiniai*, No. 829.
126. Brīvzemnieks, *Materialy*, No. 421.
127. Straubergs, *Vārdi*, p. 376.
128. Brīvzemnieks, *Materialy*, No. 422.
129. Ibid., No. 372; Straubergs, *Vārdi*, p. 376.
130. Vaitkevičienė, *Lietuvių užkalbėjimų šaltiniai*, Nos 821–9; Balkutė, *Liaudies magija* (1 variant).
131. The verb *užkalbėti* 'to charm' is a folk term for healing by means of charms and this term is not used in the Lithuanian Christian literature.
132. Vaitkevičienė, *Lietuvių užkalbėjimų šaltiniai*, No. 825.
133. Ibid., No. 824.
134. Ibid., No. 1104, 1170, 1380, 1390. Cf. *HDA*, Vol. 7, p. 1197.
135. Ibid., No. 33.
136. Brīvzemnieks, *Materialy*, No. 106.
137. Straubergs, *Vārdi*, p. 336.
138. Vaitkevičienė, *Lietuvių užkalbėjimų šaltiniai*, No. 366; Mansikka, *Litauische*, No. 28.
139. Brīvzemnieks, *Materialy*, No. 272.
140. *HDA*, Vol. 2, p. 442.
141. Vaitkevičienė, *Lietuvių užkalbėjimų šaltiniai*, No. 307; another similar variant features three kings instead of three roses (the motif of three kings is very rare in Lithuanian charms; in Latvia several variants were recorded in Latin, see Straubergs, *Vārdi*, p. 289).
142. Straubergs, *Vārdi*, p. 344.
143. Vaitkevičienė, *Lietuvių užkalbėjimų šaltiniai*, No. 601.
144. Straubergs, *Vārdi*, p. 224.
145. Vaitkevičienė, *Lietuvių užkalbėjimų šaltiniai*, No. 9; Mansikka, *Litauische*, p. 81.
146. Ibid., No. 71.
147. M. Zavjalova, who wrote on the charm types migrating in the border areas, maintains that there are very few coincidences relating the Slavic tradition with the Baltic one and practically all of them exhibit features of borrowing from Slavic charms (Zavjalova, *Problema*, p. 356).
148. R. Volkaitė-Kulikauskienė, ed., *Lietuvių etnogenezė* (Vilnius: Mokslas, 1987), pp. 124–50; Marija Gimbutas, *The Balts* (London: Thames and Hudson 1962); V. N. Toporov, O. N. Trubachev, *Lingvisticheskij analiz gidronimov Verkhnego Podneorov'ia* (Moskva: Izdatelstvo Akademii Nauk SSSR, 1962).

15
The Corpus of Charms in the Middle English Leechcraft Remedy Books[1]

Lea Olsan

In England between 1200 and 1500, a large proportion of the charms in circulation were devoted to healing.[2] These healing charms ranged widely. Latin medical texts include rituals with charms for gathering medicinal plants, amulets with charms for conception, secret charms to prevent 'cramp' and charms to staunch bleeding.[3] In vernacular remedy books, charms are provided as cures for medical conditions and against thieves. Charms to cure or protect livestock – to cure sick pigs, chickens, sheep, and cows as well as to protect their food – are also common. These often appear as addenda to remedies for humans, or in manuscripts with miscellaneous contents.[4]

Any survey of charms for medical purposes clearly shows that not every medical problem boasts a charm to cure it. In fact, relatively few conditions were treated with charms. A representative Middle English book of remedies may contain over 200 short remedies or recipes loosely arranged in anatomical order from the head downward.[5] In the remedy book from which this study began, British Library, Additional MS 33996, sixty remedies for specific symptoms occur before a charm appears (one against fevers). There are no charms in this collection for relief of headache, bad hearing, red eyes, loss of voice, lack of appetite, swollen stomach, back pain, bladder stones, or feet swollen from work and many more ailments – all treatable in this collection by other kinds of remedies. On the other hand, charms are provided as cures for blurred vision and for fevers, as a sedative for insomnia due to illness, as first-aid to staunch bleeding and treat wounds, as medicine for women during delivery of a child, as a relief (and preventative) for toothache and as a preventative for falling sickness and attacks of evil spirits. A conjuration of a plant appears as part of a ritual to determine whether a sick person will live or die. This list of ailments treatable with charms, though not comprehensive, well represents the medical problems for which charms were used during the late Middle Ages.

This chapter aims to identify a corpus of charms that circulated in manuscripts of one fifteenth-century medical recipe collection. The medical recipe collection under examination appears in British Library Additional MS 33996 (hereafter cited as A1) and twenty-one other manuscripts which have been associated with it through similarities in the recipe collections. In addition to these known texts, I have added the recipe collection in Cambridge University Library MS Dd. 5. 76, ff. 30ra–75vb (hereafter cited as CDd) to the list, because, when the recipes beginning on f. 30r were compared to those in Heinrich's edition of A1, the two collections were shown to be closely related. CDd begins with the twenty-fifth recipe in A1 and follows the order of recipes in A1, while intermittently excluding many.[6] Twenty-two of this total of twenty-three recipe collections have so far been examined and the charms from them have been compared. (See p. 231 for a list of manuscripts.)

The Leechcraft remedy book

The medical remedies represented in these manuscripts may be treated as a distinct book, as witnessed in sixteen of the manuscripts by a Prologue in Middle English. In a sense, the Prologue serves to authorize this particular collection of remedies as knowledge for the practice of 'leechcraft'.[7] The Prologue begins as follows:

þe man þat wele of lechecraft lere
Rede on þis bok & he may here
many a medicyn boþ good & trewe
to hele sores boþ olde & new

(CUL, Add. 9308, f. 2r)[8]

For this reason, and as a matter of convenience, I have referred to these recipes as the 'Leechcraft' collection, in contrast, to the collection found in manuscripts associated with the remedies titled by Robert Thornton and referred to by scholars subsequently as the '*Liber de diversis medicinis*'.[9]

Nevertheless, it is important to stress that this chapter focuses on the charms, rather than the recipes. Questions about the compilation of the remedy books or the relationship of the manuscripts are not directly addressed here. In fact, the remedy books – all of which belong to the fifteenth century – vary in length and contents. Sometimes recipes not included in A1 appear; also, individual recipes, as well as charms, found in A1 are often omitted.[10] Sometimes omissions may be the results of leaves that have gone missing, but they may also be the result of the informal (and sometimes more idiosyncratic) approach of the compilers of individual collections. Clearly scribes' tastes varied in their handling of headings. Headings of individual recipes occur in Latin with occasional French terms, as in A1, or entirely in English, as in W1. Recipe collections falling roughly in the first half of the century contain the most charms, while the recipe collections that appear to have been written later preserve fewer.[11] In three manuscripts, the charms included in the text have been systematically obliterated or obscured.[12] Such censorship may be not attributable to nearly contemporary readers. It is likely to have been caused by owners of the manuscripts as late as the 1530s and after – owners who intended to remove any 'superstitious' material suffused with the language and piety of the pre-reformation Church.

Regarding the charms in these collections, I address the following questions: How are the charms represented across the manuscripts? What charms appear most frequently? In what sense do they constitute a 'corpus'? Finally, what do these charms contribute to our understanding of medicine in its relations to magic and religion in England during the late medieval period?

The Leechcraft charms

In terms of the frequency of occurrence, none or few charms are found in seven manuscript witnesses to the Leechcraft.[13] At the other extreme, twenty-three charms appear in Sloane 374 (S1). This manuscript seems most closely related to A1. Unfortunately, all the charms in S1 have been subjected to censorship by someone who attempted to blacken them out with heavy lines. However, since the headings remain mostly undamaged and a few words are visible within the texts, it is possible to identify the individual charms with confidence. The other manuscript that contains as many as twenty-one charms is Cambridge University Library, Additional 9308 (CA).[14] Typically, the number of charms seen within the witnesses is fifteen to eighteen.[15] Thus, regarding the frequency of occurrence of charms, the Leechcraft collections fall roughly into three groups: (1) Six manuscripts contain three or fewer charms.[16] (2) Ten manuscripts contain from seven to nineteen charms.[17] (3) Three manuscripts contain twenty-one to twenty-five charms.[18]

Significantly, in the Leechcraft collections that contain seven or more charms, the same charms appear repeatedly.[19] About sixteen charms constitute the predictable set encompassed within the remedy book, at least in its fully developed form. The charm with the highest frequency of occurrence in all the manuscripts is the charm for 'hawe' in the eye, since it occurs in manuscripts which only have a few charms in them. Since it is the first charm labeled as such, it was more likely to be picked up by copyests who did not copy the whole collection. The pattern of distribution across the manuscripts is shown in Table 15.1 (below, p. 226). As shown, sixteen charms appear in eight manuscripts or more.

Below I edit the texts of all the charms that appear in the Leechcraft as found in Cambridge University Library, MS Additional 9308 (CA), because these may be readily compared with those in A1, printed in Heinrich's edition. Textual variations will therefore be evident. The order of the charms corresponds to the usual order in the witnesses. The first sixteen charms constitute a basic set, or corpus. Charms 17 through 20 in CA occur less frequently among the 'Leechcraft' collections (as seen in Table 15.2); charm 21 belongs to the last cluster of recipes in the book, which were added to the collection in another hand in the typical manner of accretion. The last charm (no.21) does not occur in any other Leechcraft manuscript, but completes the number in CA.[20]

Charm texts

Cambridge University Library, MS Additional 9308

1) f. 14v, For þe feu*e*res.[21]
Tak thre oblyes &[22] in þat[23] on writ p*a*ter e*st* alpha et oo & mak a point. & ete þat þe ferst day. Þe secu*n*de day writ on þat oþ*er* oblye fili*u*s e*st* vita & mak two titelis & ete it. Þe thridde day writ on þe thridde oblie sp*iritu*s s*anctu*s e*st* remediu*m*. & mak iii pointes and ete it. but þe first day or þu ete þe oblie sey a pat*er* noste*r* and þe secu*n*d day two & þe thridde thre wit*h*[24] as fele Ave and credo.

2) f. 22v–23r, A charm for þe hawe in the ye.
In no*m*ine +[25] p*a*tris + et fil*i*i + sp*iritu*s *s*ancti + amen. Y co*n*iure þe hawe i*n* þe name of þe fad*er* & of þe sone & of þe holy gost þat fro þis time foreward þu neu*er* greue more þe ye of þis ma*n*. N[ame]. +

Iesu[26] + Crist if it be þi wil draw out þis hawe and clense þe ye of N[ame] þi seruaunt[27] as verilich & as sothlich as þu[28] clensedest þe ye of Tobie + agios + agios + agios + sanictus[sic] + sanctus + sanctus + christus[29] vincit + christus regnat + christus imperat + christus sine fine viuit et regnat. In nomine patris etc. þis charm schal be seid thries on þe ye & at ech [fol. 23r] time a pater noster & an Aue. & writ þis charm in a scrowe and bere it. & vse þat medecyn þat is afore write for þe perle in þe ye. & also þe ious of celidoine is god to put in[30] þe ye for þe hawe.[31]

3) ff. 25r–v, A charm for tothache.

[f. 25v]Dominus noster + Iesus Christus supra petram marmoream sede-bat. Petrus tristis ante Iesum stabat et dixit ei + Iesus, quare tristis es? Petrus respondit, domine, dentes mei dolent. At ille dixit, Adiuro te migranea gutta maledicta per patrem et filium et spiritum sanctum et per xii apostolos et iiii euangelistas + Marcum + Matheum + Lucam + Iohannem et per centum xliiii milia innocentes et per Mariam matrem domini nostri Iesu Christi que talem filium portauit per quem totus mundus redemptus est vt non habeas potestatem in istum hominem. N . neque in capite neque in ullo loco corporis sui nocere valeas. Adiuro te per illum qui passus est pro [fol. 26r] nobis in cruce amen.

4) ff. 32v–33r, A charm for þe bloody flix[32].

[f. 33r] In nomine + patris + et filii + et spiritus sanctus. Amen. Stabat + Iesus contra flumen Jordanis et posuit pedem suum et dixit, Sta, aqua per deum te coniuro. Longinus miles latus domini nostri Iesu + Christi perforauit et continuo exiuit sanguis et aqua, sanguis redempcionis et aqua baptismatis. In nomine patris, restet sanguis.
In nomine filii, cesset sanguis. In nomine spiritus sancti non exeat sanguinis gutta ab hoc famulo dei N. sicut credimus quod sancta Maria vera mater est et verum infantem genuit christum, sic retineant vene que plene sunt sanguinem. Sic restet sanguis sicut restabat Iordanis quando christus in ea baptizatus fuit. In nomine patris etc.

5) f. 35r, A charm for to staunche blod.

Longinus miles latus domini nostri + Iesu Christi lancea perforauit et continuo exiuit sanguis et aqua in redempcionem nostram. Adiuro te sanguis per ipsum + Christum per latus eius per sanguinem eius +[33]

sta + sta + sta. +Christus et Iohannes descenderunt in flumen iordanis. aqua obstipuit et stetit, sic faciat sanguis istius corporis.[f. 35v]
In +Christi nomine et sancti Iohannis baptiste amen. Et dica ter pater
noster et ter Aue Maria.

6) f. 36r, A charm for same.[34]
Iesu þat was in Bethlem born[35]
& baptised was in flum Iordan.
& stinted þe water upon þe ston
stint þat blod of þis man . N[ame] . þi seruaunt
þoru þe vertu of þin holy name + Iesu
& of þi cosin swete seynt Iohn.
& sey þis charm .v. times with.v. pater noster
in þe worschep of þe fiue woundes.

7) ff. 43v–44r, For to weten if a sik man nogt[36] wounded schal leue or
deye[37]
Also.Take fiue [f. 44r] croppes of verveyne with þi rigt hand & ley in þi
lefte & sey ouer hem .v. pater noster in þe worschip of þe .v. woundes
of Crist & sey þus: I coniure yow[38] fiue croppes in þe vertu of þe .v.
woundes þat + Crist suffred on þe rode tre forto bye mannis soule out
of thraldom þat þe sik man N[ame] telle me þe sothe þoru þe vertu
of God and of yow[39] wheþer he schal leue or deye of þat siknesse. &
bless hem .v. times & ley hem in þin rigt hand agen. & tak þe sik be his
rigt hand so þat he wete nogt of þe erbes. & what þu axest he schal
telle soth of his stat.

8) f. 48v, And a man[40] mow nogt slepe for sik.
Write þese wordes on a lorer lef + ysmael + ysmael +. Adiuro vos per
angelum ut soporetur iste homo N[ame]. & put þe lef vnder his hed
nogt witeng him. & do hete ofte letuse & drink pope seed with ale.

9) f. 49r, For womman þat trauaileth of child.
Bind þis writ to here rigt thy: In nomine + patris + et filii + et spiritus
sancti amen. Per uirtutem Dei sint medicina mei pia crux et passio [fol.
49v] + Christi. Vulnera quinque Dei sint medicina mei. + sancta Maria
peperit + Christum. + sancta Anna peperit + Mariam. sancta Helizabeth peperit + Iohannem sancta Cecilia peperit + Remigium. + sator +
arepo + tenet + opera +[41] rotas + Christus uincit + Christus regnat +

Christus imperat + Christus te vocat +. Mundus te gaudet. Lex te desiderat. + Christus dixit, Lazare, veni foras. + Deus vlcionum dominus + deus ulcionum, libera famulam tuam . N[ame]. + Dextera [manus] domini fecit virtutem + a + g + l + a + alpha + et oo. Anna peperit Mariam + Helizabeth precursorem + Maria + dominum nostrum + Iesum + Christum sine dolore et tristitia. O infans, exi foras siue viuus siue mortuus quia [f. 50r] + Christus vocat te ad lucem + agios + agios + agios + Christus regnat + Christus imperat + sanctus + sanctus + sanctus + dominus + deus omnipotens + qui es et qui eras et qui uenturus es amen. + bhurnon + bhurini + blutuono + blutaono + Iesus + nazarenus + rex iudeorum + fili dei miserere mei amen.

10) f. 51v, A charm for ony werm in a mannis here.
Coniuro te vermiculum per[f. 52r] + patrem + et filium + et spiritum sanctum et per victoriam passionis domini nostri + Iesu + Christi + et per septiformem spiritum sanctum et per graciam et uirtutem huius nominis + Iesu, vt non habeas potestatem ulterius commorandi in isto famulo dei, nec in aliquo sui membro perforandi seu corrodendi licenciam habeas sed per virtutem gloriosissime dei genitricis Marie et domini nostri Iesu Christi et sanctorum martirum dei Nigasii atque Cassiani confusus ab eo discedas et contritus amen. & sey þis in his ere & do him sey .v. pater noster in þe worschip of þe fiue woundes & .v. Aue Maria in þe worschip of þe fiue ioyes of oure lady.

11) f. 52v. A charm for tothache.
Virgo serenissima beata Appollonia, ora pro nobis ad dominum. Sancta Appollonia pro domino graue sustinuit martirium. Tiranni eius dentes cum malleis ferreis fregerunt et in hoc tormento orauit ad dominum vt quicumque nomen eius secum portuauerit in terris dolorem non senciat in dentibus. Ora pro me, beata Appollonia, vt deus dolorem a dentibus meis expellat. Oremus. Deus[42] qui beatam Appolloniam de manibus inimicorum liberasti et eius orationem exaudisti, queso domine per eius intercessionem et beati Laurencii martiris tui sanum et incolumen meipsum facias per dominum.

12) f. 53r, For þe feueres.
Tak. iii. vbles & write on oon þerof, + el + elþe + sabaoth & ete þu þat þe ferst day. þe next day writ on þat oþer, + adonay + alpha &

o + messias. & ete it. þe thrid day writ on þat oþer, + pastor + agnus + fons + & ete it. & aftir ech vble eting, sey iii pater noster & iii aue Maria & .i. credo.

13) f. 53v, For⁴³ þe falleng euel.
Tak blod of þi litil finger of þi rigt hand & writ þerwith þese thre names + Iaspar + Melchior + Baltasar. & close it & hang it aboute þi necke. & put þerin gold & mirre & franc[f. 54r]encense of ech a litil. & ech day whan þu arist blesse þe with þese iii . names & sey for here fader soule & moderes iii pater noster & iii Aue. & ech day a monthe drink þe rote of pyonie with stal ale & þu schal be hol sikerly. & if it is a child tak þe blod as it is a foreseid & write þe thre names in a maser⁴⁴ & wasch it with ale or melk & do þe child drink it & he schal be hol.

14) f. 61r, A charm for woundes with oyle & wolle.
Tres boni fratres per viam ambulabant et obuiabat eis Iesus quibus dixit, Tres boni fratres quo itis? Domine, nos imus ad montem Oliueti ad [f. 61v] colligendum herbas saluacionis sanitatis et integritatis. Tres boni fratres, uenite post me et iurate mihi per lac beate virginis Marie quod non abscondetis neque in abscondito dicetis neque lucrum accipietis. Et ite ad montem Oliueti et accipite lanam nigram succisam et oleum oliue postea sic dicendo: Sicut Longinus miles latus domini nostri + Iesu + Christi lancea perforauit et illa plaga non diu doluit neque putridauit neque fistulauit neque ranclauit, neque sanguinauit neque guttam fecit + sic plaga ista per virtutem illius plage non diu doleat + neque diu putridet + fistulet + neque ranclet + neque sanguinet neque guttam faciat, sed ita sana fiat [f.62r] et munda sicut fuit vulnus quod fecit Longinus in latere domini nostri +⁴⁵ Iesu Christi quando pendebat in cruce. In nomine patris etc.

15) f. 62r, A charm for a wounde on Englisch.
Y coniure þe wounde bliue⁴⁶
by vertu of þe woundes fiue
+ Iesu Crist both god & man
with rigt he vs of helle wan
& þe tetis of seint Marie,
clene maide withoute folie
þat þu neþer ake ne swelle,

ne ra*n*cle, ne festre, ne bled
no mor þan[47] dede þe wou*n*de[48]
of Iesu Crist whan he ha*n*ged on þe rode.
But from þe grou*n*d vpward , be as hol
as were + Iesu wou*n*des eu*er*ydele.
I*n* name of þe fader of migtes most.
& [fol. 62v] of þe sone & þe holi gost.
& sey iii p*ater* nost*er* & iii Aue M*ari*a.

16) f. 62v–65r, A charm of seint Susa*n*ne.
Our lord + Iesu as sothli as Iewes tok a corou*n* of thornes & put vp on
þi blessid heued & it p*er*schid þe skin, þe flesch, þe br*ay*n, & as sothli
as neu*er* aftir þ*at* time it dede nogt longe ake ne swelle ne ra*n*cle ne
festre ne blede, as sothli lord Iesu Crist, Y biseke þe þ*at* it be þi wil þat
þis wou*n*d be hol & neu*er* aftir þis time it ake nogt ne swelle ne ra*n*cle
ne festre ne blede þoru þe v*er*tu[49] of þ*at* wou*n*de & sei a pat*er* n*oste*r
and aue. Our lord + Iesu Crist as sothli as þe iewes [f. 63r] toke a nail
of yren & p*er*sched þin rigt hand and as sothli as neu*er* aftir þat time
it dede nogt ake ne swelle & *sey forth to þe end as it is before and sey*[50]
a p*ater* n*oste*r and .i. Aue. Oure lord Iesu Crist as sothli as þe Iewes
toke a nail of yren & p*er*sched þe left hond & as sothli as neu*er* aftir
etc as afore[51] & sey a p*ater* n*oste*r & an Ave. Our lord Iesu + [52] Crist
as sothli as Lo*n*ginu*s* þe knigt tok a spere and p*er*schid þi rigt side, þe
skin, þe flesch, þe lunges, þe liuere, þe herte, & as sothli as neu*er* aftir
etc as afore.[53] & sey a p*ater* n*oste*r & Aue. Our lord + Iesu Crist as sothli
as þe Iewes token [f. 63v] a nail of yren & p*er*schid þi rigt fot & as
sothli as neu*er* aftir *etc as ferst.*[54] & sey a p*ater* n*oste*r & an aue. Our
lord Iesu Crist as sothly as þe Iewes token a nail of iren & p*er*schid þin
left fot and as sothly as neu*er* aft*er* *vt supra.*[55] & sey a p*ater* n*oste*r &
Aue. Our lord + Iesu + Crist as sothli as þu art wit*h*oute biginnynge &
schalt be wit*h*outen endinge as þat þat þu dest, wel dest & as þat þat
þu seidest, soth seidest & as sothli as þu toke boþe flesch & blod of
vi*r*gin Marie & as sothly as þu were circu*m*cised þoru þe Iewes lawe, &
as sothli as [f.64r]þu were baptised i*n* flu*m* Iordan. & as sothli as þu
leuedist here in erthe .xxx. winter & more & as sothli as þu suffredest
boþe peyne & passiou*n* for ma*n*nis trespas & nogt for þin owne & as
sothli as þu tok þi passiou*n* mekly & as þu deidest on þe crois to bye
ma*n*nis soule out of helle & as sothli as þu wentest i*n* to helle & tok
out Ada*m* & Eue & þo þat þi wille was & as sothly as þu rise fro*m* deth
to lyue þe thridde day & as sothli as þu steye vp i*n* to heuene on holi
thursday & settest þe on þi fader rigt side & as sothli as þu schal at þe

day [fol. 64v] of dome deme boþe quike & dede at þi wille & as sothli as þis is soth & as Y leue wel it is soth as sothli lord + Iesu Y bisek þe & it be þi wil þat þis wound mote be hol or þis sor & neuer aftir þis time it ake nogt ne swelle ne festre ne blede ne rancle þoru þe vertu of al þin holy passioun. In nomine patris etc. & sey a pater noster. & . l . Aue & do þe sike sey .v. pater noster in worschip of þe v woundes of Crist & .v. Aue Maria. in þe worschip of our ladi .v. ioyes & iii credes in þe worschip of þe trinite & lok þe sik be in clene lif & lat him do singen at þe beginning [fol. 65r] of his charming thre massis þe ferst .iii. dayes þe ferst masse of þe holy gost, þe secund of our lady, þe thrid for alle cristen soules and what sor þu schal tak kep to with þis charm sey it fasting ech day onis & wheþer it be wounde or ony oþer sor it schal be saf within .xv. dayes for angel Gabriel brogt it to seint Susanne to help with cristen peple.

17) f. 65r, A charm for wicked wigtes.
In nomine + patris + etc. Per uirtutem Dei sint medicina mei N[ame] pia crux et passio Christi. Uulnera quinque dei sint medicina mei + uirgo Maria mihi .N[ame]. succurre & defende ab omni malo demonio [fol. 65v] et ab omni spiritu maligno amen. + a + g + l + a + tetragramaton + alpha et o + primogenitus + via + vita. + sapientia + uirtus + Iesus + nazarenus + rex Iudeorum fili + dei miserere mei amen. + Marcus + Matheus + Lucas + Iohannes mihi succurrite .N[ame]. et defendite amen. + Omnipotens sempiterne deus hunc famulum tuum .N[ame]. hoc breue scriptum super se portantem prospe salutis dormiendo vigilando edendo potando, stando sedendo et percipue sompniando ab omni maligno spiritu et demonio custodias et ab illusionibus diabolicis protegendo ad requiem corporalem per misericordiam tuam perduras amen.

18) f. 65v, A charm for almaner feueris.
[66r] In nomine + patris etc. Virgo maria succurre mihi febricitanti amen. + Iesus + nazarenus rex iudeorum, fili + dei, miserere mei amen. Ante portam latinam iacebat beatus Petrus febricitans, et superveniens Iesus + Christus dixit illi: Petre, quid iaces hic? Beatus Petrus respondit: Domine, iaceo hic de malis febribus. + Deus atque dixit: Surge et diuitate illas. Et recepta sanitate pristina secutus est Iesum. + Deus atque dixit ei: Perge ante me. Beatus petrus dixit: Obsecro, domine, ut quicumque haec uerba super se portauerit non noceant ei febres. + Deus atque dixit: Fiat iuxta uerbum tuum + a + g + l + a + Marcus +

Matheus + Lucas + Iohannes succurrite mihi et ab [fol. 66v] omni mala
febre liberate me amen. & sey .v. pater noster þu þat art sik in worschip
of þe .v. woundes & .v. Aue Maria. for þe .v. ioyes of our ladi & iii
Credes in worschip of þe trinite.

19) f. 68r, A charm for theues.
In Bedlem God was born[56]
bitwen two bestes to rest he was leyd.
In þat stede was neyþer þef ne man
but þe holi trinite. þu self God
þat þer was born
defend oure bodyes
& our catel fro þeues
& almaner mischeues & harmes
wherso we go
be londe or be watere
be nigt or be day
be tide or be time amen.

20) f. 78r, For þe feueres.
Writ on a saugelef, Christus tonat & ete þat þe ferst day & sey a pater
noster & an aue & a credo. þe secund day, writ on anoþer, angelus
nunciat, & ete it & sey ii pater noster .ii. aue & .ii. credo. þe thridde day,
writ [fol. 78v] on an oþer lef, Iohannes predicat & ete it & sey iii pater
noster & iii aue . & .iii. credo. & whan þu art hol do singe thre masses,
þe ferst of þe holi gost, þe secund of seint Mighel þe thridde of seint
Iohannes baptist. & euer after whan þu herist þe feueres nemened,
blesse þe & sey an aue Maria.

21) f. 86v, ffor to staunche blood[57]
fferst þe behouith knowe þe mannis name & þan go to cherche & sey
þus þi charm but lok þu sey nogt þi charm before no man ne womman.
In nomine patris et filii. etc.
Whan our lord was don on þe cros
þan cam þeder Longinus
& smot him with a spere in þe side.
Blod & water com out at þe wounde
& he wiped his eyen and sey anon.
þoru þe holi uertu þat God [fol. 87r] dede þer

Y coniure þe blo[58] þat þu ne go out
of þis cristen man or womman .N[ame].
In nomine patris etc.
Sey þis charm thries & lok þu knowe þe mannis name whersoeuer
he be.

Individual charms in this corpus are well known to students of English
medicine, folklore, poetry and prose.[59] The Latin ones are perhaps less
well known. I do not pursue analysis of individual texts in this chapter,
because the main interest here is rather in the corpus of charms that
circulated within the Leechbook recipe collections.[60]

Tables of distribution

The specific pattern of charm distribution in the manuscripts is presented
in Table 15.1. The left column refers to the charms edited above from
CUL, MS Additional 9308.[61] Each of the other manuscripts containing
seven or more charms is represented by its abbreviation at the top of a
column. In the row opposite each charm, briefly indicated on the left, a
number indicates that the charm occurs in the manuscript noted at the
top of the column. The number merely tells where the charm falls in the
order of charms within its particular manuscript. It is important to understand that the charms do *not* necessarily occur in the same place among
the recipes in every manuscript. The charm order number does not show
where the charm appears among the recipes of its collection. Rather, it
simply indicates its place in the series of charms found in the collection.
For example, Table 15.1 does not show that, except for the herb prog-
nostication, the charms in Ha appear clustered together at the very end
of its recipes, as indeed they do.

Cutting off the list of charms in the group at sixteen charms is somewhat arbitrary as is shown in Table 15.2, where the last five charms in
CA also appear in other manuscripts as well. While the charm for malig-
nant spirits (or 'wikked wights') appears in six manuscripts, the preceding
charms appear in at least seven.[62] After charm seventeen the set becomes
unstable.

The Leechcraft corpus

The sense that the core of charms in the Leechcraft collections forms a set
is strengthened by comparison with charms in other recipe collections.

Table 15.1   The first column contains charms from Cambridge University Library, MS Additional 9308 (CA). Columns to the right represent the same charms as found in each of the manuscripts identified at the top of the column.

CA	A1	W1	La	Ab	S6	S5	Ha	Tr	Ar	S1	Ash	CDd
1 Fevers Pater est	1	1	1	1	1	1	1		1	[1]		
2 Hawe Toby	2	2	2	2	2	2	5		2	2	1	1
3 Toothache Iesus sedebat	3	3	3	3	3	3			3	[3]	2	
4 Bloody flux Stabat Iesus	4	4	4	4	4	4		1	4	[4]	3	2
5 Staunch blood Longius miles sta	5	5	5	5	5	5			5	[5]	4	
6 Staunch blood Iesus that was in	6	6		6	6	6			6	[6]	5[63]	3
7 Live or die Five croppes	7	7		7	7	7	2		7		6	4
8 Sleep ysmael	–[64]	8[65]	6[66]	8[67]	8			2		[7]	7[68]	5
9 Childbirth	8	9	7[69]	9	9	8		3		[8]	8	6
10 Worm in the ear	9	10			10	9	6			[9]		7
11 Toothache Virgo Apollonia	10	11			11	10	7			10		
12 Fevers El elþe	11	12	8	10	12	11	8	4		[11]	9	
13 Falling evil	12	13	9	11	13	12	9	5		[12]	10	
14 Wounds Tres boni fratres	13	14			14	13	10			[13]	11	8
15 Wound Y conjure	14	15	10[70]	12	15	14	11	6			12	9
16 Wound St. Susanne	15	16			16	15	12				13	11[71]

Table 15.2

CUL Addit. 9308	A1	W1	La	Ab	S6	S5	Ha	Tr	Ar	S1	Ash	CDd
17 Wicked spirits	16				17	16		7		[14]		10
18 Fevers Ante portam	17					17		8		[15]		
19 Thieves In Bedlam God						18	3			[16]		
20 Fevers Christus tonat[72]	18	17				19	4				14	
21 Staunch blood[73]												

For example, Thornton's *Liber de diversis medicinis* includes eleven charms of which the purpose and the general content of four charms seem familiar from the Leechcraft.[74] However, the *Liber* 'Apollonia charm' differs in text from both the 'Apollonia charms' in the 'Leechcraft'.[75] The same is true of the charm against the 'falling evil' that begins, like the Leechcraft charm, 'Tak þe blode of þe littil fynger'. The *Liber*'s directions say to write in the blood of the sick person the names of the kings of Cologne (Colayn) on the forehead and recite the verses 'Iasper brings gold' (Iasper fert aurum) etc, because 'he that bears the names of the three kings with him shal be loosed from the falling evil through the pity of God'.[76] Hanging the names around the neck in a writ is presented as an alternative. This treatment contrasts with the Leechcraft charm for falling sickness, in which the writ containing the three kings' names, written in blood on parchment, becomes an amuletic packet containing precious ingredients and, in addition, the patient is prescribed rules for a morning devotion that will serve as an apotropaic for the illness. The peony dose, though it may serve medicinal purposes as well, reminds him (and us) that his daily devotions are part of his medical regimen. The *Liber* also incorporates an elaborate ritual based on the mass.[77] In addition, the *Liber* provides instructions for making a 'cramp' ring – a ring bearing the three kings' names from the Good Friday pennies from five parish churches.[78] But cures which begin as if they are the same quickly diverge in these two remedy book traditions. The *Liber*'s remaining charm texts are two cures for fevers with wafers ('obles'), a cure for nosebleed and four short charms for childbirth. The two 'obles' charms differ from the Leechcraft charms after about two lines in each; the childbirth charms contrast distinctly with the long interlace of motifs we find in the Leechcraft.[79] While the charms in the *Liber* resemble the Leechcraft charms, covering a similar array of ailments and employing some of the same contents in several cases, the versions are realized in different styles. They do not employ the same extended formulas as those in the Leechcraft. This point is significant, since the Leechcraft charm set displays a notable consistency in its formulas as they appear across the witnesses, with the exception of a few charms in CDd.

The charms in the recipe collection in CDd differ from the other witnesses belonging to the Leechcraft group in ways that may offer insights into the development of the charm set over time. First, as the Tables 15.1 and 15.2 show, CDd lacks the two fever charms, the Apollonia charm and Latin charm for toothache, as well as the Three Kings amulet for falling sickness. Perhaps these charms were not part of the earlier Leechcraft compilations. Alternatively, the compiler of CDd may have had few occasions to cure fevers or falling sickness. CDd includes the Ismael charm for sleep, which goes missing in later collections; however, its powerful name, 'Ismael' is garbled. Second, the wound charm, 'Y conjure þe wounde bliue', follows immediately after the *Tres boni fratres* charm without the heading which appears in every other witness. It reads as if the English were meant to function as an alternative to the Latin charm, whose use in England goes back to the thirteenth century at least.[80] Third, the charm 'for wicked wightis' precedes, rather than follows, the Susanne wound charm. More significantly, the Susanne charm in CDd is less than a third as long as the standard version in CA and the other collections. In CDd it is one of three similar charms for healing wounds.[81]

Conclusions

This survey of the charms in the Leechcraft recipe collections has identified a corpus of sixteen charms belonging to this particular remedy book. The corpus includes both Latin and English charms. Evidently, those through whose hands this collection of remedies passed, including the copyists and compilers as well as practitioners and readers, viewed the charms as another form of therapy equivalent to the herbal remedies. The medical problems that the charms relieved or prevented are limited to these: bleeding of one kind or another, fresh as well as corrupting wounds (or sores), fevers, insomnia due to illness, falling sickness, 'a wicked spirit' (or 'demon'), a certain kind of blindness, toothaches, the labor of childbirth, and a 'worm' in the ear. These problems, in particular, seemed amenable to the religious words conveyed in these late medieval churchly charms.

Why were these ailments thought treatable by charms during the fifteenth century, while others were not? The answer does not lie in a single underlying characteristic common to these medical problems – for example, that all these ailments were intractable to herbal cures or susceptible to self healing, or only required prevention or were especially amenable to cure by a placebo effect. Medieval Christian charms seem to emerge for particular medical (and other) conditions, when a primary characteristic of the medical problem coincided with a culturally charged image that could be expressed in a charm. A specific charm motif may be associated with its symptom by some specific image or words. Elsewhere, I have referred to this correspondence as a 'semantic motif'.

To illustrate briefly, the charms to staunch bleeding presented below depend primarily on Christian images that foreground stopping the flow of the river Jordan at the Baptism of Christ (4) and the salvific flow of water and blood from the wound in Christ's side caused by Longinus

(4 and 5). The charm for 'hawe' (2) in the eye appropriates the image of Tobit's blindness recounted in the Book of Tobit. One toothache charm centers on St. Apollonia's torture (11). In the other (3), the effective image of a hard rock combines with the words *petram*, and *Petrus* to constitute the semantic motif for the cure. The falling sickness is cured by recourse to the Kings who prostrated themselves before Christ.[82] To prevent wounds from becoming infected, the patient and healer invoke vivid images of the wounds inflicted on the parts of the body of Christ at the crucifixion. Thus, when a specific physical symptom was felt to correspond with a religious motif that was well known in late medieval culture, the correspondence may be realized in a healing charm.[83]

Moreover, in contexts like vernacular remedy books (in contrast to learned doctors' treatises) liturgical forms are very readily transferred to private healing rituals. These rituals slip from one social environment and intentionality to another.[84] Fevers are cured (charms 1 and 20) through the ritual consumption of communion wafers or leaves inscribed with holy words in a manner reminiscent of the Eucharist.[85] To relieve a mother's fears of pain during childbirth, we find among other motifs, the formula 'Five wounds of God be my medicine'. This short formula, which occurs against evil spirits (wicked wights in charm 17) along with an invocation of the power of the cross and passion and the Virgin Mary, is incorporated into the array of formulas for safe childbirth. In sicknesses where demons were felt to be involved, expulsion by means of words was traditional.[86]

Another factor determining which ailments can be cured by charms is the availability of words or sayings, characters, or letters in the local tradition. For reasons not always clear, a motif may become attached to a specific ailment. In our formula for childbirth, powerful names ('bhurnon bhurini', etc.) and the ancient sator formula are included as traditional for reasons that are not immediately apparent. Once a charm has developed nonsensical formulas, tradition itself may preserve them. Within the circle of learned physicians, nonsensical formulas for 'cramp' and 'staunching blood' became staples for those ailments, even while they were attributed to individual physicians.[87]

In sum, the existence of a medieval charm (or prayer) to cure an ailment probably depends less on the inherent nature of the medical condition, than on cultural perceptions of the disease or symptom (i.e. how it features in the social imagination), the availability of an authorized or traditional formula for its cure, and relevant prevailing forms of religious piety. Textual traditions such as the one represented in the

recipe collections examined here and an individual compiler's prefer-
ences may influence the charms added or excluded, as witnessed by the
variability of charms (Table 15.2) after the sixteen comprising the corpus. The needs generated by a healer's clients may also determine kinds
of ailments that were treated, whether by charms or otherwise. In remedy books, charms are rarely the sole remedy offered for any particular
medical condition. As we have seen, more than one charm often exists
for any single problem. To some extent, factors as mundane as a high
frequency of occurrence for an ailment and coincident cultural interest
and social resources combine to generate formulas for healing.

Finally, these medieval verbal and written charms balance a medieval
sense of the power of words *per se*[88] with religious rituals on the one
hand and medical rituals, which are magical procedures, on the other.
It is possible in some of these charms to unwind and separate these
skeins of medicine, magic, and religion. However, the more interesting point to note is how closely the healing charms weave these three
skeins together. In other words, these charms are situated, quite com-
fortably, in an intersection of medical care, religion, and magical rite.
The closer we attend to how the crude instructions work, exactly which
prayers and how many are required as well as the possible meanings
and sources of the formulas, the better we understand their place in
medieval society. The primary purpose of the Leechcraft remedies is to
bring relief of specific bodily symptoms. From the healing perspective
of leechcraft, only a small number of medical conditions lend themselves to ritual cures. In some instances, however, the most convenient
treatments may be the verbal formulas, written amulets, images, ritual
acts, and prayers that constitute charms. Within a medical context, the
formula, 'Through the power of God, may my medicine be the holy
cross and passion of Christ' (*Per uirtutem Dei sint medicina mei pia crux et
passio + Christi*)[89] is intended to have medical significance and therefore
physical consequences. Its emotional value and intentional force will
differ when the same words are spoken within a purely spiritual or more
meditative environment.

Manuscripts containing Leechcraft remedies[90]

Ab   Aberdeen, University Library, 258, Prologue, p. 192, recipes
       pp. 6–39
CA   Cambridge, University Library, Additional 9308, Prologue,
       f. 1–1v, recipes ff. 1v–89r

CDd Cambridge, University Library, Dd. 5. 76, ff. 39ra–75vb.
Tr   Cambridge, Trinity MS O.1.13, Prologue, f. 45v, recipes ff.46–61r;
     Prologue, f. 166r, recipes 166v–172v
A1   London, British Library, Additional 33996, ff. 76v–148v
A2   London, British Library, Additional 19674, ff. 7r–34v
Ar   London, British Library, Arundel 272, Prologue, f. 1r–v, recipes
     1v–30v
Ro   London, British Library, Royal 17.A.III, ff. 119r–125v,
     134v–168r[91]
Ha   London, British Library, Harley 1600, Prologue ff. 3v–4r, recipes
     ff. 4v–41v
La   London, British Library, Lansdowne 680, Prologue 21v–22r,
     recipes 22r–73r
S1   London British Library, Sloane 374, Prologue f. 14r, recipes
     ff. 14v–85r
S2   London, British Library, Sloane 382, Prologue, f. 211r–v, recipes
     ff. 211v–246v
S3   London, British Library, Sloane 405, ff. 39r–41r, 55r–60v,
     126r–199r
S4   London, British Library, Sloane 442, Prologue, f. 43r, recipes
     ff. 43r–47v
S5   London, British Library, Sloane 468, Prologue f. 7r–v, recipes
     ff. 7v–80v
S6   London, British Library, Sloane 1314, Prologue f. 5r, recipes
     ff. 5v–40v
S7   London, British Library, Sloane 3153, Prologue, f. 2v–3r, ff. 3r–17v,
     26v–41v
W1   London, Wellcome Historical Medical Library MS 542, Prologue,
     f. 1r, recipes ff. 1r–20v
W2   London, Wellcome Historical Medical Library MS 409, ff.16r–48r
Ash Oxford, Bodleian, Ashmole 1477 Part II, Prologue, f. 1r, recipes
     ff. 1r–28v
AS   Oxford, All Souls 121, Prologue f. 1r–v, recipes ff. 1v–28v

Notes

1. An earlier version of this chapter was presented at the Charms, Charmers, and
   Charming Conference held at the Warburg Institute, London, 24 September
   2005; some parts were presented at the 41st International Congress on
   Medieval Studies, Kalamazoo, 6 May 2006.
2. Jonathan Roper's work substantiates this observation for English language
   charms. Based on his database archive of 523 charms in English dating from

the 10th to the 20th centuries, he states that healing charms not only predominate over all periods, but within every period as well. See *English Verbal Charms*, p. 61

3. See Olsan, 'Charms and Prayers' on charms found in learned Latin doctors' medical *compendia*.

4. For example, two Latin charms are added to the remedy book in B.L., Arundel 272 (hereafter cited as Ar), f. 30v, one for sick pigs and one for cows.

5. Head to toe order is complicated by sections that focus on the same kinds of cures, for example, ointments or medicinal waters. Also some prevalent symptoms, such as fevers, do not fit in any one place anatomically.

6. The first recipe in Cambridge University Library, MS Dd.5.76 (CDd), beginning on f. 39ra, 'For the chynke, Take the rote of the hogshelne', corresponds to recipe twenty-five in B.L., Additional 33996 (A1); the second in CDd, 'For akinge of swellynge in the thiese or in the feet' corresponds to recipe thirty-nine in A1; the third 'For the morfew whyte or blake', corresponds to recipe forty-five in A1. Subsequent recipes correspond to recipes in A1 and follow the same order as A1, but typically include only about three out of four recipes in ten. This observation is based on a comparison of the first fifty recipes in CDd with the A1 text. The charm texts in CDd consistently appear between recipes corresponding to those predicted by A1.

7. On the Prologue, see Keiser, 'Verse Introductions', pp. 301–9. For other occurrences, see NIMEV 3422 and Voigts and Kurtz.

8. In CUL Add. 9308, f. 1r–v, these verses end with the lines 'Be þat on & twenti dayes ben come & gon/he schal be hol boþ fesch & bon'.

9. On manuscripts containing this recipe collection, see Keiser, 'Robert Thornton's *Liber de Diversis Medicinis*' and Ogden's edition.

10. For examples, see Heinrich's introduction to the manuscripts he knew (A1, S7, Ro, A2, for which Heinrich printed an incorrect shelfmark, Ha, and S3), pp. 4–11.

11. A caveat concerning dates of manuscripts is called for here; as far as I know no systematic attempt has been made to date these manuscripts. I have accepted the dates that Keiser supplies in *Manual* vol. IX, p. 3840 and 'Verse Introductions'.

12. In Bodleian, Ashmole 1477 (Ash), charms are x'd out, but remain legible; in B.L. Sloane 374 (S1), charm texts have been obliterated by heavy lines, but headings remain and a few words of text here and there; in B.L. Lansdowne 680 (La), all the Latin words have been expunged though the texts remain undamaged otherwise. Charms in Aberdeen, University Library 258 (Ab) have been very lightly x'd out.

13. The recipe collections containing none or few charms are these: B.L., MS Sloane 442 (S4), none; B.L. MS Sloane 3153 (S7), none; B.L. MS Sloane 405 (S3), 2 charms; B. L. MS Additional 19674 (A2), 1 charm; B.L., MS Sloane 382 (S2), 2 charms; British Library, MS Royal 17. A. III (Ro), 3 charms, Oxford, All Souls MS 121 (AS) 4 charms.

14. I have discounted instructions to repeat 'miserere me Deus' (indicating a Psalm) while heating a cough remedy as a measure of time and the instruction merely to 'charm it' as no text is supplied.

15. Only variation in the number of charms is being reported here; no account has been taken of the differences in the total number of recipes in any manuscript or in the precise content of recipes. Some variations will be the result of fragmentary and piecemeal character of the Leechcraft remedies in these mss.
16. See above, note 12.
17. Ar, Tr, La, Ha, Ab, CDd, Ash, S6, W1, S5. W2 is exceptional because headings as well as charms are so thoroughly obliterated. I find evidence of five charms; recognizable are the charm for fallyng yuyl (f. 30v) and a charm for fever (f. 38r).
18. A1, CA, S1.
19. However, in CDd, the Susanne charm exists in a substantially shorter version than elsewhere. The texts of the charms in S1 have been deduced from headings and visible remnants; therefore the numbers appear in brackets in the tables.
20. Seven charms follow charm number 18 in A1: f. 133r (Heinrich, pp. 212–13), f. 138v (Heinrich, p. 220), f. 138v (Heinrich, pp. 220–1), ff. 138v–139r (Heinrich, p. 221), f.146v (Heinrich, p. 231), f. 147r (Heinrich, pp. 231–2).
21. F is blue, heading is underlined in red. This pattern of a blue initial and the rest of the heading underlined in red continues through all the charms, unless otherwise noted.
22. &] MS ampersands in the form '7' throughout. In Latin text, these are expanded as 'et'.
23. þat] MS þ^t here and elsewhere.
24. with] MS w^t throughout.
25. Crosses are red in the MS unless noted otherwise.
26. Iesu] MS 'Ihu' here and elsewhere.
27. seruaunt] MS superscript over suaut. In the margin 'uaunt'.
28. þu] MS þ^u throughout.
29. Christus] MS xs and elsewhere.
30. in] MS added above the line.
31. Directions involving fair white ginger grated on a whetstone of Norway into white wine then applied with a feather do not appear in CA with the hawe charm, as they do in A1, f. 90r, (Heinrich, p. 99).
32. flix] sic.
33. Cross is boxed in blue.
34. This is the fourth item in the string of procedures to staunch bleeding. *A* is brown.
35. NIMEV 624
36. nogt] MS has a yogh here, as elsewhere, which I have represented internally by a 'g'.
37. The heading, in red letters, precedes a string of prognoses. This is the third item.
38. yow] 'y' represents an initial yogh, as elsewhere.
39. yow] ibid.
40. a man] MS added with a caret above the line.
41. MS Cross inserted where space was not left for it.
42. *D* is blue.

43. *f* is in blue.
44. A 'maser' is a wooden cup or drinking bowl.
45. Cross is not rubricated, as others are.
46. NIMEV 1293.
47. þan] MS þt.
48. After 'wounde' the word 'gode' (good), having a long open o rhyming with 'rode' (cross) is missing in CA. The word appears in the A1 charm, f. 109 (Heinrich, p.162). The word 'hol' in A1 rhymes with 'euerydol', which is 'everydele' here in CA. These variations may be compared with the charm in W1, f. 14v, where the charm reads, 'woundes of god' (God) and 'eueridel', both of which are flawed rhymes. In W1, the Marie/folie rhyme is replaced with Marye/marie. W1 is printed in Roper, p. 115; Sheldon, p. 164.
49. MS has a stroke marked through before 'of'.
50. The words 'And sey forth … and sey a' appear in red letters. Italics are mine here and for other directive phrases.
51. The words 'as afore' appear in red letters.
52. Cross is brown, not rubricated.
53. The words 'as afore' appear in red.
54. The words 'as ferst' appear in red.
55. The words 'vt supra' appear in red.
56. See Smallwood, 211–14.
57. Folios 84r to the end of the recipe collection are in a different hand, ink, and with a different *mise en page*. Blue initials disappear and headings are written in red letters, rather than underlined in red. Thus, the charm on f. 86 was not among those belonging to the Leechcraft text.
58. Sic.
59. For recent studies of medieval charms and amulets, see Bozoky, Skemer, and Schulz.
60. For interpretations of selected charms in CA, see Olsan, 'Charms in Medieval Memory'.
61. I have used CA because it contains a large number of charms, twenty-one, most of which may readily be compared to those published by Heinrich from A1. Moreover, the CA collection is preceded by the Leechcraft Prologue.
62. Charm no. 11, an Apollonia charm occurs only six times, but that can be accounted for by the fact that Ar breaks off, recording only the first parts of the Leechcraft text.
63. Heading mistakenly reads, 'here is a charme in ynglys for the toth ache', although the text is 'Iesus that was in bedelem borne'.
64. Folios containing fifteen recipes are missing in A1 where this charm might be expected to appear as the fourteenth item. Cf. Heinrich, p. 142 .
65. The heading in W1 erroneously reads, 'speke for syke'. The charm is the same as in CA and elsewhere.
66. This adjuration in La is 'per angelum Micheolem'; the name 'ysmael' is moved to the end. Cf. charm no. 8 above.
67. The adjuration in Ab is 'per angelum Michaelem'.
68. The heading in Ash reads 'speke for syke', as in W1. See above, note 64.

69. Only the heading and two lines appear on the bottom of f. 64, after which a leaf is missing. It is possible that someone removed the leaf which contained the words of the charm to use it as an amulet.

70. A charm 'for a woman þat ys with chylde' follows as the last charm in this collection. It begins, 'Tak a masowre' (La, f. 72v).

71. In CDd two subsequent charms f. 67va–b and f. 68va, directions to staunch bleeding by writing Agla on the forehead at f. 75r, and a remedy on f. 69ra do not correspond to those in the Leechcraft.

72. A ritual on folio 83r for gathering red nettle with a Pater Noster, Ave Maria and prayer for the delivery of the patient from fevers in the stomach is excluded from the list of charms.

73. This charm to staunch bleeding f. 86v belongs to material added in a different hand on which, see above, note 57. The common practice of adding material explains why the basic set of charms becomes unstable toward the end in the longer recipe collections.

74. The charms in the *Liber de diversis medicinis* are meant to relieve 'tettre', falling evil, cramp, nosebleed, 'travailing of child' (5), and fevers (2).

75. See Ogden, p. 18, for the *Liber* 'Apollonia' charm.

76. 'He þat beris þir names of þir iij kinges with hym he sall be lesid thurgh þe petee of God of þe fallyand euyll, f. 297', Ogden, p. 42.

77. See Ogden, pp. 39–41.

78. Cf. Crawfurd, p. 173.

79. The childbirth charms in the *Liber* are these, beginning: 'Arcus forcium', 'Occeanum age', 'Beata Anna genuit', 'Sator', to be written in butter or cheese, and 'Sancta Maria peperit & matrix eius non doluit', ff. 303v 304r (Ogden, pp. 56–7).

80. Gilbertus Anglicus records the **Tres boni fratres** charm in his *Compendium medicine*, see Olsan, 'Charms and Prayers,' p. 364.

81. On charms for wounds in English, see Roper, *Verbal Charms*, pp. 113–15 and 127–30, esp. pp. 114, 115, and 127.

82. For more on how the coincidence of disease image with pious image (semantic motif) works in these charms, see Olsan, 'Charms in Medieval Memory'.

83. As shown in Table 15.2, thief charms also appear in some of these collections (CA, S5, Ha, and S1). These charms protect 'oure bodyes & our catel fro þeues & almaner mischeues & harmes'.

84. For a definition of ritual as lacking the constitutive intentionality of ordinary speech acts, see Humphrey and Laidlaw *The Archetypal Actions of Ritual*, esp. pp. 96–101. According to this theory, the intentionality of a ritual may vary while the act remains the same. This would explain how the intentionalities claimed by ecclesiastical institutions for liturgical rituals (which are primarily verbal rituals) in medieval Christianity need not remain the same for some clerics, leeches, lay persons, and patients who re-instituted certain rituals for healing purposes.

85. For a more explicit example of the mimesis of the Eucharist, see Olsan, 'The Language of Charms' p. 31.

86. On prayers and traditional incantations against demon-caused sickness, see Franz, II, pp. 421–8.

87. Olsan, 'Charms and Prayers' p. 362.

88. As in the use of powerful words and divine names on which see Skemer, *Binding Words*, pp. 107–15.
89. Charms no. 9 and 17 above.
90. I have not seen Exeter, Exeter Cathedral Library 3521. I exclude British Library, Sloane 140, noted in Keiser, 'Verse Introductions', p. 302, at this time because the fragmentary nature of its recipes, makes it uncertain whether or not it belongs to this group.
91. This last section of recipes is not continuous; e.g., f. 146v contains arabic numbers and letters of the alphabet.

Bibliography

Boffey, Julia. and Edwards, A. S. G., *A New Index of Middle English Verse*. London: The British Library, 2005 [referenced as NIMEV].

Bozoky, Edina, *Charmes et Prières Apotropaïques*, Typologie des sources du moyen âge occidental, Fasc. 86, Turnhout-Belgium: Brepols, 2003.

Crawfurd, Raymond, 'The Blessing of Cramp-Rings: A Chapter in the History of the Treatment of Epilepsy', in C. Singer, ed., *Studies in the History and Method of Science*. Vol. 1. Oxford: Clarendon, 1917, pp. 165–87.

Franz, Adolph, *Die kirchlichen Benedictionen im Mittelalter*, 2 vols. Graz: Akademische Druck- U. Verlasanstalt, 1960, rpt. of 1909 edn.

Heinrich, F., *Ein mittelenglisches Medizinbuch*, Halle: M. Neimeyer, 1896.

Humphrey, Caroline and Laidlaw, James. *The Archetypal Actions of Ritual: A Theory of Ritual Illustrated by the Jain Rite of Worship*, Oxford: Clarendon Press, 1994.

Keiser, George R., 'Verse Introductions to Middle English Medical Treatises', *English Studies* 4 (2003), pp. 301–17.

——, 'Robert Thornton's Liber de Diversis Medicinis: text, vocabulary, and scribal confusion' in, eds, *Rethinking Middle English: Linguistic and Literary Approaches*, Nikolaus Ritt and Herbert Schendl. Frankfurt am Main, New York, *et al.*; Peter Lang, 2003, pp. 30–41.

——, *Works of Science and Information*, vol. 10, in A. E. Hartung, ed. *A Manual of the Writings in Middle English 1050–1500*, 10 vols, New Haven: Connecticut Academy of Arts and Sciences, 1997.

Ogden, Margaret S., *The 'Liber de Diversis Medicinis' in the Thornton Manuscript (MS. Lincoln Cathedral A.5.2)*, EETS o.s. 207, London: Oxford University Press, 1969.

Olsan, Lea T., 'Charms in Medieval Memory', in J. Roper, ed., *Charms and Charming in Europe*, Basingstoke and New York: Palgrave Macmillan, 2004.

—— 'Charms and Prayers in Medieval Theory and Practice', *Social History of Medicine* 16 (2003), 343–66.

—— 'The Language of Charms in a Middle English Recipe Collection' *ANQ* 18.3 (2005), 29–35.

Roper, Jonathan, *English Verbal Charms*, FF Communications, Vol. CXXXVI, No. 288. Helsinki: Academia Scientiarum Fennica, 2005.

Skemer, Don C., *Binding Words: Textual Amulets in the Middle Ages*, University Park: The Pennsylvania State University Press, 2006.

Schulz, Monika, *Beschwörungen im Mittelalter: Einfürung und Überblick*, Heidlelberg: Universitätsverlag C. Winter, 2003.

Smallwood, T. M. ' "God was born in Bethlehem ...": The tradition of a Middle English Charm', *Medium Aevum* 58.2 (1989), 203–23.

Voigts, Linda Ehrsam, and Patricia Deery Kurtz, *Scientific and Medical Writings in Old and Middle English: An electronic reference.* CD-ROM. Ann Arbor: University of Michigan Press, 2000.

16
The Charms of Biljana, a Bajalica (Conjuror) in Budisava, Serbia

Maria Vivod

The village of Budisava is to be found eighty kilometres from Belgrade, the capital of Serbia, in the northern province of Vojvodina. This province represents the crossing point of three major religions, Catholicism, Orthodox Christianity and Islam. Biljana, the focus of this chapter, is a folk-healer, who, by her own account, has practised popular medicine 'all her life'. At one time she decided to leave her job of a secretary in the village school to dedicate herself to her 'God given calling', as she herself terms it.

This woman is known not only in her own village and in the wider province: her patients come from every part of Serbia (including the capital), as well as from Bosnia. Biljana practices a form of ethno-medicine characteristic for this part of central Europe and the Balkans, a method called *salivanje strave* 'melting the fear' in Serbian. This method consists of ritual behaviour and a special text known as a '*basma*' (or charm), used together with the aim of healing the patient. Another part of the technique is the melting of lead (or 'melting the fear'), which consists of the ritual melting of a small piece of lead, by means of which Biljana 'sees' the cause of the illness. This piece of lead represents the condensed illness and its cause as well. The shape the melted metal assumes is interpreted by the conjurer (*bajalica*). At the end of the interpretation, the conjurer gives this piece of lead to the patient and he must liberate himself from it by throwing it ritually back over his shoulder, without turning back his head, while pronouncing a charm.

The illness which Biljana heals and from which the term 'melting the fear' originates are defined in the folk speech as *strava* – a terror, a fear, a spell, or evil eyes. These are different psychic crises, neurosis, states of stress and nervousness. In popular beliefs, fear is personified, and is believed to be able to 'enter' the human organism, and to stay inside for a long period. In popular belief, this state is characterised by insomnia, convulsions, nervousness, lose of appetite, headaches, bed-wetting (in case of children), nightmares, etc. To 'chase out' the terror, it is necessary to determine its cause, which can be one of a diverse range. For children, it can, for example, be a large dog or a fall. For adults, there can be a variety of different kinds of causes of psychic shock and stress, such as, for example, a car accident. When its form appears in the lead, the cause is discovered, and the consequences are automatically removed.

The other state, which is more or less connected to personification of the fear, is the state defined like 'spell-boundness'. Spell-boundness is a state with similar symptoms as in the case of terror. Accordingly, we can assume common roots for the various psychic disorders, illnesses, and bewitched states, that are brought together in popular parlance under the common terms of *fear* and *spell*.

The causes of spell-boundness are similar to those found in most other European cultures: the evil eye, malign magic and negative charming. One characteristic of spell-boundness in the cultures of this territory is the connection of the spell-boundness (and its symptoms) with the creatures of other worlds, which are often parallel with the human one. Those creatures from the other world, which according to the Serbian traditional beliefs bring sickness and the spell-boundness, are anthropomorphic creatures of the female sex called *vile*, which might be translated as 'fairies'. Traditionally, these fairies send illnesses as a warning or as a punishment for the transgression of their territory, for breaking taboos connected to housework and or breaching the coded behaviour of the individual in the social structure. The conjurers are the persons who traditionally establish contact with 'their sisters' from another world and interpret their wishes, advice or discontents. A person who has not respected a particular taboo, who for example has washed the laundry or sewn on a holiday or on a Sunday, is punished with illness, with spell-boundness, because he was defied the fairies by not respecting 'their days' (these jobs are traditionally defined as 'female ones', just like the gender of the *vile*). The traditional conjurer was the mediator between these two worlds – the human one and those of the fairies. She would address them, asking for help for the sick individual and cure him according to the advices of the fairies.

In time, the Christian saints replaced the role of the fairies, as the creatures that are punishing the human beings with sickness. The saints, especially the local ones, are the creatures 'from the other side' who send 'warnings' (according to Biljana's words) in form of illness to the individuals who do not respect the taboos. In this regard, the 'familial' saints of the Serbs are especially interesting. These appear as saints – protectors of the Serb family or the kin. In the modern Serbian society, popular healers of Biljana's type interpret these saints as the mediators of the will of God; and the popular, traditional healers are the mediators between the human and the 'other' world.

The Serbian saint-protector is celebrated once a year, this is called the *slava*, 'the celebration' (or 'the glory'), defined in the Serbian Orthodox calendar (we must keep in mind that the Orthodox calendar is a Julian one, i.e. runs two weeks 'after' the Gregorian calendar). This day is dedicated to the saint-protector of the family and celebrated in the family circle with special rituals. *Slavski kolac*, 'the bread of *slava*', is prepared and is blessed in the church along with the red wine. The 'bread' is ritually broken before the meal and some parts are consumed. The guests are among the family members and friends. Traditionally, the saint-protector is connected to the fireplace of the house, and to the house itself, because the saint-protector is the personification of agrarian-god of the house and the fields, and accordingly the *slava* was linked to the house, that is the son who stayed to live in the house inherited it. Here, the patrilineal right of the firstborn is followed.

In the Serbian Orthodox calendar, we find eighty one saints, about twenty of which are celebrated as a *slava*, for example, *Sv. Stefan* – St. Stephen (9 January), *Sv. Jovan* – Saint John (20 January), *Sv. Georgije* – St. George (6 May), *Sv. Nikola* – St. Nicholas (19 December), etc. During the healing ritual, Biljana is guided by the *slava* of the patients. The person who has come for treatment is regularly asked, 'Which is your *slava*?' – which saint is his protector? The character of this saint determines the charming procedure because this saint is the one who is sent the 'warning' in the form of a sickness (just like the fairies of the past) to warn the individual or the family about the correct way of living according to the Orthodox-Christian criteria.

The conditions regarding charming are the same as in traditional charming, though some details differ. There are for example restrictions on which days of the week charming can be performed. Traditionally, charmers only charmed on Thursday and Saturdays, both of which were considered to be 'backward' days and thus suitable for the 'backward' technique of charming ('backward' in the sense of contrary to the direction of everyday life). At present, the charmers practice during the working week, and avoid doing so at weekends, especially on Sundays, because of its Christian significance. The charming itself, which Biljana calls 'prayer', takes place in a limited space, in the intimacy of a cabinet, especially furnished for this purpose inside Biljana's house.

There are some 'modern' elements as well: like the well-equipped waiting room for the patients-clients, and the obligatory 'reservation' of consultations over the phone (except in cases of emergency, when, for example, children have fallen ill).

The room for consultations is 'decorated' with different icons on the wall and the icon lamp, giving the person entering precise information about the character of the service. The 'services' of charming are not explicitly waged, but each patient leaves on the table, next to the Bible, 'as many as he thinks he should'. Under the tacit rule, the conjurer does not demand money for her services – she leaves that decision to the visitor.

In one part of this 'consulting room', there is a small corner with a central purpose: a little table with gas burner, on which Biljana melts the lead in a spoon, which, when melted, she throws into a dish of water. This kind of charming ritual consists of same elements as the traditional one: the text of the charming, the 'prayer' is spoken with bated breath, following by the repetition of exactly same moves. The same piece of lead is melted several times, until it 'cracks', that is, until it makes an explosive sound inside the water. That strong sound means that the 'prayer' was successful.

Biljana performs the whole ritual standing, while the patient sits on the place especially intended for him. The charms are pronounced when the lead is melted; the conjurer puts a dish of water over the patient's head and throws the melted lead into it. These motions are repeated alternately over the head, in front of the chest, over the knees. During one session, this procedure is repeated three times. Biljana addresses the saint-protector of the family and God himself directly. As in the traditional incantation, she represents the transmitter of the 'message' to the over world. The tone of the charm is pleading, which means that Biljana is not threatening the sickness or its author, as often happens in some texts of traditional charms.

The text of prayer varies depends upon the name of the saint-protector, and the name of the patient, for whom Biljana prays. Sometimes Biljana uses a simplified version of the same 'prayer', a fact that can lead us to conclude that mentioning of the name of the saint-protector and the name of the person for whom the charm serve is only efficient when it occurs together with the motions that follow the ritual, and that the charm text itself is not sufficient. The variations of the charm illustrate the free approach of the conjurer to its content.

Every day, right before starting her sessions, Biljana prays (The Lord's Prayer, the Apostles' Creed, etc.) in front of her altar and in front of her icon lamp. During the melting of the lead, she gathers information about her patient: age, family situation, and children and of course, the name of the saint-protector. During the first melting over the head of the patient and subsequently every time she throws the lead into the dish of water over another part of the patient's body, she is repeats this charm:

Gospode Isuse Hriste, sine	*Lord Jesus Christ, Son of God, by*
Božiji molitvama Sveti	*thy Prayers Saint*
XY [ime sveca-zaštitnika]),	*XY* [the name of the Saint-Protector],
spasi i pomiluj XY	*save and favour* [the name of
[ime pacijenta].	the patient].

The simplified version (that we heard more often) runs:

Bože presveti, Sveti XY	*Holy God, Saint XY*
[ime sveca-zaštitnika],	[the name of the Saint-Protector],
molitvama spasi XY	*by thy Prayers save XY*
[ime pacijenta].	[the name of the patient].

The text of this kind of charm represents a linguistic model of information exchange between the saint-protector and Biljana herself. The request is directed parallel both to God and the saint-protector, but in popular belief, the saint-protector is the one who is sending the illness. The will and the character of this particular saint are interpreted depending of symptoms of the illness or omens (a dream that the sick individual had). For instance, a dream about snakes is a warning from St. Nicholas about errors in ones life and deeds.

The text is murmured quietly and after each repeat Biljana crosses herself. The way in which she pronounces the charm renders the name of God and the saint-protector audible however.

We can compare Biljana's charms with some traditional texts in the form of a request:

Sveta Petko i Sveta Nedeljo i	*Holy Petka and Holy Sunday and*
svi Sveci Svetitelji i	*all the Holy Saints*
andjeli spasitelji, meni oprostite,	*and Angels' Saviors, forgive me,*
bolesnome pomozite.	*help the sick person.*
Vuković, 1981, 208	Vuković, 1981, 208

or

Sačuvaj, Bože, moga XY [ime pacijenta] od rdjavih očiju, od zločestih očiju, od svake muke i bola, od teškoce i uroka. Urok bio devet puta, od 9 8, od 8 7, ..., od 1 nijedan.	*Save, God, my XY* [the Name of the Patient] *from evil Eyes, from naughty Eyes, from every Hurt and Pain, from Difficulties and from Spells. Spell was Nine times, 9 8, from 8 7, ..., from 1 none.*
Vuković, 1981, 208	Vuković, 1981, 208

As we can see, the text of these traditional charms are in the form of a request addressed to one saint or God himself. Sometimes the request underlines the exact reason for the request: the illness or spell-boundness. The first traditional charm is highly reminiscent of the shorter version of Biljana's charm. The second charm, also a request, is concerned with the problem of spell binding. The use of 'counting backwards' to free the patient is a characteristic leitmotif of charms against spell-boundness. As Lecouteux has written: 'It function by means of a *similia similibus,* a homeopathic device which expressing the thought that directs the charms: to end some kind of evil, a referential situation functions analogically' (our own translation of Lecouteux, 1996, 105). We can remind ourselves of some other charms, which are use the model of 'counting backwards'. For the example, we will take a Hungarian traditional charm (the Hungarian minority is present on this particular territory where Biljana acts) and an example taken from a French tradition by Lecouteux:

Öt nem öt,	*Five is not five,*
négy nem négy,	*four is not four,*
hàrom nem hàrom,	*three is not three,*
kettö nem kettö,	*two is not two,*
egy nem egy.	*one is none.*
Vasas, 1985	Vasas, 1985

Dartre,	*Lichen*
Je te jure,	*I'm cursing You,*
Je t'adjure,	*I'm begging You*
Je te conjure	*I'm swearing at You*
De neuf à huit	*From Nine to eight*
De huit à sept	*From eight to seven,*
De sept à six, etc.	*From seven to six, ...*

De une à rien.	*From one to none.*
Lecouteux, 1996, 105	Lecouteux, 1996, 105

As we can see, this element of 'counting backwards', which is omnipresent in most of European and Serb charms of this form, has been lost in Biljana's so called 'prayers'. Biljana only uses the first part, the 'Christianised' form of addressing the 'higher power' (i.e. to God), through mediators, through the saint-protector for health. The simplified form of charms functions in the same linguistic-behavioural conditions as the traditional charm.

Biljana's success is a phenomenon, which is none disputably functioning after the Civil War in this part of the world. In times of personal crisis, people of all social spheres, regardless of ethnical or religious affiliations turn to her. Her reputation of being a popular healer has spread due to many factors. Serbian society is in a deep social, economic, cultural, and identity crisis. Modern medicine, partially due to a lack of material resources, is not able to provide well enough for the sick or for families in crisis. On the other hand, Serbian society following the fall of the Communist regime and the dictatorship is seeking its own identity primarily by returning to its roots. One of the motifs of turning to one's roots is the return to the traditional ways of healing. Traditional methods of medication give the necessary support to the individual in need and in the same time to the family as well. In this way, charms, which were recorded by a local ethnologist in the 1950s as being a disappearing phenomenon, are flourishing once again, in a somewhat altered way.

Bibliography

Camus, Dominique, *Paroles magiques, secrets de guérison – Les leveurs des maux aujourd'hui* (Paris: Editions Imago, 1990).

Grcović, Slavoljub, *Bajanje u kultu mrtvih kod Vlaha Severoistočne Srbije* [*Charms in the Cult of Dead of the Valach of North-east Serbia*] (Beograd: Čigoja, 2002).

Jung, Kàroly, *Gondolatok a magyar – délszlàv egybevetö néphiedelem – és mitolò-gia kapcsàn* [*Thoughts on Hungarian – South Slavic Popular Beliefs and Mythology*], (Ethnographia, A Magyar Néprajzi Tàrsasàg Folyòirata XCII), (Budapest: Akadémiai Kiadò, 1981).

Knežević, Srebrica, *Iscelitelji u svetu etnoloških istraživanja* [*Healers in the World of Ethnological Research*] (Beograd: Svetlost duha I/1, 1991).

Lecouteux, Claude, *Charmes, conjurations et bénédictions, Lexique et formules*, (Paris: Honoré Champion, 1996).

Radenković, Ljubinko, *Narodna bajanja kod Južnih Slovena* [*South Slavic Folk Incantations*] (Beograd: Prosveta, 1996).

Radenković, Ljubinko, *Urok ide uz polje-Narodna bajanja* [*The Charm Is Going Up to the Fields – Folk Incantations*] (Niš: Gradina, 1973).

Momirović, Petar, *Bajanja u Jagodini i okolini* [*Incantations in Jagodina and its region*] (Beograd: Državna Štamparija Kraljevine Jugoslavije, 1936).

Vasas, Samu, *Népi gyògyàszat, kalotaszegi gyüjtés* [*Ethnomedical research in Kalotaszeg (Transylvania)*] (Bucharest: Kriterion Könyvkiadò, 1985).

Vuković, Milan T, *Narodni običaji, verovanja i poslovice kod Srba sa kratkim pogledom u njihovu prošlost* [*Serbian Folk Customs, Beliefs and Proverbs, with a Brief Overview of the Past*] (Beograd: izdanje Milan T. Vuković, 1981).

Zlatanović, Momčilo, *Narodna bajanja iz Južne Srbije* [*Folk Incantations from Southern Serbia*](Beograd: Časopis Raskovnik, 1982).

17
Verbal Charms in Malagasy Folktales

Lee Haring

When, long before he became the *doyen* of the French literary world, the twenty-four-year-old Jean Paulhan began collecting proverbs in highland Madagascar in 1908, he noticed features of performance which were theorized only generations later. Speakers talked rapidly, yet with 'singular dignity and seriousness.'[1] One would spread his arms and lean forward; another conveyed the impression she was about to announce an accident or death; another 'went so far as to stand up every time he uttered a proverb.' Paulhan could tell that the listeners were paying close attention, the way people respond to an acrobat or the refrain in an operetta. Paulhan could not avoid noticing the ways in which performance of these special sets of words was, as an analyst today would say, 'keyed.' Keying included parallel structure, symmetry, balance, and metaphors, which 'signified on' something in the social situation (using the vernacular term for indirect, ironic speech). The old-fashioned language of proverb, *ohabolana*, spoke out of a known body of traditional discourse, a transcendent order which M. M. Bakhtin later theorized under the name of monologic speech.[2] That order was the standard against which the proverb speaker would be measured. In all these ways, 'the act of expression itself [was] framed as display.'[3] So it would be too in a verbal charm.

In Madagascar, the foreign term 'charm,' being an 'analytic category,' draws attention to 'the verbal element of vernacular magic practice,'[4] but within the ethnic genre system, it is a metaphorical extension of a material object connected to divination, named *ody*.[5] Twenty-one kinds of *ody* were listed by the British missionary lexicographers of the 1880s, who had no hesitation in using the English word: charms against hail, against being shot, against being gored when you are wrestling an ox; medicines for worms, for strengthening your sinews, or as a tonic for children.[6] Etymologically, the form *aody* means something that effects change, or returns something to its original condition. *Ody* then became a large topic for study. One missionary, the Norwegian Lars Vig, amassed enormous amounts of information on them during the last quarter of the nineteenth century.[7] His editor observes, 'This word is difficult to translate into French, for it covers a vast semantic domain. It signifies amulet, fetish, idol, and still more sacred objects: in sum, every object that is thought to possess the magical power to produce vital changes for good or ill, or to neutralise such forces by preserving a normal state.'[8] Both wooden *ody* and verbal charms are instruments in the Malagasy theory of causation. Moreover, there has long been an association between wood as a material and the upper class (*andriana*) of Madagascar's hierarchal society, so that a man coming round to sell you wood today is perpetuating a long tradition of his class.[9]

Malagasy people separate levels of language as they do classes and genders. Ordinary talk (*resaka*) is expected of women, formal style (*kabary*) of men, when they stand up to speak at formal occasions like weddings and funerals.[10] Both men and women speak *ohabolana*, which are often cited in men's formal speeches (also known as *kabary*). The speaker, whether male or female, makes a claim to entitlement merely by the citation. That same entitlement is asserted by certain fictional characters, who speak charms to return a fainting person to consciousness. If, as Wittgenstein said, 'An entire mythology is stored within our language,'[11] then an entire social system, carrying the weight of myth, is stored within the speaking of charms in Malagasy folktales, where entitlement to speak is associated with the *andriana* class, that class is associated with diviners, and the mythology coupling them can be glimpsed through narratives obviously non-mythological.[12]

Fourth largest island in the world, Madagascar is a unique amalgam of Indonesian, Indian, and African cultures, with an island-wide language. Its settlers, starting out from what is now Indonesia, probably spent time on the African coast before they moved to Madagascar. There they came into contact with the Swahili people of the coast and produced the Malagasy language of today, which contains both Indonesian-derived and African-derived words. Part of their symbol system can even be traced back to India, for three of the four Vedic social orders were visible in the strata of old Malagasy society: nobles (*andriana*), freemen (*hova*) and slaves (*andevo*).[13] Social hierarchy, one dimension of the symbol system, is asserted when charms are spoken.

A 'classic' example is a story proclaiming the nobleness of the *andriana*, collected in the western part of the island nearly a century ago. Like many Malagasy tales, this one, from the Sakalava ('People of the Long Valley'), organises its plot around a prince's search for a suitable wife. This prince, an inversion of the famous African *fille difficile* or defiant girl who rejects eligible suitors,[14] courts a girl of his own station. At her house women faint at his beauty, the princess's grandmother first, then the girl herself. Then comes the charm.

> The prince went up to her and said, 'If you have fainted for the love you have for me, arise and be in good health. But if it's only your malice and ill nature that have brought you to this, don't come back to life; die!' She came to herself and got up. Then Ndramihamiñy [Mr. Property] saw her, and he in turn was so dazzled that he fell in a faint. But the princess [Ms. Owns-Cattle] went up to him and said the same words he'd said to her. He came to himself and got up'.[15]

Their names, and their echo of each other's words, signal how well suited these two are to each other. Both are *andriana*. Performance of such a story, whether the audience was confined to nobles or included others, was a principal channel for the preservation and transmission of the class separation. I call this one a 'classic' example because the charm identifies the speaker's class membership, the speaker is standing, and his or her resuscitating words bring the object-person from horizontal to vertical.

Such narratives of the rich and famous show the class system being implied and reinforced when the *andriana* characters speak these formulas, or charms. Specialist minstrels worked over and adapted the narratives to speak clearly to the various monarchies of various ethnic groups.[16] The class separation they allude to shows in the earliest narratives recorded. Sieur de Flacourt, who founded the first European settlement, attests to the separation of the *noirs* and the *blancs* already in the mid-seventeenth century. He even cites the earliest recorded Malagasy myth as an explicit charter for social hierarchy.[17] Officially, Malagasy ideology allows unions only between persons of the same status. Further to the north, the Merina of the central highlands, where Jean Paulhan lived, have always maintained 'a rigid class structure with strict rules about intermarriage,' even when recurrent and overwhelming political exigencies have obliged men to marry women of lower status.[18]

Even the relatively egalitarian Bara group of southern Madagascar show the influence of the class system. The formula appears in Bara stories about the members of their royal family, as when the prince's favored wife is cast out into the forest, after giving birth, by her jealous co-wives. The husband sends people to overtake her; she faints. 'Ah,' he says, 'is it loving or hating me that caused you to faint? 'She answers not in words, but by coming back to life. 'Who killed you?' he asks. 'Your wives', she replies. He repudiates those who 'kill my wife' (*ni valiki niteraki*), and thus it is, the narrator adds, that the wives of a polygamist hate one another.[19] The terse style might reflect less-than-ideal circumstances of recording, or shifts in Bara social organization at that time, but the entitlement of a princely speaker links Bara to other Malagasy groups like the Merina.

The Merina have a stronger sense of class distinction. The quoted charm in one of their narratives, which was also known to the Bara-Tanala to the south,[20] more emphatically proclaims the nobleness of the *andriana*. It is a true history (*tantara*), one of many such that were collected in the 1870s by the sedulous Jesuit Fr. Callet, and no trivial tale for entertainment (*tafasiry*). 'Andriambavirano came down from heaven,' writes Fr. Callet. 'According to the legend, the leaf of a tree fell into the lake atop Angavo,' a hill about twenty-five kilometers east of Antananarivo, the capital city. A young slave spies the leaf, but he is not to grasp it: it will belong to his master, Andriamanjavona, who speaks the charm: '*Raha andrian-dray andrian-dreny aho*, If truly I am noble from [or by] my father and noble from my mother, I'll get it easily.' The prince's charm signals his status: he is a royal prince by a double filiation.[21] 'He succeeded in grasping it,' the story goes on, 'carried it home, and put it in a box.' There it grows arms and legs and becomes a woman. She refuses the slave's attempts to grasp her and marries the prince.

> But one day, his *vadibe* (first wife) killed Andriambavirano. Andriamanitra [God] resuscitated her by sending his messengers Andriampanointointaolana, Andriampanafosafoninofo, and Andriantomponiaina. She came back to Andriamanjavona. The *vadibe* was surprised and said, 'She is truly a daughter of Andriamanitra! She was dead, now she lives.'[22]

It is a true story because she is the mother of a clan. Fr. Callet already noticed that the story resembles at least eight other Malagasy tales.[23] The hero's command of the charm seems to assert conceptions of politics and kingship which originated from the Indonesian strand of Malagasy settlement.[24] The folklorist sees, however, that the story is not exclusive property of the Malagasy. For example, in one episode, the *vadibe* casts out the divine wife's three children, who are adopted by a foster father. This and other elements attach this Merina tale to the worldwide story type known as The Three Golden Children or Three Golden Sons, which the Grimms called The Three Little Birds (ATU 707).[25] But the charm is a distinct Malagasy touch.

Related narratives confirm the notion that only nobles are entitled to speak verbal charms. A tale of the Betsimisaraka, who live in the eastern part of Madagascar, portrays a non-noble husband and wife making a vow to each other:

> 'I have only you as a wife. If I ever take another, may the *pirog* [boat] sink me into the water!' Faravavy [wife] for her part said, 'I have only you as a husband. If I ever give in to the desire for another man, may lightning carry me up into the clouds!'

But when he drowns, she breaks her vow – which was no charm anyway, to be sure.[26]

Tangential to the study of charms is the Madagascar variant of Ovid's tale in which Apollo punishes Midas by giving him ass's ears. Ovid writes,

> The slave who was wont to trim his long hair beheld his shame. And he, since he dared not reveal the disgraceful sight, yet eager to tell it out and utterly unable to keep it to himself, went off and dug a hole in the ground and into the hole, with low, muttered words, he whispered of his master's ears which he had seen.[27]

The Antanosy narrator begins, 'There was once a horned king. His people didn't know their king had two horns.' His secret physical peculiarity is discovered by a lower-class character, a honey-gatherer, who worries (all Malagasy worry, say foreign observers) at what might happen if he reveals the king's secret. Instead of telling what he knows, he digs a hole and vomits into it; a golden, gold-bearing tree grows in that spot. While the honey-gatherer hides, the king attempts a charm: 'As I am a famous king and your owner as well, you must come down at my command, so that I gather your gold.' When the charm is unsuccessful, the king realizes someone else must be the real master of that tree. 'So each of the people said, "If I am your real master, who grew you, come down so that my king can gather your fruits".' Again no effect. The king summons the honey-gatherer and orders him to lower the tree. The honey-gatherer, at first terrified of telling his story, finally says,

> 'There was a secret I once found out, but I didn't want to tell it to anyone. Then the desire to tell that secret made me sick to my stomach and I vomited into a hole. A week later, this tree started to sprout; I was the first to see it. I was surprised to see golden flowers on it. Finally I decided it came from my vomiting.' The king said, 'What is the secret

you didn't want to tell?' The honey-gatherer said, 'Pardon, sire, I can't tell it to you, because if I tell it to you, I'll be condemned to death.' The *mpanjaka* [king] kept pressing him, and the honey-gatherer said, 'One day I was out looking for honey, and I saw you taking your bath in the pond, and I saw that you have two horns, and that was the secret I didn't want to tell anybody, but I'm telling you now because you force me.'

Revealing the awful truth entitles this low-class character to speak a resuscitating charm and command the tree.

The king fainted from shame, but the honey-gatherer now said, 'If it is true that you have the two horns I saw, come back to life.' The king revived immediately.

Then the honey-gatherer said to the tree, 'If you come from my vomiting, which was caused by my desire to speak, and if I am thus your master, descend so my king can gather your fruits.' The tree descended low down. The king's subjects were surprised and gathered the gold from the tree. Then the honey-gatherer said, 'If you come from my vomiting, which was caused by my desire to speak, ascend back up, higher than before.' And the tree ascended higher than it had been.

Again the effect is to raise the object. The moral contradicts normal Malagasy taciturnity:

That's why they say you can't keep from telling or saying something you've found, even when it's bad or shameful, and especially if it's good.[28]

The commoner earns his entitlement by correctly handling special knowledge in privileged language.

Confirming the entitlement are two 'if-then' formulas cited in a tale of the Tanala ('Forest People'), who live in south central Madagascar. The first is uttered by the princess Renikombareva, who revives a suitor:

Renikombareva [the princess] sent for water which she put into a horn, and sprinkled the man with the water, saying without modesty, 'Come, my good man! If it is my ugliness that has caused you to faint away, die! But if it is my beauty, live!' Then the king jumped up and cried, 'What a long time I've been asleep!'

The charm is a warrant for the match; her three brothers award him the princess. The second 'if-then' formula comes in a later episode, when a messenger bird must be revived to give his message. The king offers the bird rum and water, saying, 'If you are bringing us good news, drink this water and rum and come back to life! But if you are bringing us misfortune, die!' The bird knows never to refuse a free drink, revives, knocks back a few, and delivers his message.[29] All the characters in this story are nobles; even the bird is a royal symbol.

A beautiful illustration of this use of formularised charms to warrant class membership comes from one of the greatest of Malagasy stories, a version of the international tale The Twins, or Blood Brothers (ATU 303),[30] which the Grimms called The Two Brothers (no. 60). Too long and elaborate to summarise here, the piece was recorded from a very accomplished Sakalava narrator, who brings in the charm after the hero has spent a long, long time alternating between disguise as a leper and victory on the battlefield in beautiful clothes and armor. His wife, whom he has already secured, finds him so disgusting that she acquires herbs, one for him to drink, the other to bathe in. Once her servant has removed his outer coating in the bath, she tells her mistress that his body is healthy, not leprous; indeed it shines like gold. 'Don't be telling me lies', says the wife, 'go back and bathe my husband.' 'I'm not lying,' says the servant, 'come and see.' When she finally does see him after his bath, she faints. Then comes the charm:

'If the cause of your faint is the love you have for me,
    rise up and be well,
but if it is your malice and wickedness that brought it on,
    do not arise, and die!'
The young woman then opened her eyes and arose. Seeing her, Big-Leper fainted away in turn, and his wife said to him,
'If it is your malice and wickedness
    which have made you faint away so,
    do not arise, but die,
for I have money and cattle to bury you
    according to the customs of your ancestors.
But if it is your goodness and the love you have for me.
    arise and live,
    to enjoy with me all the riches I possess!'
Saying these words [the narrator goes on], she took a silk kerchief, moistened it in cold water and then passed it over her husband's face. He immediately came to, got up, and kissed his wife very tenderly.[31]

The charm does seem to have been accurately translated: Dandouau, the collector, transcribed this and his dozens of other Sakalava stories almost as if taking dictation. The obeisance paid by the narrator's elaborate style to the high rank of his characters goes far to associate the *andriana* with power, as that is manifested in the word. Spokespersons for their rank, they have only to quote a couple of classical lines to remind the other characters in the story, and us their audience, of their identity.

In antiquity, the sovereign and the diviner were of almost equal importance. By the time these narratives were recorded and translated, the *andriana* characters in them are acting out in words a stylized, verbal, somewhat secularized version of what *ombiasy*, diviners, do in real life with objects. Evidently a 'charm' in Madagascar is a key to a belief system, which associates the upper class with the diviners. According to a creation story by one of Dandouau's Sakalava informants, *ody* are prehistoric, which suggests that their symbolic force antedates settlement in Madagascar. Equally prehistory, said this narrator, are rivalries and verbal duels among *moasy* (healers), whose symmetry is reminiscent of the inseparable Malagasy tricksters Ikotofetsy and Imahaka.[32] But their spells are weapons, not medicines, and their ancient grudges produce topographical features seen today.

Once, they say, there were two famous magicians gifted with extraordinary power. One of them lived in Madagascar, the other on the opposite shore in Africa. Both were celebrated for their *ody*, and being very jealous, they cordially detested each other. Each one would have liked to remain the only one on earth, so as to be the most powerful *moasy* in the world. They decided to fight until one of them was on the ground. So they goaded each other: 'Let's have a terrific war!' said one of them.

'Very well,' said the other, 'but not with guns or spears. Let's make war with our *ody*.'

Each one prepared his most powerful evil spells and threw them across the way against his adversary. But it was no use. Each one found more effectual *ody* to counter them.

Then they wanted to fight by throwing stones. They pulled up rocks as big as mountains and threw them with extraordinary force. They threw so many so hard that finally they wounded each other, and both died.

It's the stones that they threw that still, today, form all the big and small islands facing Madagascar: Nosy-Be, Mayotte, Anjouan, and so on, as well as the big rocks and hills along the coasts. They say there are also a lot on the other side of the sea, along the African coast.

When the two *moasy* died, their blood spread and formed the sea. Their tears became the rain, their bones the trunks of trees, their skin the bark on the trunks, and their hair became leaves and grass. That's why today, to make *ody*, you take water, leaves, bark, and bits of wood.

As for their heads, Zanahary took them home with him. He distributed the mind they had in them among all human beings, but he didn't distribute it equally. That's why there are wise men and fools, intelligent and stupid men, men who know how to make *ody* and others who don't.[33]

Both those pieces of wood and the verbal formulas that go with them possess the most powerful concept of the belief system, which is called *hasina*, an 'intrinsic or supernatural virtue.'[34] Its power shows in another of Dandouau's Sakalava tales. The hero Rena (Rich) is tested by performing a childlike service: he courteously removes the gum from an old lady's eyes. When he asks her for food, she sends him out to fetch bran and bones, for she will reverse the natural sequence of cooking. She feeds him rice, which she makes out of the bran, and meat, which she makes from the bones. Only then, having established her supernatural powers, does she confer on him an *ody* that will help him overcome a cannibal monster, whom he has been charged to capture and take back to his future father-in-law. 'Take this little stick,' she says. 'When you see *Lahimarena* [the cannibal monster], climb a tree. He will come right under you to devour you, and you strike him with this stick, saying, "Eat what I give you and don't eat what I don't give you!"' In the event, the formula succeeds: the monster becomes like a pet dog, follows him to town, and obligingly devours the girl's recalcitrant family, thus depriving her of relatives her husband might have to deal with later. She agrees to marry him, and he dispatches the monster back to the forest.[35] Wood and word are equally saturated with *hasina*, a 'force of penetration,' a 'persuasive virtue,' but also a 'therapeutic virtue.'...
Thus, according to one authority, '*hasina* is an analogic notion taking as many forms as there are beings.'[36] Recently another authority, an elder of the east-coast Betsimisaraka, confirmed the real-life *hasina* present in a ritual stick: 'When you hold the stick, there isn't anything you don't know. The stick holds it all – it comes out in dreams and tells you how to complete the ceremony the following day.'[37]

Restoring someone to consciousness is a kind of cure, so that the charm is analogous to *fanafody*, medicine, which cures disease. In one Merina historical account, when visitors asked their host to cure one of their party, he disclaimed the power: 'I am not the one who can make an *ody*, but there is a god [*Andriamanitra*] at my house, and if you want him to do the cure, then make an offering to the god. I'm not looking for reward, for it isn't I who keep charms, but Andriamanitra himself.'[38] The modest, class-conscious disclaimer is echoed in a Sakalava legend: a diviner successfully resuscitated a dead boy whose body was cast ashore after he has been eaten by a shark. (Many Malagasy stories, both fictional and historical, narrate the rescue of victims from the belly of a swallowing monster).[39] The diviner applies a 'charm' to the boy's body, the boy comes back to life, and the crowd of people who witnessed it exclaimed: 'This is indeed an effectual remedy.' Andriamanta [the diviner] then said with great solemnity: 'It is not mere medicine, but God himself.'[40] Not all diviners can be counted upon to be so unpretentious or monotheistic. A great many *ody* are love charms. The most potent ones in history were royal talismans, the *sampy* of the Merina sovereigns, which were destroyed, under European Christian influence, by assertion of royal prerogative.[41]

In life, it is the diviners, *ombiasy*, who possess esoteric knowledge and control both the material *ody* and the verbal formulas that go with them. For them as for European healers, language helps to bring about healing.[42] Still today, at least among Tanala, *ombiasy* show strict respect for inherited ritual, are credited with immemorial knowledge of divination techniques, and hence have a crucial political role which associates them with kings (*mpanjaka*). The *ombiasy* are the guarantors of a divine order; the *mpanjaka* preside over a social order that endeavors to be a reproduction of it. The ideological–political synthesis is the basis for social unity.[43]

Speaking charms in narratives, the *andriana* appear as spokespersons of that waning social order. A Sakalava prince, Andriantoakafo, having succeeded his father Andriamandisoarivo and wishing to invoke the protection of the gods and ancestors, submitted his newborn daughter to an ordeal by exposure. Placing her in a box in the waves, he uttered the charm,

'O my daughter,
> if I am to maintain the kingdom of the Zafimolena in the land of Boina,
>> do not be carried off by the water,
>>> and let the sea bring you to the dry land where I shall reign.

But if I am not to maintain this kingdom,
>   if it is to pass into other hands,
>>   may the will of the gods and ancestors show itself
>>>   by having you swept off by the water and never return
>>>>   to dry land.'

Not content with the mere words of this oracular pronouncement, the prince's subjects made sure the princess came safe to land. Thus they ensured the founding of a city in that place.[44] The narrative captures the unevenly resolved conflicts between sovereign and subjects and between language and the world.

The entitlement claimed by that prince claimed is visible in a frequent motif of Malagasy folktales, the stretching tree. In a Sakalava tale, the elder of two girls, abandoned by their father in the forest, says to a big tree, 'If you are a god or a goddess, come lower so we can get on you.' The tree descends, and when the girls have cut branches for their bed, the elder dismisses the tree, again claiming her entitlement: 'If you are a god or a goddess, stretch back up again.' This frequent motif would be merely fanciful if not for the inherited word-power attributed to *andriana*. Entitlement to the performance of formal speech is of course not confined to Madagascar;[45] performance theorists reformulate it as 'the acceptance of responsibility to perform, to do the thing with acceptance of being evaluated.'[46] Within a fictional narrative, however, the function of the charm – to revive a person to consciousness – parallels the function of the narrative in its performance situation.

Performance of a narrative or a charm is a frame, a species of quotation, and a switch from one mode of verbal interaction to another, in which a set of old words is brought into a new setting.[47] When the 'masters of words' (*mpikabary*) in Madagascar cite the proverbial words of the ancestors, they reach 'the ultimate stage of reverence,'[48] but they also build the future out of the past, upholding their conviction that words do affect the world.[49] The charm spoken in a narrative does that in miniature. In its context, it parallels the words of the story in the performance event. Both are expected to have an effect on the listener, to bring him or her back to life.

Notes

1. Jean Paulhan, 'L'expérience du proverbe,' *Commerce* 5 (1925), 23–77: 29.
2. Paul Ottino, 'Les discours oratoires *kabary* et les "joutes de paroles" *hainteny*,' in *Le scribe et la grande maison. Études offertes au Professeur J. Dez*, ed.

N. J. Gueunier, N. Rajanarimanana, and P. Vérin (Paris: Institut National des Langues et Civilisations Orientales, 1992), 93–104: 97; Claudia Mitchell-Kernan, 'Signifying', in *Mother Wit from the Laughing Barrel*, ed. Alan Dundes, reprint, 1971 (Englewood Cliffs (NJ): Prentice-Hall, 1973), 310–28; Mikhail Bakhtin, *Problems of Dostoevsky's Poetics*, ed. and trans. Caryl Emerson, intro. by Wayne C. Booth, reprint, 1929, Theory and History of Literature, Vol. 8 (Minneapolis: University of Minnesota Press, 1984), 79–85.

3. Richard Bauman, *A World of Others' Words: Cross-Cultural Perspectives on Intertextuality* (Oxford: Blackwell, 2004), 9; Richard Bauman, *Verbal Art as Performance* (Prospect Heights (IL): Waveland Press, 1977).

4. Jonathan Roper, ed., *Charms and Charming in Europe* (London: Palgrave Macmillan, 2004), 1.

5. Dan Ben-Amos, 'Analytical Categories and Ethnic Genres,' in *Folklore Genres*, ed. Dan Ben-Amos (Austin: University of Texas Press, 1976), 215–42.

6. John Richardson, *A New Malagasy–English Dictionary* (Antananarivo: The London Missionary Society, 1885), 453–54.

7. Jean-Pierre Domenichini, *Les dieux au service des rois: histoire orale des sampin'andriana ou palladiums royaux de Madagascar* (Paris: Centre de Documentation et de Recherche sur l'Asie du Sud-Est et le Monde Insulindien. Éditions du Centre National de la Recherche Scientifique, 1985); Lars Vig, *Charmes: Spécimens de Magie Malgache* (Bergen: Universitetsforlaget, 1969).

8. Vig, *Charmes*, 12.

9. Jean-Pierre Domenichini, 'Les andriana dans l'histoire,' paper presented at Nanisana (Nanisana, Madagascar, 1987), 4, Photocopy.

10. Elinor Ochs Keenan, 'Norm-Makers, Norm-Breakers: Uses of Speech by Men and Women in a Malagasy Community,' in *Explorations in the Ethnography of Speaking*, 2nd edn, ed. Richard Bauman and Joel Sherzer, reprint, 1974 (Cambridge: Cambridge University Press, 1989), 125–43: 126–7; Maurice Bloch, *How We Think They Think: Anthropological Approaches to Cognition, Memory, and Literacy* (Boulder: Westview Press, 1998), 156.

11. Ludwig Wittgenstein, 'Remarks on Frazer's *Golden Bough*,' in *Philosophical Occasions, 1912–1951*, ed. James Klagge and Alfred Nordmann, reprint, 1931 (Indanapolis: Hackett Publishing Company, 1993), 115–55, 133.

12. Paul Ottino, *L'étrangère intime: essai d'anthropologie de la civilisation de l'ancien Madagascar* (Paris: Éditions Des Archives Contemporaines, 1986).

13. Ottino, *L'Étrangère*, 559–60.

14. Veronika Görög-Karady and Christiane Seydou, comp. & ed., *La fille difficile, un conte-type africain* (Paris: CNRS Éditions, 2001).

15. André Dandouau, *Contes populaires des sakalava et des tsimihety de la région d'Analalava* (Algiers: Jules Carbonel, 1922), 261.

16. Françoise Raison-Jourde, 'Introduction,' in *Les souverains de Madagascar: l'histoire royale et ses résurgences contemporaines*, ed. Françoise Raison-Jourde (Paris: Éditions Karthala, 1983), 33.

17. Etienne de Flacourt, *Histoire de la Grande Isle Madagascar* (Paris: Gervais Clouzier, 1661), xxi-xxii; Paul Ottino, 'La hiérarchie sociale et l'alliance dans le royaume de Matacassi des XVIe et XVIIe siècles,' *ASEMI* 4, no. 4 (1973): 53–89, 72–3.

18. Ottino, 'La Hiérarchie Sociale,' 74; Mervyn Brown, *Madagascar Rediscovered: A History from Early Times to Independence* (Hamden, Connecticut: Archon Books, 1979), 128.

19. Jacques Faublée, *Récits bara*, Travaux et Mémoires de l'Institut d'Ethnologie (Paris: Institut d'Ethnologie, Musée de l'Homme, 1947), 173–5.
20. R. P. Callet, *Tantaran'ny andriana*, Originally Tantara ny andriana eto Madagascar, G.-S. Chapus and E. Ratsimba, reprint, 1908 (Antananarivo: Librairie de Madagascar, 1958), 1:17n.
21. Ottino, *L'Étrangère*, 161.
22. Callet, *Tantaran'ny andriana*, 1:16n.15.
23. Lee Haring, *Malagasy Tale Index*, FF Communications (Helsinki: Suomalainen Tiedeakatemia, 1982), 416–17.
24. Paul Ottino, 'Les andriambahoaka malgaches et l'héritage indonésien,' in *Les souverains de Madagascar*, ed. Françoise Raison-Jourde (Paris: Karthala, 1983), 71–96.
25. Hans-Jörg Uther, *The Types of International Folktales, a Classification and Bibliography*, FF Communications (Helsinki: Suomalainen Tiedeakatemia, 2004), 381–3; Jacob Grimm and Wilhelm Grimm, *The Complete Fairy Tales of the Brothers Grimm*, trans. Jack Zipes (New York: Bantam Books, 1987), 353–6.
26. Charles Renel, *Contes de Madagascar*, Collection de Contes et Chansons Populaires (Paris: Ernest Leroux, 1910), 2: 270–3.
27. Ovid, *Metamorphoses*, trans. Frank Justus Miller, Loeb Classical Library (London: William Heinemann Ltd, 1916), 2: 132–3.
28. Raymond Decary, *Contes et légendes du sud-ouest de Madagascar* (Paris: G.-P. Maisonneuve et Larose, 1964), 109–13.
29. Renel, *Contes de Madagascar*, 1: 228–39.
30. Uther, *The Types of International Folktales, a Classification and Bibliography*, 1: 183–5.
31. Dandouau, *Contes populaires*, 201.
32. Gabriel Ferrand, *Contes populaires malgaches*, Collection de Contes et de Chansons Populaires (Paris: Ernest Leroux, 1893), 201–48.
33. Dandouau, *Contes populaires*, 288–9.
34. Richardson, *A New Malagasy–English Dictionary*, 236.
35. Dandouau, *Contes populaires*, 271–5.
36. Alain Delivré, *L'histoire des rois d'Imerina: interprétation d'une tradition orale* (Paris: Klincksieck, 1974), 142–3.
37. Jennifer Cole, *Forget Colonialism? Sacrifice and the Art of Memory in Madagascar* (Berkeley: University of California Press, 2001), 130.
38. Domenichini, *Les Dieux au Service*, 372–3.
39. Haring, *Index*, 131–5.
40. A. Walen, 'The Sakalava, Concluded from Annual no. VII,' *Antananarivo Annual* 8 (1884) 52–67: 58–9.
41. Domenichini, *Les Dieux au Service*, 418–45; Delivré, *L'histoire des rois d'Imerina: interprétation d'une tradition orale*, 192–9.
42. Roper, *Charms and Charming*.
43. Philippe Beaujard, *Mythe et société à Madagascar (Tanala de l'Ikongo): le chasseur d'oiseaux et la princesse du ciel*, preface by Georges Condominas (Paris: L'Harmattan, 1991), 422; Philippe Beaujard, *Princes et paysans: les tanala de l'Ikongo. Un espace social du sud-est de Madagascar* (Paris: L'Harmattan, 1983), 388.
44. Dandouau, *Contes populaires*, 386–7.

45. Amy Shuman, *Other People's Stories: Entitlement Claims and the Critique of Empathy* (Urbana: University of Illinois Press, 2005).
46. Dell Hymes, 'Ways of Speaking', in *Explorations in the Ethnography of Speaking*, ed. Richard Bauman and Joel Sherzer (Cambridge: Cambridge University Press, 1974), 433–51: 443.
47. Dell Hymes, 'The Contribution of Folklore to Sociolinguistic Research,' in *Toward New Perspectives in Folklore*, ed. Américo Paredes and Richard Bauman (Austin: University of Texas Press, 1972), 42–50: 49.
48. This is Dominique Jullien's phrase for Marcel Proust's frequent quotations from the memoirs of the Duc de Saint-Simon Dominique Jullien, *Proust et Ses Modèles: Les* Mille et Une Nuits *et les* Mémoires *de Saint-Simon* (Paris: José Corti, 1989), 101.
49. Cole, *Forget Colonialism?* 147, 155–61.

18
The Structure and Use of Charms in Georgia, The Caucasus

Meri Tsiklauri and David Hunt

Introduction

The Republic of Georgia is situated in the Caucasus, between the Great Caucasus range in the North and the Little Caucasus range in the South. Thus the country contains both the valleys between these mountain ranges and the mountains themselves; and the population consists both of valley dwellers and mountain people. These differences are also reflected in terms of cultural development. The culture of the valley dwellers, although distinctly Georgian, is comparable to that of other parts of Europe or the Near East, and includes such high cultural phenomena as written literature, art and music. On the other hand, the cultural development of the mountain people was, until less than a century ago, largely based on the oral transmission of beliefs, customs, literature, music and all else. Much of the contact between these two groups was based on religion, which here is mainly Christian. This latter statement, however, must be qualified by the realization that Christianity here includes elements of the previous, 'pagan' religion, and the relative proportions of Christianity and paganism have varied both with time and location according to the degree of cultural development of the people, being more pagan in the mountains, more Orthodox Christian in the valley. The relative proportions of pagan to Christian beliefs and customs are also reflected in the relative proportions of charms to prayers. Generally the Georgian charms span a broad range between pure charms and pure prayers, as some of the examples below demonstrate. Charms were traditionally a characteristic part of the life of Georgians, which is proved by the fact that we meet them in the old Georgian manuscripts from the tenth century. (Georgian written literature is preserved from the fifth century.)

The etymology of the Georgian word for charm

The generally accepted definition of charms in the Georgian scientific world is as follows: 'a charm is a firmly-organized verbal formula having a magic force, which aims to achieve a desired result by influence on the object or on the phenomenon'.[1] In Modern Georgian the word used for 'charm' is *shelotsva*; its root is the word *lotsva*, with the prefix *she*. *Lotsva* is a word equivalent to the English 'pray' and 'prayer'. *Lotsva* in Georgian is both a noun and also a verb: it is both a divine church act and it is also the words spoken during this service. By adding the prefix *she* to *lotsva*, the resulting word gains the new sense of 'charm'. The prefix *she* shows the direction of the magic force of the charm towards the sufferer. The term *shelotsva* is recorded in the manuscripts of the tenth to eleventh centuries. During the same period we meet another word for 'charm': *sakhvra*, which was widely used in literary language of Arab origin. *Sakhvra* denotes both 'charm' and 'witchcraft'.

We can also etymologically examine the terms for 'charm' in the other languages of the Georgian language group called Kartvelian Languages – in the Laz language, spoken in Lazeti (Georgian territory that is now controlled by Turkey), in the Mingrelian language (spoken in a region of West Georgia), in the Svan language (spoken in highlands in western Georgia) and in the Abkhazian language (a people not of Georgian origin, but living on the Georgian territory historically). In the Laz language for charm they use the word *okitkhu*; etymologically this term is connected to the word *kitkhva*, which has two meanings 'ask' and 'read'. In Mingrelian, they use *shelorsa* which is phonetically different, but semantically the same as the Georgian *shelotsva*. In Svan, they use three words: the first – *haluish nin* means 'the language of the magician', the second *limezre* means 'charm', and the third *lichudi*, whose root *lichvdani* has two meanings 'ask' and 'read' as in Laz *okitkhu*. In Abkhazian they use the word *atihva*, the sense of which is 'a blow'.

We must presume that in pagan times the Georgian language must have possessed a term corresponding to 'charm', which was replaced under the influence of Christianity by a word having a Christian colouring – pray, prayer.

Classification of charms according their aims and meaning

Georgian charms can mostly be divided into two classes: economic charms that can influence the development and improvement of economic life, and healing charms that can bring good health. Both groups can be divided into smaller groupings. Economic charms can be divided into those concerned with agriculture, animal husbandry, hunting, fishing, and weather. Healing charms can be divided into the following groupings: those used against infections, pediatric, obstetrical–gynecological, neurological, psychiatric, surgical, traumatic, stomato-logical, oncological, therapeutic, dermatological, ophthalmological, and also universal charms for all diseases.

In older texts, we find also 'charms of a social character' connected to social or public relations, such as charms causing love and respect from the master, chief, or king; charms bringing money or wealth, charms bringing good luck to the family and spoken while starting to build a house or when entering a new house, charms bringing safety when trav-elling, charms of battle or war for defeating the enemy, charms against thieves, love charms, and so on. These types of charms are not nowa-days a part of active folklore repertoires, but are rather termed 'literary' charms. It is difficult to say whether they reflect the oral tradition or not; while it is not clear if they sprang up relatively recently, and have since dropped out from the repertoire of folklore, their existence must still be noted.

Most Georgian charms can also be classified according to the following aspects:

1. Whether they are accompanied by actions and objects (the use of such actions or objects is, nowadays at least, associated with a minority of charms).
2. How they are articulated (e.g. whispered, pronounced loudly).
3. Whether the words are written down (and if so, whether they are written on paper, or on other objects having prophylactic functions. Such amulets were applied to sore places, and sometimes also they were fixed on the wall of the house. Georgia is in the area where belief in the evil eye exists/-ed, and thus some people would always carry an amulet against the evil eye with them).
4. According to their form (prose, verse, rhythmical texts).
5. According to their religious content (pagan, or a syncretism of paganism and Christianity).

Structure of verbal charms

Here we can present examples of some of the structures found in Georgian charms:

1. A Christian introduction formula is often met with. These can be seen as attempts to disguise a charm's pagan origin. After the formula

is the name of the disease or phenomenon, against which the charm is directed. At the end of a charm, words such as 'In the name of the Father, of the Son and of the Holy spirit' and 'Amen' can be found.

2. Epical beginning:

> I speak a charm for the evil eye,
> For my eye
> For my people's eye,
> For a stranger's eye ...
>
>> (See also charm text example no. 12, below)

3. Pairs of rhyming words are often used at the beginning of a charm:

> 'Alisa, Malisa I curse the eyes of ...',
> 'Ashina, Mashina the heart, who made you frightened ...'

It may be that some such rhyming words, while meaningless today, were addressed to the spirits causing the problem in former times.

4. Dialogue charms:
Very often the texts of the charms are built on dialogues. Formulae of dialogues differ, but can be divided into two main groups according the characters of the dialogue. Firstly we have examples of dialogue formulae between God and the disease, or the Virgin Mary and the disease, and secondly we have examples of dialogue formulae built on dialogues between good forces such as Christian Saints.

5. Abracadabra:
Some formulae are built on abracadabras. These incomprehensible words, which have no meaning in the Georgian vocabulary, give charms more mystery and intensify the magical action and the influence of the words.

6. Impossibility formulae:
Patterns of lies based on impossibilities are widely spread in folklore. A charm against a piece of food stuck in the throat is the following:

> A dove was sitting
> On the top of the tree,
> I climbed up without feet
> And took it down,
> Roasted it without fire
> And ate it without mouth.[2]

7. Frightening or banishing formulae:
   The charmer very often uses words to frighten and banish the evil spirits. An example of a charm against a carbuncle:
   'If you are a carbuncle, go out, if not, I'll take you out, I'll put you in the iron jug and send you through wind and water'.[3]
8. Formulae of curse or damnation:
   The curse words have a negative attitude or destructive ability, which is used by a charmer against evils.
9. Formulae of healing advice:
   In these formulae, advice is given by Christian Saints, or sometimes the evil spirit is forced to give advice after some cursing words. Sometimes the items of advice are enumerated and named.

> Evil spirit of disease says:
> 'Don't prick my iron eye,
> Don't break my glass foot
>
> . . .
>
> I came quickly and quickly will go,
> Your medicine is the gall of the wolf
> And the white of egg'.[4]

or:

> 'Christ, tell me what is the medicine?'
> 'Three times make prayer, three times spit,
> Three times blow, this is the medicine'.[5]

Actions used in the process of telling charms

Charms are either spoken loudly or said in a whisper. They can also be accompanied by mimicry and gesture with a special intonation. Spitting and blowing is used during pronunciation of charms, mostly at the end of formulae, but sometimes in the middle of the oral text. Spitting and blowing is thought to be a good means for banishing evil spirits.

Very often charmers perform the action of making circles. The charmer goes round the bed of the sick person and makes a circle with a stick, believing that then the disease will not be spread out of the bed. 'One witch (charmer) agreed to dictate the text of the charm to a stranger. The charmer made a movement of a circle on the ground with a stick around herself, sat on a small chair in the middle of the circle and then dictated the text. The explanation of this action was so that the charm (the text of the charm) will not lose its force.'[6] Otherwise the charmer would not be able to use the charm text for healing in future, because its magic force would be lost.

During the reciting of charms other magic movements are used, such as ritual actions – for example, painting a circle with charcoal on the diseased place, or painting a cross with charcoal on the face of the sick person. Instead of charcoal, ashes (cinders) may be used.

Objects used while reciting charms include black-handled knives, needles, iron or other metal objects, alum, sulphur, pig-lard, salt, silk, water, various herbs, corn, or a walnut-tree stick.

Some charms are used during the evening of a new moon (e.g. charms against warts), some charms must be pronounced three times, seven times, or for three successive days, or seven successive weeks. Some charms can be pronounced without the presence of the sufferer, but it is still necessary to say the sufferer's name.

Modern charmers are mostly older peasant women from the villages. While men may know charms, only very few of them practice charming, more so in the highlands than in the valleys.

Poetic language of the Georgian charms

In those charms that are intended to be heard, poetic methods are generally used to increase their impact on the listener. Of course the aesthetic influence of charms during their pronunciation is only secondary in the cases when they are pronounced in a whisper, and the words are hardly heard. In this case the manner of pronunciation is of primary importance, and the manner and action have a hypnotic, magic function.

Among the many poetic methods used, we find: pairs of rhyming words (e.g. charms nos. 5 and 10, below), alliteration, tropes (no. 4), onomatopoeic words or words of mimicry (no. 1), simile (see below), metaphor (e.g. 'Red old man ploughed the sea, sowed the sand'),[7] personification (no. 3), ellipsis (no. 3), anaphora (see below), and gradation. Not all of these effects survive translation into English.

As an example of a simile we can take the following:

Let my charm be of benefit for you
As mother's milk for a baby.
Let my charm be of benefit for you
As milk of a cow for a calf.[8]

And as an example of anaphora, we have the following:

So I act, so I do:
I deprive a handsome man of strength,
I deprive a beautiful woman of beauty.[9]

An important role is played by colours. In folklore generally, colours are symbols of universal forces and processes. Three colours have a dominant function in Georgian charms (black, red and white) according to the level of strength of evil forces, and at the same time having a protective meaning. The colour used indicates the complication or simplicity, and the strength or weakness of the evil phenomenon or disease. The magic force weakens as follows: from black to red to white. The colour black is associated with the highest degree of force of an evil spirit. On rare occasions the colour blue replaces black. The colour green is mostly associated with health and wealth. Weakness and illness is implied by the colour yellow. In example no. 9, below, the colour red is used in connection with the fire, which may have caused the burn.

According to data in the charms, the places of residence of evil spirits are woods, rocks, rivers, seas, lakes, fields, islands, and ravines.

To conclude our introductory overview of Georgian charms and charming we can present thirteen charms from the collection of Mikho Mosulishvili:[10]

1. Against a cold (in the head)

Surdo metsvia sadilad,	*Cold visited me at dinner.*
Ra gavuketo sadilat?	*What shall I make it for dinner?*
Arkili, Barkili,	*Arkili, Barkili,*
Sami tagvis barkali.	*Three legs of mouse.*
Magrad shevkar, shevpachiche,	*I tied it* [i.e. the cold]
Shavsa dzaglsa gadavkide.	*Hung it on the black dog,*
Dzagli Khidzed gavarda,	*The dog fell over the bridge,*
Surdo tskalshi chavarda.	*The cold fell in the water.*[11]

While pronouncing these words the charmer washes the face of the sick person with running water.

2. Against scab (skin disease)

Sakhelita mamisata da dzisata	*By the name of the Father and the Son*

da sulisa tsmindistata, Amin.	*And the Holy Spirit, Amen.*
Muno ielo, ielo, usakhlkaro da mshiero.	*Scab without shelter and hungry,*
Muni khnamda chalasa, udabursa alagsa.	*Scab ploughed in the grove in a desert place,*
Mgeli eba Kharata, gveli apeurata.	*A wolf instead of an ox to pull the plough,*
Gveli gatskda, chamovarda ...	*And serpent for a yoke ...*
Muni amovarda dzirita da pesvita.	*The serpent was torn and fell down. Scab was torn up by the roots.*

After the words charmer puts on the scab of the sick person sulphur and specially ground herbs mixed with vinegar.[12]

In some cases the medicine against scab must be prepared and the charm must be spoken on a Tuesday, while the medicine must be put on the scab on Thursday and on Saturday, and the diseased place must be washed on Sunday.[13]

3. Against haemorrhage

Dzmam dzma mokla,	*Brother killed brother,*
Kainma Abeli ...	*Cain killed Abel ...*
Siskhlo, gekopa	*Blood, it is enough*
Magdeni, nadeni	*Bleeding so long.*

These words must be written on the piece of paper three times in the blood that is issuing, and the paper must be tied up on the forehead of the sufferer.[14]

4. Against migraine

Shakiki shemoechvia satibisa bolosa,	*Migraine visited our field,*
Egre schamda rkinasa,rogorts khari tivasa.	*It ate iron as the ox eats hay,*
Gautskra tsminda Giorgi,	*Saint George got angry with it*
Geipara dilasa.	*And it did a bunk in the morning.*

After pronouncing the charm, the charmer takes salted ground stinging-nettle wet with wine and ties it upon the forehead of sick person with a silk handkerchief.[15]

5. Against cow disease:

> Aluani:
> Geluani:
> Gergegetsuani:
> Uphum:
> Gerch:

This charm is an Abracadabra – the words in it have no meaning.[16]

6. Against lumbago:

Sakheli sakhelita,	*Name with name,*
Shagilotsam chvilisasa,	*I speak charm of waist aching,*
Ra aris sheni tsamali?	*What is your medicine?*
Tsiteli batsari da kanapi,	*Red thread and hemp,*
Gadausvi makhati,	*Touch it with a needle,*
eshveleba mchvalesa.	*it will help the waist-ache.*
Ar gamokval nebita,	*If you will not go out,*
Gamogikvan dzalita ,	*I shall make you come out by force,*
Dagtsem shavtara danasa	*I shall strike you with a black-handled knife.*
Migtsem mdinare tskalsa.	*And throw you in the river.*[17]

7. Against a wart

Sakhelita mamisata	*By the name of the Father*
da tsmindisa sulisata.	*and the Holy Spirit.*
Mechechma utkra mtvaresa,	*Wart told the moon:*
Me gjobivar shena.	*'I'm better than you'*
Mzem chahkra tavshia,	*The sun hit it on the head*
Chaadzvrina dzirita.	*And pushed it down.*

The wart charm is to be said in the evening when the moon is new.[18]

8. Against hiccupping

Ia-Makhsenebelsa,	*Violet – who speaks about me,*
Vardi-magonebelsa,	*Rose – who remembers me,*
Shvidi tslis tsieb-tskheleba,	*Seven year's fever;*
Anteba da Khurveba	*Inflammation and fever*

Chems avad makhsenebelsa.   *To the person who says bad words about me.*

(The formula must be pronounced three times).[19]

9. For a burn (scald)

Tsitel Khutsessa tsiteli Khari sheeba,	*Red priest had a red ox to pull the plough,*
Gaiara Christe gmertma, hkitkha:	*Christ passed by and asked:*
– Khutseso rasa khnam da rasa tesam?	*'Priest, what are you ploughing and sowing?'*
– Kldesa da kvasa vtesam.	*'Rock and stone I am sowing'.*
Damtsvaro ase shen ikhare,	*Burn, so flourish*
Rogorts khldeshi kvisham ikharos.	*As sand on the rock!*

While speaking a burn charm, a charmer holds coal and a needle.[20]

10. Against hydrophobia

Here-Bere, Sere-Sere,	*Here-Bere, Sere-Sere,*
Avtelo, Kavtelo,	*Avtelo, Kavtelo,*
Kristev,	*Christ,*
Shen Khar Tsamali tsopisa.	*You are the medicine of hydrophobia.*[21]

11. Against erysipelas (St. Anthony's Fire)

Viarebodi Kalaksa, kalakis kalaks,	*I walked down to the town.*
Vkrepdi tsamals, tsamlis tsamals,	*Picked medicine, medicine of medicine*
Avi karisasa, karshevanisasas,	*Against wind,*
Tsiteli karisasas, tetri karisasas,	*Red wind, white wind,*
Lurdji karisasas.	*Blue wind.*
Gamodi, dambadebels madloba,	*'Go out, thanks to the Creator*
Torem gamogikvan.	*Go out, if not I'll make you come out*
Chemi shavtariani danita.	*With my black-handled knife,*
Tu ar gamokval	*If you will not go out,*
Chemi dzalit gamogikvan,	*I'll take you out by force,*
Tsmindis samebis dzalit,	*By the force of the Holy Trinity,*
Kvabs chagagdeb sinisasa,	*I'll throw you into the bronze saucepan*

Tsetskls aginteb Lalisasa.	*And I'll set fire to it,*
Gamo!²²	*Go out!'*

Erysipelas in Georgian is called *Tsiteli kari*, which means 'red wind'. After speaking a charm against erysipelas, the charmer makes a mark around the diseased part with a strap of deer's leather, so as not to let the swelling become bigger. He or she then rubs the swelling with sugar drops (a kind of sweet) and cream, and puts the *Phelypaea coccina* on it.

12. Against the evil eye

Shegilotsav tvalisasa,	*I say a charm against eye,*
Utsin chemi tavisasa,	*Against my eye,*
Shinaurisasa, gareulisasa,	*Against your people's eye, against the stranger's eye,*
Tvalshavisasa, tvalchrelisasa,	*Against the black and many-coloured eye*
Katsisasa Kalisasa.	*Of a man and of a woman.*
Shensa tvalsa tvalavi	*To your eye an evil eye,*
Gulta Lakhvari,	*To your heart a spear,*
Tvalshi tskali,	*To your eye water*
Kona nemsi,	*And a bunch of needles,*
Nems-Makhati imis tvalebs;	*Needles to his eyes,*
Banit mekhi, karit tsetskhli!	*Thunder on the roof, fire at the door!*
Gmerto, shen dastsere	*God, sign of your grace,*
Sheni tskalobis djvari!	*Make by a cross!²³*

13. Against Ujhmuri (night evil spirit)

Ujhmuri modioda shuagamis bindisasa,	*Ujhmuri was walking down at night*
Moiknevda Kavarjensa-tangrdzelsa da gishlisasa.	*Waving its long crook*
Dakhvda deda Mariami.	*It met Mother Mary*
– Sad midikhar, Ujhmuro?	*'Where are you going Ujhmuri?'*
– Balgebis sashineblada, ded-mamis satireblada.	*'To frighten children, to make parents cry'.*
– Balgebs vin gatirebinebs,	*'Nobody will allow you to make children cry,*

dagtsemen shavtara danasa.	*They will strike you with a black-handled knife*
Pui, tsminda Giorgim dagtskevlos!	*Pah! Let Saint George curse you!*
Lotsva chemi, rgeba Gvtisa!²⁴	*My charm and God's support!'.*

Some people believe that Ujhmuri causes fever if a person stays at night out of doors, in which case, it will enter the body and cause fever. When I [Tsiklauri] visited my grandmother, Luba Intskirveli, in Guria (a region in Western Georgia), if I stayed playing till late in the yard with the neighbour's children, my grandmother warned us to come indoors because Ujhmuri would enter our body and would cause fever. This was in 1955–60.

During the pronunciation of the charm above, the charmer takes charcoal and a knife, then paints a cross with the charcoal on the face of the sick person and throws the rest of the charcoal into the bosom of the sufferer.

Notes

1. Okroshidze 1972: 182.
2. Gagulashvili 1983: 108.
3. Ibid.: 113.
4. Ibid.: 115.
5. Loc. cit.
6. Ibid.: 130.
7. Loc. cit.
8. Ibid.: 89.
9. Ibid.: 91.
10. Mosulishvili 1992.
11. Ibid.: 25.
12. Ibid.: 38,39.
13. Ibid.: 35,38.
14. Ibid.: 43.
15. Ibid.: 46.
16. Ibid.: 56.
17. Ibid.: 76,77.
18. Ibid.: 70.
19. Ibid.: 172
20. Ibid.: 191.
21. Ibid.: 71.
22. Ibid.: 91.
23. Ibid.: 127.
24. Ibid.: 139.

Bibliography

There are very few works specifically on Georgian charms. Generally the texts of charms are scattered in a variety of books, or are unpublished (and scattered in the folklore records of collecting expeditions, kept in the folklore archives in various scientific centres in Georgia, most especially the archive of the Folklore Department of the Shota Rustaveli Institute of Georgian Literature, in Tbilisi). The few existing references follow, including Suladze's work which was not cited in this chapter.

Gagulashvili, I. Sh., *Gruzinskaya Magicheskaya Poezia*, (Tbilisi: Tbilisi State University, 1983).

Mosulishvili, M. (edited by Amiran Arabuli), *Gveli Movkal Uplisatvis. Kartuli Shelotsvebi*, (Tbilisi: 1992).

Okroshidze, T., *Zagovori. Gruzinskoe Narodnoe Poeticheskoe Tvorchestvo*, (Tbilisi: Merani, 1972).

Suladze, Mzia, *Shelotsvata Poetica*, (unpublished Shota Rustaveli Institute of Georgian Literature dissertation), (Tbilisi: 1997).

19
Manteras: An Overview of a Malay Archipelagoes' Charming Tradition

Low Kok On

The Malay word *mantera* is derived from the Sanskrit term *mantra* (also, *mantr* and *matar*), which has been defined as 'that part of each Veda which comprises the hymns; a passage of Vedas, a holy text; a formula sacred to any particular deity; a mystical verse, a magical formula; an incantation, a charm, spell, philter; secret consultation or spiritual instruction.'[1] The Sanskrit word is also the ultimate source of modern English *mantra*. When the Malay borrowed this term into their own language, its use was restricted to the somewhat narrower field of 'charms, incarnations, and secret prayers' (as a dictionary from two hundred years ago has it)[2] or 'words or sentences when chants that give rise to magic power in order to cure sickness etc.' to quote a more contemporary dictionary, the *Kamus Dewan*.[3] The terms *jampi* and *serapah* have more currency in present-day Malay. For generations, *jampi* meant those *manteras* used by the Malay witch doctor to cure sickness. *Jampi* will usually be chanted over the traditional medicine, water, oil etc. before it is used on the patients. A *serapah*, on the other hand, which literally means 'curse', is commonly used to chase away bad spirits or wild animals by means of cursing. Nevertheless the focus of this investigation are *manteras*, or charms.

According to Harun Mat Piah, the Malay people began to compose *manteras* in prehistoric times.[4] In that animistic period, they believed that every living and non-living thing had a spirit. If someone offended such a spirit, then he or she would fall sick, or get into trouble in some other way. When their belief system have changed from animism, firstly to Hinduism-Buddhism, and latterly to Islam, the *mantera* continue to develop until the present day, though with some modifications. As Za'ba has stated, we find that the names of certain Hindu gods and goddesses are invoked in Malay charms.[5] When the Malays became

Muslim, Islamic greetings and prayers like *assalam ualaikum, lailahaillal-lah*, etc. and Islamic terms such as *Allah* (God), *Rasullulah* (Muhammad), and *roh* (soul) were added to their *manteras*. Thus Malay *manteras* can be further subdivided into three main categories: (a) the original Malay *manteras* (which are expressions of animism), (b) Hindu-Buddhist influenced *manteras*, and (c) Islamic influenced *manteras*. Besides these, there are also Malay *manteras* which contain a syncretic mixture of animism, Hinduism and Islam. The first text given below is an animist *mantera*, while the second example contains a mixture of animism, Hinduism and Islam characteristics:

Sungai Nipah Sungai Gemuruh	*River of Nipah River of Gemuruh*
Tiga dengan Sungai Ati-ati	*Third with River of Ati-ati*
Bagai dikipas engkau tubuh	*Your body like being fan*
Bagai dilambai engkau hati	*Your heart like being wave*
Kalau engkau tak minum susu ibu	*If you have never drunk your mother's milk*
Tak kena buatan aku	*You will be fine*
Kalau engkau minum	*If you have drunk it before*
Engkau kena buatan aku[6]	*Surely my charm will bestow upon you*

[Notes: *Nipah* is the plant *nipa fruticans*, a *gemuruh* is a loud sound, and *Ati-ati* is another plant, *coleus atropurpureus*]

Assalamualaikum,	*Assalamualaikum,*
Hai berna kuning,	*Hey, yellow berna,*
Mu tumbuh di bukit Gunung Siguntang Mahameru,	*You reside at Mount Siguntang Mahameru,[7]*
Berdaun perak, berbatang suasa, berbuah emas,	*With silver leaves, bronze branches, gold fruits,*
Aku nak minta jadi anak panah Seri Rama,	*Let me turn into the arrow of Seri Rama,*
. . .[8]	*. . .*

[Notes: *Assalamualaikum* is Arabic for 'peace be with you all', and *berna* is a kind of spirit]

The first of these two love charms lacks any Hindu-Buddhist or Islamic terms or greetings. The natural objects which appear in the charm, such as the River of Nipah, River of Gemuruh and River Ati-ati can be seen to be motivated by the aim of the charmer to gain magical love power through certain spirits residing in those three rivers. The second of the

two *mantera* above contains Islamic greetings – *assalamualaikum*, as well as Hindu features such as Mount Siguntang Mahameru, Seri Rama, and additionally, an animistic feature, the yellow *berna*.
For the Balinese people of Indonesia, who remain 95 per cent Hindu, the two senses of *mantera*, i.e. both charm and sacred Hindu text, are not distinguished. In the *manteras* used in Hindu worship, we find the frequent occurrence 'om,' a syllable which symbolizes 'life'. The Hindus believe that the utterance of 'om' in *manteras* will give rise to a supernatural power.[9] As a result, 'om' occurs in most Hindu *manteras*, such as the following:

Om Siva yang maha kuasa om	*Om the great Siva om*
Om Siva, Siva, Siva berkuasa	*Om Siva, Siva, the powerful Siva*
Om segala sakti dalam Siva	*Om all the supernatural power in Siva*
Om segala sakti dalam	*Om all the supernatural power in*
Dewi Sakthi	*Goddess Sakthi*
Om segala dewa om	*Om all the deities om*
. . .[10]	. . .

Likewise, *manteras* used in worship in the ancient Java language of Indonesia also featured 'om'. But not all the *manteras* found among the Malay tribal groups in Indonesia contain the utterance 'om'. For example, the Gebong Domas, one of the Balinese tribal groups who follow Hinduism but do not adhere to the Hindu caste system, produced *manteras* lacking any utterance of 'om', such as the following:

Ya, aku memohon ampun	*Yes, I am asking for pardon*
Ini aku memberi engkau sesaji	*Here I am, serving you food*
Sebanyak ini	*This much food*
Kerana sekarang Tumpek Landep	*Because today is Tumpek Landep's*
Hari kelahiranmu	*Birthday*
Semoga engkau berguna	*Wishing that you are useful*
Sebagaimana mestinya[11]	*Like you supposed to be*

Most of the Malay *manteras* are poetic in their form, and functional in their nature. The length of a Malay *mantera* can be similar to an ordinary contemporary poem or merely comprised of a few words, such as the following *mantera* used to weaken the strength of one's enemy:

Bismi
Bukmu mawa umur[12]

This *mantera* is particularly difficult to translate: *Bismi* is derived from the Arabic for 'In the name of God,' *buk* denotes a sound, such as that of fruit falling on the ground, *mu* means 'you,' *mawa* is a leaf monkey, and *umur* means 'age.' The full meaning of this short *mantera* is beyond the present author.

The shaman of the Malay is known as *bomoh* or *pawang*. Such people are the keepers of the Malay *manteras*. They memorize various *manteras* from the oral teaching of their *tok guru* (master), and use them for achieve certain goals, such as curing sicknesses, bringing success in hunting, avoiding danger, and so on. For the Malay, a *bomoh* who knows both the *manteras* (charms) and how to use them for various purposes and conditions (charming) is said to be *berilmu*. The root word of *berilmu* is *ilmu*, a word which literally meaning 'knowledge', but which has developed a more specialised meaning as Clifford Geertz explains:

> *Ilmu* is generally considered to be a kind of abstract knowledge or supernormal skill, but by the more concrete-minded and 'old-fashioned'. It is sometimes viewed as a kind of substantive magical power, in which case its transmission may be more direct than through teaching.[13]

Just as the main role of the Malay *bomohs* is in curing sickness, so they are also the ones who have the expertise to decide which is the correct *mantera* to apply for a specific illness. To begin with, the *bomoh* may use certain *manteras* to trace the origin of a particular sickness, as seen in the following example:

Asal kuntum akar raja selum	*Petal originated from the King's* selum root
Batang raja berdiri	*King's branch is standing*
Daun raja ngepa	Raja ngepa *leaf*
Buah raja mengunduk	Raja mengunduk *fruit*
Kuntum cari sekun, rasi jadi temuan[14]	*Petal trying to match, the match found*

Different *manteras* will be used for different sickness. To remove poison from one's body for example, the *bomoh* will use the following mantera:

Kekek cendawan kekek	Kekek *mushroom* kekek
Tumbuh cendawan hilang rupa	*Growth the mushroom lost the appearance*
Titik air tigak titik	*Dropping three drops of water*

Aku mengeluarkan bisa	*I am going to take out the poison*
Dalam tubuh si anu ini	*From the body of so and so*
Masuk segala tawar	*Putting in all the magic spell*
Keluar segala bisa	*Out it comes all the poisons*
Hu Allah[15]	*Hu Allah*

[Note: *kekek* could be interpreted as 'loud laughter' but its sense here is unclear]

In former times, and still to some extent even today, most diseases were believed to be caused by harmful spirits. In such cases, the *bomoh* will act as a middle man negotiating with these harmful spirits or exorcising them from the patient's body. The *mantera* given below serves just such a purpose:

Hai hantu, hantu jembalang	*Hey ghost,* jembalang *ghost*
Datang di bukit balik ke bukit	*From hill back to hill*
Datang di pusu balik ke pusu	*From pusu back to pusu*
Datang di pohon balik ke pohon	*From tree back to tree*
Datang di gunung balik ke gunung	*From mountain back to mountain*
Sekarang kau pulang ke tempat asalmu	*Now you shall go back to your place of origin*[16]

[Note: a *jembalang* is a kind of spirit that can change itself into animal form, e.g. deer, buffalo, etc j *pusu* is a pile of earth in the wild]

Spirits can also be used by their owners to gain something or to achieve a certain purposes by its owner. People believed that some *bomohs* (and even some ordinary people who know *manteras*) could acquire the services of a particular spirit. The 'Black Warrior Mantera' exemplifies this well:

Hai Panglima Hitam	*Hey, Black Warrior*
Aku nak mengguna kau untuk . . .	*I need your favour to . . .*
Sebutkan hajat	[here the one's wish is stated]
Panglima Hitam dari seberang	*Black Warrior from over there*
Dibawa orang dari tanah Jawa	*Brought over by people from Java*
Panglima Hitam sungguh gagah	*Black Warrior is very brave*
Apa dikehendak berjaya	*Whatever I desire will be fulfilled*
Dengan berkat doa	*With the blessing of special prayer*
Lailahaillallah Muhammadar Rasulullah[17]	*Lailahaillallah Muhammadar Rasulullah*

[Note: *Lailahaillallah Muhammadar Rasulullah* denotes 'There is no other God than Allah and Muhammed is his prophet']

If an expectant mother encounters difficulties, the *tuk bidan* (the traditional Malay midwife) will rub her abdomen with oil while repeating the following charm:

Bukan aku yang buka pintu rajat	*It's not me who open the door of rajat*
Allah yang buka pintu rajat	*Allah will open the door of rajat*
Bukan aku yang buka pintu rajat	*It's not me who open the door of rajat*
Muhammad yang buka pintu rajat	*It's Muhammad who will open the door of rajat*
Bukan aku yang buka pintu rajat	*It's not me who will open the door of rajat*
Lokman Hakim yang buka pintu rajat	*It's Lokman Hakim who will open the door of rajat*
Tuk bomoh ketujuh yang buka pintu rajat	*The seventh tuk bomoh will open the door of rajat*
Bukan aku yang buka pintu rajat	*It's not me who open the door of rajat*
Tuk bidan ketujuh yang buka pintu rajat	*The seventh tuk bidan will open the door of rajat*
Dengan berkat doa	*With special prayer*
Lailahaillallah Muhammadar Rasulullah[18]	*Lailahaillallah Muhammadar Rasulullah*

N.B. 'the door of rajat' here means the door used to ward off evil. Compare *Kamus Dewan, s.v.* 'rajah (rajat)': 'a kind of writing (like in the forms of description, letter, sign, etc.) to be made as a talisman to ward off evil etc.'

Another sphere that *manteras* are used in is that of love. To gain or regain the affections of a certain person, one can turn, once again, to the *bomoh*. Here are two such Malay love charms:

Hei om pali	*Hey om pali*
Hei hantu tanah	*Hey ghosts of the soil*
Jembalang bumi	*Hey jembalang of the soil*
Kau pergi mengambil semangat roh si anu	*go and bring back the spirit of my loved one*
Bawa gila kepada aku	*bring back to me that kind of madness*

Menyala seperti api	burning like a fire
Seperti nasi mendidih	hot like boiling rice.
Jika engkau tidak membawanya	If you fail to bring back that kind
gila kepada aku	of madness
Seperti api yang menyala, nasi	burning like a fire; hot like a
yang mendidih	boiling rice
Kusumpah engkau	Then I will put a curse on you
Derhaka engkau kepada Allah	To Allah you are a betrayer
Bukan dengan kuasa aku	Not from my own power
Dengan kuasa Allah[19]	But the power of Allah

[Note: *om pali* is an exclamation sound borrowed from Thai. In Sanskrit, *om* means 'life,' and this word is believed to have magic power both in Hinduism and Buddhism.]

Hai, malaikat kudus qidam	Hey, sacred angel of qidam
Keempat puncak bertemu aku	Of all the four peaks allow me
dengan si anu	to meet [the beloved]
Jika si anu memandang,	If he/she stares
Aku di dalam renungan matanya	I will be in his/her view,
Jikalau si anu bercakap	If he/she speaks
Aku di dalam cakapnya	I will be in his speech,
Jikau si anu berjalan	If he/she walks
Aku di dalam langkahnya	I will be in his/her steps,
Jikalau si anu makan	If he/she eats
Aku di dalam nasinya	I will be in his/her rice
Akulah memakai gendangan	I am the one using prophet
Nabi Muhammad	Muhammad's beating drum
Dengan berkat sidi guruku[20]	With effective blessing from
	my master

[Note: *qidam* means existing originally like the attributes of God.]

As most of the Malays have been farmers from ancient times, and have been greatly involved in paddy planting, we can find many Malay *manteras* related to planting paddy. Right from the moment the Malay farmers sowing the paddy seeds, they will chant the following *mantera*:

Assalamualaikum	Assalamualaikum
Hai nabi Sulaiman, raja sekalian	Hey prophet Solomon, king of
bumi	the earth

Assalamualaikum	*Assalamualaikum*
Hai jin tanah, jembalang bumi	*Hey earth djinn, earth ghost*
Assalamualaikum	*Assalamualaikum*
Hai bapaku, langit	*Hey father sky*
Assalamualaikum	*Assalamualaikum*
Hai ibuku, bumi	*Hey mother earth*
Hai bapa kawal, ibu kawal	*Hey father guard, mother guard*
Aku nak kirim anakku	*I would like to send my children*
Anak Maharaja Cahaya pada ibunya	*The children of the Light King to their mother*
Aku suruh belayar ke laut hitam,	*I will ask them to sail to the black sea, green sea,*
laut hijau, laut biru ke laut ungu	*blue sea, and to the purple sea*
Bukan aku menurunkan benih	*I am not putting in the seeds*
Aku menurunkan padi[21]	*But I am putting in the paddy*

Before the farmers start to plant their paddy in the paddy field, there is a ceremony of arranging nine clumps of paddy, during which chant the following *mantera* in order to obtain a good harvest:

Bismillahir-Rahmanir-Rahimi	Bismillahir-Rahmanir-Rahimi
Merpati terbang seribu	*Fly, thousand of pigeons fly*
Singgah tidur di Kuala Perlis	*Stop and put a night at Kuala Perlis*
Tanam padi sembilan perdu	*Planting nine perdu of paddy*
Keluar padi sembilan nalih[22]	*Harvesting nine nalih of it*

[Note: *Bismillahir-Rahmanir-Rahimi* is Arabic for 'In the name of most loving and generous God'; *Kuala Perlis* is a place situated in the state of Perlis, in northern Peninsular Malaysia; a *perdu* is a *nalih* is a Malay unit of measurement – one *nalih* is equivalent to sixteen *gantang*, and one *gantang* is equivalent to 4.54 litres].

Malay farmers also believed that the paddy have spirits known as *semangat padi*. If the spirits stay with the paddy then a good harvest will ensue, but if the spirit of paddy do not want to stay there, then the outlook for the paddy plants is poor. One of the ways to please the paddy plants is to chant certain special *manteras* for these spirits:

Seri Dangomala, Seri Dangomali	Seri Dangomala, Seri Dangomali
Hendak kirim anak sembilan bulan	*With intention to send 'anak sembilan bulan'*
Segala inang, segala pengasuh	*To all the baby sitters*

Jangan beri sakit, jangan beri demam	*Allow no sickness, allow no fever*
Jangan beri ngilu dan pening	*Allow no feeling ill and faint*
Kecil menjadi besar	*From small become big*
Tua jadi muda	*From old become young*
Yang tak kejap diperkejap	*From not strong to become strong*
Yang tak sama dipersama	*From uneven to even*
Yang tak hijau diperhijau	*From non-greenish to greenish*
Yang tak tinggi dipertinggi	*From short to become tall*
Hijau seperti air laut	*As green as the sea water*
Tinggi seperti bukit Kaf[23]	*As tall as the Kaf Hill*

[Note: *Seri Dangomala* would seem to be an invocation of the deities; *anak sembilan bulan* is a nickname given to the paddy that literally means 'nine month-old child']

Whenever the paddy plants are attacked by insects, the farmers will first burn incense made from a fragrant tree known as *kemenyan* in the middle of the paddy field, and they will then burn, *rabun-rabun*, which is a mixture of sulphur, onion skin, pepper and chili. While the burning goes on, the farmer will begin to chanting the following *mantera* while keeping *gula kelapa* (sugar made of coconut syrup) in his mouth. This sugar is referred to in the words of the charm:

Bismillahir-Rahmanir-Rahimi	Bismillahir-Rahmanir-Rahimi
Bangkak Yeng Yeng	Bangkak Yeng Yeng
Belalang pianggang, belalang angin	*Grasshopper of all kinds*
Jangan hisap sari padi	*Do not suck the essence of paddy*
Hisaplah sari api	*Suck the essence of fire instead*
Lemak manis rasanya seperti gula kelapa	*It's sweet like coconut sugar*
Sama-sama mengenyah dan menyingkir	*Together we chew and let go*
Jangan dijadikan mangsa terhadap tanamanku	*Let not my plants be your victims*
Akan kena denda Allah	*If not God will punish you*
Kalau hendak mencari mangsa,	*If you intend to find a victim*
di sana, jauh di sana	*They are there, far away*
Aku melarang tidak, menyuruh pun tidak[24]	*I will not stopping you from going there*

[Note: *Bangkak Yeng Yeng* (literally 'green rice-buds') is the name given to the king or queen of grasshoppers (*Leptocoriza varicornis*) that destroy paddy]

Manteras can be practiced by ordinary people as well as by *bomoh*. In the past, for example, if the sunset had an especial glow about, then an ordinary person could take water into his mouth, and dislodges it in the direction of the brightness, and at the same time throwing ashes saying:

Mambang kuning, mambang kelabu	*Yellow divinity, grey divinity*
Pantat kuning disembur abu	*Ashes to be thrown to yellow buttock*[25]
Mambang kuning, mambang kelabu	*Yellow divinity, grey divinity*
Pantat kuning disembur abu	*Ashes to be thrown to yellow buttock*[26]

If a person wishes to look attractive and to get noticed, he or she may use the 'Si Awang Lebih' (*Awang the Extraordinary*) *mantera*, may try to beautify one's face by means of a *mantera*, or may make his body smell good by means of a *mantera*:

'Mantera Si Awang Lebih'

Bismillahir-rahmanir-rahim	Bismillahir-rahmanir-rahim
Seri gurun, seri bintang, seri matahari	*Shining, shining stars, shining sun*
Seri naik ke mukaku	*The shine will be on my face*
Cahaya limpah ke tubuhku	*Light will be on my body*
Cahaya Allah cahaya Muhammad	*The light of Allah, the light of Muhammad*
Cahaya baginda Rasulullah	*The light of the prophet*
Duduk aku seperti raja	*I will be seated like a king*
Berdiri aku seperti menteri	*I will be standing like a minister*
Berjalan aku seperti baginda	*I will walk like your Majesty*
Duduk akulah yang lebih	*When seated I look so extraordinary*
Berdiri aku lebih	*And so extraordinary when I stand*
Siapa yang berkata?	*Who says so?*
Akulah yang lebih	*I am the extraordinary one*
Berkat aku memakai	*I am blessed by using*
'Si Awang Lebih'	*'Si Awang Lebih'*[27]

There is even a *mantera* to be said when putting on talcum powder:

Bedak olak olek	*Powder keep on revolving*
Mari pakai hujung gunting	*Let it be at the edge of scissor*
Kupakai bedak di luar kulit	*I put talcum powder on my skin*
Mesra dalam daging	*Getting well with my fresh*
Dengan berkat doa	*With blessing from special prayer*
Lailahaillallah Muhammadar Rasulullah[28]	Lailahaillallah Muhammadar Rasulullah

All in all, the Malay *manteras* cover almost aspect of their life depends on the need in whatever situation, whatever motive they have and whatever problems they are facing too. Another purpose they can be used for is to avoid meeting a tiger in the jungle:

Hei Besenu, Hei Berkaih	*Hey* Besenu, *Hey* Berkaih
Aku tahu asal kaujadi	*I know your origin*
Syed Abuniah Lahah Abu Kasap	*Syed Abuniah Lahah Abu Kasap*
Pusatmu pucuk ubun-ubun	*Your navel is the shoot of* ubun-ubun
Susukau di tapak tangan	*Your milk is at your palm*
Simpankan petala tujuh langit	*keep the seven heavens*
Simpankan petala tujuh bumi	*keep the seven earths*
Kalau tak simpan	*If you do not keep them*
Derhaka kau kepada Allah	*You are betraying Allah*[29]

[Note: *Besenu* and *Berkaih* would seem to be nicknames for the tiger; *Syed Abuniah Lahah Abu Kasap* is a personal name; *ubun-ubun* denotes the soft spot at the crown of a baby's head.]

Even nowadays, the *bomoh* or *pawang* still plays an important role in lives of some of the Malays, in both city and countryside. When Malays suffer from an unusual sickness for example, they will consult their *bomoh* or *pawang*, who will chant *manteras* in attempt to cure such spirit-caused sicknesses. Some people resort to *manteras* if modern biomedicine fails them. *Manteras* are can be used by football teams, who may hire a *bomoh* or *pawang* to chant in front of the goalposts in order to win a game. Likewise a *bomoh hujan* (rain witch doctor) may be sought out to ensure good weather for football games (or indeed, for outdoor parties and functions). Even politicians are not averse from hiring a *bomoh* or *pawang* to ensure they win an election or secure a top post in their political party.

While modern biomedicine is accepted by people in almost every walk of life in Malaysia, the role of the *bomoh* is still significant. Mohd Razali Salleh has conducted research on the consultation of traditional healers by psychiatric patients and general outpatients in Malaysia. He finds that:

> Seventy-six (73.1%) psychiatric patients had consulted a *bomoh* prior to their visit to the clinic as compared to 26 (25%) OPD patients. The number of *bomohs* consulted was significantly higher among the psychiatric patients than the OPD patients. The strength of social support, the availability of a *bomoh* and the belief of the patients, friends and/or relatives in the *bomoh* have been suggested as the main factors that influenced the Malay patients in seeking *bomoh* treatment. The belief that mental illness is due to supernatural causes is firmly held by *bomohs* who reinforce this notion in those who seek their advice. The importance of understanding the patient's cultural background in treating psychiatric patients is highlighted.[30]

In this era of globalization, Malay *manteras* continue to develop and attract the interest of the Malay people, even though most of the Muslim religious leaders have stated that the practice of *manteras* is against the teachings of Islam. This final *mantera* is intended for a person wishing to start his business in this modern age:

Hei, Gedung!	*Hey, warehouses,*
Aku seru engkau!	*I plead with you!*
Gedung segala harta,	*Warehouses of all kinds,*
Harta nampak, harta tersembunyi.	*Visible properties, hidden properties.*
Harta berat, harta ringan,	*Heavy properties, light properties,*
Bukalah pintumu!	*Open up your door!*
Aku masuk dengan doa,	*I shall enter with prayers,*
Aku masuk dengan tawakal!	*I shall enter with good wishes!*
Aku bekerja siang malam,	*I work day and night,*
Aku masuk dengan tulang empat kerat.	*I enter with my entire body.*

Aku masuk dengan usaha,	*I enter with hard work,*
Dapatlah harta kepadaku.	*Property comes to me.*
Biar penuh tempayan yang kosong,	*Let the vase be full,*
Biar berat uncang yang ringan.	*Let the light money sack become heavy*
Biar kenyang anak yang lapar,	*Let the stomach of all my children be full,*
Biar gembira isteri yang sedih.	*Make my wife happy too*
Kalau emas biar berbungkal,	*If it is gold let it be much,*
Kalau harta biar bertimbang.	*If it is a property let it be balanced.*
Kalau ladang biar menjadi,	*If it is an estate let it be fruitful,*
Kalau sawah biar berpadi.	*If it is a field let it have paddy.*
Harta yang sedikit biar menjadi banyak,	*Let a little bit of property become more,*
Yang banyak biar bertimbun-timbun.	*Let lots of properties become more and more,*
Menjadi rezeki yang halal,	*Become a* halal *source of income*
Menjadi rezeki yang berkat,	*Blessed be all sources of income,*
Semuanya datang kepadaku.	*Yes, all will come to me,*
Berkata sidi guru aku,	*My master said* sidi
Berkata aku lailahaillallah.[31]	*And I say* lailahaillallah

[Notes: *halal* denotes something permitted by Islam, *sidi* is an answered prayer, and *lailahaillallah* means there is no other God than Allah.]

Notes

1. Plattas (1960: 1071).
2. Marsden (1812: 334).
3. *Kamus Dewan* (2005: 997).
4. Harun Mat Piah (1989: 478–9).
5. Za'ba (1980:105).
6. Harun Mat Piah (1989: 493).

7. In Hinduism, Mount Si Guntang Mahameru.
8. Harun Mat Piah (1989: 483).
9. Harun Daud (1995: 14).
10. Harun Daud (1995: 14).
11. Loc. cit.
12. Harun Mat Piah (1989: 489).
13. Harun Daud (1995: 15).
14. Harun Mat Piah (1989: 490).
15. Harun Mat Piah (1989: 513).
16. (Source: unknown).
17. (Source: unknown).
18. Harun Mat Piah (1989: 520).
19. Harun Mat Piah (1989: 485).
20. Harun Mat Piah (1989: 521-2).
21. Winstedt 1920, cited in Harun Mat Piah (1989: 507-8).
22. Amat Juhari Moain (1990: 74).
23. *Warna Sari Sastera Melayu Tradisional*, (1996: 349).
24. Amat Juhari Moain (1990: 75).
25. Skeat (1984: 93).
26. Skeat (1984: 93).
27. Harun Mat Piah (1989:521).
28. Harun Mat Piah (1989: 492).
29. Skeat (1984), cited in Harun Mat Piah (1989: 491).
30. *www.mma.org.my/info/1_original_89* accessed on 1 January 2007.
31. *http://www.pts.com.my/modules.php?name=News&file=article&sid=162* accessed on 1 January 2007.

Bibliography

Amat Juhari Moain. 1990. *Kepercayaan Orang Melayu Berhubung dengan Pertanian (The Belief of Malay Related to Plants)* Kuala Lumpur: Dewan Bahasa dan Pustaka.

Harun Daud. 1995. 'Mantera Sebagai Karya Sastera: Definisi yang Digunakan oleh Masyarakat Nusantara' (Mantera as a Literary Products: The Definition Used by the Malay Archipelago) in *Dewan Sastera*. February.

Harun Mat Piah. 1989. *Puisi Melayu Tradisional: Satu Perbicaraan Genre dan Fungsi (Malay Traditional Poems: Genre and Functions)*. Kuala Lumpur: Dewan Bahasa and Pustaka.

Marsden, W. 1812. *A Dictionary of the Malayan Language in Two Parts: Malayan English and English Malayan*. London: Longman.

Plattas, John T. 1960. *A Dictionary of Urdu, Classical Hindu and English*. Oxford: Oxford University Press.

Sheikh Othman bin Sheikh Salim *et al.*, eds, *Kamus Dewan [Dewan Dictionary]*. 2005. Kuala Lumpur: Dewan Bahasa and Pustaka.

Skeat, W.W. 1984 [1911]. *Malay Magic, Being an Introduction to the Folklore and Popular Religion of the Malay Peninsula*. New York: Dover.

Warna Sari Sastera Melayu Tradisional (The Essence of Malay Traditional Literature). 1996.

Kuala Lumpur: Majlis Peperiksaan Malaysia. Dewan Bahasa dan Pustaka, Penerbit Fajar Bakti.

Winstedt, R.O. 1920. In Harun Mat Piah. 1989. *Puisi Melayu Tradisional: Satu Perbicaraan Genre dan Fungsi* (*Malay Traditional Poems: Genre and Functions*). Kuala Lumpur: Dewan Bahasa and Pustaka.

Za'ba. 1980. 'The Malays and Religion' in *Tamadun Islam di Malaysia* (*Malaysia Islamic Cicilization*). Kuala Lumpur: Persatuan Sejarah Malaysia.

Websites

'Mantera Membuka Perniagaan' (Mantera to Begin Doing Business). *http://www.pts.com.my/modules.php?name=News&file=article&sid=162* (accessed June 2007)

Mohd Razali Salleh. 'The Consultation of Traditional Healers by Malay Patients'. *http://www.mma.org.my/info/1_original_89* (accessed June 2007)

Index

Jerusalem 201
Jerusalem you town of pain 177,
184 n15
Jesus Christ xix, 27–30, 33, 39, 41,
43, 44–5, 54, 62–3, 65–7, 83, 89, 91,
92, 94, 95, 148–150, 152–155, 157,
159, 167, 169–70, 172, 177–181,
199–205, 207, 217–25, 229, 231,
264, 269
Jesus and the fiery torch 177, 181,
184 n15
Job 155, 196
John of Greenborough 88, 96 n3
John the Baptist 154, 158, 205, 219,
225, 240
Judas Iscariot 91

Kerbelite, B. 76
kerchief, used when charming 147
King Lear xx, Ch. 8 *passim*
Kittredge, George Lyman 101–2
Krohn, Kaarle 176
Kuusi, Matti 168, 170

lard 265
Latyr stone, the 31
Lazarus 220
lead melting xxiv, 238, 241
Leechcraft remedy book Ch. 15 *passim*;
distribution of charms within
225–7; fewer charms in later copies
of 216
'let her not eat or drink' formula
127–35; evolution 127–8; in Early
Modern and Modern Europe
129–131; Greek/Russian parallels
132–4; semantics 134–5
Liber de diversis medicinis 215, 227
lidérc 38, 43–4, 46
Lilith 105
limited goods, theory of 5
literariness of many Middle English
charms 94
Lithuanian and Latvian charms,
limited parallels between 187
lizard 164
Longinus 98 n19, 218–20, 225
Longinus' spear 92, 95, 222, 229

Lord's Prayer, the 30, 62–3, 68, 88,
90, 148, 149, 151, 153, 154, 217–25,
235 n72, 241
love charms xxi, 81–2, 84, Ch. 10
passim, 255, 274, 278–9
love, the fiery nature of 127, 133,
136–7
Low Saturday 147
luonto 3, 8–9

Magi 221, 227–9
magic books, printed 156, 176, 179,
183 n3
magic/religion dichotomy,
dissolved 63
magical practitioners: *bajalica* 238,
bomoh 276–8, 282–4, *bomoh hujan*
283, *cunning folk* 15, *druzhok*
126, *juzo* 109, *kolduny* 136,
loktyzo-puzhykcho 109, *moasy*
253, *muzhangche* 109, *ombiasy*
253, *pawang* 276, 283,
shinchanuzhsho 109, *shüvedyshe*
109, *tietäja* Ch. 1 *passim*,
uzhsho-kolsho 109, *welho* 12
Maikov, Leonid xv, 80, 82
manuscript books: English 214–16,
229; Russian 123–4; Slovene
146–7; compilers of 216
manuscripts, containing charms:
xxii, MSS Cambridge UL Dd.5.76
215, 232 note, UL Kk.6.33 89,
UL Adds 9308 216–227, 232 n8;
MSS London BL Adds 33996 94,
Ch. 15 *passim*, BL Harley 273 92,
BL Royal 12.G.iv 88, 91, 95,
BL Sloane 374 216, 233 note,
BL Sloane 962 90, 92; MSS Oxford
Bod Ashmole 1477 233 n12, Bod
Ashmole 1378 97 n11, Bod Laud
Misc. 553 91, 95–6, Bod
Rawlinson C506 107 n4
manuscripts, full list of those
containing *Leechbook* charms
231–2
Mansikka, Viljo 31–2, 34, 121
Maranda, P. and
E. Köngas-Maranda 71
Marcellus of Bordeaux 31–2, 34

CPSIA information can be obtained
at www.ICGtesting.com
Printed in the USA
BVHW040220101220
595355BV00005B/142